Autobiography and Black Identity Politics
Racialization in Twentieth-Century America

Why has autobiography been central to African-American political speech throughout the twentieth century? What is it about the racialization process that persistently places African-Americans in the position of speaking from personal experience? In *Autobiography and Black Identity Politics: Racialization in Twentieth-Century America* Kenneth Mostern illustrates the relationship between narrative and racial categories such as "colored," "Negro," "black," or "African American" in the work of writers such as W. E. B. Du Bois, Zora Neale Hurston, Malcolm X, Paul Robeson, Angela Davis, and bell hooks. Mostern shows how these autobiographical narratives attempt to construct and transform the political meanings of blackness. The relationship between a black masculine identity that emerged during the 1960s, and the counter-movement of black feminism since the 1970s, is also discussed. This wide-ranging study will interest all those working in African-American studies, cultural studies, and literary theory.

KENNETH MOSTERN is Assistant Professor in the Department of English at the University of Tennessee.

Chart p. 34
§ re Marshall
Di Leonardo

Cultural Margins

General editor

Timothy Brennan
Department of English and Comparative Literature, University of Minnesota

The series Cultural Margins originated in response to the rapidly increasing interest in postcolonial and minority discourses among literary and humanist scholars in the US, Europe, and elsewhere. The aim of the series is to present books which investigate the complex cultural zone within and through which dominant and minority societies interact and negotiate their differences. Studies in the series range from examinations of the debilitating effects of cultural marginalization, to analyses of the forms of power found at the margins of culture, to books which map the varied and complex components involved in the relations of domination and subversion. This is an international series, addressing questions crucial to the deconstruction and reconstruction of cultural identity in the late twentieth-century world.

1   Ann Marie Smith, *New Rights Discourses on Race and Sexuality: Britain, 1968–1990*   0 521 45921 4

2   David Richards, *Masks of Difference: Cultural Representations in Literature, Anthropology, and Art*   0 521 47972 X

3   Vincent, J. Cheng, *Joyce, Race, and Empire*   0 521 47859 6

4   Alice Gambrell, *Women Intellectuals, Modernism, and Difference: Transatlantic Culture, 1991–1945*   0 521 55688 0

5   Francis Barker, Peter Hulme, and Margaret Iversen (eds.), *Cannibalism and the Colonial World*   0 521 62908 X

6   Neil Lazarus, *Nationalism and Cultural Practice in the Postcolonial World*   0 521 62493 2

Autobiography and
Black Identity Politics

Racialization in Twentieth-Century America

Kenneth Mostern

CAMBRIDGE
UNIVERSITY PRESS

PUBLISHED BY THE PRESS SYNDICATE OF THE UNIVERSITY OF CAMBRIDGE
The Pitt Building, Trumpington Street, Cambridge CB2 1RP, United Kingdom

CAMBRIDGE UNIVERSITY PRESS
The Edinburgh Building, Cambridge, CB2 2RU, UK http://www.cup.cam.ac.uk
40 West 20th Street, New York, NY 10011-4211, USA http://www.cup.org
10 Stamford Road, Oakleigh, Melbourne 3166, Australia

First published 1999

Printed in the United Kingdom at the University Press, Cambridge

Typeset in 9.5/12pt Palatino [VN]

A catalogue record for this book is available from the British Library

Library of Congress cataloguing in publication data

Mostern, Kenneth.
Autobiography and Black identity politics: racialization in
twentieth-century America / Kenneth Mostern.
        p.   cm. (Cultural margins: v. 6)
Includes bibliographical references.
ISBN 0 521 64114 4 (hardback). ISBN 0 521 64679 0 (paperback)
1. Afro-Americans – Race identity.   2. Afro-Americans – Politics and
government.   3. Autobiography – Political aspects – United States.
4. United States – Race relations.   5. Autobiography – Afro-American
authors.   I. Title.   II. Series.
E185.625.M685   1999
973'.0496073 – dc21   98-36538   CIP

ISBN 0 521 64114 4 hardback
ISBN 0 521 64679 0 paperback

What I thought was love
in me, I find a thousand instances
as fear. Of the tree's shadow
winding around the chair, a distant music
of frozen birds rattling
in the cold.
                    Where ever I go to claim
my flesh, there are entrances
of spirit. And even its comforts
are hideous uses I strain
to understand.
                    Though I am a man
who is loud
on the birth
of his ways. Publicly redefining
each change in my soul, as if I had predicted
them,
                and profited, biblically, even tho
                their changing weight,
                                erased familiarity
                                from my face.
                                        A question I think,
                                        an answer, whatever sits
                                        counting the minutes
                                        till you die.

        When they say, "It is Roi
        who is dead?" I wonder
        who will they mean?

LEROI JONES, IMMEDIATELY BEFORE BECOMING AMIRI BARAKA

Categorization is not the sin; the problem is the lack of desire to explain
the categorizations that are made.

Some of our greatest politicians have been forced to become ministers or
blues singers.

PATRICIA WILLIAMS

Contents

Acknowledgments   *page* ix

Part one: Theorizing race, autobiography, and identity politics

1   What is identity politics? Race and the autobiographical   3

2   African-American autobiography and the field of autobiography studies   28

Part two: The politics of Negro self-representation

3   Three theories of the race of W. E. B. Du Bois   57

4   The gender, race, and culture of anti-lynching politics in the Jim Crow era   83

5   Representing the Negro as proletarian   112

Part three: The dialectics of home: gender, nation and blackness since the 1960s

6   Malcolm X and the grammar of redemption   137

7   The political identity "woman" as emergent from the space of Black Power   164

8   Home and profession in black feminism   189

Notes   217
Works cited   262
Index   275

vii

Acknowledgments

When reading works produced within the contemporary academy, acknowledgments are a particularly significant autobiographical space. Especially in those texts in which the author's self-position is not rigorously theorized (as either object or subject), acknowledgments may provide a window onto issues that are otherwise taken for granted. I do not claim to be stating anything especially clever in saying this: many of us realize that thanking universities and fellowship foundations for institutional support is a central *ideological* component of our lives, and that the least subtle of "vulgar" analyses of "manufacturing consent" are not misplaced, however ultimately inadequate they may be. Others of us are also in denial about this. I can say nothing about that here. Nor am I claiming that the publicly-private personality expressed by various scholars in their acknowledgments contains a relationship of immediate determination with the content of their books in every case. (One interpretation of this book would be that its topic is, precisely, "mediation.") But, among other things, the argument that follows, including its quasi-autobiographical coda, is that it is never a good idea to avoid asking the question of the acknowledgments, in whatever form they appear, *especially* when reading the two literary genres addressed herein: autobiography and critical theory.

This, then, is the relatively unrigorous version of my autobiography:

Most of this book was drafted while I was in Oakland, California, having its origins in my second semester at Berkeley in 1990. There is a specific ambivalence in that sentence – retrospectively, I date my present life in terms of my entry to graduate school, yet at the time I

Acknowledgments

thought of myself as an off-campus activist at least as much as a professional intellectual. For this reason, the basic structuration of the book, its practical formation, was influenced in specific ways by the people I was doing anti-racist political work with *outside the academy* in a way that will undoubtedly never again be true of my intellectual work. In 1990 I was not some kind of model activist; in 1998 I maintain nonprofessional connections and commitments which continue to influence me: the two kinds of work are not in binary relation. Yet they have been materially distinct in my life, and this distinction cannot be disavowed by pretending to "go beyond" it. I make it here to prioritize the activists and the work that first motivated this book. In this regard I want to thank first the people least likely to read it, some of whom I remain in contact with, others who I have not spoken to for years: Jose Carasco, Mickey Ellinger, Harmony Goldberg, George Lipman, Kareima McKnight, Simone Rowe, Ikuko Sato, Rhodney Ward, generally John Brown Anti-Klan Committee, Immigrant Rights Action Pledge, Direct Action Against Racism, Roots Against War, and the Campus Coalition Against the Gulf War. Closest among my California activist friends for the last eight years is marxist autodidact and all around superior human being Rene Francisco Poitevin, who read much of this book in earlier forms. He enrolled in graduate school in sociology in the fall of 1997.

In my professional life, two individuals followed this book from beginning to end, and have, in every sense, made my career possible: Barbara Christian and Abdul JanMohamed. Each, through their rigor and their personal commitment, centered me at times when my research was floundering. I do not think you can go very wrong, when reading this text, thinking carefully about the particular mix: a white anti-racist activist, in long-term conversation with Barbara's commitments to the narrative text or "work," to black women's autonomy, and to the centrality of *movements*; and Abdul's commitment to a revised psychoanalytical marxist theory. All of us have politics that could be described as third worldist, though only I use the term. I make no claims to follow either one in particular ways; they both disagree with numerous things that I say here. I claim that they have been incredible catalysts for me, and a wonderfully supportive faculty.

Percy Hintzen is the other faculty member who helped me find the argument of this book over many years. Other faculty and graduate students at Berkeley who read work of mine or from whom I have received help, support, and friendship, or merely conversed with me

x

about theory, during the period of initial writing included Arturo Aldama, Victor Bascara, Rakesh Bhandari, Mitch Breitwieser, Oscar Compomanes, Donna Jones, Montye Fuse, Arlene Kaiser, Viet Thanh Nguyen, Catherine Ramirez, Leslie Salzinger, Amrijit Singh, Victoria Torres, France Winddance Twine, Jonathan Warren, Sau-Ling Wong. My dissertation writing group – Jyoti Hosagrahar, Mia Fuller, Arthur Riss, Jennifer Shaw, Jan McHargue, Rebecca Dobkins, and Tamra Suslow-Ortiz – supported and fed me, in addition to reading several chapters, during a key year. David Szanton, Dean of Interdisciplinary Studies, organized us and gave us funds for dinner.

I will always be grateful to my undergraduate advisor, Lucy Maddox, who first caused me to think about "American" "identity."

After moving to Knoxville, Tennessee, I met both of the people who have given me most intellectually and personally, Heather Dobbins and Carter Mathes, as students in my black literature classes. (Carter has gone on to a Ph.D. program at Berkeley and Heather, an accomplished poet, swears the last thing in the world she will do is get a Ph.D.) Among my colleagues, my weekly lunches with Mark Hulsether, completing his first book at the same time as I have been, have provided particularly steady grounding, while George Hutchinson, Chris Holmlund, and Handel Wright have also been serious interlocutors. Krisztian Horvath and Susan Hilderbrand's extensive help in preparing the final manuscript was truly service beyond the call. Other Tennesseans who have contributed substantially to my intellectual life are: Misty Anderson, Shannon Anderson, Joy Asekun, Janet Atwill, Charles Biggs, Erik Bledsoe, Allen Dunn, John Evelev, Jesse Graves, Chris Hodge, Ron Hopson, La Vinia Jennings, Leslie LaChance, Jeanne Leiby, Chuck Maland, Keith Norris, Betsy Sutherland, Randi Voss, and John Zomchick. Thank you also to my English 443 (African-American Autobiography) seminar in the spring of 1996 for being such excellent discussants for much of this material, as well as for humoring my desire to have the class on Nikki Giovanni at the entrance ramp to the James White Freeway, once 400 Mulvaney Street.

Thanks to my friends at Solutions to Issues of Concern of Knoxvilleans (SICK), Tennesseans for Fair Taxation, and Tennessee Industrial Renewal Network.

In recent years – and especially since moving to Knoxville – my intellectual community has been partially made on the net. Most critically important is Bruce Simon, who I began arguing with on a postcolonial studies reading list in 1993 and who did me the service of reading this entire manuscript in draft. He also introduced me to Wahneema Lubiano, whose help in the completion of this project was enormous. Other friends or helpful interlocutors who are initially, or primarily, from the net include Michael Bibby, Anthony Rucker, and Kali Tal. Generally speaking, interaction with others on the Spoon Collective's postcolonialism and marxism lists, the American Studies Association's H-AMSTDY, the Marxist Literary Group list, and the UI-Chicago based AFAMLIT list, has been of great assistance in the initial articulation of many ideas.

Others to whom I am grateful for corresponding with me about specific sections of my book include Gina Dent, Colleen Lye, William Maxwell, and Alan Wald.

This book could of course not exist without my year off, provided by the Charlotte W. Newcombe Dissertation Fellowship, Woodrow Wilson National Fellowship Foundation, in 1994–5. The John O. Hodges Better English Fund at the University of Tennessee provided two courses release time and occasionally other expenses. Otherwise, thanks to those who have hired me to teach.

Thank you to the old and close friends whose names don't appear in any of the above categories, to my family, and to anyone who reads this.

And thank you to Ruth Mostern for, well, everything. Maybe we'll even get jobs in the same city sometime. (And, because it is theoretically relevant to chapter eight: Mostern is *not* my father's last name, but one we made up. And if we knew how defensive it'd make us, we'd never have done it. Now you know.)

Part one

**Theorizing race, autobiography,
and identity politics**

What is identity politics? Race and the autobiographical

I believe in the recognition of devices as *devices* – but I also
believe in the reality of those devices. In one century men
choose to hide their conquests under religion, in another under
race. So you and I may recognize the fraudulence of the device
in both cases, but the fact remains that a man who has a sword
run through him because he will not become a Moslem or a
Christian – or who is lynched because his is black – is suffering
the utter reality of that device of conquest. And it is pointless
to pretend that it doesn't *exist* – merely because it is a lie.

Lorraine Hansberry[1.]

O my body, make of me always a man who questions!

Frantz Fanon[2]

Representation has not withered away.   Gayatri Spivak[3]

Identifying "identity politics"

It has become typical to see the widest variety of writers of both
popular and academic work arguing against, or discussing the limitations of, something which they call "identity politics." The positions
which are grouped together by this name are not generally categor-
ized that way by anyone who actually holds these positions: such
people might refer to themselves, variously, as "nationalists," "feminists," "Afrocentrists," or "multiculturalists," with further adjec-
tival modifications referring to specific modes of nationalism or feminism ("cultural," "economic"), or specific political modifiers, like
"liberal," "radical," or "critical," the last term of which once denoted
marxist sympathies, but does not anymore. It is, by contrast, exceptionally rare to see someone arguing in favor of a position which they
refer to as "identity politics," since the term, as Micaela di Leonardo

has pointed out, is "innately a term of opprobrium."[4] This fact should cause the reader sympathetic to the idea that power is not distributed equally under postmodern capitalism,[5] with some categorical consistency among lines often referred to as "identities," to wonder what the implications of such a category having so many opponents – di Leonardo among them – might be. Indeed, the specific politics I named do, in some way, all suppose that there is a structural relationship between the field of subjectivities widely termed "identities," and the field of activities widely termed "politics." But the meaning of these terms, and the forms of the connection made, vary widely from critic to critic and argument to argument, with people who have passionately denounced identity politics in one context often accused of engaging in it in others.

June Jordan's work, which I take as an example of a particularly elegant contemporary radical humanism, will provide my first example. Jordan is periodically cited for being a (specifically) black woman who opposes identity politics, a fact which first of all should be taken as a sign that the field of identity politics is always already identified with women of color.[6] Jordan has argued, obviously correctly, that stated political positions and the fact of being black and/or female are not necessarily connected, and that for this reason her own earlier assumption that political organizing ought to occur around such identifications can no longer be maintained. It is easy to agree with the critique of this simplified version of "identity politics" – the claim that, for example, since all women have common interests, feminist organizing only occurs when women join to fight for these interests. But, of course, it is difficult (though perhaps not impossible) to find any contemporary writer who maintains this simplistic position. In fact, this absolutist position was quite rare and widely maligned even in the period that supposedly typified it, that of the social movements of the period 1956–80: it has always been most common as a straw argument against which people work.[7] For all that, I have used a recent Jordan text, an essay republished in the same volume in which she criticizes identity politics, called "Wrong or White"[8] in a multi-racial classroom, and no piece of writing that I have taught has ever provoked the racist fury (or liberal patronization) against black women intellectuals for ostensibly engaging in "identity politics" than that piece did. To at least some of the students in the class where I used it, Jordan's willingness to use the labels "black," "white," "male," "heterosexual," "people of color," etc., in talking about political phenomena was *a priori* evidence of something that academics (though not my students) call "essentialism." As such, these terms challenged my students' implicit individualism, their often honest attempts to "take people for who they are." From my point of view, in opposing "identity politics," instead of, for example, masculinist black nationalism, Jordan helps to obscure what is at stake in the term, the ways in which her opposition to identity politics is itself received *on the basis of her race and gender.* Jordan's career in black feminism itself demonstrates Toril Moi's point that *"even when they say the same things,* women are not speaking from the same position as men, and consequently are not arguing the same thing at all."[9] This is especially true for black women in the academy right now. It is because our speech is always received, in the rhetorical situation, as being from an identity-position, that identical political statements by me or by Jordan are, whatever their identity, understood socially in nonidentical fashions. Our identities literally *cannot* be disconnected from our politics.[10]

Di Leonardo traces the concern with identity politics in the contemporary US back through the "women's culture" discussions of the 1970s to its "ultimate source in modern nationalist ideologies."[11] From the point of view of the argument I will be sketching throughout this book, this tracing is historically inadequate inasmuch as it dwells on one lineage of identity politics that has, for historical reasons, become exceptionally simple to attack. In this book I trace identity politics through writings about the racialization process by members of the group whose minoritization is key to the structure of all major/minor positioning in the US – those visibly of African descent. My lineage will, like hers, intersect with the rise of third world nationalisms as constructed, generally bourgeois phenomena related to the full integration of global capitalism in this century. However, since di Leonardo's position on cultural nationalism is unable to distinguish between the specific constructions of nationalism in Europe in the nineteenth century and in the decolonizing world in the twentieth (like her major source, Benedict Anderson's *Imagined Communities*), I will continually insist that power/value relations, and not "culture," determine the limits of what she calls "the shifting nature of identity,"[12] and thus the significance of identity politics at a given moment. This is why Patricia Williams can state simultaneously, in the concluding "Word on Categories" in *The Alchemy of Race and Rights*, that "while being black has been the most powerful social attribution in my life, it is only one of a number of governing narratives or presiding fictions by which I am constantly reconfiguring myself in the world" and then, in the very same context, that

> I do believe that the simple matter of the color of one's skin so profoundly affects the way one is treated, so radically shapes what one is allowed to think and feel about this society, that the decision to generalize from such a division is valid. Furthermore, it is hard to describe succinctly the racial perspective and history that are my concern.[13]

We must learn to think both sides of this at the same time: race is not the sum total of Williams' subjectivity; yet it is a "perspective"; what is unique about this perspective cannot be described succinctly or narrowly, yet the set of racialized experiences she has had have become the "valid" "concern" of an entire book of critical legal theory. Judith Roof and Robyn Wiegman write, "perhaps it is only a scholar, only a member of an oppressed group, who could feel trapped enough to intellectualize herself beyond the collective psyche of her group."[14] Writing a critical history of African-American identity politics is narrating the history of this "perhaps."

All politics can be described as an engaged relationship between the social location of particular political actors and the social totality in which their action takes place. Since this is the case, I will not suddenly be the first person to defend "identity politics" from its attackers; often I agree with arguments against specific identitarian political claims; often I don't. Rather I will try to describe the many and complicated ways in which intellectuals from a community both already constituted and always being reconstituted have attempted to work with existing racial positions in the formation of their political identities. "Race-ness" in the US is to this day primarily attributed to black and other nonwhite Americans, though, as African American intellectuals since W. E. B. Du Bois published "The Souls of White Folk" in 1920 have pointed out, white people "have" it too. That it is always being reconstituted in practice in no way eliminates the implications of the fact that it is always already constituted as an identity, an "always already" which implies (contrary to much recent opinion) its *relative stability* and *reproduction*. Thus I will argue that however differently we can demonstrate that "race-ness" was constituted in 1903, when Du Bois made his justly famous statement that "the problem of the 20th century is the problem of the color line," from the way it is constituted today, it has remained an ever-present lens by which the world is viewed and has continued to be a primary force in social struggle. That something as biologically insignificant as skin-

6

color has, in becoming raced, maintained such a role is precisely what should provide the impetus for an inquiry into the historical interrelations between the socioeconomic and psychological meanings of identity as it structures and determines politics.

Identifying "Black Autobiography": determination, articulation, and the racial object

Imagining identity politics this way means adequately conceptualizing the verb "determine" in the previous sentence. Much recent political theory, since Laclau and Mouffe's *Hegemony and Socialist Strategy*,[15] resists marxist accounts of determination, which are seen as reductionist because of the observation that no automatic link can be made between a given subject's relation to the means of production and her/his stated politics. Therefore, in the account of Laclau and Mouffe and those, like Stuart Hall, most influenced by them, the notion of "determination" has largely been replaced by the more relatively volunteerist term "articulation," whereby it is said that while a cultural pattern of articulation may exist between various subject-positions and various political statements, this relationship is arbitrary, conforming to no objective conditions of social enforcement. (Indeed, for Laclau and Mouffe there is nothing that can be usefully termed "society" at all.) June Jordan's discussion of race/gender position as implying no necessary politics follows a pattern consistent with Laclau and Mouffe's thinking, and this position is typical of much recent academic writing – and nearly all cultural theory – about women of color. This has served to accomplish the widespread articulation of social theory that takes the attack on "essentialism" as its primary object, generally called poststructuralism, to race and gender theory, in a formation professedly "postmarxist."

In race theory, it is Hall's formulations that have been most consistently influential. After twenty years of working in a generally marxist problematic,[16] Hall decisively abandoned marxist parameters in the theorization of race after declaring "new times" with the fall of the Soviet bloc in 1989. In his postmarxist period, the notion of race has been produced through emphasis on four elements: articulation, process, culture, and fragmentation. Thus:

> [1] An articulation is the form of the connection that *can* make a
> unity of two different elements, under certain conditions. It is a
> linkage which is not necessary, determined, absolute and essential for all time.[17]

7

[2, 3] Perhaps instead of thinking identity as an already accomplished fact, which the new cultural practices then represent, we should think, instead, of identity as a "production" which is never complete, always in process, and always constituted within, not outside, representation. This view problematizes the very authority and authenticity to which the term "cultural identity" lays claim.[18]

[4] [Citing the work of photographer Armet Francis:] Such images offer a way of imposing an imaginary coherence on the experience of dispersal and fragmentation, which is the history of all enforced diasporas.[19]

My book will not *disagree* with any of the above formulations. I will, instead, propose repeatedly that (1) while the concept of articulation defined above is useful and necessary, it supplements but certainly does not displace structural determination in thinking race, class, and gender; that (2) the rhetoric of "perhaps" and "never complete" in the discussion of the real processes of identity production serves to obscure the persistence of specific identity positions, which, while of course not "complete" (whatever that would mean) nevertheless could not become other than they are without a generalized rewiring of the identity-production machinery; that (3) this fact is masked further by the all-too-quick slippage from "identity" to "cultural identity," as though this took care of the distinct question of "racial identity"; and finally that (4) the last passage quoted could just as easily read: "such images offer a way of forging a symbolic coherence on the experience of dispersal and fragmentation, one necessary to the political process of all enforced diasporas." This sentence would not be better than Hall's. But understanding that his sentence, and my rewriting of it, deserve each other is essential to the production of a genuinely radical analysis of political identities.

In the same two years that *Hegemony and Socialist Strategy* was published, Eric Olin Wright's *Classes* and the English translation of Pierre Bourdieu's *Distinction*, the former a work of highly unorthodox marxism, the latter not marxist at all, gave elaborate statistical accounts demonstrating that patterns of consciousness – tendencies – based on class position do in fact exist.[20] Indeed, Wright's account even provided some (by no means adequate) means for reading the US working class as predominantly female and nonwhite, and thus its political articulations as not only implicitly anti-capitalist in certain ways, but tending toward feminism and anti-racism as well.[21] Theoretically, however, the point is not that for Wright (let alone

8

Bourdieu) there is some kind of pure oppositional consciousness embedded in an already defined aggregate called "the working class," but rather that there is a relevant structural *tendency* for certain objectively positioned groups to articulate certain positions, a tendency that conforms perfectly to Raymond Williams' flexible, non-reductive double definition of structural class determination: for Williams, to say that consciousness is determined by economic location is to say simply that the economy "sets limits" and "exerts pressures" on what any given individual may think.[22] Stated this way it is hard to know what is controversial: if one is unable to purchase expensive consumer goods, one will be limited in the opinions one may have of them; if one works chopping chicken parts in a locked building ten hours a day, there are specific physical and material events one's thinking will be pressed to understand – like the experience of consistently poor health. In all cases there are multiple cultural and political ideologies that intersect these limits and pressures – but these ideologies will not be distributed in the same patterns as among middle class intellectuals. And indeed, the same point has been made available for race and gender theory, with nonessentialist accounts of determination a persistent presence, often under the name "standpoint epistemologies."[23]

We must be committed to defining identity politics – perhaps you will afford me with some better neologism, but I am content with this term for the moment – in a way that respects both identity and politics, which does not imply that identity *is* politics but rather recalls that identity and politics are not independent variables, and therefore that solidarity always stands in the complicated relationship between the two. One of the things that has been obscured by the contemporary presumption – especially strong in ethnic studies – that marxist theory is a relic of the past with nothing to teach us,[24] is that this is what marxism has attempted to do since at least *The Eighteenth Brumaire of Louis Napoleon*.[25] In this context it is simply ignored that there have been serious pro-black nationalist and pro-feminist political positions generated from marxist ontologies throughout this century, accounts which have themselves described a structure for the determinate emergence of multiple identity positions. They differ from poststructuralist accounts not in their ability to account for race and gender, but in their insistence on systematicity. Since marxism derives class not from "discourse" but from the economy, when a marxist notices that race and gender, like class, are centrally important political categories, s/he asks what structure or

9

system of material determination produces these categories as discourses.[26]

Cedric Robinson's *Black Marxism* embarks on this project precisely.[27] For Robinson, the inadequacy of Marx's argument in *Capital* is that, by researching (with great perspicuity) the way in which surplus-value was wrest from the English working class during the mid-nineteenth century, he created a theory of capitalism which emphasized exploitation as first of all a diachronic issue: capital expands when the bourgeoisie controls value created in the course of the working day. In so doing, he neglected to see that capitalist exploitation began not in Europe at all, but in the development of the modern world system[28] via the settlement and expropriation of America (including the genocide of its residents), and the employment of a superexploited class of laborers: African slaves. As a result of being the first, and most exploited, class of proletarians, Robinson proposes that black diaspora peoples created the tradition of opposition most able to respond to capitalism at its weakest points; for this reason, black working class struggle for nationalist autonomy – which itself depends on the facts of already existing segregation – is the necessary point of reference for socialist politics. The persistence of race, in this analysis, is assumed rather than explained; because the labor force was split racially at the inception of capitalism, it must continue to be until the end of capitalism – and perhaps beyond. While Robinson's historical narrative is certainly correct in defining the origins of racialization, I am not convinced that contemporary capitalism requires continued segregation in the terms Robinson's analysis suggests. In fact, race is relatively unlikely to be determined by the needs of late capitalist production. However, once constructed, important discursive systems like race tend to take on lives of their own; thus this book accepts the category of the "memory of slavery," conceived by Gilroy as a determinate trauma – a psychoanalytic category, here sociologized – as an explanation for the persistence of "blackness" as a mechanism in US politics.[29]

It is in this context that I employ the category of "autobiography," which is *not* "personal experience," but rather an articulation based on the determinate memory and recall of experience via the lens of traumatically constrained ideology, to describe the continuing racialization of politics.[30] Becky Thompson and Sangeeta Tyagi suggest that "autobiography illustrates why racial identity formation occurs at the intersection of a person's subjective memory of trauma and collective remembrance of histories of domination."[31] Yet autobiogra-

phy does not illustrate this intersection in a simple way, as bell hooks
reflects: after writing her autobiography she "felt as though [she] had
an overview not so much of my childhood but of those experiences
that were deeply imprinted in my consciousness. Significantly, that
which was absent, left out, not included also was important."[32] In
particular, autobiography is that *process* which articulates the determined subject so as to actively produce a newly positive identity. To
the extent that racial trauma is, precisely, what autobiography recalls,
racial identity politics is determined, and a variety of other politics
may, as hooks knows, be repressed. Yet the recognition of the limitations of the process, like the identity itself, can only emerge through
the process, to which there is no alternative.

African-American literary history begins with the self-consciously
politicized autobiography. Paul Gilroy's recent statement, that African-American autobiography "express[es] in the most powerful way
a tradition of writing in which autobiography becomes an act or
process of simultaneous self-creation and self-emancipation"[33] has
been demonstrated over the last two decades in work by William
Andrews, Joanne Braxton, Stephen Butterfield, David Dudley, V. P.
Franklin, Sidonie Smith, Valerie Smith, and numerous others.[34] James
Olney, indeed, has claimed that the very development of autobiography as a field of study has depended on the entrance of African-
American as well as other minority and feminist literatures into
academic study.[35] Gilroy's text continues:

> the presentation of a public persona thus becomes a founding
> motif within the expressive culture of the African diaspora...
> Eagerly received by the [abolition] movement to which they
> were addressed, these [autobiographies] helped to mark out a
> dissident space within the bourgeois public sphere which they
> aimed to suffuse with their utopian content. The autobiographi-
> cal character of many [public] statements is thus absolutely
> crucial.[36]

The tradition of African-American writing is thus one in which political commentary necessitates, invites, and assumes autobiography as
its rhetorical form. This is simultaneously the result of oppression,
where, as Andrews states, the white reading public will not trust
anything but the (supposedly) transparent testimony of the slave,
who is presumed only to report, not theorize; but, dialectically,
through the success of numerous slave narrators in making the testimonial space culturally available for the purpose of theorizing selves.
Gilroy's claim that the autobiographical mode of political representa-

tion is, then, a culturally-based ethical pattern, is borne out by the extent to which *nearly all* African-American political leaders (regardless of politics; self-designated or appointed by one or another community) have chosen to write personal stories as a means of theorizing their political positions: Frederick Douglass (three times), Booker T. Washington, W. E. B. Du Bois (as least three times, depending on how you count), James Weldon Johnson, Ida B. Wells Barnett, Paul Robeson, Martin Luther King, Jr., Malcolm X, Angela Davis, and the list goes on.[37] Thus Gates' influential formulation: over and over "the narrated, descriptive 'eye' was put into service as a literary form to posit both the individual 'I' of the black author as well as the collective 'I' of the race."[38]

Narrating the contours and maneuvers that make up this practice from the point of view that these maneuvers are neither corrupt, nor correct, but are the determinate practice of racial politics, is the major strategy of this book. The book consists of seven chapters, after this one, organized along the following lines: chapter two extends the introductory material of this chapter into a review of various theoretical positions in the field of "Autobiography Studies." My goal in chapter two will not be to define "autobiography" as it is used in this book, as my last several paragraphs have already done that, but rather to locate work in African-American autobiography studies, including my own, as a particular "minority" space in the larger field. Chapter two may be considered optional reading for those not interested in Autobiography Studies as such. My main narrative of racialization picks up again in chapter three, where I discuss the extremely important theoretical and autobiographical contributions of W. E. B. Du Bois, and the difficult oscillations of his writing with regard to the meanings of his own racialization. In chapter four I discuss black liberal autobiography before World War II as it is cut along gender lines, emphasizing in particular the representation of lynching as a galvanizing force for racial identification and resulting political action. In chapter five I describe the relationship between Communist politics and black subjectivity as it is illustrated by several little-read black Communist texts, and suggest that the history of 1960s concepts of black nationalism should not be written without a consideration of Communism. Chapter six explores the contemporary significance of *The Autobiography of Malcolm X* through an analysis of its internally warring subject positions and changing narratives. Chapter seven reads gender and subjectivity in the two major women's autobiographies to emerge from the black power period, Nikki Giovanni's

Gemini and Angela Davis' *Autobiography*, neither of which is self-identified as "feminist." Finally, in chapter eight these two autobiographies are mapped among several autobiographical works of black feminism, a politics that, in the work of bell hooks, attempts to account for autobiography as a moment of its own self-becoming. Ultimately this chapter narrates how the entry of black feminism into the academy has led to disputes about the effectiveness of hooks' autobiographical method.

The above, I hope, stands as the theoretical justification for the approach taken in this project. Before I begin the narrative described in the last paragraph, the remainder of this introduction will commence three further arguments that make up the key political content of the book: the relationship of feminism to the contemporary revision of black identity politics; the bifurcation of race and culture, and the confusion over terminology that results from this bifurcation; and the question of narrative as a fundamental moment of political action.

June Jordan and black feminism: the construction of independence

The majority of the texts discussed in this book are by black men, a fact which is the necessary outcome of my intent to explore *dominant* meanings of racialization this century, and my tendency toward the analysis of texts by well-known political "leaders." This should not be taken as a lack of commitment to feminism, but rather as compatible with a specific, and so far relatively uncommon, feminist argument.

There is no question that the basic tendency of all the great male narrators of racialization is to be patriarchal in specific ways which I address in detail. However, it is my contention that far from feminism (or anti-patriarchy) providing the excuse to call into question racial identity, what will be required is a feminist analysis of the specific social dynamics in which *black men's oppression is a specifically gendered oppression*. That is to say, the imagery of black men in the US depends not only on their blackness, but also on the specific fear of their gender, or *raced-gender*. As a strategy to rectify this specifically gendered problem, anti-racism for much of this century took the specifically patriarchal forms of the dominant society, to its own detriment. Thus this book is in part an exploration of how radical anti-racism in both integrationist and nationalist forms became, in the 1ᵣ⁶⁻⁻ specifically and arrogantly patriarchal discourse. In making thi ment, I am following broadly the work of Hortense Spillers, for whom the African-American man does not fully attain patriarchal gendering due to his lack of possession of the patronymic, and Robyn Wiegman, who devotes a chapter of *American Anatomies* to discussing lynching as a prime figure for the enforcement of black male gendering.[39] In this book, I seek the origins of contemporary anti-racism in the necessary and excellent political struggle against lynching, begun by Ida B. Wells Barnett in an explicitly feminist manner; and then trace how the analysis of lynching became the analysis of the constriction of something called "black manhood," the reconstruction of which would then constitute racial equality or liberation for black *men*.

Saying this cannot be a retrospective criticism of Ida B. Wells Barnett or Walter White for their focus on anti-lynching in its own historical context, since, in fact, lynching really was one primary mode of terror used in the disenfranchisement of African-American men *and* women. Nor even should we dismiss the anti-racist importance of the specific articulation of manhood-as-such in *The Autobiography of Malcolm X* in 1965, even as we find ourselves trying to undo this model of manhood today. Because the *gender oppression* of black men by white men and women continues, the way for contemporary feminism to avoid being rearticulated as racism toward black men is for it to focus not only on opposition to black men's gender privilege (which of course it must do), but additionally to attend to black manhood as a dominated social location. Paying attention to the racist and sexist rhetoric of "Welfare Mothers" must be made compatible with attention to the racist *and sexist* rhetoric of "violent criminals who need to be put in prison." If this is the case, tracing the emergence of a specific, racialized feminism as an identity politics in the 1970s becomes essential to the contemporary reconstruction of blackness-as-such. This is true both because of the space it creates for black women's autonomy – which, as will become important late in this book, should not be confused with "separatism"[40] – *and* because of its centrality in the reconstruction of black male gendering, a project brought underway in the academy by Phillip Bryan Harper, bell hooks, Kobena Mercer, and Marcellus Blount and George Cunningham.[41] In spite of its currency in the academy, however, it seems likely that this project has not yet entered a broader social movement, which, as Barbara Smith reminds us, is the necessary condition of long-term political effectivity.[42]

While the later chapters of this book, especially six, seven, and eight, narrate this gender dynamic with much more care, I would like to introduce the dynamic of black feminist autonomism and its effect on racial identity politics by returning to June Jordan via an analysis of the pivotal essay "Declaration of an Independence I Would Just As Soon Not Have." This essay was originally published in *Ms.* in 1976 with the title "Second Thoughts of a Black Feminist," but my reading of it here is based on the version reprinted in her collection *Civil Wars*.[43] Though it declares black women's independence, this short essay does not suggest at any moment that there is something necessary connecting its political argument with the social fact that its writer is black and female. On the contrary, according to the second and third sentences of the essay, "there must be hundreds of other women [and] . . . maybe hundreds of men who want the same drastic things to happen."[44] The essay is an open appeal to all these people, women and men of whatever race, to "interlink" with her. The next three paragraphs lay out objective statistical information regarding the "famine afflicting some 800 million lives," the "majority of Black [children] doomed to semi-illiteracy and/or obsolete vocational training for jobs" that have "disappeared," and the fact that from the point of view of the people in power "you are damned as Black, damned as a woman, and damned as a quote female head of household un-quote."[45] Only in the last of these three paragraphs does Jordan suggest that there is some sense in which her race and gender contributes to the writing of these facts: she states that "if you happen to be a Black woman, as I am," then "you undoubtedly recognize" these damnations.[46] But the fact of the damnations is clearly still separable from her apprehension of them. Only the essayist's consistent rhetoric of emotional connection – the idea that these facts might leave one "nauseous, jumpy, and chronically enraged" – makes it clear that an identitarian, and not merely a rational argument, is being made.[47]

It is in the question of linking with other people that the issue of identity becomes central in the second half of the essay. Jordan states that for a period of time she worked "alone," writing poems and articles, eventually deciding that this accomplished nothing. At this point she sought to join collectivities of struggle which were fighting to change these objective conditions, groups organized as "the Black Movement, the Third World Movement, and the Women's Movement." In these movements, unfortunately, she "encountered a woeful magnitude of internecine, unfortunate, and basically untenable conflicts of analysis."[48] As we would (now) expect, Jordan reports that the black movement defined issues around the needs of black men, and worse, black "manhood"; that the third world movements were unable to cope with corrupt leaders and institutions in the third world which engage in class and gender warfare and make coalition with first world, white-dominated corporate capital; and that the women's movement has granted "exceedingly little attention to the problems of working class or poor people, to the victimization of Black women who head families."[49] In each case, Jordan states, the participants in these movements expect her to leave part of herself at the door, leading her to conclude:

> I would hope that the sum total of the liberation struggles I have attempted to sketch, and briefly criticize, would mean this: That I will be free to be who I am, Black and female, without fear, without pain, without humiliation. That I will be free to become whatever my life requires of me, without posturing, without compromise, without terror... That I can count on a sisterhood and a brotherhood that will let me give my life to its consecration, without equivocating, without sorrow...
>
> Toward these ends, I have written this account of one woman's declaration of an independence I would just as soon not have. I believe I am not alone. Please verify.[50]

Clearly, the strategy of assuming both that identity is and is not central to the politics of the entire essay is central to this conclusion. Politics has the responsibility to create the space for Jordan's assertion of identity, which is both singular and also black and female. That is, the facts of race and gender are not incidental, but necessary to politics, even as they are insufficient for the full accomplishment of identity. Meanwhile this politics, to be effective, will not limit itself to those who have Jordan's race and gender.

However, the key moment in understanding the nature of the emergence of black feminist articulation, toward which this essay is historically pivotal, is in the part of the essay I intentionally skipped until this point: the headnote composed for its 1981 republication. It reads:

> If it is not apparent from the text, then let me make it clear that I wrote this from the inside. As a Black woman, and as a human being within the First World Movement, and as a woman who loves women as well as she loves men... My question at the end of this piece was answered by *Black women* who wrote to me, care of *Ms.*, from all over the country. Yes, they said, you are not alone![51]

The words "Black women" are not incidental, nor are they "wrong," possible to condemn as a political mistake in retrospect. At least two things are likely to be true. First, it is likely that, even though Jordan may have received a small number of letters of agreement from people who were not black women, the ones that mattered *to her* were those by black women. This is speculation; perhaps she received no others to begin with. In either case, the fact that black women are at the center of rearticulating a politics is itself the central factor in a newly emerging and changing raced-gender identity. Second, to the extent that Jordan's own writing has "gone beyond" this moment, it would be foolish and inappropriate to assume that this could have happened *except through the politics of identity*. It has not suddenly become optional for black single mothers, who continue twenty years later to be oppressed in many of the same ways Jordan describes, to simply self-generate solidarity with others. The process of black feminist autonomism is – among other things – a personal and psychological one that will get repeated by every generation for as long as social identities are socioeconomically produced along particular, and predictable, lines; it cannot be "gone beyond" unless the material condition which produces it – the psychological marginalization of all who are not white men in the service of capital – ends.

Racial space, cultural space

I am overdetermined from without. (Frantz Fanon)[52]

"Negritude" was never perceived as a mere essence that could be distilled down to a way of shaking hands or to the food we eat. *It was not only a shout in church, but the entire history of the ability to shout out loud.* (Jewelle Gomez)[53]

The materiality of race-ness

A dialectical attitude toward the understanding of the social world always requires the critic to think two things – subjectivity and objectivity – at the same time. This attitude is quite distinct from the one that claims to "go beyond" the "binary" of subject and object, an attitude which time and again is used as a means of ignoring materially operative distinctions between the focalizing subject and the preponderance of the objective forces. When thinking the system of racial subjectivity and white supremacy at present, one must always minimally think two things, which stand at different points between enforcement and focalization: skin-color visibility as such, and the entire set of dispositions that make up what we might, applying Bourdieu, call the "racial habitus."[54]

17

There is no way not to persistently return to "gross morphological" features which determine job, housing, and economic and cultural opportunities when talking about racial identity in a system whose disciplinary mechanisms are white supremacist.[55] "Racial identity," as I've already discussed, emerged in the psycho-socioeconomic valuation of people *based on skin color* as the identifiable object which conditions patterns of exchange; its continued effectivity results from the fact that such evaluative moments on the part of people with (psychological, economic, or police) power are no less present in the psychic formation of contemporary blacks as previously.[56] In turn, these patterns of exchange have generated patterns of cultural disposition and political affiliation, patterns which split the middle of class, gender, and religious, sexual, and other positionalities, without calling into question their simultaneous operations. As Robyn Wiegman states:

> [R]ace as a constituted "fact" of the body – as a truth that not only can but must be pursued beyond the realm of visible similarities and differences – characterizes the methodological proclivities of the modern episteme, and ... under its disciplinary gaze ... an elaborate discourse purporting the African's inherent inhumanity is most productively ... waged.[57]

What needs elaboration is precisely the extent to which the critique of the natural readability of the racialized body – which is, in Wiegman's terms (taken from Foucault), the critique of the visual presumptions of modernity in general – has itself been the product of that overdetermined body in its experiences. This is why, in Du Bois' *Dusk of Dawn* (discussed in chapter three), the critique of modernity *is* the "autobiography of the race concept."

The common attempt to eliminate skin-color as the object within this historical system, because we know that there is no biological reason for skin color and hair to matter, will always fail because while it can explain how "cultural identity is considered an achievement,"[58] it cannot explain why cultural identity, on one hand, and socioeconomic success, on another, are achieved in statistically consistent patterns with regard to skin color, and remain enforceable *as* skin-color in so many social locations. Sartre, an early advocate of performative models of subjectivity, argued that "there can be no doubt that *one makes oneself* a bourgeois ... but in order to make oneself bourgeois, one must be bourgeois."[59] *Cultural* identity can only be considered as a particular achievement of particularly *raced* individuals.

It should, for example, be obvious at this late date that if there is a "general" United States popular culture it is, if it is anything, "African," having been infused with the performance styles and musical beats of people of African descent for centuries to the point that these styles are clearly a large part of all performing traditions here. One certainly cannot make a clear delineation between "African-American" culture and "white American" culture. Yet this fact has never led to a moment where taste for a particular, new, cultural artifact was not largely split along racial lines. That Elvis Presley sings "black" music in 1955 does not mean that black and white people, then or now, respond to his doing so, as if by impulse, in the same ways. (This is particularly striking as soon as his music travels outside Memphis.) And while there are, clearly, musical subcultures (most notably dance subcultures, often overlapping substantially with subcultures of sexual dissidence) that are racially integrated for periods of time and within particular class fragments, the vast majority of music produced continues to be consumed along racial lines – so much so that when specific white people attempt to escape our own conditions of racialization, we are likely to cross musical-racial lines in particular. In doing so, we later learn, we most often explore black musical styles of five to ten years in the past, rather than the breaking ones to which we may have no access. In becoming "black" in this way we therefore often exhibit most clearly our connection to specifically white forms of dissidence. Our genuine cultural hybridity thus coexists with our unchanged racial situation.

Brackette Williams has identified this pattern as a relationship of misrecognition of skin color as culture within the national community:

> [In the case of whites in "black culture":]
> Class-stratified "real culture producers," within the logic of the same ideological precepts, are conjoined with their "betters" in such a manner that when they adopt the products of the marginalized others they are able to do so without experiencing the same pragmatic and ideological consequences to which the marginalized others are subjected.
> [In the case of blacks in "white culture":]
> Whether they are good-bodied, lower-class cultural passers imitating their way to Oneness or they are bad-bodied cultural and racial passers engaged in the same affirmative actions, their sacrifices are made individually but assessed in terms of their categorical identities. As tolerated subordinated or acceptable inappropriates, cultural passers can be integrated into the national community but they are not to be confused with the national community.[60]

Racism, and the presumptive existence of a "white race," is part of the "culture" of the US; when these social forces which form race are internalized by black Americans – "the social forces which menaced me had become interior," as James Baldwin puts it[61] – racialization, a structurally determined political and cultural event, takes place. Freudian theory also makes possible this relation of exteriority to interiority in the elaboration of group formation – "a primary group . . . is a number of individuals who have put one and the same object in the place of their ego ideal and have consequently identified themselves with one another in their ego."[62] For Freud such an object, through which group members recognize a "common quality" in themselves,[63] requires a charismatic "leader" in its initial psychological formation. Yet in the kind of visually structured field under investigation here, skin color itself may provide the charismatic object for the identification of a group. Taken together, these descriptions of racial group formation depend on an anthropology of culture and caste in the US national context which is, obviously, "multicultural," but is also systematically stratified into what Spillers calls our "grammar," which operates without reference to the "facts" of our hybrid cultural history.[64]

The overall effect of this structure is the spontaneous tendency of the subject produced within the US to map "whiteness" onto that which is thought of as culturally European-derived, and "blackness" onto that which is African- or at least not European-derived, even when the mapping corresponds to no historical referents. Thus, in the broad culture system dominant positions may be coded "white," and insurgent positions "black," regardless of their content. The enforcement of the system works because it does not depend on the content of these positions, but on the skin color of those who take them; thus a fascist statement made by a given black intellectual (say, Louis Farrakhan) will become coded "black," and as a result "insurgent," while the conscientious attempts of white radicals to do anti-racist work over a long period of time will not eliminate racial splitting in our own institutions. The result of this series of agentless, because general, codings is that, over time, black and white fascisms develop distinct (even while hybrid) tendencies and dispositions, which can be graphed as both part of the same ideological system (fascism) and as distinct tendencies within it.

The enforcement of discrimination which goes on in left-wing groups, though usually in muted and unintentional forms (white people not realizing they have more power), has tended to lead black people to form autonomous organizations of revolt, and different traditions of writers in revolt (who themselves form a "tradition" because, through the generations, they too were so drawn), even as they share many of the same assessments of what is objectively wrong in the society. In saying this, I am certainly not arguing that there are no genuinely mixed racial communities or subcultures; rather what I am saying is precisely that, to the extent they exist, they *are* subcultures, and far more short-lived than the tendencies they combat. Those of us who really do live more or less interracial lives can neither insist that others do so, least of all when we come from dominant socioeconomic positions, nor neglect to analyze the forms in which racial difference reappears within our social locations. In a highly segregated society, there is no excuse for us to feel good about the fact that some of our best friends are black. As a practical matter political actors continue to operate in mixed-race or single-race settings, or both, as a matter of (first) social circumstance and (second) active preference. There is no abstract or pre-practical position from which one can insist on one or the other form of action.

Thus, contrary to many people's assumptions, I will demonstrate that self-conscious "nationalism" – which, in any event, I call "autonomism" whenever possible – has frequently been based on strategic or tactical concerns, rather than so-called "essentialism." Further, the belief in some kind of racial essence has been perfectly compatible with advocacy of integrationist positions (and arguments for the hybridity of culture). Indeed, the most effective and significant autonomist arguments, from my point of view, have tended to be those, like Du Bois' in *Dusk of Dawn*, that take as their premise the social construction of race, and build their anti-integrationist argument on the basis of the need to respond to social formations which insist on racial essence when in fact there is none. Indeed, the best argument for a contemporary black nationalism (which does not exist at present) would be likely to come from the combination of a dialectical humanism and the analysis of the intransigence of racial dynamics in US society, as described by Joel Kovel or Derrick Bell.[65]

In the twentieth century US, all people are socially determined by race. An underlying theme of a book about racialization is necessarily the racial position of its writer, especially if its writer is white and the racial identity under discussion is black. Certainly my cultural and racial theory here, if it is to be meaningful, must be able to account for the appearance of my own work; the neutrality of the scientific investigator is a thoroughly implausible explanation. In working through the autobiographical texts of Malcolm X and bell hooks, toward the end of this book, we begin to see that unlike earlier African-American writers like James Weldon Johnson, who often accepted the premise that racial identity is a Negro problem, at present any understanding of black race-ness can only occur in concert with the understanding that (1) racism is a white problem and (2) whiteness is first of all defined in the articulations of blacks. I break with "whiteness studies" to the extent that it focuses on whiteness without the detour through black writing; I am interested in whiteness inasmuch as it is an object of African-American critical gaze in Du Bois, X and hooks.[66] Thus my "autobiographical" coda is a preliminary attempt to imagine my analytical position as object, not subject.

The terminology of race-ness

After this long description of the race/culture system, I am finally prepared to explain my choice of signs for race. I use V. N. Volosinov's *Marxism and the Philosophy of Language* as a jumping-off point for understanding the sign.[67] For Volosinov, to discuss the materiality of the sign is first of all to have a sociology of language which reflects the awareness that signs are both shared, intersubjectively, and also refracted ideologically along class, which for Volosinov is to say *sociological*, lines. As a result, although the meaning of a given sign may differ in historical place and time, the job of the analyst is to understand its "specific variability"[68] – the extent to which it can be made to change, from within a specific class position, at a given moment. Thus the sign reflects experience, and also refracts it, in relatively consistent ways, which necessarily produce "we-experiences," or common understandings of the sign's meaning.[69] Without positing such a we-experience language itself could not exist, and no intersubjective communication could happen. To discuss the we-experience of a given term – say "black," or "African American" – is, then, precisely to discover the "different degrees and different types of ideological structuring" this particular sign is capable of manifesting over a period of time where it is used to structure social meanings.[70]

These considerations will permit me here to explain certain terminological choices in this book. Because terms like "black" and "African American" are used to describe two distinct things at once – skin color/hair, and a multiplicity of differing cultural choices – the community created by specific signs is in all cases difficult to gauge. Colored, Negro, black, African American, all have different specific variabilities at different historical moments. Rather than attempting to adjudicate between these choices, and preferring one term throughout, I attempt to strategically standardize meanings in a different way. With regard to usage in the context of my own narrative voice in 1998, I am following the excellent suggestion of Joe Wood: "Since, *color*, James Baldwin says, *is not a human or personal reality; it is a political reality*, we might call our cultural communities African American, and the political community Black."[71] I use "black" – the principle subject of this book – to refer to the racial/political/visual aspect of practice, and "African American" – a present, but lesser subject of analysis here – to refer to the cultural/habitual aspect of practice, even while recognizing that the autobiographers I analyze are usually (but not always) both raced "black" and enculturated "African American." In practice, this distinction makes sense only some of the time, and I could not justify every single time I make it in this book.

At the same time, in order to avoid anachronism, and for their differential rhetorical value, when I refer to the subjectivities of the intellectuals I write about in this book, I use their own terms of choice, most often "Negro" – you simply can't understand race-ness in Du Bois without understanding that he is referring, in particular, to "*Negro*ness" – and occasionally "colored" (as in *The Autobiography of an Ex-Colored Man*). When describing Malcolm X and bell hooks, I use "black" and "African American" interchangeably, as they each do, though not necessarily using the same pattern that I use for myself.[72] This book never addresses "nigga," though this term is unquestionably necessary to the analysis of a variety of contemporary texts by African Americans.

Writing narrative about political practice

This book is, self-consciously, a narrative. I do not, for example, recommend reading its chapters out of order. Though there are substantive and identitarian reasons to doubt I am capable, what I hope to achieve corresponds to this quotation from Hortense Spillers, taken wildly and willfully out of context: "As *dated* as this narrative process is, and more, as 'unprogressive' as the relevant reading sensibilities are, the 'hermeneutic narrative' ... matches – perfectly – the 'end' of the world; in the black community, this is Freedom, and the 'beginning.'"[73] The narrative of racial identity in the United States is neither the largest nor the smallest narrative that can be conceived, and my attention to it does not constitute a unique commitment to this and only this narrative, but rather is a considered attempt to understand its contours within present global development, structured by the needs of capital.[74] I have found it beneficial to adopt Frederic Jameson's strategy of juxtaposition with the end of "restructur[ing] the problematics of ideology, of the unconscious and of desire, of representation, of history, and of cultural production, around the all-informing process of *narrative*, which I take to be (here using the shorthand of philosophical idealism) the central function or *instance* of the human mind."[75] Multilevel "local" and "global" narrations exist in a complex interrelation such that it is rarely useful to claim that a particular autobiographical narrative, is "wrong" or "right" so much as that it stands in a particular relationship to the possibility of social struggle at a particular psycho-socioeconomic moment. To say this is to say no more than that the fight for African-American identity is "but one phase in a larger *global* conflict stretching from the United States to Asia, Africa and the islands of the sea," as Gilroy paraphrases W. E. B. Du Bois.[76] Or, as Grace Lee Boggs put it in a moment of optimism greater than Du Bois ever experienced, the black movement is "a movement toward involving ever deeper layers of the oppressed masses whose grievances are deeply rooted in the nature of the system and who are ready for increasingly desperate acts against it."[77] There is no revolution at present. The US-based intellectual, as intellectual, can attempt to narrate a plausible set of links between the political location s/he inhabits and the layers of subalterity not materially present to her/him.

Inasmuch as racial meanings change, they do so only as the result of racially explicit social movements. Though it has changed character several times, race-ness has never been an arbitrary term which could be filled up by anything at a given moment. Each time its character has changed it has been as the direct result of mass action begun by African Americans. There have been three basic shifts in the meaning of race-ness this century, only one of which can be said to have effected the US as a whole. The first occurred primarily with the construction of a black professional class whose modes of self-representation are established by Du Bois' *The Souls of Black Folk* and in his *Crisis* writings, and through the political agitation of the NAACP; the second, during the era of global decolonization (and represented, within the narrative of the book, largely by Paul Robeson in chapter 5), made race-ness become widely recognized as an international issue; and the third, exemplified in the text which continues to be the hegemonic text about blackness today, *The Autobiography of Malcolm X*, was the development of an autonomous pride in race-as-such among US blacks. (A narrative attending to white people's understandings of race in response to each of these rearticulations ought no doubt to accompany this claim; but it is not the narrative of this book.) The period we are now in is the period of the feminist rearticulation of this entire narrative, the success of which (like the success of the three changes already listed) is both uncertain and uneven.

To posit social change – "revolutionary" or "reformist" – is in principle to narrate. Like the Du Bois of the 1930s and with Fanon, whose humanist narrative of opposition to imperialism has been brilliantly described by Sekyi-Otu,[78] I understand racial autonomism to be a moment within a marxist narrative which, for only being a moment, literally cannot be "gone beyond" so long as the social conditions in which racial identification arises continue to exist. Likewise, class has not disappeared. Capitalism, as a system of exploitation and oppression, now requires the permanent unemployment of 700 million people, and the structural underemployment of perhaps a billion others, to keep wages down and the rate of return on capital up. The collapse of the inadequate state socialisms of the Soviet bloc has sped up this process on both the international and domestic levels; no one should be fooled that the present ability of capital to move at greater and greater rates and to destroy organized workforces en masse is unrelated to the collapse of even the meager systemic challenge that existed before 1989. Indeed, I am, with Ellen Meiksins Wood, committed to the notion that "this is the moment when Marx should and can come fully into his own *for the first time*," precisely because

> capitalism has become a truly universal system. It's universal not only in the sense that it's global, not only in the sense that just about every economic actor in the world today is operating according to the logic of capitalism, and even those on the outermost periphery of the capitalist economy are, in one way or another, subject to that logic. Capitalism is universal also in the sense that its logic – the logic of accumulation, commodification, profit-maximization, competition – has penetrated just about every aspect of human life and nature itself, in ways that weren't even true of so-called advanced capitalist countries as recently as two or three decades ago. So Marx is more relevant than ever, because he, more effectively than any other human being then or now, devoted his life to explaining the systemic logic of capitalism.[79]

The practice of everyday life, the existence of subcultures that refuse participation with the system, and the important positive histories and agencies of (among others) black Americans which others emphasize and which are, in fact, central to this book do not displace the need for massive, indeed total, challenge: that is, *opposition* as such. I can see no reason to avoid responsibly constructing this "binary."

The style of marxist narrative I am trying to describe here went under the name of third worldism or Maoism thirty years ago, and suggested that the decolonizing regions of the world, being those with the weakest forms of capitalism and the strongest revolutionary armies, were the privileged locations of socialist struggle. Black American nationalist struggle was to be powerful inasmuch as it was one moment in this *international* movement.[80] That this theoretical narrative did not occur no doubt speaks to certain inadequacies in the narrative, and in narratives of social change generally; it speaks even more strongly to the reality that capitalism has, so far, won. Insisting on this metanarrative not as an example of where we are now, but as an example of that which we have repressed (inasmuch as very few contemporary writers, and almost none in Cultural Studies, seem to remember it at all), is insisting that globally and locally the continued immiseration of most women and most people of color – indeed, the increasing immiseration of most white men – has depended in part on the ability of the hegemons to convince us that there is no possible narrative of social change, that hundreds of millions of people did not engage in movements for decolonization and socialism. When I am in despair I believe Bourdieu (and Ice Cube) and not Marx (or Digable Planets), who require a certain amount of optimism. I never believe the self-centered triumphalism that is present in so much neo-Nietzscheanism (even though I do, in fact, listen to Ice T).[81]

I do not disagree with those who claim that this third world marxist narrative is no longer current, and that in general the old forms of opposition are no longer possible, and indeed, this book points in the direction of black feminism, a social movement that has, on a systemic scale, yet to be, as a plausible space to start. Such black feminism is a conscientious narration of black women's identifications in the past and present; it also should be an invitation for the conscientious narration of all identities in the US with respect to race and gender position; and it should, of course, place the analysis of identity within the system of economic equivalences, where our identities, once narrated, become bought and sold. A black feminist identity narrative, even such a narration by a white man, is potentially allied to social change (though the triumphalism of theory must be avoided at all costs) inasmuch as it helps point the way toward a response to what hooks calls white supremacist capitalist patriarchy. Any social movement against capitalism must start with the critique of racism and sexism not because ending these will necessarily lead to the termination of capitalism, but because race and gender (and nation, at an international level) are, as Gilroy says, the modalities through which class in the US is presently lived[82] – and the origins of revolt are always necessarily in people's self-understanding of their lived conditions, their autobiographies.

2

African-American autobiography and the field of autobiography Studies

Only the techniques of the *Bildungsroman* could enable us to show how collective crisis and personal crisis provide each other with a mutual opportunity, how political revision is accompanied by personal regeneration, attested by the changes in vestimentary and cosmetic symbolism which consecrate a total commitment to an ethico-political vision of the social world, erected into the principle of a whole lifestyle, private as much as public.   Pierre Bourdieu[1]

In spite of the fact that autobiography is impossible, this in no way prevents it from existing. Perhaps, in describing it, I in turn took my desire for reality; but what I had wanted to do, was to describe this reality in its reality, a reality shared by a great number of authors and readers.   Philippe Lejeune[2]

A schema for reading contemporary theories of autobiography

Scholars who take autobiography as their subject necessarily position themselves according to two distributive axes: an axis of referentiality, and an axis of subjectivity.[3] "Referentiality" refers to the question of whether autobiography is to be understood as representing, or as nonrepresentational with regard to, a real world external to the text. "Subjectivity" refers to discussions of the position of the speaking subject, the "I" (or, in those few cases without "I", the point of view) which narrates the autobiographical text – its social positioning and construction, its number, its autonomy, its relationship to other subject-positions. No definition of autobiography is possible without some explicit or implicit position along each of these axes. Each axis provides a continuum, rather than a set of discreet positions; the precise definition of any given writer does not necessarily fall neatly into one side of an issue. But most authors choose to analyze particular autobiographies according to their preferences within the space of the grid. In 1999, professional critics are generally aware of these issues, and place themselves in relationship to others on these questions.[4] Before describing the range of theoretical positions that have been enunciated along these axes, several introductory points about the field need to be made.

First, pointing to referentiality and subjectivity as questions which pervade the study of autobiography does not, of course, distinguish such study from other contemporary critical practices. Indeed, that these terms call directly upon the foremost critical theories of the last generation, grouped broadly as poststructuralism, and the most important growing fields of literary study of the last generation, gender, race, and ethnic studies, permits anthologists of autobiography studies from James Olney to Leigh Gilmore to suggest that the study of autobiography may solve key theoretical questions. Whether or not autobiography can in fact provide translatable answers to questions in other fields of literary studies is of less immediate interest to me than the particular doubling which results from this notion throughout autobiography theory, including the present book: wherever a given theorist describes the position of a given autobiographer, as in whatever sense referential and/or subject-constructing, the theorist is also describing what s/he takes to be the referential and/or subjective status of her/his own work. It is this phenomenon, which has its deepest roots in feminist critical work like Nancy Miller's well-known account of "personal criticism,"[5] that permits readings of particular autobiographies, time and again, to allegorize the practice and experience of reading. In this way, the criticism of autobiography is particularly close to the autobiography of the critic.

Second, I am not claiming that the discussion of these distributive axes will be sufficient to answer all possible questions in autobiography theory, merely that all autobiography theory must, minimally, address these axes. There is at least one question that is central to contemporary theory of autobiography that will go largely unaddressed in this chapter: the material form of texts that may be called "autobiography" in the first place. At least two subfields I have surveyed, Women's Autobiography Studies and Native American Autobiography Studies, pose the question of form in a way that challenges the discussion in this chapter. In the former case, certain writers, like Goozé, stress the particular importance of including diaries and fragmented collections within the category of autobiography in order for it to be useful as a framework for surveying women's self-representations;[6] in the latter, Brumble and Wong are most well-known for speaking of oral, and in Wong's case pictographic, forms of autobiography.[7] Without engaging with their arguments in detail, it seems relevant for me to acknowledge up front that this chapter, and this book as a whole, is written with skepticism that one brings precision and attentiveness to the genre by referring to nonbook, nonpublic, and nonnarrative forms as "autobiographies." I am, obviously, supportive of all efforts to examine diaries and blankets according to the question of how they may help us understand self-representation in their specific cultural contexts. I am, additionally, sympathetic to the probability that, given the institutional constraints of the academy, these studies are only possible when framed in terms of a previously legitimated literary discourse. For all that, I do not accept Wong's statement that "if one assumes that self-narration is the fundamental act of autobiography, one must recognize a variety of forms besides literary autobiography."[8] It is not obvious that self-narrative is more "fundamental" to the theory of autobiography than its material context (i.e. the rise of the published self-reflective book), nor is it obvious that interest in the category "self-narration" should be made identical to interest in the category "autobiography." In the meantime, as should be clear from chapter one, it matters a great deal that for African-American Autobiography Studies (including African-American Women's Autobiography Studies), the linear narrative book, or book of essays, which relates a self for public identification *is* worth discussing in itself, as a category separate from other kinds of texts.

Finally, what follows in this chapter is a survey of theories of autobiography; it is not a new theory of autobiography. This book provides several, partial, versions of such a new theory: in chapter one, where I position autobiography in an identitarian political schema which goes determination, articulation, movement; in chapter three, where I present the dialectical theory of autobiography that might be generated from a close reading of W. E. B. Du Bois' *Dusk of Dawn*; in chapter eight, where I discuss the relationship of the emergence of black feminism to the writing of autobiographical criticism. By contrast, the argument of this chapter concerns the relationship of African-American Autobiography Studies to other versions of the study of autobiography. I will suggest that African-American Studies has tended to place autobiography in a relatively stable location in the field: where "I" tends to have a determinate relation to a specifically racial "we"; and where the text provides for its audience a way to symbolize racialization as a version of the real.

The axis of referentiality

Along the axis of referentiality there are definitions of autobiography that can be described as primarily nominalist, nonreferential, or (according to the sociologizing bias of my own position) "institutional" understandings of the term; and there are definitions which presume at different levels that autobiographical narrative is directly reflective of real patterns in a life, and thus knowing whether or not something is an autobiography depends on knowing first that it corresponds to reality (or, in the case of fraud, that it does not but claims to). A variety of positions which adopt both institutionality and referentiality at different theoretical moments are possible – in the case of Lejeune, as we will see, institutionality is ultimately considered necessary as a background for defending referentiality. Also, referential realism, at this late date, is most often constructed as a second-order matter of correspondence to psychoanalytic, affective or ideological form; it need not rest on an unmediated understanding of the one-to-one correspondence of signifier and signified.

I use the word "institution" broadly. In my schema, an institutional theory of autobiography need assert nothing more than that when someone in a position of sufficient cultural authority to do so has labeled something an "autobiography," one has an autobiography. Thus anything which, as part of its title, or through the identity of author and narrator, or the labeling by a publishing company, or the labeling by a literary critic, has come to be called an autobiography falls within the category. Arguably any narrator can assert such a position of authority; Paul DeMan's argument that autobiography is best described as a rhetorical trope would thus fall into this category.[9] The basic ambiguity of such a definition is the question of whose authority is to be accepted, and theories of struggle and resistance will tend to see this definition, like all definitions, as one site of the workings of power. For this reason, a dialectical realism will argue that an institutional definition of a term does not get one away from questions of referentiality; rather it may bump the question of referentiality up a level from the text itself to the space of the economy of competing representations. When the accuracy of the text (its consistency with other textual representations) then comes back into focus, it does so as part of the mapping of a larger social space rather than in terms of the opinions of one or another friend or challenger of the autobiographer.

The axis of subjectivity

It is widely assumed that autobiography refers always to an "I," even by those who most want to show the constructedness of that "I," or its particular relationships to determinate "not-I's." This is interesting, because one need not assume that *any* part of the world itself, neither "auto" nor "bio" nor "graph" refers to the category of the individual. There is no semantic reason to presume that auto-reference could not be to a group of people who form a collective subjectivity ("we"), and indeed collective autobiographies, like the New York 21's *Look For Me in the Whirlwind*, have been written. However, the word autobiography arises in the nineteenth century with Romanticism's public depiction of the individuated, private self, and this ideology continues to pervade it. Thus the basic form of the text is the *bildungsroman*, in which the author explains the peculiar circumstances that explain how he (gender intended) became himself and not any other self. Of course, the adequacy of the "I" to account for itself may come under question, and individualism may be shown to deconstruct itself (or, in psychoanalytic terms, repress its unconscious). The attribution of individualism to autobiography may be made by someone whose intention is to critique that individualism; the defining characteristic of critical individualist accounts of autobiography is their accounting for the failure of individualism via the category of the single author. Thus in the individualist definition, "I" always refers only to itself, without a collectivity *ever* being implicated by it.

Other alternatives are possible, however; autobiographies may be defined to include texts written with "we" as their subject. More commonly, it is possible to construct a definition in which every time the word "I" appears, the text implicitly or explicitly references one or more supraindividual subjectivities. Because this is so counterintuitive, I will jump ahead of my argument for a moment to refer to the most famous instances of this phenomenon, the Latin American *testimonios* analyzed by Doris Sommer – I quote at this point only her first example, from Domitilia Barrios' *Let Me Speak!*: "I don't want anyone at any moment to interpret the story I'm about to tell as something that is only personal ... What happened to me could have happened to hundreds of people in my country."[10] Sommer herself is ambivalent about whether to call such a statement and such a textual practice "autobiographical," since she worries that the term implies individualist narrative.

Such "testimony on behalf of," which is clearly one element in all African-American Autobiography Study (though how significant an element is something about which critics differ), is precisely that which permits us to see what is generally considered definitive by individualist scholarship: thus, regardless of the "success" or "failure" of the "I," its testimony is only about itself. The major *structural* (or sociolinguistic) question of my book as a whole, as distinct from my historical argument about race as a particular category of autobiographical subjectivity, is when, and for whom, "I" may be said to implicate a larger category like race, or used to create explicit links between actions and characteristics within the scope of a collectivity.

Figure 2.1 charts the range of ways people under discussion here define autobiography.

Some representative theoretical positions

Lejeune/DeMan

It is necessary to start this analysis with reference to the definition of autobiography by Philippe Lejeune in the essay "The Autobiographical Pact," a commonsense definition that may be said to inaugurate the above problems: "Retrospective prose narrative written by a real person concerning his own existence, where the focus is his individual life, in particular the story of his personality."[11] This definition, it seems clear, would quickly take us into the referential problematic on the side of the necessity of reference to a thing called a "personality," probably (though one need not assume this to adopt Lejeune's definition) an already given and unconstructed reification. However, this assumption of referentiality, which Lejeune implicitly requires, doesn't work in any obvious or straightforward way. With attention to the modernist literature and literary theory that provides his intellectual backdrop, Lejeune immediately asserts that such a retrospective prose narrative often traffics under the name of "autobiographical novel"; in other cases, where no such name is given, the fact of reference is left undecidable to the reader of the autobiography. Within mere pages of giving this definition, Lejeune has acknowl-

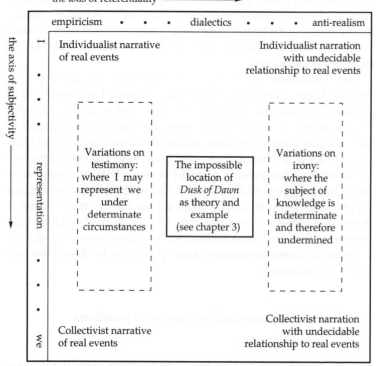

Figure 2.1   Positions in the theory of autobiography

edged that it is insufficient as grounds for testing whether a text is an autobiography. The solution he offers, then, for what we actually call autobiography is the essential speech act which he calls the autobiographical "pact."

The autobiographical pact, according to Lejeune, comes in several forms; what all of them have in common is "their intention to honor" the "signature" of the autobiographer.[12] Most commonly one demonstrates this intention with reference to the title page of any given book; it is here that "we make use of a general textual criterion, the identity ("identicalness") of the *name* (author-narrator-protagonist). The autobiographical pact is the affirmation in the text of this identity, referring back in the final analysis to the *name* of the author on the cover."[13] In this argument, the use of the word "autobiography" itself is not relevant to how we consider the book,[14] and while this may tip us off, the existence of novels which refer to themselves as autobiographies (one of which, *The Autobiography of an Ex-Colored Man*, is canonical to African-American literature) makes the presence or absence of the term an unreliable piece of evidence. On the other hand, a match of names is sufficient evidence to show intention of the author, and where some aspect of the proper name is missing (as in the 1912 *Autobiography of an Ex-Colored Man*, which was anonymous) the text becomes undecidable. It is this match, Lejeune emphasizes, that the carefully chosen word "pact" intends to focus on – the pact is *not* a contractual metaphor which implies enforcement mechanisms outside the locally constituted field of criticism, but rather an explicitly metaphysical notion – as in a pact with the devil – requiring a peculiar form of trust, or identification, from the reader. Participating in the institution becomes a question of membership in the self-defined institution of autobiography-reading.

Paul DeMan misses this in his critical response to Lejeune, stating that for Lejeune "autobiography is not only representational and cognitive but contractual, grounded not in tropes but in speech acts."[15] Later essays by Lejeune reiterate that he *wants* to find representationality in autobiography, and that is clearly DeMan's major gripe; however, in all his essays he acknowledges that it is impossible to justify a representational definition. (Indeed, only in response to DeMan does he even begin to wonder if the definition of autobiography is a representational issue. I will return to this.) In this context what is interesting to me is that DeMan's own description of autobiography as primarily a rhetorical trope, far from removing us from the notion of the pact (as opposed to the contract), actually clarifies Lejeune's definition.

For DeMan, Lejeune's pact requires that the reader assert the role of transcendental authority. If no outside enforcement mechanism exists, then the "transcendental authority that allows him to pass judgment" causes us to "reenter a system of tropes at the very moment we escape from it."[16] This is an altogether sound criticism, and Lejeune's extremely *rhetorical* response to it (discussed below) is evidence that he is convinced, though he believes that this has no particular consequences. Our alternative, according to DeMan, is to see that

> Autobiography is not a genre or a mode, but a figure of reading or of understanding that occurs, to some degree, in all texts. The autobiographical moment happens as an alignment between the two subjects involved in the process of reading in which they

determine each other by mutual reflexive substitution... This specular structure is interiorized in a text in which the author declares himself the subject of his own understanding, but this merely makes explicit the wide claim to authorship that takes place whenever a text is stated to be *by* someone and assumed to be understandable to the extent that this is the case. Which amounts to saying that any book with a readable title page is, to some extent, autobiographical.[17]

Note that the principle means of determination in this passage remain identical to those in Lejeune's gloss on his definition: "reading," "author declares," "readable title page," "author" (which is Lejeune's signature), "*by* someone" (which is how DeMan gets in the proper name through the back door).[18] Now, it may be that the difference between DeMan's and Lejeune's terminology is significant; it is plausible, for example, that we might choose DeMan's specific language if we want to open up autobiography to texts without protagonists.[19] My point as of now is that in both Lejeune and DeMan certain public *practices* and *institutions* are basic to the definition of autobiography *without regard to referentiality*. This unites these writers in offering a position opposed to those who presume that autobiography is defined by its manner of representing life; that Lejeune assumes that autobiography will probably also be referential, and DeMan does not, in no way changes this similarity.

The implications of this institutional sense of definition extend to the forms by which studies of autobiography are published. For example, the editors of the anthologies *The Culture of Autobiography*, *De/Colonizing the Subject*, and *Autobiography: Essays Theoretical and Critical* have made no attempt to restrict the essays included in their volumes to any particular sense of the meaning of "autobiography." Olney is the only editor, of the three texts named, to attempt any sort of reading of the meaning of the term at all in the introduction; Folkenflik, Smith, and Watson simply proclaim the "diversity" of their collections as being central to their strength.[20] Olney, more invested in bringing unity to the field, nevertheless recognizes that numerous essays in his volume transgress his own canonical version of what autobiography is, whether by illustrating collectivity, collaboration, and the lack of individualism (Rosenblatt, Eakin, Mason), media previously unstudied (Bruss), or the nonexistence of a coherent reference to the term (Sprinker). Meanwhile, a contributor to Smith and Watson's volume, Caren Kaplan, bypasses the question of "autobiography" altogether to speak of "outlaw genres," which permit subjectivities that fall outside the zone of authorship to be accounted for within the field of autobiography studies. My point is that "autobiography" is implicitly defined, in these cases, as an object of literary *critical* gaze which can countenance anything that the critic is positioned to claim within its bounds. The institutional meaning of autobiography, whether the institution is the academy or the trope, refers to a set of economic relations, symbolic or material, that can permit contradictory objects within my charted space of autobiography.

Eakin/Gunn/Lejeune (bis)

Toni Cade Bambara, after being pressed by interviewer Claudia Tate on the question of autobiographical writing, states that "I don't do it ... except, of course, that I do; we all do. That is, whomsoever we may conjure up or remember or imagine to get a story down, we're telling our own tale just as surely as a client on the analyst's couch, just as surely as a pilgrim on the way to Canterbury..."[21] Similarly, Houston Baker, discussing his own critical method, remarks that

> For a theorist to acknowledge autobiography as a driving force is for him or her to do no more than tell the truth. When I "analyze", for you my reader, a poem or a novel ... I am merely offering you a determinate recall of my experiences under the conventions of criticism, or theory – a peculiar and covering style, as it were.[22]

If DeMan's tropic criticism permits us to take these comments seriously as tropes (and DeMan concurs that once autobiography is a trope, all texts are "readable" as autobiographies), it does not, yet, allow us to view them in terms of the determinate recall of aspects of the critics inhabited social space. For the context of both of these quotations is the attempt by Tate, Bambara, and Baker to think through characters and theories as black. The invocation of the autobiographical within the nonautobiographical is, specifically, a means of referring to the racialized space in particular as a source of writing. For both Bambara and Baker their "autobiographical" texts are constructions, conscious reformations of some splintered and highly problematized set of experiences, not a unitary narrated consciousness. And for all that, reference (and specifically race and gender reference) reappears at the moment of the exploration of motivation.

Another way of making this point is: if, as DeMan says, "that the autobiographical project may itself produce and determine the life"[23] – an entirely reasonable claim that anti-referential critics take as central – then in turn it must be asserted that the social means of accomplishment of "the autobiographical project," which include (but are not limited to) the objective existence of the life, are not distributed equally. In this context Wahneema Lubiano's distinction, with regard to the tropic use of the "real" in contemporary African-American culture is valuable: the rise of "real" blackness emerges from the scarcity of representations of blackness and the specific locations in which these representations appear. While it would be, then, a mistake to permit a specific claim of the "real" to stand in for a general analysis of the economy of representation for African Americans, the latter is nevertheless *real*.[24]

The two critics who have worked hardest to define autobiography in referential terms resembling these claims are Janet Varner Gunn (whose book is subtitled "A Poetics of Experience") and Paul John Eakin.[25] Eakin starts with a disclaimer: "Poststructuralist criticism of autobiography characteristically – and mistakenly – assumes that an autobiographer's allegiance to referential truth necessarily entails a series of traditional beliefs about self, language, and literary form"; and again, "contemporary theory, with all its sophistication, needs to be reminded that there is nothing perfunctory about the referential claims of autobiography. Most autobiographers these days certainly know – to one degree or another – that autobiography is a kind of fiction."[26] Autobiographers may be perfectly aware that language cannot guarantee the truth of anything, and yet use the trope of autobiography specifically because in the legal and political community they inhabit, they choose to document their references. That is to say, there are public (artistic, cultural, political) reasons for telling a publicly comprehensible truth. Critics, by contrast, trained to read fiction, and to read rhetorically, don't know what to do when confronted with an "imaginative literature based on referentiality,"[27] and so come up with ever more elaborate ways of pretending that our considerations do not include referentiality.

Gunn's *Autobiography: Toward a Poetics of Experience* accounts for the construction of autobiographical truth in phenomenological terms, as a historical progression of "impulse" to "perspective" to "response." The specifics of her account, which relies on Proust, Wordsworth, and Thoreau, are thoroughly bourgeois individualist: her version of narrative assumes an anti-determinist position with respect to the writer recreating her/himself at the moment, but also appears to assume that the writer works with no determinate outside social forces impinging on the process of self-narrativization – canonical narratives, being universal, are not produced in a specifiable habitus. For this reason she concludes that the ultimate threat to phenomenological reference is politics: "the problem of autobiography lies in the threat of ideology."[28] In spite of this, her developmental theory supposes that autobiography itself is the outcome of a process of coming to self-consciousness and then, ultimately, writing about it, corresponding in some ways with the account of political articulation that I suggested in chapter one. Thus it is not surprising that in a more recent essay she indicates that working with Palestinians during the *intifada* has led her to reassess not the process of narrative-identity creation in autobiography, but the question of what such identity production might mean outside the European canonical tradition, in the writing of third world women.[29]

Just as Eakin's work requires an author who intends her/his work to be referential, it requires a reader whose interest in the referential work is, explicitly, identitarian:

> Loesburg's purpose in describing the reader's tendency to project into an extratextual realm of authorial intention is to warn against it. To the contrary, I am arguing that this proto-autobiographical tendency – this identification of reader with autobiographer – constitutes the fundamental motive for the reader's interest in autobiography in the first place.[30]

If this is the case, the existence of "anti-autobiography," like *Roland Barthes by Roland Barthes* (Eakin's example), is simply inconsequential to the social structure of identification that exists where writer and reader share the anti-autobiographer's (professional or aesthetic) interest in anti-identification. (Anti-identification is then simply a specialized form of identification.) However, while Eakin insists on reference as necessary to identification in reading autobiography, he provides no theory of how, or under what circumstances, this identification of the reader and autobiographer takes place. Such a consideration would, in turn, lead to an examination not only of reference in autobiography, but also of the selection process by which Eakin chooses specific autobiographies to study. It is conspicuous that while he can laud the recent work of feminist scholars like Sidonie Smith for their differential attention to women's textual self-construction from that proposed in male-dominated theory, he feels no compulsion to address or even refer to the political goals that such projects imply. For Eakin this would seem to be irrelevant to the study of autobiography: he identifies with all versions of the autobiographical subject as part of his job as critic and theorist. Thus he can run together the question of fragmented subjectivity, as Smith might understand it in a writer like Cherrie Moraga (discussed below), with his own analysis of Richard Rodriguez's *Hunger of Memory*. Since referentiality is theorized separately from, and as a category beyond, that of subjectivity, that Moraga and Rodriguez might be bitter political opponents is not connected to the *forms* of split-identification in their narratives.[31]

Eakin's insistence on referential aesthetics as the ground of autobiography parallels Philippe Lejeune's rewriting of "The Autobiographical Pact" in "The Autobiographical Pact (bis)" in an interesting way. Following DeMan's criticism of his work, Lejeune offers an ironic restatement of his position which makes clear the paradox of his initial definition by acknowledging his own complicity in the ideology of autobiography. Here Lejeune states:

> Yes, I have been fooled. I believe that we can promise to tell the truth; I believe in the transparency of language, and in the existence of a complete subject who expresses himself through it; I believe that my proper name guarantees my autonomy and my singularity (even though I have crossed several Philippe Lejeune's in my life); I believe that when I say "I" it is I who am speaking. But of course it also happens that I believe the contrary... "In the field of the subject, there is no referent." We *indeed know* all this; we are not so dumb, but, once this precaution has been taken, we go on as if we did not know it.[32]

As long as we remain on the referential axis, a statement like this one is as complete a picture of autobiography as we can make. Lejeune is now, by his own account, interested in "working class autobiography"; Gunn is writing about Palestinian women; Eakin is impressed by Sidonie Smith's work on "women's autobiography" (without himself taking any position on feminism). Something is happening here that reference alone cannot explain. We need to switch axes and address issues of subjectivity in the definition of autobiography.

Gusdorf/Stone/Heilbrun/Rampersad

Consideration of subjectivity in autobiography is not somehow new and postmodern; Georges Gusdorf's canonical description of specifically "autobiographical concerns" as "the conscious awareness of the singularity of each individual life," provided a definition of autobiography in terms of the form of the subject in 1956.[33] For Gusdorf, what was definitive in autobiography was never the axis of referentiality, since he always understood narrative to be the invention of a life; rather, it always specified a particular relation of text and subject. While Gusdorf values autobiography (and the individual) as the product of a progressive history, it would be a mistake to accuse him of not recognizing that this textual individualism is local and ideological. Unambiguous about the "us" who are his audience, Gusdorf claims that

> The concern, which seems so natural to us, to turn back on one's own past, to recollect one's life in order to narrate it, *is not at all universal*. It asserts itself only in recent centuries and only on a small part of the map of the world. The man who takes delight in thus drawing his own image believes himself worthy of a special interest. Each one of us tends to think of himself as the center of a living space: I count, my existence is significant to the world, and my death will leave the world incomplete.[34]

In this context, it would be a mistake to criticize Gusdorf of universalizing the European male subject and assuming that others do not write autobiography, as Caren Kaplan does;[35] indeed, the discovery that there is something peculiar about western self-histories of subjectivity is precisely what we should praise Gusdorf for. The specific textual individuality that Gusdorf describes is, of course, not so ennobling as he seems to believe, but it is in fact descriptive of the character of autobiography as it has been performed implicitly or explicitly by a certain variety of western, primarily male, writers.

Counterhegemonic autobiographical narratives are always already competing with, and in many cases reusing for their own purposes, this pregiven individualist form: this is the most important truth of scholarship on the slave narrative, where the political effectiveness for abolition may depend on the ideological reconstruction of the slave as (male) heroic or (female) sentimental subject. As critics we are capable of the twin mistakes of assuming that autobiography must reproduce these notions of subjectivity, or of assuming that any text written by a person outside the correct race, nation, gender or class position will inevitably provide a different perspective. In this context, Gusdorf's full analysis of the "distance," "enlightenment," and "destiny" of the subject may retain significance in any description of how an autobiography creates the self;[36] these terms may be useful in analysis of, for example, the way certain US immigration narratives measure the distance of the unenlightened preimmigration self to the destined "American" self; they may also help us to see how the famously disjunctive destination of Jacobs' *Incidents of the Life of a Slave Girl* – ending with freedom, not marriage – breaks from convention. Precisely what does not differentiate Jacobs from Gusdorf is that for her, too, the subject's distance, enlightenment, and destiny "confer a meaning on the event which, when it actually occurred, no doubt had several meanings or perhaps none."[37] It would be a mistake to argue that Gusdorf's "conditions and limits of autobiography" are thus *wrong*; they are to this day the best description of one location in the field of autobiography.

That we are always confronted with individualist ideology when studying autobiography is best illustrated with reference to writers whose field of study is narrower than "autobiography" but whose assumptions are as equally individualist as Gusdorf's. Looking at Carolyn Heilbrun on the problems of writing women's "life stories," Arnold Ramparsad's essay on African-American autobiography, or Albert Stone's elaborately multi-ethnic *Autobiographical Occasions and Original Acts* will illustrate, if nothing else, that for the willful reader *any* autobiography can be read through the framework of an all-important individual subject, regardless of its explicit content.[38]

Heilbrun's basic argument is useful: since the basic forms of writing the self have always consisted of enunciating the "public" role of the implicitly male individual, and the orthodox role of women is to cater to the "private" lives of males, the language and narrative form that could usefully describe the life of any given woman needs to be invented. So far this analysis is consistent with that of poststructuralist feminists like Smith or Watson; but rather than suggesting that narrative life stories could actually exhibit an entirely different mode of identity construction than the one Gusdorf provides, Heilbrun supposes that the problem is not the notion of the subject, but the form of the narrative which produces it. Women's identities are still individual identities; it's just that these identities are better understood through the invention of a language of privacy to supplement publicity. The point of referring Gusdorf's narrative to a writer about *feminism* is not, then, to denounce Heilbrun as limited and Gusdorf as sexist (though both are true), but to point out that writing life stories really does engage one in the problematic of presenting an explicitly public identity, even when such an identity fails to fully explain the life. Western individualist ideology may be implicitly recreated in any reference to the "I" in a published life story. Ultimately, when we read Albert Stone's claim that *The Autobiography of Malcolm X* demonstrates that "not only *individualism* [is] a common cultural value, but also that *identity* [is] a vital personal achievement"[39] it is both obvious that this is a willful misreading of the politics and argument of the text (which I take up at length in chapter six), but also that individualism – which is not "individuality" – plays such a hegemonic role in the definition of autobiography that *The Autobiography of Malcolm X* may provide an example of it. Precisely because what we have is X's life story, we are positioned, if we want, to read *this* revolt as documentably "unique."[40]

Sommer

Doris Sommer, not Georges Gusdorf, taught me the necessity of the implication of individualism in autobiography by analyzing texts that attempt to break from that ideology, thus illustrating what would constitute the most distant position on the axis of subjectivity from Gusdorf. She is so concerned with destroying any possible individualist readings of her genre, the Latin American *testimonio* (testimonial), that she suggests that in spite of our knee-jerk assumptions, it might be thoroughly inappropriate to use the term "autobiography" at all in thinking about them. She cites Gusdorf's definition of autobiography, and then, comparing the testimonial, she remarks that:

> My own casual impulse to recuperate testimonials into autobiography … dramatizes at least one danger for First World readers. By understating the difference, we may miss the potential in what I am calling the testimonials' collective self: the possibility to get beyond the gap between public and private spheres and beyond the often helpless solicitude that has plagued Western women even more than men since the rise of capitalism. To read testimonials as if they were merely a variation of autobiography would reinforce [our] habit of conflating human culture and history with the lives of extraordinary individuals.[41]

In terms of location within the western academy, actually making a genre distinction based on the location of subjectivity in a text has not proved viable, as Sommer certainly knows; her article, after all, appeared in an anthology devoted to women's "autobiography," is likely to be cited only by students of "autobiography," and all discussion of the testimonial form will be submerged into the imperial genre. This may be an appropriate metaphor for cultural imperialism in literary studies. It is precisely because testimonial – the individual speaking explicitly as representative of the collective subject – remains always already trapped in the space of autobiography studies within the US academy that Albert Stone's inability to read an affective black collectivity in Malcolm X's not always so personal identity is possible.

Sommer's article is so central to imagining the kind of political possibility opened up by autobiography that I need to go through her analysis of testimonial in some detail. The autobiographies that interest me in the black tradition are definitely not testimonial, as will be clear below; but Sommer's analysis of the *plausibility* of collective textual subjectivity in the testimonial is necessary in any model that hopes to read autobiographies of black individuals in a way that will run counter to individualism.

To start, testimonial often begins, as I quoted above, with a disclaimer concerning the reason for the writing of autobiography, a disclaimer frequently seen in the US slave narrative as well: "I'd like to stress that it's not only *my* life, it's also the testimony of my people" (Menchú); "Eugenia, exemplary model of self-sacrifice and revolutionary heroism, is a typical and not an exceptional case of so many Salvadoran women" (Alegria).[42] One significance of this, in Sommer's view, is that unlike the autobiographical voice in Gusdorf, which being individual is also to be identified with universally, these texts do not invite the western reader to identify with the author at all. On the contrary, since the "I" stands in for "we," in such a text, it in no way can imply '*you*.' (This disrupts Eakin's "fundamental motive" for reading autobiography, see above. Unlike, perhaps, with Rodriguez or even Moraga, "we" will not read about Menchú as a way of learning about ourselves.) The text, far from being permeable and having unstable identity categories, as Sidonie Smith claims that many minority and women's texts have (see below), in fact sets up intentional and highly specific political and national boundaries. Indeed these boundaries already exist in the procedure by which the book is written, since testimonials are not written by the narrator; rather they are written by a metropolitan leftist who generally has initiated the contact and suggested the collaboration. The expected autobiographical motives are thus overturned: "They are written neither for individual growth nor for glory but are offered through the scribe to a broad public as one part of a general strategy to win political ground."[43]

Sommer suggests that a true counterhegemonic position, rather than asserting that the third world produces autobiographies too, might be to attempt to view all western autobiography as an unusual case of testimony, with the peculiar difference being that western autobiography produces the illusion of singularity, when in reality it speaks the raced, classed, gendered, or otherwise collective identity of a western subject. While this is a tempting suggestion, my preference for creating a spatial description that places both Gusdorf and Sommer on a table which includes a continuum between them comes from my sense that African-American autobiographies are generally neither one nor the other, but rather the constant and conscious negotiating of the "I" with a variety of racialized engagements. While it would make no more sense to mythify *The Autobiography of Malcolm X* as a work of collectivity (even notwithstanding that the structure of collaboration between Haley and X resembles the one described by Sommer), it might be reasonable to read that text against Stone for its testimony about a black subjectivity many readers are not invited to share. In doing so we would want to negotiate the complex interaction between the "I" of the autobiographical subject and the implicit or explicit collectivities (examples of "we") that it (factually) represents. We would be under no obligation to see the text as engaged in identification in Eakin's sense – we always identify with the subject – or failure of identification in Sommer's sense – we have nothing to do with the subject of the text. Rather in any given reading situation we would be searching for the mediating terms appropriate to the invitation for, or refusal of, identification at hand, terms which include, but are not limited to, race.

Gilmore/Lionnet/Smith

Appropriately angered that Gusdorf and a host of other white men take hegemonic ideology for universal truth, Leigh Gilmore, Francoise Lionnet, Sidonie Smith, and a range of other writers of postmodern autobiography theory deny the stability of Gusdorf's identifications altogether, and claim that the process of narrating gender autobiographically can be used to expose the impossibility of women developing stable identifications. Indeed, in a recent article, Gilmore takes the marginal position of the genre of autobiography within literary studies at large as a means of finding it an advantageous space for the theorization of margins generally:

> Autobiography has often been seen as insufficiently objective because the eyewitness may be simultaneously the most sought

after and suspect interpreter of events. At the same time, autobiography has been spurned as insufficiently subjective (or imaginative) because it relies too much on the constraints of the
real to be taken as art. Thus autobiography has fallen outside
both fiction and history... Constructing autobiography as a
genre has depended, at least in part, on domesticating its specific weirdness... What we can call autobiography's resistance to
genre can now be taken as a crisis in genre itself, rather than the
cause of autobiography's dismissal or rehabilitation.[44]

From the point of view taken in this chapter and this book as a whole,
this argument is a strange one. It is certainly true that autobiography
is, as it should be, suspicious within judicial contexts, and is marginal
to the disciplines of history and literature, but this in no way justifies
why a form which has a specific history of representing male individuals should provide a privileged location for the instability of all
subjects under all circumstances. This is a much broader, and much
less careful, argument than the useful suggestion that women's fragmented voices under patriarchy may be represented in women's
autobiography. It is simply sloppy to find some intrinsic categorical
connection between the marginality of autobiography studies and the
marginality of Women's Studies; if there is such a connection (and I
believe there is) arguments for it have to be made in historical and
institutional terms. Yet the failure to see this in certain theories of
autobiography which call themselves postmodern is related to their
failure to see that, as I have been arguing, the space occupied by
autobiography studies within Women's Studies, and the space occupied by autobiography studies in African-American Studies, are
themselves different. In short, these theories privilege concepts like
"mixture" and "split subjectivity" *of themselves,* rather than in terms
of any specific set of identifications that, factually, mix; as a result
they see political value primarily in the confusion and impossibility
of identity in the texts of specific women and men rather than in the
means by which this confusion develops specific positions from
which the formation of social collectivities is possible. This is no more
a general theory of the politics of autobiography than is Gusdorf's.

Lionnet's *Autobiographical Voices: Race, Gender, Self-Portraiture,* begins with a chapter on the poetics of "metissage," a word taken from
the Martiniquan poet Edouard Glissant, which she translates loosely
as braiding. Since there is a "long Western tradition ... which conceives of writing as a system that rigidifies,"[45] then, for Lionnet,
colonialism provides the metaphors and French poststructuralism

provides the theory which demonstrates the impossibility of this rigidity. In this context, the analysis of Pan-African women writers demonstrates alternative possibilities for narrative by illustrating the mixing of voices from various oral and intellectual traditions within their work. Work engaged in such metissage is always work that combines and recombines identity in complicated ways, destabilizing assumptions. Such destabilization is then made the center of a theory of politics relying on such mixing – "solidarity" through metissage.[46] Such a politics is, no doubt, desirable; however, Lionnet never makes it clear exactly what the grounds for solidarity will be: either we must make the presupposition that women of color will find universal solidarity in the fact that they are the privileged subjects of mixture – an option Lionnet explicitly rejects – or we must have a theory which recognizes that any number of people are happy to "mix" "identities" by eating the foods of the world and buying African art, while using white male privilege and/or the possession of capital privilege to gain and maintain dominance. Braiding, without some guidelines regarding what is to be braided, implies nothing whatsoever. That Lionnet can provide no such guidelines is indicated by the fact that her first two chapters on autobiography discover the principle of braiding in two canonical texts of the study of autobiography, Augustine's *Confessions* and Nietzsche's *Ecce Homo*. These chapters are placed before (this is not innocent, though she makes claims about the nonlinearity of her text) any analysis of the writings of women of color. I am certain, of course, that metissage is present in these texts; my concern is that the will to rigidify or derigidify these texts is independent of them, and it is precisely this that needs to be assessed in making claims for them.[47]

While Sidonie Smith's theoretical apparatus in chapter one of *Subjectivity, Identity, and the Body* is altogether better elaborated than Lionnet's or Gilmore's, her position seems to lead her in the same basic direction when she actually reads autobiographies.[48] In her readings of texts, the question of split or inconsistent subjectivities is again privileged. Women, in Smith's account, are more likely than men to have to "struggle to become a subject,"[49] and thus the texts in which they recount their lives become a location in which they may illustrate the process of subject-formation, the complicated nature of the "I," more clearly than the men who presume, and thus naturalize, the process of subjectification. As a result (and this is a point I both endorse and think of as very important), women's texts tend to "embody" subjectivity in a way that men's may not: whereas the universal subject in Gusdorf's narrative is located in an idealized mind, the sources of struggle for women that they exhibit in order to arrive at a subject require, at the start, the exploration of the ways in which the body is acted on by language and ideology. Smith's critical objective, then, becomes to explore "the destabilizing strategies of the 'others,'" who have refused the "alienation from the historically imposed image of the self" and instead "talked back." She hopes to demonstrate that "these subjects enter the scene of autobiographical writing ... dialogically with the cacophonous voices of cultural discourses." Thus analysis requires questions like "what kind of subject speaks throughout the autobiographical text? How does the writer manipulate the 'I' so as to fill it, not with the prescriptive history of female essentialism, but with her own experientially based history? How does she redefine for herself the identity contents of the 'I'?"[50]

These are excellent and necessary questions, questions which must be included in any discussion of the construction of self by writers from dominated groups, and questions which I will address in different ways throughout this book. From the point of view of politics, however, the implication remains that since the female subject is always first and last described as split, she is permanently denied the promise of group solidarity (intentional or culturally created community) that is a premise of Sommer's account of testimonial. By looking for the ways in which the "I" is rewritten, rather than the plausible locations of the "we" in the text, Smith ends up posing (albeit from a somewhat different political position) essentially the same question as Heilbrun – what kind of subject can an individual woman express? Even though the "I" is recognized as nonnatural and unstable, there is no sociological or economic subject theorized to supplement it.[51]

That in spite of explicit reference to solidarity and linkages among women Smith has the same problem as Lionnet – an inability to theorize the *content* of solidarity, or why it might be typical of certain groups – can be best demonstrated by comparing her analyses of Zora Neale Hurston's *Dust Tracks on the Road* and Cherrie Moraga's *Loving in the War Years*. Both texts are offered by Smith as politically exemplary cases of the difficult placement of subjectivity by radical women of color, women who transgress boundaries. Yet what they actually say about their lives, by Smith's account, is contradictory. The contradiction might, of course, be explained by placing the two texts within the historical and spatial contexts in which they were written, in which case we might find that each woman was compelled to write by rather different circumstances; or it might turn out that one actually has politics we might want to endorse while the other does not. Finally, we might appreciate the intellectual work of each woman, difficult in accomplishment as it was, and yet reject parts of each of their positions. Unfortunately, Smith provides no indication that there is a problem; mere construction of subjectivity in ways that differ from Gusdorf is the end of her analysis, and there are no grounds for negotiating the differences that might actually prevent solidarity between these two writers.

Smith, like many recent critics, is particularly concerned to demonstrate the instability of expected subject-formations in Hurston's autobiography. Hurston is quite explicit about destabilizing herself from the point of view of race ("The word 'race' is a loose classification of physical characteristics. It tells us nothing about the insides of people"),[52] gender ("the narrator emphasizes the disjunction between the cultural meaning assigned her sexed body and her independently constructed identity as tomboy"),[53] and most centrally, community ("Hurston repudiates the communal history of victimization as the unified ground upon which the essential difference of 'the Negro' can be established").[54] Such destabilizations challenge both dominant assumptions about blacks, and also those of the dominated (specifically black or black female) group, permitting Hurston to mark out a space for the "individual" through the linguistic positionings and repositionings of these categories. What is not clear is whether such repositionings, which are not merely multiple (as all positionings are) but always in flux, provide the grounds for any politics in particular. One answer is Smith's invocation of "diasporic" subjectivity, the subjectivity of black women's metissage internationally. If this is the case, it should be reasonable to ask the (vulgar, materialist) question of whether this links Hurston more firmly to "indigenous folk proverbs" or "the system of white patronage of black artists in which she was so entangled."[55] I do not, at this point, ask this question as a means to reflect on Hurston at all; rather, I want to know in practical terms why Smith advocates "diaspora" over "racial" consciousness at a specific historical juncture.

But perhaps Smith doesn't. In her discussion of Cherrie Moraga's text (itself an autobiography only in the loosest sense – it does not contain an autobiographical pact), Smith lauds Moraga for "bring[ing] the autobiographical body out from under the process of erasure, assuming her body as a narrative point of departure."[56] Note that Hurston, when she explicitly rejects the sign of the flesh on her body, is properly rejecting essentialism, but when Moraga centers her body, she is doing the same. Indeed, we find here that "the narrator's engagement with her specific body forces her to confront the palpability of color and the politics of chromatism."[57] Moraga's light skin, which does in fact put her in a (somewhat) privileged position with regard to other Chicanas, produces "what is inside her" in concrete ways, not by virtue of biological determinism but as a result of the construction of her experience over time; this is one of the central themes of *Loving in the War Years*. Further, this middle, *mixed*, position with regard to identity is regarded by Moraga *not* as transgressive (in itself), but initially *oppressive*: "The narrator considers this instability of identification an oppressive rather than a liberating condition: 'You call this a choice! To constantly push up against a wall of resistance from your own people or to fall away nameless into the mainstream of this country, running with our common blood?'"[58] Smith is correct in pointing out the ways that Moraga's work insists that we understand the specificity of oppression, especially as it results from particular forms of hybridity. Yet we are a far cry from the politics of metissage. Because skin color identity (and sexuality) affect Moraga in specific, and *relatively fixed* ways within her major communities of identification, Chicana, lesbian, white (such that even when she passes as a white heterosexual she has to grapple, consciously, with the fact that she is not one) it forces her to make specific political choices, choices which differ concretely from those made fifty years earlier by Hurston.[59] Moraga's is explicitly a text which names the identities of its politics; she creates we-collectives out of fragmentation in a way that resembles many of the authors I will be discussing in this book – Hurston *not* among them.

A theory of autobiography caught inside the "I," that only notices the differences within it, is doomed to see only the split subjectivities of Hurston and Moraga. A theory that recognizes that all autobiography includes, in some measure, testimony – the construction of a "we" – will notice their difference.

Criticism of black autobiography

In the second section of my first chapter I discussed the relationship of African-American political writing to autobiography via Paul Gilroy's work; much of that discussion could have been placed here. There I pointed out the prevalence of autobiographical writing by individual subjects who, for whatever reason, insist on their relationship to a "we" in African-American history – including those whose primary political activities were not writing. Indeed, if this essay in the theory of autobiography can, finally, be taken to mean anything, it is that what has always been implicitly known by writers on African-American autobiography – specifically, that autobiography often stands in for the political scientist's or sociologist's negotiation of individual history with already given community identities, of "I" and "we" – has been rarely or only intermittently considered within the general theory of autobiography. The fact that autobiographies express the relationship of individuals to communities has been noted on and off since Gusdorf, but has nevertheless only rarely led to questions about how particular individuals relate to *which* communities; the fact that the western subject is a reified, mythical concept and that minority autobiography can be used to mount a challenge to that subject has been argued, yet only rarely has anyone attempted to define how, materially, this challenge happens. Doris Sommer's essay is the only exception to this statement in the scholarship analyzed above. Yet black autobiography studies has done just this, over and over. Stephen Butterfield noted in 1974 that "in black autobiography, the unity of the personal and the mass voice remains a dominant tradition." He then argued that

> The appeal of black autobiographies is in their political awareness, their empathy for suffering, their ability to break down the division of "I" and "you," their knowledge of oppression and discovery of ways to cope with that experience, and their sense of shared life, shared triumph, and communal responsibility. The self belongs to the people, and the people find a voice in the self.[60]

This is, of course, not an unproblematic statement. My point is that such a position, unlike most scholarship on autobiography, leads the critic first toward the question of understanding the construction of particular social identifications – conceived as positive identifications – between reader and text. In opposition to Butterfield, I will demonstrate in this book that "characteristic black modes of thought" do *not* "run through all periods almost unchanged";[61] yet it would be foolish to take this as a sign of the instability of identification categories; rather, as with Gilroy, it needs to be investigated how race remains an always present and nearly always self-chosen sign even when the "mode of thought" has changed from bourgeois to radical, or misogynist to feminist.[62] What we must confront when looking for racial identity in an autobiography is then not so much difference itself (which is always there) but "what difference that difference makes."[63]

In the aftermath of the Black Power period – the moment of the institutionalization of both African-American Studies and Autobiography Studies – the tendency among those writing about black autobiography, white and black, was to assume a reified vision of blackness – one that was by no means typical of earlier periods. Of course all autobiographical texts themselves could never have borne out the sort of generalizations made by Butterfield. But it must be remembered that this reified version of blackness was not simply bad but rather was, in particular ways, productive. Because of this, to say that it is not over – that authoritarian forms of blackness continue to be consequential – is neither to endorse nor condemn such forms but to understand in a determinate way what would be minimally necessary, in the future, to transform them. That it is possible that no place can be found for women in the particular version of blackness identified by Butterfield (though, interestingly, he acknowledges his neglect and indicates that rectifying it *would require an entirely separate book*) is actually a peculiarity of a patriarchal construction of blackness at a particular time, the form of which itself has a history that earlier had been noticeably *less* masculinist; it is not a necessary result of the fixing of textual 'identity.' Thus the inclusion of black women's texts, and theory, does not necessarily lead to the break-down of racial identity; it may illustrate other determinate complexities and variations on such identity. It should not surprise us that Joanne Braxton, in *Black Women Writing Autobiography*, has no more difficulty in constructing a book about black women's autobiography out of a Piagetian narrative of personal development than Francoise Lionnet has in constructing her book from metissage. Or that both Braxton's and Lionnet's choices are articulable to identity politics.

It is, then, particularly conspicuous that William Andrews, whose interests in black autobiography are far less overtly ideological than mine, emphasizes in a recent essay the relative stability of concerns of critics of black autobiography. From the first work on black autobiography, by Rebecca Chalmers Barton in 1948, the opportunity to analyze the political relation of writer to community has been a central draw for critical work.[64] In the 1980s critics looked, especially at the slave narrative, to develop theoretical models concerning the rhetorical nature of that political relation, but politics continued to provide an explicit – *not implicit*, as with many white women writers – backdrop to all constructions of the black autobiographical subject, women as well as men. As to the future of Black Autobiography Studies? "It is hard to imagine that critics and scholars of black

autobiography will veer sharply away from the interests and concerns that preoccupied criticism of this genre in the 1980s."[65] If this
statement can be made sense of (not "if it is true"), it speaks to the
specific role of autobiography in African-American literary studies,
in which the first texts are autobiographies, and where all scholars
already have the institution of autobiography imposed on us.

Part two

The politics of Negro self-representation

Three theories of the race of W. E. B. Du Bois

It is generally recognized today that no scientific definition of
race is possible ... Race would seem to be a dynamic and not a
static conception, and the typical races are continually
changing and developing, amalgamating and differentiating.
W. E. B. Du Bois[1]

The only possible objective definition of consciousness is a
sociological one.   V. N. Volosinov[2]

Autobiographies do not form indisputable authorities. They
are always incomplete, and often unreliable. Eager as I am to
put down the truth, there are difficulties; memory fails
especially in small details, so that it becomes finally but a
theory of my life, with much forgotten and misconceived, with
valuable testimony but often less than absolutely true, despite
my intention to be fair and frank.   W. E. B. Du Bois[3]

Introduction

At the opening of his 1940 book *Dusk of Dawn: An Essay Toward an
Autobiography of a Race Concept*, W. E. B. Du Bois places an "Apology"
which is first of all an apology for his vacillation on the question of the
generic status of the text: autobiography or sociology? He tells us that
this book was initially intended as a third "set of thought centering
around the hurts and hesitancies that hem the black man in America,"[4] following 1903's extremely popular *The Souls of Black Folk* and
1920's less successful sequel, *Darkwater: Voices From Within the Veil*.
But, he says, the celebration of his seventieth birthday provided him
with the opportunity to compose an autobiographical speech, which
he then decided could be used as a framing narrative for a book of
general essays.[5] This narrative would not encompass the whole book,

however, since "in my own experience, autobiographies have had little lure; repeatedly they assume too much or too little: too much in dreaming that one's own life has greatly influenced the world; too little in the reticences, repressions and distortions which come because men do not dare to be absolutely frank." If reading about a life as self-represented is not interesting, nevertheless composing such a text may be forgiven if the author acknowledges at the start its partiality, specifically through the choice of a theme other than the "self" but of which the "self" provides some sort of reflection:

> My life has had its significance and its only deep significance because it was part of a Problem; but that problem was, as I continue to think, the central problem of the greatest of the world's democracies and so the problem of the future world ... I seem to see a way of elucidating the inner meaning and significance of that problem by explaining it in terms of the one human life that I know best.[6]

In introducing the text this way Du Bois is aware that, if his reader has read one other of his books, it is *The Souls of Black Folk*, written thirty-seven years earlier, which is prefaced in prescient terms, "the problem of the twentieth century is the problem of the color line," and the main text of which opens with the question asked of himself, "How does it feel to be a Problem?"[7] It is in this context, Du Bois asserts, that his life may be seen as a privileged representation of racial themes; and this in turn explains the form of his narrative, which rotates continually between the "concept of race" and the "personal interest" in his life story. In this context it can hardly surprise us that when we turn to "The Plot" (as chapter 1 is called), we learn immediately that 1868–1940 are "incidentally the years of my own life but more especially years ... that rush from the American Civil War to the reign of the second Roosevelt" and then encounter a list of historical events encompassing Europe, Asia, and Africa.[8] If this *is* autobiography, it is neither the story of individuality which invites the identification of the reader with the narrator described in Gusdorf's analysis of the genre, nor, alternatively, is it a simple occasion of the African-American testimonial with its ironizing of the dominant "I was born" narrative (Andrews) and reliance on a distancing between reader and narrator (Sommer); rather it has the structure of a dialectical account which presumes to locate the individual in a world history, and a specifically anti-colonial account which, unlike those by European theorists of the period, is able to locate the colonial world as part of this history.[9]

The structure of the text, in which events in his life are followed by local events, which are followed by international events, which always circle back to describe their local meanings, reflects Du Bois' understanding of the ambiguous position of being inside and outside the dominant progressive narrative of world history as taught in his Harvard Ph.D. program at the end of the nineteenth century, in ways that determine the existential fact of being within race: "in the folds of this European civilization I was born and shall die, imprisoned, conditioned, depressed, exalted and inspired."[10] This doubleness, it is important to remember, is in Du Bois' account not merely defining of his subjectivity but already objectively given, a problem he "did little to create" but "did exemplify."[11] Thus to say that Du Bois "has" a race, acts in a raced manner, is to conceive race primarily in terms of the existence of different levels of social existence, in which race is formed socially as a sort of common sense explanation of skin color which, as an autobiographical matter, has placed Du Bois in certain social positions and not others. In this narrative race obtains its historical necessity within the economic (i.e. in the formation of a particular labor force for the purpose of capital accumulation) and is fetishized through racist "scientific" and ideological practice, which takes already given assumptions about the existence of race and literally makes them true. By the time Du Bois is able to write a book about race, it is already a fully internalized psychic structure,[12] an agency quite apart from its now scientifically understood nonexistence. Reflecting on this, Du Bois then writes his autobiography *as a Negro man*, and scare quotes would be particularly inappropriate around this phrase. Because of the complex autobiography of the racial concept, then, political action regarding race must always operate simultaneously at the levels of economy, culture, and psychology. Textually, *Dusk of Dawn* itself is intended to provide a model for the exploration of "the interaction of this stream ... on my work and in relation to what has been going on in the world since my birth."[13]

Thus, the first concern of this chapter is the manner in which *Dusk of Dawn* provides the most significant illustration of my claim in chapter one that books by African Americans about race theory are often written in the form of autobiography. If Du Bois claims to find "little lure" in autobiography in general, he nevertheless proposes that his autobiography's interest will lie in its narrative-theoretical apparatus, which examines the particular relationship between autobiographical truth and political-theoretical truth. In this light, no account of the seventy-year old Du Bois' autobiography can stand to ignore that it is but one of Du Bois' numerous other autobiographical texts which, by his own account at age ninety-one, contain at least three distinct "theories" of his life.[14] Each theory relies on a strikingly different apparatus of self-representation, corresponding at the formal and argumentative levels to three specific political formations common to twentieth century African-American intellectual history – those of liberalism, Pan-Africanist marxism, and orthodox communism. The divergence in form and content of these multiple autobiographical accounts, none of which is *just* an autobiography, lead me to reflect further on the meaning of autobiography.

Beyond this, as the peculiar subtitle of *Dusk of Dawn* makes clear, the text is not merely the "autobiography" of a "self" but is also representative of the "concept" of the category "race" – and this is a distinct claim from "is representative of the black race." Indeed, Du Bois' various autobiographical representations cannot be understood without the further analysis of the meaning of "race," since this is precisely what he suggests that his life best represents: this will be my second concern in this chapter. Given the recent attacks on the use of the concept of race as an analytical tool from several theoretical standpoints, it will become necessary for me to explain and specifically defend Du Bois' careful usage of the word, in contemporary terminology, as a "social construction," but as one which, having long been constructed, has ongoing real effects. Race, then, in Du Bois' usage, is best understood as a particular formation of social marginality, one with a logic that consistently cuts through other social formations in the United States.[15]

Thus the issues which drive my analysis of *Dusk of Dawn*, as well as the two other autobiographical texts discussed at somewhat lesser length below, are the questions "what is an autobiography?" and "what is a race?" When articulated together, these two questions join to raise once again the more general question of "identity politics." The limitations of Du Bois' understanding of racial identity politics will appear in his failure to address gender as an aspect of race in *Dusk of Dawn*; gender is a concern of Du Bois' only in the *Autobiography*, where it becomes divorced from race, and thus in Du Bois' theory from socially determined and determining consciousness. While I see Du Bois' practice of autobiography as still suggestive for contemporary political analysis, it is clear to me that his practice can only be exemplified and extended in the current period by those writers who further address the genderedness of autobiography.

The three theories

Darkwater: The individualist theory of the veil and identity politics

As I will show below, *Dusk of Dawn* provides a theory of identity politics reliant on the notion that collective political action always supposes a relationship of identification, and that in the United States all identification is funneled first through racial identification. In general, this is also my position; but the best way to introduce this argument in Du Bois' life is not to describe the argument of *Dusk*, but rather to recount the politics of Du Bois' most successful form of self-representation, the one which led, however unintentionally, to his political leadership. The notion of racial identity during his liberal period, stretching from before *The Souls of Black Folk*, through the early autobiographical account that opens *Darkwater*, until the late 1920s when he entered his period of serious engagement with marxism, can be understood as a version of existential and intellectual individualism whose rhetoric is Emersonian, as in the striving individual within a capitalized "Nature." Within African-American history this differs sharply from Frederick Douglass' artisan class-based commercial individualism. It suggests that what attracted so much of the black professional class to Du Bois' ideas in the beginning was not the account of racial identity *per se*, but the representation of individual heroism in its American form *as* Negro.[16]

Darkwater's autobiography starts with a line Du Bois liked so much he repeats it in each later autobiography: "I was born by a golden river and in the shadow of two great hills five years after the Emancipation Proclamation."[17] The line is conspicuous for the slightly anachronistic attempt at elegiac significance that Du Bois' writing maintains deep into the twentieth century. It becomes even more conspicuous given the explanation of why, exactly, the river was golden, which appears pages later: "That river of my birth was golden because of the woolen and paper waste that soiled it. The gold was theirs, not ours; but the gleam and glint was for all."[18] If the negative truth of pollution and economic domination helps to explain his politics later in the essay, the gold color is positioned rhetorically to afford Du Bois' birth, and perhaps his light brown skin color as well, great importance. This specific rhetoric, often visual, always about the personal or clan-based worth of the people in Du Bois' family tree, can be seen in the introduction of every new thought for several pages: "My own people were part of a great clan"; "Mother was dark shining bronze"; "Alfred, my father must have seemed a splendid vision"; "Long years before [my father] Louis XIV drove two Huguenots, Jacques and Louis Du Bois, into wild Ulster County, New York."[19] The reader here is asked to glory in the aristocratic beauty and character of these people who are of African descent, though race is not stressed in particular, inasmuch as the rhetoric is retained in describing white ancestors in the last example. The family's poverty is not entirely missing from this account (nor, of course, is coming from a situation of poverty an embarrassment in American-ist narrative), but much of what one notices about it is that the narrator expresses amazement that he could have been impoverish-ed, as is illustrated by the peculiar use of exclamation points: "I never remember being cold or hungry, but I do remember that shoes and coal, and sometimes flour, caused mother moments of anxious thought in winter, and a new suit was an event!"[20]

Over a third of this rather short narrative is taken with his back-ground, almost pleading against itself that it is "respectable."[21] When he does, finally, turn to his own abilities, he positions himself as very much "one of the boys," and at the same time magically better:

> Very gradually I found myself assuming quite placidly that I was different from other children. At first I think I connected the difference with a manifest ability to get my lessons rather better than most and to recite with a certain happy, almost taunting, glibness, which brought frowns here and there. Then, slowly, I realized that some folks, a few, even several, actually considered my brown skin a misfortune; once or twice I became painfully aware that some human beings thought it a crime. I was not for a moment daunted, – although, of course, there were some days of secret tears – rather I was spurred to tireless effort. If they beat me at anything, I was grimly determined to make them sweat for it! ...
>
> As time flew I felt not so much disowned and rejected as rather drawn into higher spaces and made part of a mightier mission.[22]

Interest in Du Bois' person, in this passage, does not derive from an interest in race; here the reader is positioned as someone who should be interested in the race problem primarily because it has intersec-ted, arbitrarily, with Du Bois, whose extraordinariness does not de-pend at its base on any sort of racial consciousness. While Du Bois' later autobiographies are not without the sense that his individual achievement is significant, they do not maintain this narrative of the extraordinary, instead referring far more to a narrative of luck –

compare *Dusk*, where he reports that his high school principal, not mentioned in *Darkwater*, was a major figure in his getting an academic education and, had he had a different principal, could easily have set Du Bois to a trade.[23] Here he barely acknowledges anything but exceptional accomplishment: "I suspect that beneath all my seeming triumphs there were many failures and disappointments, but the realities loomed so large that they swept away even the memory of other dreams and wishes."[24] On the other hand, "I *willed* to do. It was done. I *wished!* The wish came true."[25] The adult life has been divided into four conspicuously capitalized parts, "the Age of Miracles, the Days of Disillusion, the Discipline of Work and Play, and the Second Miracle Age," but even the Days of Disillusion, the period of his early professional existence before he lands the job at Atlanta University, turn out to be "not disappointing enough to discourage me."[26]

In 1920, at this moment of editing *Crisis* and of being the best-known Negro official of the integrationist, still white-led NAACP, Du Bois provides an explicitly *American* myth which contains within it a large constituency of people who will be race-assertive precisely because the content given blackness in the psyche is portrayed as indistinguishable from any other form of human existence. It is especially indistinguishable with concern to gender: in these twenty pages of *Darkwater* Nina Gomer Du Bois appears in a manner that one associates with masculine narratives of success: "in 1896, I married – a slip of a girl, beautifully dark-eyed and thorough and good as a German housewife."[27] Du Bois, like Douglass before him, was a liberal feminist whose life as an agitator happened in close collaboration with white women; indeed, later in *Darkwater* there is a chapter on the importance of women's rights to Negro politics. Yet it will take Du Bois until the *Autobiography*, after Nina's death and his remarriage, for a public accounting of his gender identity.

Finally, what differentiates the *Darkwater* account from Du Bois' later narratives is that it contains no "apology" – no explanation of the reason for his own self-representation, no suggestion that people should read about him for any other reason than admiration of him as an individual. Autobiography in American ideology has never needed any apology because writing the exemplary self has been a moral imperative of individualism since the Puritans.[28] Arnold Rampersad claims that this moral sense, the idea that through work and politics he would be setting an example, was the driving force through Du Bois' life, through all his changes in organizational and political affiliation.[29] I would, on the other hand, suggest that since Du Bois' relatively consistent, and compelling, imagery of race was generated by the social space which became the explicit form of his political subjectivity (with which his audience necessarily identified), *Darkwater*'s moral vision, disconnected from race, is appropriately described as an "uncompleted argument," in the sense Anthony Appiah regards *Dusk of Dawn*.[30] The individualist and liberal narrative of *Darkwater* is the one Du Bois tries repeatedly to escape through the claim to exemplify collective racial subjectivity later on.

Dusk of Dawn: race and/as the autobiographical

What is a race?

In contrast to *Darkwater*, in *Dusk* Du Bois insists that his "autobiography is a digressive illustration and exemplification of what race has meant" – that is, a sociology of race.[31] More strikingly, he argues that the content of his intellectual thinking is itself tied to, or determined by, his skin color: that intellectual thought is (among other things) a function of race. We are now used to calling this position "essentialist." Yet Du Bois knows that skin color itself is a thoroughly arbitrary sign, with no *natural* relationship to the ability of any individual to understand or accept the content of the arguments he makes. Race, for Du Bois in this narrative, is a social *construction* in the strictest sense of the term possible. Biological or scientific race does not exist; nor can race be given any global sense at all, since its psychic meaning is always defined in a specific local and intersubjective context in which one person is, as it were, "behind a barrier"; but, because this barrier is in fact *constructed* systematically in the widest variety of localities, its psychological form effects all who live inside it, even when they experience its meaning in different specific ways.[32] In such circumstances, because the racial barrier is already formed, black scholars (as one example) live their race in such a way that it causes them to make conscious and unconscious decisions *separately* from those defined outside their group, thus creating racial formations with, over time, distinct cultural and political manifestations. Thus, while there is no reason to believe that, for example, any given black person will become a socialist, or that a black American will always care more about Africa than a white American, one nevertheless cannot describe the path by which a given individual adopts socialism or African solidarity in any terms other than as a result of various psychic events in which felt racial differential led to a choice in a particular direction. It is then precisely because the "scientific definition of race is impossible" that the concept of race, in the sense of the determined adoption of what Omi and Winant call "racial projects" is called by Du Bois the "greatest thing in my life and absolutely determine[s] it."[33]

Du Bois had the most distinguished education available to any American in the late nineteenth century, including a Ph.D. at Harvard (the first granted to an African American), two years at the University of Berlin, and three years at Fisk University in Tennessee. Du Bois' reflections on the climate of this intellectual milieu where "above all science was becoming a religion" suggests, at the outset, the workings of race:

> When I was a young man, so far as I was concerned, the foundations of present culture were laid, the way was charted, the progress toward certain great goals was undoubted and inevitable. There was room for argument concerning details and methods and possible detours in the onsweep of civilization; but the fundamental facts were clear...
>
> Apparently one consideration alone saved me from complete conformity with the thoughts and confusions of then current social trends; and that was the problems of racial and cultural contacts.[34]

It is important to emphasize at the outset that this discussion views the process of the acquisition of knowledge to be identical among humans at the outset; Du Bois, a New England boy from a town with few Negroes who has a personal affect that continues to be conservative long after he becomes a radical intellectual, is clear that race has not prevented him from initially accepting the premises of his education. The very fact that he is successful in the New England educational setting, where he knows no other Negro High School students, demonstrates his basic conformity. However, a social fact – the problem of racial and cultural *contacts* – requires him to examine the way that the social system is constructed. Thus the racial barrier becomes the sufficient cause for a preliminary investigation of the assumptions of his education.

In the previous chapter, Du Bois has already taken pains to demonstrate that he is first of all a New England child, and not a black child – we learn that for him there was simply no racial we-subject with which he could identify as there might have been had he been born in the south. For example, in describing his youth, Du Bois' first conception of the "problem of inheritance" is neither biological nor racial, but rather economic and regional: a local fortune (of a family for whom Du Bois worked), "the Hopkins millions" passed into the "foreign hands" of a scheming English architect, thus removing capital from the local Great Barrington economy.[35] The use of "inheritance" here is worth noting because social scientific testimony about race would take this word as its key category; Du Bois is suggesting that race is precisely that which he does *not* "inherit" as a child. In his childhood "the color line was manifest and yet not absolutely drawn," and to the extent it is defined "the racial angle was more clearly defined against the Irish" than against him.[36] His culture is absolutely indistinguishable from that of white New England, his views of property are vague and conventionally American, and, to the extent that he had a manifest attitude toward race at all it was one of "exaltation and high disdain" of the white kids for being less smart than himself.[37]

In retrospect, he reports, race manifested itself in small ways, through a certain implicit awareness that he should avoid placing himself in circumstances where he would not be wanted. Only as he reached high school graduation and faced the problem of college – ironically, he claims that he was able to go to college only *because* he was black, since a smart white boy of his class position would have tended to apprentice for positions in the local elite – was race made explicit, as money was raised from local philanthropists to send Du Bois south to "meet colored people of [his] own age and ... ambitions." It is in this context that Du Bois first hears the southern black music that he would become famous writing about, about which he "*seemed to* recognize something inherently and deeply my own."[38]

This last sentence is ambiguous, but I believe that the emphasis must be placed on the word "seemed." The context of the quote reads as follows:

> I became aware, once a chance to go to [Fisk] was opened up for me, of the spiritual isolation in which I was living. I heard too in these days for the first time the Negro folk songs. A Hampton Quartet had sung them in the Congregational Church. I was thrilled and moved to tears and seemed to recognize something inherently and deeply my own. I was glad to go to Fisk.

The process of psychic racial formation in Du Bois' youth, then, is as follows: there is no manifest content to being Negro, just a minor, but socially enforced, sense of not being like others, a sense with consequences so great that at a certain point it begins to control the entire set of possible choices. *Once this is recognized*, the Negro subject unconsciously fills up the outward sign of this difference, skin color, with apparently arbitrary signs, cultural manifestations s/he does not necessarily possess, "seeming to recognize" them as "my own." This structure of argument is repeated several times in *Dusk of Dawn*, especially with regard to identification with Africa, as I will demonstrate below.[39] What will become most significant for understanding the way that "blackness" ultimately becomes socially constructed on a global scale is that, having had this sensation, this "seeming to recognize," Du Bois becomes an agent of its reproduction. Since this process is being multiplied throughout the United States, "a" race is formed and indeed re-formed, since it has already been, in the twentieth century, long since formed. It should not, then, surprise us when the initially arbitrary formation "Negro identity" comes to develop cultural, political, and economic significance in the overtly political argument later in the text.[40]

The generation of this racial feeling or persona in turn leads Du Bois to changes in political/ideological allegiance, based on specific events which are coded in various ways as racial; the history of his racial formation leads to the particular theorizing he engages in. This is best illustrated by the three major changes in his intellectual position, in which he moved away from "complete conformity" with the ideas of his age, and, starting around 1910, developed a highly original third worldist perspective which would in fact become common among Pan-Africanist intellectuals in the late 1930s and 1940s.[41] These changes were a redefinition of and move away from the notion of progress through scientific practice, the development of an interest in Pan-African studies, and his ultimate analysis of racial imperialism as an element of (though not specifically derived from) capitalism.[42] In the first case, Du Bois asserts that long before he started to develop the social analysis of race he wanted to study (and indeed to help invent) the discipline of sociology because of his "firm belief in a changing racial group" which allowed him to "easily grasp the idea of a changing developing society rather than a fixed social structure."[43] Social science would in turn be the hegemonic tool through which he could fight racism. But being a Negro sociologist at the turn of the century was essentially impossible for one structural reason – essentially all funding on research or education for Negroes happened through Booker T. Washington's Tuskegee Machine, and the white philanthropists responsible for Washington's power. But

Washington opposed Negroes engaging in scholarly research, preferring "industrial education" and the concentration on expanding the race's economic resources. In this context, Du Bois found the resources for doing research more and more constricted by Washington's machine, and necessarily found himself, in spite of specific intentions to the contrary, engaged in the sort of racial politics which he sincerely felt had nothing to do with his work as a scientist (however much his subject matter was already the result of race). Du Bois ends up being the accidental leader of a black community faction in opposition to Washington.

His conflict with Washington is not the only reason his views of the effectiveness of science in fighting racism change. Rather he asserts, "two considerations ... broke in upon my work and eventually disrupted it: first, one could not be a calm, cool, and detached scientist while Negroes were lynched, murdered and starved; and secondly, there was no such definite demand for scientific work of the sort that I was doing."[44] The first compulsion, given the phrasing *one could not*, is an ironic invocation of race in particular; obviously "one" could engage in a variety of strategies, but Du Bois couldn't and he was literally the *one* experienced Negro social scientist in the country during the decade 1900–10; and the second depended concretely on the approval of Washington's funders. Through these mechanisms which affect only dark-skinned people, and only because they are dark-skinned, developing a forum for agitation (or else abandoning all intellectual interests) becomes the only *racially* possible course.

In the second case, the construction of a Pan-African discourse, it is very important that we read the discussion of Countee Cullen's famous question, "What is Africa to me?" in its context in *Dusk*.[45] The first point to be made is that in the thirteen pages which follow this question, in which Du Bois describes what he has learned in his several trips to Africa, he doesn't invoke a racial identity between himself and residents of West Africa, except within a quotation from a speech given sixteen years earlier, in 1924. (This quotation is itself not about Africans at all, but about Negro American "pride in their race and lineage," the peculiar American subjectivity always under discussion here.) On the contrary, from our present perspective, one shudders in regard to the way Du Bois invents the "primitive" African with whom he does *not* share an identity.[46] The sentence which concludes this section is "Now to return to the American concept of race," which is to say, the discussion of Africa is *not* to be confused with the discussion of race in the US.[47] So what is this description of Pan-African ideology doing in the middle of a chapter called "The Concept of Race"? Primarily it is describing how, as a young African-American intellectual, Du Bois developed a psychic imagination of Africa, an affective kinship which leads him to perceive and learn particular things from his connection to Africa and its intellectuals through the Pan-American movement that is particular to an American racialized self.

This is not to say that earlier in his life Du Bois never believed that he shared a "race" with Africans. In *Dusk,* he specifically refers to his early writing which argues for this commonality, like the 1897 essay "The Conservation of Races," in order to disavow it. What remains for him to explore *autobiographically* is precisely how the earlier belief in a shared race constitutes a moment of his blackness which can ultimately be described in terms of the "*American* concept of race." In *this* context, Du Bois writes that the African descendants of his distant African relatives do share *something* with him:

> [They] have suffered a common disaster and have one long memory ... The physical bond is least and the badge of color relatively unimportant save as a badge; the real essence of this kinship is its social heritage of slavery the discrimination and insult; and this heritage binds together not simply the children of Africa, but extends through yellow Asia and into the South Seas. It is this unity that draws me to Africa.[48]

It is easy to see the problems in the idea of "one" "racial memory," though there are certainly equally important ways of conceiving this issue which are worth defending.[49] I find it more compelling, given the context, to notice the stress on power relations and social marginality uniting African Americans and Africans in addition to other "colored" peoples of the world. During the entire period of his editorship, between 1910–1934, *Crisis* was one of the better popular sources for information on decolonization movements in *Asia.*

How do you know a race when you see it?

Du Bois, then, has not been trying to show that Africans and African Americans are members of "a" common race (though under some specific social circumstances it may be most accurate to articulate them together as such), but rather to show the "full psychological meaning of caste segregation,"[50] which made the invention of the Negro race necessary and useful for the African Americans who participated in it (quite regardless of the racial projects of white people) and which sustains this racial formation without reference to biology. "Negro" may not be a race in any coherent sense, but the psychic implications of the veil, which cause people to live "as Negroes," are themselves unifying characteristics. I am aware of the tautology; it is unavoidable. Du Bois, abandoning both "autobiography" and "science," attempts to provide a generalizing metaphor:

> It is difficult to let others see the full psychological meaning of caste segregation. It is as though one, looking out from a dark cave in a side of an impending mountain, sees the world passing and speaks to it; speaks courteously and persuasively, showing them how these entombed souls are hindered in their natural movements, expression, and development; and how their loosening from prison would be a matter not simply of courtesy, ... but aid to the world... It gradually penetrates the minds of the prisoners that the people passing do not hear; that some thick sheet of invisible but horribly tangible plate glass in between them and the world. They get excited; they talk louder; they gesticulate... Then the people within may become hysterical. They may scream and hurl themselves against the barriers, hardly realizing in their bewilderment that they are screaming in a vacuum unheard and that their antics may actually seem funny to those outside looking in...
> All my life I have had continually to haul my soul back and say, "All white folk are not scoundrels nor murderers. They are, even as I am, painfully human."[51]

The positive characteristics given to "Negroness," which does not define a "culture" as such, are the result of this negativity, the normative condition of being beneath, behind, under. A race is invented because such invention is the only means of articulation, of proceeding positively:

> Perhaps it is wrong to speak of it at all as "a concept" rather than as a group of contradictory forces, facts, and tendencies... It was for me as I have written first a matter of dawning realization, then of study and science; then a matter of inquiry into the diverse strands of my own family; and finally consideration of my connection, physical and spiritual, with Africa and the Negro race in its homeland.[52]

I cannot trace the argument of the next chapter, "The White World," with the detail I have approached the previous one, since it repeats a great deal of the same ground through Du Bois' humorous description of two fictional "friends," both white, both of whom consider themselves not racist, or at least not unusually so. What is important about this chapter in the argument of the text is the explanation it gives for how race works as a psychic *differential* in conversation between Negroes and whites regardless of the fact that in the sample conversations the black voice (which is Du Bois') is primarily arguing that race does not exist – or more precisely, that he himself is actually a white man (and fully complicit in the culture and ideas of the dominant majority) by the white man's own definition. bell hooks has remarked that white people are generally amazed that black people look at us with an ethnographic eye, themselves scrutinizing our whiteness.[53] Du Bois' procedure here is to accomplish such scrutiny by inhabiting the position of whiteness, and thus ironizing the white race, to the horror of his (fictional) white interlocutor. For example, at the end of a long exchange, the white man asks in exasperation (I have witnessed this question in the 1990s, and probably you have too): "Why don't you leave [us], then? Get out, go to Africa or the North Pole?" Du Bois responds:

> I am as bad as [you] are. In fact, I am related to [you]...
> "By blood?"
> By Blood.
> "Then you are railing at yourself. You are not black, you are no Negro."
> And you? Yellow blood and black has deluged Europe...
> "What then becomes of all your argument, if there are no races and we are all so horribly mixed as you maliciously charge?
> Oh, my friend, can you not see that I am laughing at you?...
> Human beings are infinite in variety, and when they are agglutinated in groups, great and small, the groups differ as though they, too, had integrating souls. But they do not... Race is a cultural, sometimes a historical fact...
> "But what is this group; and how do you differentiate it; and how can you call it 'black' when you admit it is not black?"
> I recognize it quite easily and with full legal sanction; the black man is a person who must ride "Jim Crow" in Georgia.[54]

The social irony which inhabits race in *Dusk* pervades all racial interaction for Du Bois' later work. You cannot make sense of this passage without understanding that, in any biological sense of the word, racially the white and black participants are the same; simultaneously their inability to understand one another, even to agree to a discursive framework, results from occupying different racial spaces. Because this phenomenon is the normal form of interaction between educated, liberal, black and white Americans, teaching people the biological meaninglessness of race is largely irrelevant to political strategy. It does not matter whether race is "scientific" in most contexts. Politics in the US is *necessarily* built around racial identity precisely because such identity is first of all defined and enforced by such politically charged interactions.

The Negro political subject in *Dusk of Dawn*

At the time *Dusk* was written Du Bois had recently completed, in collaboration with a few students at Atlanta University, a lengthy and elaborate political platform they called the "Basic American Negro Creed"[55] which attempts to create a political subject. From an ideological point of view it is the most elaborate attempt to combine the assumptions of three major tendencies in African-American political thought of the time: liberalism, "nationalist" self-segregation,[56] and socialist economic planning. The premise of Du Bois' plan for action is that what African Americans want, in the abstract, is political rights, economic growth and full equality, and participation in public culture. These things are not specific to race, and are not claimed as somehow being "black." But because of the fact of blackness, the already given existence of segregation, the path to achieving these things must be specifically black, and draw specifically on the cultural and political icons of black and African history. It is precisely at this point of presenting a complete political program, that Du Bois' reliance on autobiographical method fails him, for he knows that he speaks for no one except perhaps a few intellectuals (so few that he will be chased from Atlanta University, as he was from the NAACP, because of his growing engagement with socialist and anti-war politics within just a few years). The objective structure of blackness that has had so much subjective impact on his life and theorizing has placed him, at age seventy, in a profoundly different position than many other blacks, whose own self-accounts tend to articulate any one of the three positions he is attempting to combine, but not the three together.

As he has for most of his life, Du Bois speaks first as a member of the black professional class (he has dropped the term "talented tenth" and the commonly used "bourgeoisie" was never appropriate from a marxist point of view) in the context of racial uplift, a category that corresponds specifically to the liberal tendency of his thinking. Unlike in his self-account in *Darkwater*, however, he no longer identifies with this class, which, he argues is essentially self-hating, sharing the suspicions of whites about the inadequacies of the race.[57] Du Bois argues, for example, that "younger educated Negroes" are spurred by this self-hatred to widely divergent personal strategies:

One avoids every appearance of segregation... He will take
every opportunity to join in the political and cultural life of the
whites. But he pays for this and pays dearly. He so often meets
actual insult ... that he becomes nervous and truculent through
expectations of dislike. And on the other hand, Negroes ...
suspect that he is "ashamed of his race."

Another sort of young educated Negro forms and joins Negro
organizations; prides himself on living with "his people"; with-
draws from contact with whites, unless there is no obvious
alternative... Between these two extremes range all sorts of
interracial patterns, and all of them theoretically follow the idea
that Negroes must only submit to segregation "when forced." In
practically all cases the net result is a more or less clear and
definite crystallization of the culture elements among colored
people into their own groups for social and cultural contact.[58]

Just as race had produced him, it has spontaneously produced a
segregated black group with an autonomous culture formed not in
spite of but because individuals are split by ideology and class in much
the same way they are in other recognizable social groups. At the same
time, a partially segregated black economy already exists, due to the
capital furnished by the group for churches, segregated schools,
professional services, and a variety of in-community business that
always offer the best opportunity for black investment in a racist
society. Thus he proposes, in place of the political movement with
which he has so long been identified (that is, the NAACP), an argument that would not become influential until at least the mid-1960s
under the rubric of Black Power: "Instead of letting this segregation
remain largely a matter of chance and unplanned development, and
allowing its objects and results to rest in the hands of the white
majority or in the accidents of the situation, it would make the
segregation a matter of careful thought and intelligent planning on the
part of Negroes."[59] Such an economy is plausible precisely because the
professional group has a nationalist motivation – their own psychic
self-hatred and white-enforced embarrassment about being identified
with an oppressed race. Rejecting this depends on racial identification
with the whole group, on developing a racial consciousness.

What such a proposal does not address is why an identifiable
group, even a group with which people demonstrably identify, will
be able to drop the various and incoherent strategies which have led
to its formation and adopt Du Bois' strategy in 1940. Having developed an elaborate dialectical argument connecting his own autobiography, to race, to a particular analysis of political economy and practice,

Du Bois is left with the concrete fact that he speaks for *absolutely no one*. In contrast to when he co-founded the NAACP, representing a definable segment of the black American population, Du Bois is not able to show that in 1940 in *exemplifying* the concept of race he also *represents* it politically. It is only at this stage of the argument that he finds himself moving, arbitrarily, back to Africa, pleading for a sort of ethical racial identification that he knows perfectly well is not generalizable to the black American group:

> In the African communal group, ties of family and blood, of mother and child, of group relationship, made the group leadership strong... In the case of the more artificial group among American Negroes, there are sources of strength in common memories of suffering in the past; in present threats of degradation and extinction; in common ambitions and ideals; in emulation and the determination to prove ability and desert. Here in subtle ways the communalism of the African clan can be transferred to the Negro American group... We have a chance here to teach industrial and cultural democracy to a world that bitterly needs it.[60]

It is impossible to read this without the sense that Du Bois is grasping at straws. He knows that race is not culture, but spatial limitation; and that while autobiography explains the existence of the racial formation, it does not unify it politically.[61] While engagement with this particular form of identity politics may in fact be useful as a proposal, Du Bois, the scientist, continues to have no analysis of the formation of political blocs and social movements which might indicate under what conditions his proposal may be realized.

Last words on the argument of *Dusk of Dawn*

The first three chapters of *Dusk of Dawn* narrated the life of W. E. B. Du Bois to exemplify the formation of racial consciousness; the second three chapters have taken humorous anecdotes, fictional encounters, and family genealogies to define the political meaning, in the United States, of this personal story. The last two chapters complete the dialectical structure by returning to Du Bois' life story, now in the years 1920–1940, amid a global analysis, for the portion of his life he now narrates is that of his study of economics and his marxist analysis of the colonization of the third world. Black American subjectivity, with its centrally important political component, is nevertheless also necessary to contextualize as one part of a larger struggle against the

74

cultural and economic subordination of peoples of color internationally. While the political analysis is useful, a contradiction in the
structure of autobiographical representation comes clearly into focus:
as the subject matter becomes that of global capitalism, the autobiographical narrative becomes far more individualized than in the first
two thirds of the text, since it is the narrative of the scholar who
studies and *knows*. While the objective argument becomes clear, subjectivity becomes less and less a framework for understanding social
formations and more and more an account of his fights within and
without his political organization. It is not just that his political
analysis becomes framed in objective terms for the first time in the
text; it is that the rejection of his political analysis, the failure of the
Basic American Negro Creed to generate an audience, is also faceless
and nameless: "This creed proved unacceptable both to the Adult
Education Association and to its colored affiliates. Consequently
when I returned from abroad the manuscript, although ordered and
already paid for, was returned to me as rejected for publication. Just
who pronounced the veto I don't know."[62]

Autobiography: The communist theory and the end of identity politics

The *Autobiography of W. E. B. Du Bois* provides a radically new frame
for Du Bois' life, despite the fact that about 200 of its pages are taken
nearly word for word from the two previous autobiographical texts.
About half of the *Autobiography*'s 423 pages are new, addressing
material not published in either previous text; a nearly 200-page
structure which addresses almost exclusively the changes in his
theory of self-representation during his last twenty years of life has
been added. Thus the new account is constructed in such a way as to
maximize attention to a new view of politics, race, and the historical
significance of his life. The new material in effect folds the theory of
race, which provides *Dusk*'s largest framework, into the narrative of
working class revolution which he has adopted, arguing that the
earlier notion is simply subjective, and of no "historical" significance;
while his participation in communist politics at the end of his life is
the only politically viable framework for the social deconstruction of
race. In this context, for the first time in his autobiographical work he
attempts to analyze his individual motivations, in a fascinating
chapter called "My Character" which is stuck, apparently arbitrarily,
amid the narrative of his life at age seventy (which is to say, the point

where *Dusk of Dawn* leaves off). This chapter, it seems, provides the outline of an answer to the question of what autobiographical issues exist outside *Dusk*'s narrative of racial identity.

The communist superstructure superimposed onto the life is quite different in style from that of the racial autonomist superstructure in *Dusk*, because this time Du Bois does not claim that his life in particular allows for privileged access to the narrative of revolutionary social change. He is a member of a coherent, but small segment of the international division of classes, in which no special place is provided for American Negroes; and his joining of the international movement is non-identitarian, if not quite a "choice." In the first paragraph he is literally escaping from the United States:

> August 8 was a day of warm and beautiful sunshine, and many friends with flowers and wine were at the dock to bid me and my wife goodbye. For the 15th time I was going abroad. I felt like a released prisoner, because since 1951, I had been refused a passport by my government, on the excuse that it was not considered to be "to the best interests of the United States" that I go abroad. It assumed that if I did, I would probably criticize the United States for its attitude toward American Negroes. This was certainly true.[63]

Du Bois was one of many leftists denied passports during this period, ostensibly for being Communist Party members (in fact in Du Bois' case he officially joined the party only after leaving the country). His opposition to the United States as an imperialist power had roots that were outlined in the anti-colonial texts dating back to the 1910s, and which were quite distinct from any interest in the political program of the Comintern.[64] Though my argument differs from Gerald Horne's – that his decision to join the party is not an aberration but a logical consequence of the political position he outlined in the early 1930s[65] – it is clear that the Cold War opened a sharp split between Du Boisian socialism (which was acceptable, if eccentric, within the pre-Depression NAACP) and Du Boisian liberalism – a split between the black middle class with whom he was affiliated for so long, and the predominantly white left, who would provide his only community now. From the point of view of the new textual strategy, the result is to marginalize the narrative of personal identity, placing in front of it a narrative of international travel, in which Du Bois looks at the rest of the world as an outsider, a privileged observer. The first five chapters of the *Autobiography* are called "My 15th Trip Abroad," "Europe," "The Pawned Peoples [of Eastern Europe]," "The Soviet Union" and

"China," textually decentering the story of Du Bois' identity within a global narrative.

The travel narrative promised by the chapter titles isn't especially fleshed out with much description of travel, however. Rather, we are given a fairly straightforward account of twentieth-century history in each of these places that, while often merely accurate ("There is no European labor party ready to help emancipate the workers of Asia and Africa"[66]) is structured around an immensely predictable rhetoric showing none of the complications and contradictions engaged in *Dusk*'s investigation of subjectivity ("In the Soviet Union the overwhelming power of the working class as representing the nation is always decisive"[67]). These chapters, in turn, lead comfortably into what can only be called the statement of religious conversion, "Interlude: Communism" on pages 57–8 of the text, which replaces the complicated and local engagement with the political economy of black America in the earlier autobiography with a statement of "belief" so abstract and unargued as to erase subjectivity (to say nothing of race) as an element of dialectical narrative:

> I have studied socialism and communism long and carefully in lands where they are practiced and in conversation with their adherents, and with wide reading. I now state my conclusion frankly and clearly: I believe in communism...
>
> I shall therefore hereafter help the triumph of communism in every honest way that I can: without deceit or hurt; and in any way possible, without war; and with goodwill to all men of all colors, classes and creeds. If, because of this belief and such action, I become the victim of attack and calumny, I will react in the way that seems to me best for the world in which I live and which I have tried earnestly to serve.[68]

It is impossible not to see in these passages a Christianity which Du Bois abandoned for something he called science as a youth.[69] One of the results of this move to a Christian doctrine of conversion and proselytization is that *Dusk of Dawn*'s "Apology," phrased in the earlier text as a doctrine of autobiography as sociological representation, is now rephrased as enlightenment narrative:

> Who now am I to have come to these conclusions? And of what if any significance are my deductions?... The final answer to these questions, time and posterity must make. But perhaps it is my duty to contribute whatever enlightenment I can. This is the excuse for this writing which I call a soliloquy.[70]

In contrast to Du Bois' earlier argument that the black self is in some way always constructed by the social institution of the racial veil, an idea that appears in some manner at every point of Du Bois' career from 1897 (whether the veil is described as less or more important to individual agency), here he is arguing that in the movement of world history such social construction of the subject is of no account. If Du Bois has had something to say to the world, having asked certain questions and come to certain conclusions, we are not to account for it by his racial experience, as he previously claimed, but from his enlightenment.[71] On the other hand, self-representation does not disappear altogether from the scientist's text; rather it returns in its most traditional form, the question of "that older generation which formed my youth," "character," about which Du Bois provides the most interesting new material in the book.[72]

For the little that Du Bois actually relies on anything we would understand as Freudian theory, he mentions Freud by name in *Dusk of Dawn* as having influenced his claims for what might be understood as a racial unconscious. In that context the rejection of such an unconscious in the *Autobiography* seems especially significant:

> When I was a young man, we talked much of character ... It is typical of our time that insistence on character today in the country has almost ceased. Freud and others have stressed the unconscious factors of our personality so that today we do not advise youth about their development of character; we watch and count their actions with almost helpless disassociation from thought of advice.
> Nevertheless, from that older generation which formed my youth I still retain an interest in what men are rather than what they do.[73]

This distinction between "are" and "do" simply does not appear in *Dusk* or in *Darkwater*, and is impossible if our investigation intends to discover the subject as racialized. Here, the list of characteristics that Du Bois can be said to be proud of includes honesty, unwillingness to go into debt, unwillingness to make money on immoral businesses even given the specific opportunity – all fairly predictable. What appears next, and strikes me as of particular importance for the ways it retrospectively reflects on Du Bois' understanding of blackness, leaves the reader quite unprepared: the "one aspect of my life I look back upon with mixed feelings [is] on matters of friendship and sex."[74] Du Bois was publicly outspoken as an advocate of gender equality all his life; but here, in the midst of a discussion of what he "is" rather than what he "did," appears the first discussion of his own *sex*, which he is not prepared to address in sociological terms.

Du Bois explains that his coupling of "friendship" and "sex" in the passage just quoted is sensible because he has "always had more friends among women than among men." If so, this is not obvious from reading the autobiographies, although because he speaks little enough about friends, it doesn't seem implausible. Certainly in the Peace Movement of the 1940s and 1950s, the horizon in which the *Autobiography* was written, this is true – but the need to make it a general statement about his life should be greeted with suspicion. Continuing this self-analysis, he states, "this began with the close companionship I had with my mother. Friends used to praise me for my attention to my mother; we always went out together arm in arm and had our few indoor amusements together. This seemed quite normal to me; my mother was lame, why should I not guide her steps?" The analytical mode is quickly dropped, however, with no attempt at explaining these "indoor amusements" nor at connecting the relationship with his mother to later friendships: "Later in my life among my own colored people the women began to have more education, while the men imitated an American culture which I did not share." Quickly changing the subject again, Du Bois moves on to his early sexual experience:

> Indeed the chief blame which I lay on my New England schooling was the inexcusable ignorance of sex which I had when I went south to Fisk at 17. I was precipitated into a region with loose sex morals among black and white, while I actually did not know the physical difference between men and women... This built for me inexcusable and startling temptations. It began to turn one of the most beautiful of earth's experiences into a thing of temptation and horror.

Finally, Du Bois relates these things to his marriage:

> I married at 29 and we lived together for 53 years. It was not an absolutely ideal union, but it was happier than most, so far as I could perceive. It suffered from the fundamental drawback of modern American marriages: a difference in aim and function between its partners; my wife and children were incidents of my main life work.[75]

Set in light of the absence of gender in previous accounts of his life, it is clear that "character" and "sex" have not been coded as aspects of "racial" life at any point in the three theories. (From a strictly political point of view one would want to know if the reason why the mainstream anti-lynching campaign, as represented, for example, by Du Bois' *Crisis* writings, consistently attempted to sidestep its most talented and persistent writer, Ida Wells Barnett, it is because of her insistence on talking about sexuality along the racial border.[76]) In this light one can see the theory of race in *Dusk* as necessarily masculine, because race, unlike other psychic issues, is uniquely sociological, while "character" and "sex" are apparently not analyzable at the same level.[77]

To state this is not merely to state the obvious; rather it is to say something about the structure of representation in autobiography which, though Du Bois tries to overcome it through a dialectical sociology, continues to plague his narrative. He works particularly hard, in the manner of the best contemporary theory, to account for the conditions which produce himself as autobiographer, within *Dusk of Dawn*. Yet the category of subject production continues to occur through masculinist notions of production through the maintenance of the public/private split,[78] a split which itself corresponds to Doris Sommer's distinction between metaphoric (representation as replacement) and metonymic (representation as membership) representations in autobiography. Only through the ironically "old-fashioned" category of character is Du Bois able to make even the smallest incursion into this separation, and then to state that he wishes he had married someone as politically involved as himself.[79]

Conclusion

The three theories of the race of W. E. B. Du Bois follow this pattern:

> race as peculiar shading, or veil, on the achievements of the great individual →
>
> race as determining feature of the subject →
>
> race as of some importance in his life, but of no particular importance to the narrative of history, which is toward the elimination of race

This chart permits me to suggest tentative and specific answers to my original questions, "what is a race?" and "what is an autobiography?" in the context of African-American identity politics in the twentieth century.

What is a race? It seems to me that the methodology of *Dusk of Dawn*, really inaugurated in 1897 with the question "How does it feel to be a Problem?," but elaborated with the greatest sophistication only in 1940, is a useful starting point for addressing the social construction of race. Du Bois' method provides the most plausible means for avoiding the notion that "racial consciousness" of the sort that Du Bois' life enacts is corrupt, and understanding its workings. Specifically, because *Dusk* goes back and forth between the historical and personal events and rules that enforce racial distinctions, and demonstrates the ways in which the actions of individually raced people are the agency of these events and rules, it provides a dialectical vision of race without imagining that there is some moment of transcendence at which point we all stop being raced. (Dialectics does not obligate the social analyst to predict moments of transcendence.) Race is, in this sense, a habitus, and anti-racism (which is never color-blind) can only proceed through the continual working within it. Housing in the United States is as segregated now as it was in 1940,[80] and there is no more room for pretense in our political proposals today than there was then.

Because of this I take the particularly unpopular position that identity politics is not something that "we" can somehow "go beyond," as nearly all liberal, marxist, and poststructuralist arguments within the theory-driven academy have claimed recently. *Dusk of Dawn* illustrates that the case for black nationalist (as an example of identity) politics has never depended on so-called "essentialism"; numerous other examples of this can be found. But *Dusk of Dawn* is significantly less helpful in getting us to the point where we can understand the workings of bloc formation that identity politics depends upon, than it is in helping us understand the meaning of racial identity. For the same argument in which Du Bois demonstrates that there are grounds for the coherence and mutual trust of the Negro middle class as a class, and additionally ties its interests to the improvement of conditions for all black people, also depends on an initial description of the diversity of this class's political activities and assumptions. Du Bois is able to show that people may act as they do by working through a fully reified – indeed, *centered* – racial identity, and their actions can only be interpreted on that basis; but this in no way implies that they will act collectively or in the same ways. Put differently, the black person who refuses to be segregated and the black person who self-segregates are both acting *racially*, and will experience the results racially (i.e. through the experience of racial subordination within a white supremacist system). Social movements will necessarily be cut through by such relations of identification; as a result the formation of cross-identity movements depends on the conscious promulgation of a form of volunteerism which in contemporary terms is best understood as "coalition."[81]

For liberals, nationalists, and communists of the first half of this century, including those who are explicitly (in whatever sense) feminist, race is generally not a category that is gendered. That gender is untheorized in *Dusk of Dawn* does not, of course, mean that it doesn't appear, and another account of the book might stress a great deal more its presence as an absence. It has become typical to note the relationship between certain notions of blackness popularized in the 1960s to masculinism, but what I would want to emphasize in this case is that gender exclusiveness in Du Bois' case seems tied not to his proto-nationalism but rather, ironically, to the gender-blind version of feminism to which he adhered. Thus the women who appear as named activists in his texts have no existence as women. Nina Gomer Du Bois is not named in *Dusk*'s world history. Du Bois' mistress, Jessie Fauset, remains unspoken when discussing "My Character." What this means, finally, is not that the methodology of autobiography around which Du Bois constructs his analysis of race is untenable, but that a feminist project would necessarily consider "black male" as a raced-gender category and would insist that all future Du Boisian racial practice center gendered experience.

What is an autobiography? After abandoning liberalism, Du Bois practices autobiography as the dialectical representation of the self's habitus in a multiply determined social space. "Negro" appended to the category "self" is the central category through which, at the level of consciousness, he experienced himself in the United States in the twentieth century. Marxist political economy is used, first as background, later as foreground, to link this level with a global totality. An autobiography becomes that text in which the determinate recall of self and the determinate recall of history are consequences of one another; this should be true even in a text, like *Darkwater*, where the author is unconscious of the fact. This is why ideology can be read in any given autobiography.[82] In this context consciousness of race in self-representation (for "colorless" white people as well as already racialized people of color) is required for political effectivity; this is the reality of racial identity politics. Yet when you write an autobiography with no intention other than to theorize this point, the self's resistance to nonracial psychic determinations provides the specific limitations of racial identity politics.

4

The gender, race, and culture of anti-lynching politics in the Jim Crow era

As an American Negro, I consider the most fortunate thing in my whole life to be the fact that through childhood I was reared free from undue fear of or esteem for white people as a race; otherwise, the deeper implications of American race prejudice might have become a part of my subconscious as well as my conscious self.   James Weldon Johnson[1]

From what I had read and heard, Negroes were supposed to write about the Race Problem. I was and am thoroughly sick of the subject. My interest lies in what makes a man or a woman do such-and-so, regardless of his color.   Zora Neale Hurston[2]

I am not white. There is nothing within my mind and heart which tempts me to think I am. Yet I realize acutely that the only characteristic which matters to either the white or the colored race – the appearance of whiteness – is mine.
                                                                    Walter White[3]

We have associated too long with the white man not to have copied his vices as well as his virtues.   Ida B. Wells Barnett[4]

Middle class politics in the first half of the twentieth century

This chapter is about raced-gender formation in the broad African-American professional class during the long period that extends from the 1890s, which saw the solidification of the legal foundations of Jim Crow with *Plessy v. Ferguson* and the promulgation of the new southern state constitutions, through World War II. It is productive to think of this time period as a specific political era: while conditions for African Americans on the whole changed substantially over these fifty years, as is best represented by the mass migration out of southern agrarian areas to urban areas of both the south and the north, nevertheless specific political struggles enunciated in the 1890s – over access to education, integration of public facilities and occupations, and the struggle for federal anti-lynching legislation – remained the principle concerns of the middle class. While education and integration, intrinsic to the politics of "uplifting the race," occupy much of the time of middle class political figures, in this chapter I focus on anti-lynching, and more specifically autobiographies which depict lynching as a crisis which moves middle class actors toward racial identification. From the point of view of textual representation of blackness in both autobiography and fiction, the anti-lynching struggle is the one most conspicuously definitive of the period: for Ida B. Wells Barnett, James Weldon Johnson, and Walter White the awareness of the possibility of lynching is, in particular, the framework by which the category of racial identification *as such* is articulated.[5] I will claim, too, that there is a determinate relationship between the representation of lynching in the autobiography of a particular ex-colored narrator, as well its nonrepresentation in the autobiography of Zora Neale Hurston, and these texts' removal from racial identification. In both of these texts, racial identification is narrowed to a related but nonequivalent term, cultural identification. This move tends to efface race's existence as a discourse of power.

This chapter builds on the work of Robyn Wiegman and Sandra Gunning, who have demonstrated that lynching is the enforcement mechanism by which the threat of presumptively hypermasculine black manhood is successfully contained via symbolic emasculation.[6] This is turn generates "manhood" as a space into which black politics directs itself. Wiegman's argument sets the stage for this chapter, and to some extent for the remainder of this book, in a very particular way. For Wiegman, the feminist analysis of the objectification of black masculinity in the sadism of the lynching ritual[7] helps to provide a nuanced explanation of the pursuit of a specifically black *masculinist* politics in the period following World War II. In other words, the development of what I'd call a *black male gender politics*, patriarchal in form, emerges from the model of lynching-as-emasculation-as-racialization. If so, this has specific implications for a contemporary feminist politics:

> The increasing use of castration as a preferred form of mutilation for African-American men demonstrates lynching's con-

nection to the socio-symbolic realm of sexual difference. That this realm pivots on scripting the body as a visible terrain is perhaps an incontestable assertion in the 1990s... And yet, feminist theory's lengthy and crucial exploration of the visible economy that governs sexual difference has most often remained stranded within a reduction of the body to the figure of woman.[8]

What attentiveness to the lynched black male body adds to feminist analysis, for Wiegman, is the possibility of comprehending the specificity of black male gendering as a form of *gendering*. Feminist politics would need, then, not to challenge only patriarchy, but the particular forms of racial masculinity constructed in white supremacy, a particular form of patriarchy:

> In this regard, Black Power's overemphasis on black masculinity and black male entitlements might be viewed less as a simple re-creation of patriarchal logic than as an extrapolation and, to some degree, politically resistant *intensification of America's intersecting legacy of race, sexuality, and gender*. At the same time, of course, Black Power's rhetorical inversion – to assert the black phallus in the context of metaphorical and literal castration – elides black liberation struggle with a universal masculine position, thereby displacing both the specificity and legitimacy of black female articulations of political disempowerment, as well as a variety of claims from African-American sexual minorities.[9]

Sandra Gunning argues, through a reading of Pauline Hopkins' representation of white male rape of black women in *Contending Forces*, that *rape* is the term specifically elided by the literary representation of blackness via the figure of lynching/castration typical of other turn-of-the century texts.[10] If so, what is at stake here in the articulation of autobiographical race-ness in its gendered forms is the traditional dichotomy of public and private around which racial politics has been built: lynching, as white supremacist public carnival, in supposed defense of the privacy of whiteness, can be opposed politically precisely because of its ostentatious display; the form of direct white patriarchal oppression on black women, rape, with the simultaneous invention that black women pursue white men, is not subject to agitation in the same way, because of its relegation to individual, private, or invisible acts.[11]

The significance of this chapter will be to address the forms by which specifically gendered individuals represent themselves in public opposition to this vision of the black male body. In doing so, they map the relationship of "culture" – the sphere of ritual practices (whether lynching or storytelling) – onto "race" – the sign of psychological subjectification and subjection – in different ways. Thus the fact that James Weldon Johnson is both director of the NAACP, and also a songwriter, author, and anthologist with a well-articulated cultural politics; that, while both political figures, Walter White wrote two novels and Ida B. Wells Barnett's diary imagines several; and that cultural activist Zora Neale Hurston repeatedly needs to *explain* her disinterest in writing about "the race," is at the center of this analysis. In my opening chapter I argued that a certain amount of contemporary confusion would be eliminated if we were to differentiate between "black racial politics," in which "black" and "white" might be seen as having differential (and nonhybrid) relations to the law, and "African-American culture," which is hybrid, like all culture, and engagement with which is not predicted simply by skin-color. In distinguishing Ida B. Wells Barnett and Walter White's racial blackness, from James Weldon Johnson and Zora Neale Hurston's cultural "coloredness," this chapter suggests something of the history of this distinction. It bears repeating that my distinction between race and culture does not form an opposition, but attempts to propose historically plausible configurations of their relation.

Finally, racialization is reproduced in anti-lynching narratives in terms of what James Weldon Johnson, in my epigraph, refers to as "the deeper implications of ... prejudice [which] become part of [one's] subconscious self." I retain Johnson's "depth" metaphor as a way of portraying the psychic manifestation of racial thinking that provides certain Negro authors with political or cultural perspective, as illustrated within their texts through a certain "density of representation" of the self-as-racialized.[12] Thus, the choice to read these autobiographical statements in juxtaposition will be revealing in ways that attention to the political statements of Walter White or Ida B. Wells Barnett, taken as isolated "opinions," would not be. Consistent patterns of continuity and hierarchy in the American racial matrix can be made visible, however circuitously, through such analysis; we can theorize the methods by which dark-skinned African Americans, especially women, are placed at the bottom of the system of the production of knowledge.

In other words, what will emerge is the problem that complicates the production of black women's autobiography when racialization is the product of lynching: Wells Barnett, the founder of anti-lynching politics, and Hurston, whose texts deny that lynching has any specific effect on the culture of southern Negroes, are the two major points of

reference for contemporary black feminism in the period under discussion. I believe that the plausibility of the current wave of black
feminism lies in a historical moment, the 1970s, when each woman
can be represented as having made significant contributions to the
development of a common history: a moment where the hard-line
racial politics of Wells Barnett and the ironic cultural politics of
Hurston no longer seem incompatible in Alice Walker or Toni Cade
Bambara's reconstructions of raced-gender identity. At the same
time, the fact that prior to World War II they *were* incompatible has
been suppressed – with political effects that have obscured important
issues in the contemporary construction of black feminism.

Coloredness and whiteness in the autobiography of passing

We have long since come to understand *The Autobiography of an
Ex-Colored Man* as a novel by James Weldon Johnson, loosely based
on the life of D-, a personal friend of Johnson's who appears in
Johnson's actual autobiography, *Along This Way*. It must be remembered, however, that the book was published anonymously in 1912
while Johnson was out of the country, working as American consul in
a Nicaraguan port. While several people knew that Johnson was its
author prior to his public acknowledgment of the fact, his identity
was not known generally until the second edition, with Carl Van
Vechten's introduction, in 1927.[13] Quite unknown in 1912, by the time
of the second edition Johnson had become one of the most widely
recognizable intellectuals in African America. That is, in 1927 it had
become possible to question the relationship between author and
narrator in a way it had not been at the earlier date, especially given
the presumption that Negroes tend to write autobiographies, not
imaginative fiction. Most criticism of the text to date has concerned
the forms of irony (which have, based on the historical moment of the
critic, been turned into forms of "symbolic action" or "subversion"[14])
which can be read into the clear differentiation between the narrator
and that which is known about the author. However, Benjamin Lawson provides the helpful suggestion that the book published without
Johnson's name on it is a different book from the one that comes
down to us as the canonical novel (which Lawson, suggestively,
refers to as the autobiography's "sequel").[15] Following Lawson's
suggestion, for the purposes of my reading I will attempt to take the
later Johnson at his word, noting that he stated that he intended the

book to be read as a "human document" as *distinguished* from a "novel,"[16] and attempt to read the book nonironically as autobiographical narrative. No doubt there is a certain irony in this. Without making the pretense that such an activity is fully achievable, I rely on the text's status as autobiography (albeit the autobiography of a fictional character) as a means of theorizing the book's relevance to a moment in racial identity politics.[17]

This autobiography is, among other things, a conscious political intervention. Political pronouncements about "the race," pronouncements which must be made to reflect explicitly on the subjectivity of the anonymous, passing narrator, abound in this slim volume: for example, the ex-colored man provides a long narrative of the (exactly) three types of colored folk in the south circa 1890.[18] Indeed the narrator apologizes later that his first-hand knowledge of New York's colored community is insufficient for him to repeat this sociological procedure for that city. Here the text resembles Du Bois' description of the Negro middle class in the middle section of *Dusk of Dawn*. This ex-colored man – whose personal pain as one who passes, and wonders whether he should, is at the center of the ambivalent idea of racial identity in the text – has no hesitation about describing, without ambivalence, the racial identities of others.

Thus we need to recognize that the fact of passing complicates but in no way calls into question the existence of race in *The Autobiography of an Ex-Colored Man*.[19] Instead, race becomes displaced into new forms of ambivalence not yet described in *The Souls of Black Folk*, a book the ex-colored man names as one he admires greatly. The book is framed on both sides with this expression of ambivalent racial identification – indeed, the decision to write the book depends on it, because of the narrator's "feeling of unsatisfaction," indeed, an impulse similar to that of the "un-found-out criminal" (first two paragraphs of the text) that perhaps he believes that he is.[20] He feels less guilty about this criminality as it relates to American society, however, than as it reflects on him personally since it constitutes the "selling out of [his] birthright" (last paragraph of the text).[21] If the narrative then leads to a life of material success (coded white) rather than cultural creativity (coded colored), it is not that the racial conditions which could have provided the alternative possibility were unavailable to him.[22] The positivity of race is thus coded throughout as the rush of affective intensity associated with the reasons for writing in the three paragraphs I have just quoted, and distinguished from the staid, almost clinical prose that forms the ex-colored narrator's more general style. Race, and particularly the revelation of racial difference, is identified with *affect as such*.[23] Without blackness there would be no intensity, only logic and calculation. Blackness first of all (though not, perhaps, to the exclusion of gender, as we will see) is the locus of deep emotional life. Race is the depth of one's race, which is to say the intensity of one's affect, regardless of its content.

Such race-emotion is itself contingent on a paradoxical positioning of the meaning of race as simultaneously the unspoken-traumatic and the intellectually unimportant in childhood. In this context the narrator gives an elaborate account of two classmates, his friend Red, the stupid but loyal white boy, and Shiny, the dark-skinned boy who is the brightest student at the New England school they attend. Race, the narrator strongly implies through this reversal of stereotypes, has no effect on the relative accomplishments of these two individuals as intellectuals at any point in their lives; and in different ways the narrator remains close to both throughout the book. In this context no psychic portrayal of the difficulties of Shiny's position is offered; however, witnessing the open prejudice Shiny periodically faces is effective in bringing pain to the *narrator*, who first encounters this prejudice before he knows that he's colored. For the ex-colored man early in life was a "perfect little aristocrat,"[24] surrounded by multi-racial and many-hued schoolmates, comfortable living arrangements, extensive lessons in European music, and books. Yet after being called a nigger in the schoolyard, and unexpectedly identified with Shiny, these books become an important means of escape from the race he has no self-identification with: "I had had no particular like or dislike for these black and brown boys and girls ... [but] I had a very strong aversion to being classed with them."[25] The racial politics that arises from this contradiction appear something like this: behaviorally and in terms of the ability to succeed in New England schools, Shiny demonstrates that race is inconsequential; but there is less turmoil and more freedom in being able to be disassociated from it *emotionally*. This disassociation is available first of all to white people, who do not think of themselves as raced; and perhaps occasionally to successful dark black men, who may at least live without ambiguity, even under the attack of prejudice. The narrator as passer, here, is the person for whom racial identity turns out to have somewhat greater depth of affect than he would prefer.

At the same time the book supports the positivity of minority culture according to another configuration of ideas central to the narrator's life: that of the significance of music to black folk. At the start, the narrator turns out to be an especially talented creative musician whose mind always wanders off his lessons:

> My teacher had no small difficulties at first in pinning me down to the notes. If she played my lesson over for me, I invariably attempted to reproduce the required sounds without the slightest recourse to the written characters. Her daughter, my other teacher, also had her worries. She found that, in reading, whenever I came to words that were found difficult or unfamiliar, I was prone to bring my imagination to the rescue and read from the picture.[26]

The reason why this is important has to do with the particular way the narrator contextualizes the music of the folk against the lessons in art he learns and the particular synthesis of the two he later attempts, during his time as a professional rag time pianist. "I do not think it would be an exaggeration to say that in Europe the United States is popularly known better by rag-time than by anything else it has produced in a generation... These [ragtime and the cakewalk] are lower forms of art, but they give evidence of a power that will some day be applied to the higher forms." Ragtime, the cakewalk, the Uncle Remus stories, the Fisk Jubilee singers: these are the "four things which refute the oft-advanced theory that [colored people] are an absolutely inferior race."[27] Black creativity and art are already approaching the highest standards of Euro-American art, but unfortunately, this folk art, suffering under the limitations of the racial habitus, doesn't allow those with the most talent (like the narrator himself) to achieve a daring synthesis of the two. If one could say proudly "I am colored" and live life as an artist in the best circles, then no doubt the ex-colored man would do so.[28]

Combining the emotive (subjective) and the artistic (objectification of the subjective), a culturally-rather than politically-based race agenda becomes primarily a problem of the development of class and civilization. Colored people are "forced to take [their] outlook on all things, not from the view-point of a citizen, or a man, or even a human being, but from the view-point of a *colored* man"; indeed, southern whites – but *not* northern US or European whites – are similarly limited by race because they take "the point of view of the white man."[29] While for Du Bois, in this early period, the attempt to see in a way that would then be specific to Negroes and/or the oppressed was desirable because he assumed that the problem of perspectival vision was a problem for all people (and a problem generated by heroic individuality generally), for the ex-colored man this leads to a politics whereby admission to the society of the white north is the only conceivable goal, and the material condition of mixedness, which includes the intimate, experiential knowledge of the lower forms of colored life, remains a source of unrest which thoroughly objective, nonpassing northern racialization does not contain. Thus, the "broadest-minded colored man I have ever met," the narrator tells us, states that "I don't object to anyone's having prejudices so long as those prejudices don't interfere with my personal liberty ... When prejudice attempts to move *me* one foot, one inch, out of the place where I am comfortably located, then I object." New England middle class colored people are "genuine yankees."[30] Black society, at its best, really is white society at its best, which in the end is precisely why passing *should* be possible, and why the decision to publicly identify oneself as colored when one's skin is not colored *makes no sense*, however emotionally tied up the narrator is about it.

In the last chapter the ex-colored man explains his decision to pass, which is to become "judicious": "I had made up my mind that since I was not going to be a Negro, I would avail myself of every possible opportunity to make a white man's success; and that, if it can be summed up in any one word, means 'money.'"[31] Perhaps the ex-colored man would have remained colored and performed his musical synthesis had he been independently wealthy, but finally, not having been left sufficient property, he is as judicious as a white man, marries white, and prospers.

Why does the ex-colored man finally, in spite of all ambivalence and a reasonably successful run as a young colored artist, choose ex-coloration? Because in the midst of what appears to be a perfectly happy visit to the south, where he no longer lives, he witnesses a lynching. He gives no explanation of the circumstances of this lynching, but merely a stark description of his experience of horror. He immediately leaves the south, and while on the train from Georgia to New York he contemplates the event as follows:

> I understood that it was not discouragement or fear or search for a larger field of action and opportunity that was driving me out of the Negro race. I knew that it was shame, unbearable shame. Shame at being identified with a people that could with impunity be treated worse than animals. For surely the law would restrain and punish the malicious burning of animals.[32]

This passage proposes that it is more shameful to be identified with an oppressed race (presumably by whites, since no agency is given to colored people in the paragraph) than to be accepted as part of the race that engages in the lynching (presumably also by whites). The lynching calls into question the ex-colored man's manhood, since his putative race is treated worse than animals; passing for white will allow him his specific, gendered role in the economy of family and national life. Shame is not the duty of the masculine.

The foundations of anti-lynching politics: Ida B. Wells Barnett and Walter White

Sandra Gunning argues that, whatever the white liberal's stated revulsion toward lynching, by the first decade of this century racial discourse had moved such that the white claim that lynching occurs in response to the unusually brutal criminality of black men was widely accepted even by white opponents of the practice.[33] If so, the ex-colored man's shame must be seen as the product not only of failure to identify with a race that can be "treated like animals," but as positive identification with at least this aspect of white racial discourse – its identification of blackness and bestiality. But by 1912 national anti-lynching agitation had had a twenty-year history; and a generation later two individuals especially famous for anti-lynching activism, Ida B. Wells Barnett and Walter White, would write retrospective autobiographies whose narratives of identification were built around identification with the lynched, not the lynchers.[34] Wells Barnett inaugurated the anti-lynching campaigns through her newspaper reportage in 1892 and her pamphlet *Southern Horrors: Lynch Law in All its Phases*, which organized and elaborated her journalism, the following year. Anti-lynching activity continued through the ongoing NAACP campaign, led after 1920 by the much younger Walter White, for federal intervention against local authorities in lynching cases, and later still in the activism that sprung up around the Scottsboro trial in 1934 and pitted the Communist Party and the NAACP against each other. Significantly, in both Wells Barnett's and White's autobiographical narratives, witnessing and being threatened with lynching is the event through which they establish their identities as raced political activists.

Wells Barnett was born in Mississippi during the civil war into a family which, by her account in *Crusade for Justice*, valued education as a means for their children to rise in the world, an idea at least in part connected to the relative class mobility afforded by her father's skills as a craftsperson.[35] She spends very little space describing her youth, moving quickly on to her success in school, becoming a teacher, and then a journalist in Memphis. Independent and brash, in 1890 she tried to prevent newly promulgated Jim Crow laws from taking effect by suing a Tennessee railroad company for discrimination, and forty years later she lashes out in her autobiography about how the race leaders of Memphis refused to join in agitation around her suit. In 1892, three black grocery store owners, personal friends of Wells Barnett from the professional class of Memphis, were lynched by a posse led by the white owner of a competing store. Wells Barnett, then editor of the *Free Speech*, organized a boycott of white businesses and began writing columns against lynching. While attending a conference in Philadelphia she published an editorial in which she responded to the well-known charge that lynching was a spontaneous and necessary response to black men who rape white women. She states:

> Thomas Moss, Calvin McDowell, and Lee Stewart had been lynched in Memphis, one of the leading cities of the South, in which no lynching had taken place before, with just as much brutality as other victims of the mob; and they had committed no crime against women. This is what opened my eyes to what lynching really was. An excuse to get rid of Negroes who were acquiring wealth and property and thus keep the race terrorized and "keep the nigger down." I then began an investigation of every lynching I read about. I stumbled on the amazing record that every case of rape reported in that three months became such only when it became public.[36]

In addition to reporting this fact, and quoting from a variety of statements she collected as a reporter, Wells Barnett added the flourish that made her immediately notorious and caused her exile from Memphis, under the threat that she herself would be lynched – she wrote in the *Free Speech* that "nobody in [the north] believes the old thread-bare lie that Negro men assault white women. If Southern white men are not careful they will overreach themselves and a conclusion will be reached which will be very damaging to the moral reputation of their women."[37] These statements made Wells Barnett a full-time "race leader" for approximately three years, until her marriage to Chicago newspaperman Frederick Barnett. And while by no means did she give up politics after 1895, the centrality to her identity of this event and its immediate aftermath is manifest in the fact that fully half of the (admittedly unfinished) autobiography concerns those three of her sixty-eight years.[38]

The politics of Negro self-representation

For White, who describes himself as blond-haired and blue-eyed in the opening sentence of his autobiography, *A Man Called White*, the lynching event is itself the moment which provides racial identity; "I Learn Who I Am" is the title of the first chapter, in which the lynching story is told. White describes his light-skinned, prideful family (in which he was the lightest) as consciously separating themselves from other Negroes by their perfect cleanliness;[39] but there was a particular night when the family was "taught that there is no isolation" from other Negroes.[40] That is the night in September 1906 of the Atlanta riot – the same one that caused Du Bois to write his most famous poem, "A Litany at Atlanta" – in which mobs beat every Negro they could and burned numerous homes in the Negro sections of town, leaving an estimated twenty-five dead.[41] White, thirteen at the time, was riding with his father from the post office (where his father was a clerk) when they found themselves pursued by the mob; they were saved only because they lived relatively far from other Negroes and because White's father was carrying a shotgun. White writes:

> In the flickering light the mob swayed, paused, and began to flow toward us. In that instant there opened up within me a great awareness; I knew then who I was. I was a Negro, a human being with an invisible pigmentation which marked me a person to be hunted, hanged, abused, discriminated against, kept in poverty and ignorance, in order that those whose skin was white would have readily at hand a proof of their superiority ... No matter how low a white man fell, he could always hold fast to the smug conviction that he was superior to two-thirds of the world's population.[42]

This event opens White's narrative, and is followed by the narrative of his birth; the book likewise concludes by harking back to the meaning of that event in his life. The Atlanta riots, in *A Man Called White*, literally establish in textual form the depth of White's race identification, as the Memphis lynching defines the racial politics of Wells Barnett's life. Yet lynching also clearly affects the light-skinned, male, White and the dark-skinned, female, Wells Barnett differently: unlike Wells Barnett, White has little interest in angrily comparing his commitment to anti-lynching politics to the lack of such commitment among other Negroes, believing that it is inappropriate to use the fact that he "feels" completely Negro as an ethical point. Still, White's and Wells Barnett's representations of anti-lynching are united in the urgency brought by this practice. White thus provides an account of racial identification specifically in contrast to the representation of lynching in *The Autobiography of an Ex-Colored Man* and the politics of passing generally.[43]

Waldron says of *A Man Called White* that more than an autobiography it is "a biography of the NAACP during White's leadership,"[44] and it is this suggestion in particular that seems important as we consider the trajectories of Wells Barnett's and White's narratives. During White's tenure the NAACP became a major national lobbying group, while Wells Barnett, who was there (but too radical) at the founding of the group, had split with it for decades and never developed a comparable institutional affiliation to write a book about. Her lack of relationship with the NAACP, and its particular importance in understanding the history of anti-lynching politics, becomes the crux of my comparison between the two autobiographies.

Sexuality, gender, and the anti-lynching argument: Ida B. Wells Barnett and the NAACP

I have already quoted Wells Barnett's public suggestion in 1892 that a suspicious mind might interpret lynching as having something to do with white southern women's illicit attraction for black men – or at least white men's fantasies that such an attraction might exist. Indeed, as an investigative journalist she claims to have found several specific events where lynchings occurred because white women, who had been having consensual sex with black men, are forced by white men to claim rape to avoid being abused themselves – and it is for this claim that Wells Barnett is herself masculinized, and threatened with lynching.[45] Thus the theorization of sexuality on the racial border is not original to contemporary theory, but over a century old. The Ex-Colored Man describes, among the groups of white people who could be seen "slumming" in colored gambling halls, white women who paid black men for sexual services, and includes a story of a black man murdering his white mistress, suggesting the volatility of such liaisons and perhaps contributing to white male hysteria.[46] Johnson, in telling the story of how he, too, was nearly lynched, for being seen walking in a park with a colored woman whose skin color was light enough to pass, writes in *Along This Way* that "in the core of the heart of the American race problem the sex factor is rooted."[47] Walter White, in 1929, published *Rope and Faggot*, "a study of the complex influences – economic, political, religious, sexual – behind [lynching]." Indeed, White claims that his book is "the first attempt to analyze the causative factors of lynching,"[48] sexuality being one of the main ones. It is the significance of White's claim of primacy among histories of anti-lynching that I want to investigate here.

Rope and Faggot is, indeed, an intellectually serious attempt to discuss lynching not only of itself but as "a symptom of a malodorous economic and social condition" in the southern United States.[49] In White's account, because the phenomenon exists at the intersection of so many other pressing problems not only for the Negro, but also southern civilization in general, agitation, legal change, and education around this issue should be a pressing national concern. After presenting the current statistical data on lynching and some representative horror stories, state by state, White develops in successive chapters three arguments in particular: that lynching is the logical outcome of the religious outlook of evangelical Protestantism ("the evangelical Christian denominations have done much towards creation of the particular fanaticism which finds an outlet in lynching"); that, as already mentioned, long-cathected patterns of desire and jealousy are the central psychic determinants of lynching ("With the most intransigent Negrophobe it is possible to conduct a conversation on certain phases of the race question and do so with a measured calmness of manner. But when one approaches, however delicately or remotely, the question of sex or 'social equality,' reason and judicial calm promptly take flight"); and finally, and by White's own (very pro-capitalist) account *foundationally*, that lynching occurs for the protection of white economic interests (*"Lynching has always been the means for protection, not of white women, but of profits."*).[50] Finally, because he is trying to give the broadest possible account of lynching, White provides a survey of the scientific racism and eugenicist arguments of his period in order to suggest the complicity of science in lynching, while describing to his readers why these theories have been discredited by true men of science.

I am not interested in questioning the usefulness of *Rope And Faggot* as an analysis of lynching; nor do I particularly care to dwell on certain obvious criticisms we might make of its position today – for example, of White's idea that the south "overemphasizes" sex due to its lack of moral and commercial development; of the notion that lynching is primarily in the interest of a white agricultural elite, and not of liberal urban dwelling elites; and of the claim that evangelism as such is a dangerous perversion of the masses, implying his personal distaste not only for the sexual-emotive but also for black and white popular cultures. The argument I'm specifically interested in making is that for all its formal properties as a book of history and social theory, White's book recapitulates the identical arguments of Ida B. Wells Barnett in her less formally constructed, less apparently "theoretical" pamphlets of the period 1892–5, *Southern Horrors* and *A Red Record*. That is, *each* of White's major arguments appears already, if in somewhat different form, in Wells Barnett's writing. After being the first investigator in the US to research and tabulate lynching statistics – statistics that included the discovery that rape was not even claimed by white southerners as the cause of more than seventy percent of lynchings – Wells Barnett goes on to indict southern Christianity as barbaric (even while showing considerably less disdain for popular religion than White); elaborates far more explicitly on the mythic aspect of the black male rapist than White dares thirty years later, since the argument about sexuality is Wells Barnett's major argument; and argues that lynching is often a means of white people protecting their economic interests from the encroachments of black people.[51] She even makes the same threat to lynchers as White – that capital holders (she refers to British, White to northern US) will not invest in the south unless it civilizes itself.[52] Much of White's text merely recapitulates these earlier arguments while claiming explicitly that no one has yet theorized lynching at all; and White does not mention Wells Barnett once. Wells Barnett was quite conscious of having already been written out of African-American history when she sat down to write *Crusade for Justice*, one year after *Rope and Faggot* was published.[53]

The pattern of exclusion I'm depicting here is not simply another example of "reclaiming" black women; it is a theoretical account based on the argument of Barbara Christian's much misunderstood "The Race for Theory," as follows: white editors at a "major" publisher put out an intellectually fine analysis of a problem (i.e. lynching), one that is, among other things, distinguished by the way it draws on reserves of symbolic capital. The content of the argument is identical to one already made in a more obscurely published form by a black woman. This is called "new." The black woman is not cited.[54] White gives the impression of never having heard Wells Barnett's name, and in truth, it seems plausible that he hardly gave her existence any thought in his life, in spite of the fact that she was the most well-known anti-lynching figure in the United States prior to himself. Gloria Hull has documented how male intellectual networks circulated Harlem Renaissance publishing opportunities to the exclusion of their female contemporaries, and ties this to the threat that black women, given the opportunity, will discuss sexuality in threatening ways.[55] Wells Barnett, a generation older than White, in Chicago, and long since excluded from the ranks of "race leaders," cannot be heard writing about sexuality; but by 1929 it has become, tentatively, possible for a light-skinned man in mainstream pro-corporate politics to be heard doing so. When this happens, anti-lynching, no longer pursued by a woman, is disengaged from numerous other issues that turn of the century women's groups address, such as temperance and the sexual abuse of black women. It is not the "our men are being emasculated" narrative of anti-lynching politics, which Wells Barnett shares, that leads intrinsically to the masculinization of race politics; it is the disengagement of this narrative from the complementary analysis of the politics of black women's sexualization.

If Walter White's autobiography is less about himself than about the NAACP during his leadership, Wells Barnett's also deals primarily with her public persona during the main period of her activism. As I have said, nearly half of the manuscript addresses just the years 1892–5. Wells Barnett implies strongly that this is the really important moment of her public life, the life one recounts in an autobiography which has no personal aspect to it, but is entirely an account of her public career. And it is during this long, central section of *Crusade For Justice* that one notices all the signs of the marginality that her political career will take, for it is in the midst of the dozens of her own newspaper columns from that period inserted in the text that one learns that in August 1894 "a delegation of the men of my own race asked me to put the soft pedal on charges against white women and their relations with black men." She concludes "I indignantly refused to do so."[56] It is, in particular, the public acknowledgment of some women's cross-racial sexual desire – even by a woman who herself denies having any such desire – that is beyond the bounds of the speakable and requires the suppression of Wells Barnett from anti-lynching's history – even at the potential cost of withdrawing attention from black male emasculation.

The historical narrative of Wells Barnett's exclusion from the NAACP, which this is not intended to be,[57] shows a succession of black and white male leaders, including the older principals of my own narrative to this point, Du Bois and Johnson, finding her far too contrary for their own moderate tastes in the first decade of the twentieth century. Then, in its first decade the white-led NAACP did not primarily occupy itself with anti-lynching issues in particular – indeed, this issue was brought to the center when the organization became principally black-led in the 1920s. Du Bois edited the *Crisis* as a journal not only of racial uplift and the development of Negro culture, but as an explicitly internationalist journal of politics. The first leaders of the association, other than Du Bois exclusively white, saw themselves as part of the progressive movement and concentrated on educational and labor reform issues. By the time Walter White became a staffperson in 1918 as the organization's first representative of the generation younger than Wells Barnett, her exclusion from "race leadership" by the older political leaders was already accomplished, and when White started his own investigations of lynching, traveling to the south and passing for white in order to talk to the participants in the lynchings themselves, he may really have assumed that he was the first person to do so risky a deed. This confirmed for him the world-historical significance of his being both Negro and light enough to pass. Mainstream historians of anti-lynching had, until the current wave of feminists reclaimed Wells Barnett, usually taken Johnson and White's word for it that they had only minor precursors, relatively unimportant to the discourse of race and sexuality. Wells Barnett's biographer, in 1990, notes accurately that "Ida Wells' activity in the civil rights movement has until recently been lost to the collective memory of the race and the nation."[58]

Along This Way: Negro *bildungsroman*

There is no more perfect *bildungsroman* in African-American literary history than James Weldon Johnson's *Along This Way*; to say this is to begin with the premise that it is an atypical African-American autobiography. Unlike autobiographies discussed in this book by everyone from Du Bois to Hurston to hooks, it makes no attempt to establish individuality in contradistinction from racial and political participation; instead it presumes that individuality is the proper focus of any autobiography and that there can be no question of the quality and significance of Johnson's own. It thus has no "narrow" political, social scientific, or identitarian argument, and while, in the manner that famous old men will, Johnson muses throughout about the issues of the world he lives in, the issues which interest him have every bit as much to do with the running of the US foreign service (of which he was an officer for eight years) as with uplifting the race. And while uplifting the race is, obviously, a major issue on which to spend one's time, it is notably displaced from the book's conclusion, precisely when we think it will be used to sum up his life. Instead, Johnson prefers to state his theological position on the last two pages of the book: "I do not see any evidence to refute those scientists and philosophers who hold that the universe is purposeless."[59] I find particularly evocative a comment from a contemporaneous review of the book by New England liberal Carl Van Doren which appears as enticement on the inside front cover of the recently published Penguin edition: "A book any man might be proud to have written about a life any man might be proud to have lived." Indeed.

Of course Johnson's political position, with which it is possible to neither agree nor to disagree of itself, is that the purpose of Negro political, social, and artistic activity is to make possible distinguished autobiographies that any man, and not any black man, might write. This variety of liberal individualism must be distinguished not only from the racialized self in Wells Barnett, White, and Du Bois' *Dusk of Dawn*, but also from that of Du Bois' liberal individualism in *Darkwater*. For Du Bois in 1920, race-as-essence is the necessary local circumstance within which the accomplished individual works and thereby exemplifies; individuality is possible, in Johnson's narrative, by contrast, only inasmuch as race does not play a role in one's thinking. Race must not be deeply implanted, as it is for too many unfortunate Negroes and whites. He explains, in response to the question that "every Negro" has faced, "what wouldn't you give to be a white man?"

> I find that I do not wish to be anyone but myself. To conceive of myself as someone else is impossible, and the effort is repugnant. If the jinnee should suddenly appear before me and, by way of introduction, say, "Name the amount of wealth you would like to have, and it shall be given you," I, gauging my personal needs and a sum sufficient to enable me to do freely the things I should like, should reply, "Give me three hundred thousand dollars in (if such there still be) sound securities." ... If ... he should say "Name any race of which you should like to be a member, and it shall be done," I should be at a loss.[60]

This is not to say that there are no racial traits, according to Johnson – indeed, the possibility of such traits arises a few times, as when, in a discussion of Atlanta University's sexual repressiveness Johnson refers to, of all things, the "idealism" of the school's sexual policy as "something of an innate racial trait."[61] No mind; innate racial traits are not determinate; to the apparently minor extent they exist, they can be overcome and thus made the subject of rational commentary.

Johnson conceptualizes race as a socially and perhaps biologically shared problem, shared such that the rhetoric of "my people" is deployed when useful, such as when "we of the vanguard" must "learn to know the masses of [our] people" so that we can learn from their "instinctive knowledge of their possession of" the power to survive.[62] Thus a fairly predictable black collective identity is conceived, but with an autonomous vanguard that is to be cosmopolitan, similarly cultured to the European vanguard, and thus essentially deracinated, deracination being a historical project in which only the best Europeans and Africans participate. If this feels contradictory, consider that (as in *The Autobiography of an Ex-Colored Man*) art is perceived as central to racial uplift and the members of the vanguard might do the race a particular service by taking an interest in folk music and turning it into something attractive to the dominant art world. But, since cultural vanguards themselves are always necessarily international and aracial, white musicians are just as prominently represented in this important work as black; any effort by a cosmopolitan white musician is therefore uplifting to the race in the same sense as if the effort were made by a black musician.[63] The increasing generality of African-American culture is thus the progressive factor that defines transcendence in and of the Negro race.

That Johnson's autobiography is the story of a life, which is to say upbringing, education, hobbies, pleasures, and theology, rather than a public or institutional history or sociology, differentiates it from Wells Barnett's and White's accounts. Unlike their abbreviated accounts of childhood, Johnson spends nearly a quarter of his book – one hundred pages – describing in detail his childhood. It is in this context that he repeatedly insists, not only on the separation between his own family and the mass of Jacksonville Negroes, but even more on the racial tolerance of the white city-dwellers during and immediately after reconstruction, a tolerance which disappears only after he leaves the city for Atlanta University. Race comes and goes quickly in the childhood narrative, usually by means of comparing its unimportance to something more significant: "I was not afraid of [Mr. Cole] because he was white – his or anybody else's being white had no special significance for me at that time – I was afraid of him because everybody said he was crazy"; "My religious experience preceded any experiences of race"; "Long after the reconstruction Jacksonville was known as a good town for Negroes."[64] Repeatedly, assurances of the *noblesse oblige* of the aristocratic leadership of Jacksonville (a leadership which has since given way to the rabble) are given so that the reader understands Johnson as having consistently benefited from upper class white support. Johnson does not claim typicality in this – unlike, say, Booker T. Washington in *Up From Slavery* – rather, he stresses the differences in experiences among blacks, especially as they reflect class. In this context he contrasts himself in a self-congratulatory way with those for whom moderation is not probable, who believe that "there will be only one way of salvation for the race ... through the making of its isolation a religion and the cultivation of a hard, keen, relentless hatred for everything white."[65] Conspicuously, *Along This Way* does have a personal near-lynching story, about being seen in public in Jacksonville with a Negro woman light enough to pass and being confronted by a militia. In line with the will to balance in the text as a whole, this story *is* politically and emotionally meaningful to Johnson, but without having any of the extreme psychological determination that it has for the ex-colored man, Wells Barnett, and White.[66]

The mixed racial vanguard of Johnson's political point of view, and the individualist subject of his autobiography, is gendered male by tacit assumption; gender is unlike race here and in other autobiographies of the time because it requires no explanation. Further, that this vanguard will be built by the intermarriage of darker men with supportive, light-skinned women is strongly implied not only by Johnson's own marriage to an all but white woman, but by his remarkable commentary about his friend D-, the only person whose real name is not given in the *Along This Way*, because he is passing, and the model for the ex-colored man:

> He introduced me to a very beautiful girl who was with him, as the young lady he was going to marry ... As soon as the young lady opened her mouth, I noted her Southern drawl ... She was from Louisiana. The information surprised me in no manner. D-, in the confessions he used to make, had more than once confided to me the strange and strong attraction that Southern white women possessed for him. There was certainly nothing unnatural in his experience. A situation which combines the forbidden and the unknown close at hand could not do less than create a magnified lure. White men, where the races are thrown together, have never, for themselves, taken great pains to disguise that fact. There is no sound reason to think that this mysterious pull exerts itself to only one direction across the color line, or that it confines itself to only one of the sexes; the pull is double and inter-crossed. It is possible that dame Nature never kicks up her heels in such ecstatic abandon as when she has succeeded in bringing a fair woman and a dark man together, and vice versa.[67]

That the races will combine is not only acceptable but natural, and a process long since under way. Wells Barnett, learning of the love of her white English friend Catherine Impey for the Ceylonese doctor George Ferdinands, a love which was not reciprocated, also wondered publicly why anyone should question Impey's sexual or romantic attraction. She lost as much support among British women for saying so as she lost among white and black men in the US for stating that white southern women have such an attraction.[68] Now, since Johnson does not care to discuss skin color politics among Negroes in *Along This Way* (unlike the narrator of *The Autobiography of an Ex-Colored Man*), it is not clear in his narrative what the political meaning of this attraction, from the point of view of a dark-skinned black woman, should be. That is to say, political equality between the races in Johnson's narrative depends on black men being allowed their attraction to white and/or light women, just as white men have been allowed their attraction to dark women. Likewise, inasmuch as Johnson believes that women have sexual agency, he presumes that white women will also be attracted to black men. (Note that his key example here, D-, is himself *passing*, which is to say socially represented as white. The southern woman's attraction for the black man who looks white is then permitted to stand in for the attraction of white women for black men, since the attraction is based on *ideological* titillation regardless of visual stimulus.) But will dark-skinned black women be attracted to white men? This schema leaves out any question of the agency of Wells Barnett, who, with an affect deeper than Johnson's, finds white men unattractive not as such but because they are the agents of lynching, and light skinned-black male leaders untrustworthy because they consistently find her willingness to tell the truth threatening to their own positions.

Reading Zora Neale Hurston's disavowal of race

Because what I am about to say will get me in some trouble in the contemporary academy, I am going to start with some informal context. When I sat down to rewrite, for the last time, this section on *Dust Tracks on the Road*, I also reread, for pleasure (rather than for teaching preparation) *Their Eyes Were Watching God*, including Mary Helen Washington's well-known account of the urgency of black women intellectuals' rediscovery of that book in the early 1970s, which introduces the widely used Harper edition.[69] I needed to remember, to internalize most deeply, that necessity: *Their Eyes* is a great novel because of the depth and richness of its language, and is a political intervention of the strongest form because of its absolutely unique centering of the question of *pleasure* for a rural black woman. No other artist in Hurston's period could imagine such a center for a novel. Precisely what is at issue here is *affect*: black feminism needed, and needs, Hurston's cultural affect more than it needs Wells Barnett's stern Christianity. The book's disappearance from black literary history between 1940 and 1970 can, in the end, only be satisfactorily explained through the analysis of misogyny.

Hurston has now been canonical for at least a decade; Michele Wallace famously and brilliantly explored the implications of the Hurston explosion in 1989, and if anything, critical attention to the novel is just now letting up a little. In fact, if the new volume edited by Elizabeth Abel, Barbara Christian, and Helene Moglen, *Female Subjects in Black and White*, in which Hurston's work is not mentioned except for Ann DuCille's account of the historical importance of its rediscovery, can be taken as a sign of anything, it's that as the psychoanalytical component of gendering becomes the focus of more white and black feminist work on black women, Hurston's work becomes less central. (This is a fact that would not have surprised Richard Wright, who, by the way, was quite sexist – would you have accused me of sexism if I didn't say that, immediately?) Whether or not this is the case, there is no risk of Hurston disappearing from my, or anyone else's, literature classes as I write, even as the black women who will write the next generation's novels are still being denied basic education as a result of the continued race and class war. Might it now be possible for a leftist to point out that Wright, and Sterling Brown, and Arna Bontempts, and the other 1930s' men and women who disliked Hurston might have not been *mere* misogynists, but might have been critical of the fact that her political positions were in *direct contradiction to their own*? Might it be possible to suggest that marxian cultural politics of the 1930s, for all its deeply problematic sexism, actually has something to teach us, in the 1990s, as the distance between rich and poor enlarges at a rate not seen since the 1920s? Hurston had something big to teach in the 1970s; entering graduate school in 1989, those things were canonical to my training. Might academic cultural studies, including its black feminist form, have other things to learn now?

Here, before I enter the text of *Dust Tracks*, is how I would like you to read the politics of my intervention: this essay is not written against those scholars, like Deborah Plant and Francoise Lionnet, who understand that Hurston's career is deeply individualizing and, to the extent it is "political," it is, in strictly Nietzschean terms, about the care of the self.[70] That I consider such a politics not wrong, but severely inadequate, will have been clear by now, but the grounds of my disagreement with these scholars is not in their interpretations of Hurston. On the other hand, these pages are written very directly against statements that appear in two pieces on Hurston: Priscilla Wald's essay "Becoming 'Colored': The Self-Authorizing Language of Difference in Zora Neale Hurston," and Samira Kawash's chapter on Hurston in *Dislocating the Color Line*.[71] I single these two pieces out for making an identical move that is, as made, quite symptomatic of our moment: in essays that are, appropriately, about how Hurston prefigures poststructuralism, Wald states apologetically, not once but twice, that "Hurston does not translate her subversive use of double-consciousness into an effective political strategy";[72] Kawash likewise apologizes, concluding her essay with "Hurston's turning to what might be called a politics of contagion does not provide us with a program of action."[73] Hurston has become such a figure of awe that these critics need to believe that if she doesn't provide us with a liberal or leftist politics of opposition to power it is a fault to apologize for, rather than a fact needs no apology: Hurston simply opposes left politics. Either you do too, and stop apologizing for Hurston's failure; or you take left politics seriously, and stop arguing that Hurston was intrinsically more "advanced" than her contemporaries.

This essay interprets *Dust Tracks on the Road* in terms of her specific undermining of the politics of anti-lynching. It will suggest that "My People! My People!" has a politics indistinguishable from texts that no one likely to be reading this would defend at present, like Shelby Steele's *The Content of Our Character*, a book one might equally excuse with the claim that it was written to make money, as is sometimes claimed for *Dust Tracks*. (What is historically significant is that in 1942 there was not yet an interest among white conservatives to pay a black woman to take such a position, and Hurston died in obscurity.) Ultimately, what seems important to me is just this: in spite of all Hurston's (and Steele's) claims that she is tired of writing about the race question, she is formed in the same paradox as everyone else: she has to write, incessantly, about the problem of being a Negro who does not care to write about being a Negro. As a result, *Dust Tracks*, far from avoiding the issue, becomes a series of tirades against the racial left. *Dust Tracks* is simply another example of the phenomenon this book describes over and over: black people have to write political statements in the form of autobiographies. The only difference is that this political statement, instead of using this fact for the creation of an anti-racist politics, blames other black writers for the situation.

Deborah Plant, in *Every Tub Must Sit on its Own Bottom*, the only book-length study of Hurston's politics to date, makes two central arguments about Hurston, and about her autobiography, that will frame my work. First, Plant argues that Hurston's "uncompromising individualism ... helped her survive systemic sexism, racism, and classism, strengthened her will to resist negative controlling images, and empowered her to overcome Anglo-American cultural hegemony."[74] I take this statement to be true, with the caveat that it should not be assumed that "uncompromising individualism" is the only possible strategy for any given black woman in fighting back, merely that it is the path that worked, for some time and with extraordinary results, for Hurston. The particular importance of this claim to my larger argument is that it matters, if we are to ask under what conditions black feminism and left politics may be articulated in conjunction with one another, that we agree with Plant that the conservative politics of individual transcendence through grit and personal superiority can be generated indigenously within African-American, and in particular African-American women's, culture. Second, Plant says of *Dust Tracks on the Road*, that it "did not deal with the racist, sexist, and classist world that other sources tell us confronted Hurston. But when the autobiography is viewed as a documented teleology of the self and a creation of the will, the fictional quality undergoes a transformation where it becomes truth."[75] In other words, as *Their Eyes'* second paragraph says of women generally, "the dream is the truth."[76] It is precisely at this moment that what is at stake, politically, in the continued separation of "novel" and "autobiography" as generic categories becomes most clear: if the truth does not inhere in the representation of racism, sexism, and classism (which is itself not the same as capitalism, of course), but in the fantasized self, we will have to ask what the effect of the entry of such "truth" into the field of autobiographical representation (i.e. "non-fiction") signifies for those who claim other, competing, truths.

Obscuring white supremacy in the south

It is not enough to point out that *Dust Tracks* does not, unlike all other texts in this chapter and essentially all black autobiographical texts of the period, tell a lynching story; in fact, the book goes out of its way to tell stories about racial peace in the south, and to remove agency for white supremacy from the violence of white people. At the opening of the book we learn that blacks moved to Maitland, Florida, because there was "good pay" and "sympathetic white folks," and set up the black town of Eatonville entirely voluntarily, in spite of the lack of racial tension which allowed a black man to win election as Mayor of Maitland.[77] On the other hand, blacks can't seem to succeed because "humble" Negroes "do not resent a white man looking down" on them, but hate "Big Niggers."[78] In fact, the only person in the book who is beaten for "impudence" is poor white – this is in the chapter "My People, My People," and frames part of the illustration of why there is no point in bringing up race categories when addressing the everyday lives of blacks in the south.[79] Finally, in her conclusion Hurston goes beyond the argument that the descendants of slave-holders are not responsible for slavery (which is itself a straw argument, of course), to suggest that there is no point in talking to such a descendant about slavery, for "he has heard just as much about the thing as I have."[80] So much for the need for curricular reform, or for that matter, for my presence teaching African-American literature at a large public university in the south.

Dehistoricizing the folk

William Maxwell, in a balanced essay laying out the disagreements between Richard Wright and Zora Neale Hurston, has contextualized something very important to me here: Wright was deeply influenced by the (highly problematic) Chicago school of urban sociology, Hurston by (highly problematic) Boasian anthropology.[81] Yet only Hazel Carby, whose work is as unflattering to Hurston as mine, has even bothered to ask critical questions about the relationship between Hurston's professional work as a folklorist and Hurston's politics.[82] Yet a cursory look at *Dust Tracks* reveals that it does precisely what is endemic to imperialist cultural anthropology: it removes the category of "their" culture from the context of "our" history, such that "they" simply "tell stories." Hurston's account of her anthropological work is highly flattering to the rigor and "pure objectivity" of Franz Boas, and presents a rather conventional case against "theories" which impinge on such objectivity.[83] She refers, it appears without any irony (unlike the supposedly unironic Du Bois, as noted in the previous chapter) to "primitive minds" who are "quick to sunshine and anger."[84] And then she goes on to tell a series of folk stories she collected about subjects "from love to work, to travel, to food, to weather, to fight, to demanding the return of a wig by a woman who has turned unfaithful."[85] In this list, the absence of poverty or oppression as subject matter, in spite of the fact that she has just quoted from a song dealing with these issues, is conspicuous. But this is completely consistent with how she addresses her own "travels" in the book: this is the moment when the rural black south loses half of its population, *including Hurston*, to the urban north, and yet Hurston's interpretive account of black folklore neglects this central issue![86]

Class as culture, not poverty – let alone relation to the means of production

Indeed, for a writer reputed to have brought a new class of black characters to African-American literature, Hurston's autobiography makes her a very poor candidate for working class hero. Lighter-skinned than most others in her natal community, Hurston was the daughter of an Eatonville Mayor; even when *Dust Tracks* places her in the working class it does so with a consistent air of discomfort and distaste for other black women who work.[87] This is especially note-worthy during her description of the "fat, black old woman who had nursed the master of the house" she worked in, about whom she says, repeating everybody's favorite racist and sexist cliché, "nobody is so powerful in a Southern family."[88] But this shouldn't surprise us, because her white patron in Eatonville, the man who took a liking to her at birth and constantly helped her out in growing up, has already been portrayed positively giving young Zora a long speech built around the phrase "Sniglets, don't be a nigger." Hurston's footnoted comment – the only footnote in the whole book – is "The word Nigger used in this sense does not mean race. It means a weak, contemptible person of any race."[89] Contempt is not expressed toward those whites who use what is conventionally known as a racial slur, if they use it stylishly and well; but contempt is in weakness, and weakness is always to be found in working people who spend their lives getting by. (Why is contempt for weakness not, to Nietzscheans, itself a kind of resentment? Who is being threatened here?)

So: "the Negro population of Maitland settled simultaneously with the white. They had been needed, and found profitable employment. The best of relations existed between employer and employee," spoken like a true member of the employing class. A scene in a barbershop demonstrates that black barbers will not cut black men's hair because "theories go by the board when a person's livelihood is threatened." Charlotte Osgood Mason, despite being a rich patron who wields money to produce her own fantasy of black culture, is not simply portrayed as good, but as a true woman of the people. Folk stories about Brer Monkey, who in Hurston's account stands in for blacks, always seem to turn on how monkeys really aren't capable of doing responsible jobs.[90] The claim that all it takes to avoid being a nigger, or lower class, is the refusal to be humble, is what Du Bois, writing about Booker T. Washington, called a "dangerous half-truth" for the poor – in its aversion to asking structural questions about the economic roots of class differential, it provides a convenient ideological cover for those who really are fearful of collective action.

"Culture" without "race"

Finally, *Dust Tracks* does have an explicit politics: it is cultural politics in its weakest possible incarnation. Hurston is quite explicit about having an agenda to spread the "wealth and beauty" of black cultures.[91] She is, simply, the only significant figure of the 1930s who imagines that African-American culture, spread to white elite spaces (like the theaters of New York), can bring social change in the absence of a sense of collectivity that emerges from the acknowledgment that "what makes a man or a woman do such-and-so" is not a variable "regardless" of "color." That passage continues: "it seemed to me that the human beings I met reacted pretty much to the same stimuli. Different idioms, yes. Circumstances and conditions having power to influence, yes. Inherent different, no."[92] This, like so many so-called "anti-essentialist" arguments, is simply a straw argument, made against no one. Isn't the existence of racism and race caste "different stimuli"? Doesn't having different levels of power to influence things change the behavior of people? In any event, it should be clear to this point that no one I've written about consistently assumes that blacks are "inherently" different from whites; what is at stake are the various strategies for conceiving of difference after that has been agreed. What is specific about Hurston is that *all* difference must be conceived through the most ahistorical version of the category "culture," and the possibility of a psychology or sociology of race must be denied.

Hurston's cultural politics is a genuine *aspect* of any radical political framework, a fact not lost on any writer I've discussed in chapters three and four. Du Bois and Johnson are famous for asking how to transfer black cultural performances to the New York stage; and while Du Bois' tastes may be too stodgy for Hurston, the same cannot be said of Johnson, whose claims for the autonomous aesthetic as universal are as strong as Hurston's.[93] But while happily claiming it has no effect on him, Johnson, the perfect liberal multiculturalist, doesn't feel the need to obscure the way the racial line impinges on the psyches of others – white and black.

On the different roads to black feminist theory

Wells Barnett, it will be said, has completely bought into the norms of white middle class professionalization. As such, her version of race uplift politics is centered around race activism without a sense of the autonomy of culture. If this is the case, the question that must inform studies of the emergence of black feminism in the early twentieth century is no longer "does it exist?" – this question has been answered, in the last twenty years, with an unambiguous "yes" – but what are the tensions that made it necessary for the greatest of black feminist intellectuals to *choose* either race or culture? What are the processes of psychic and institutional exclusion which create self-protective moral normativity in Wells Barnett's fight against the racial line, and the equally self-protective refusal to recognize a racial line at all in Hurston's celebration of African-American culture? How has the construction of "tradition" as male worked to complicate the connection between female intellectuals of different temperaments, until it appears they have nothing to say to one another at all? In my readings of Nikki Giovanni and Angela Davis (also southerners, though Giovanni, importantly, exists in a world where she has the choice to not migrate) in chapter seven, I will explore the repetition of these same tensions at the moment when, historically, they finally begin to dissolve, in part because they are at last made explicit.

In the meantime, one way of mapping what I have developed in chapters three and four is to build a chart, of the sort that can be found in Pierre Bourdieu's *Homo Academicus* and *The Rules of Art*, for plotting the relationship of intellectuals within a bounded field.[94] In this case the boundaries are formed in the logic of Jim Crow, with its strict drawing of racial lines of intellectual association. The following is, of course, spectacularly insufficient for such an understanding of the field as a whole; it should be understood as preliminary, and focused on the middle class. Yet without being able to read it, contemporary writers will continue to act as though specific positions on the chart –

whether Hurston's, or the ex-colored man's, or Du Bois' – have greater independence than they actually have. *Dusk of Dawn* – but not any other autobiography of the period, or even Du Bois' later *Autobiography* – demonstrates an awareness of this nonautonomy, whether or not it charts it adequately.

	gender	race	skin-color	race identification	emphasis	congeniality
ECM	male	white/ex-colored	light	weak	business	varies with race
WW	male	Negro	light	strong	politics	high
JWJ	male	Negro	tan	weak	culture/politics	high
WEBD	male	Negro	tan	strong	politics/culture	low
ZNH	female	colored	tan	weak	culture	high
IBWB	female	Negro	dark	strong	politics	low

Finally, while my position differs in certain specifics from Barbara Christian's, it is important to recognize that my jumping-off point for the Bourdieuian analysis of the emergence of black feminism appears in her two essays "The Race for Theory," and "The Highs and Lows of Black Feminist Criticism." The emergence of black feminism must be plotted in both "high" and "low" forms; the thing we currently call "black feminism" is of itself compatible with a highly variable class politics.[95]

5

Representing the Negro as proletarian

The Negro problem is basically a labor problem. The labor problem is organically bound up with the Negro problem. The Negro problem cannot be solved save through the solution of the labor problem. The labor problem cannot be solved unless the race problem is solved.   Richard B. Moore[1]

The trouble is that between them and the Revolution ... there is no idealogic distance which would secure artistic perspective. The want of both desire and capacity on the part of the literary "fellow-travelers" to grasp with Revolution by merging with it, and yet not to dissolve in it ... is a social and not an individual trait.   Leon Trotsky[2]

He was constrained by logic to accept Marxism as an intellectual instrument whose absence from the human mind would reduce the picture of the processes of modern industry to a meaningless antheap ... Above all he loathed the Communist attempt to destroy human subjectivity; for him, his subjectivity was the essence of his life.   Richard Wright[3]

It is not the *act of positing* which is the subject ... it is the subjectivity of *objective* essential powers, whose action, therefore, must also be something *objective.*   Karl Marx[4]

Mediating black studies, the history of the Communist Party USA, and contemporary marxist theory: an outline of issues

I have been arguing that the claim that historical marxism is inadequate to the theorization of race and gender – which, broadly speaking, I agree with – cannot entail the trashing of the marxist critique of political economy, which remains correct in its essentials. I have further suggested that the methods of historical marxism have been effective, if not fully adequate, in helping us to frame certain kinds of questions about race and gender. In this chapter I further present the value of actually reading historical marxism's various attempts at presenting raced and gendered subjects, something rarely done by those for whom it is simply received knowledge that marxism is inadequate. One does not have to believe that Communist and Labor Party organizations have had an adequate account of race, nor that they have treated their black members uniformly well, nor that they have organized in a universally perspecuitous manner, to recognize that, as Mary Berry and John Blassingame state, "the CPUSA was in the vanguard of American whites demanding equality of economic opportunity for blacks."[5] Even more importantly, such organizations always had many African-American members; these members, on the whole, received "affirmative action" in training and promotion because the organizations generally, in good liberal fashion, cared about "race representation"; they – and their white allies and friends – wrote about the politics of race and class, and did so in widely divergent ways; and finally, these writings influenced the course of black political identity in the twentieth century. Many of the black nationalisms of the 1960s are more related to the history and politics of the Comintern-originated thesis that the "Black Belt" – the series of counties running from the Atlantic coast to the Gulf of Mexico in which over 70 percent of the population is black – *should* – not might or could – in the course of socialist revolution, emerge as an autonomous nation-state, than they are to the history of the (also important) bourgeois nationalisms traced most elaborately by Wilson Moses. Indeed, when one understands that the Black Belt thesis was promulgated by the USSR-dominated Comintern, not the CPUSA, and that US Negro Party officials themselves were deeply divided by it – Harry Haywood being its strongest proponent, James Ford one of its greatest opponents – then presumptions about the subservience of US civil rights issues to Moscow within the CP become much more difficult to maintain.

Manning Marable argued in 1984 that the conditions that led to the emergence of the Civil Rights Movement in Montgomery in 1955 already existed in the immediate years after World War II. He states:

> The sit-ins, the non-violent street demonstrations, did not yet occur; the facade of white supremacy was crumbling, yet for almost ten years there was no overt and mass movement which challenged racism in the streets. This interim decade, between World War II and the Montgomery County, Alabama, bus

The politics of Negro self-representation

boycott of December 1955, has also generally been ignored by black social historians. I think that the answer to the question, "Why were mass popular protests for desegregation relatively weak or non-existent in the period 1945–54?" is precisely the answer to the second question, 'Why have historians of the black Movement done so little research on the post-war period?' The impact of the Cold War, the anti-Communist purges and near-totalitarian social environment, had a devastating effect upon the cause of blacks' civil rights and civil liberties.[6]

Among social historians in particular, the situation in which Communist movements, including their relationship to blacks, goes unstudied was already changing when Marable wrote those words. There are now good books about CP organizing among African Americans in the 1930s by Mark Naison and Robin D. G. Kelley, and in the post-War period by Gerald Horne.[7] Additionally, recent work by Horne, Brenda Plummer, and Penny Von Eschen has demonstrated that the Cold War divided an African-American intellectual and political community that had, in the 1930s and through the war, a shared agenda of fighting simultaneously segregation and caste domination at home, and US imperialism abroad, into camps that were for or against US foreign policy.[8] Finally, Communist- and left-identified, primarily white, writers of the period have been the subjects of major new work by Barbara Foley, Paula Rabinowitz, and Alan Wald among several others.[9] Still, only Horne among historians, and no literary critic at all, has attempted to ask what was specifically African-American about the social and cultural theory of marxist movements, pre- or post-World War II. Participation in these movements is always perceived to marginalize intellectuals from the history of black subjectivity, except where they break loudly and unequivocally from the party, as in the well-known Cold War accounts by Richard Wright and Ralph Ellison. Wright, if anything, is criticized for retaining his post-CP interest in marxist theory; Langston Hughes' *I Wonder as I Wander*, which continues to treat his time working with the party as significant and positive and his trip to the Soviet Union as the experience of a better economic system, is ignored.

This chapter is an initial, and rather skeletal, attempt to write an older form of marxism into the history of racialization, the production of black subjectivity, from which it has been almost entirely absent. I read the 1937 autobiography of CP member and labor organizer Angelo Herndon, *Let Me Live*, and the 1959 autobiography of fellow traveling actor and folk-singer Paul Robeson, *Here I Stand*, because these autobiographies are of specific relevance to the narrative of racialization developed in this book – my account of them will, among other things, cite them as direct precursors to *The Autobiography of Malcolm X*.[10] Before I get to them, the first half of this chapter will provide an overview of the issues one needs to confront in order to attempt a new narrative of black Communism. Nowhere in this chapter is it my intention to make grand claims about the centrality of Communism to racial identity politics in the twentieth century; I merely refuse its marginalization. It is necessary that Herndon's and Robeson's texts, and the Negro marxist theorization of race and class, be readable as part of African-American literary and intellectual history, without apology, and without the kinds of distancing acts that demonstrate over and over how successful the Cold War has been in obscuring the reality of US marxist history, and the continued usefulness of marxist theory in political work.[11]

Writers as supporters and members of the CPUSA

There are a number of reasons why party members wrote, and encouraged workers to write, autobiographically, reasons which correspond in part to why African Americans have written autobiographies. Confronted with the question of praxis marxism has frequently been an identity politics, in the most obvious of ways: subjectivity has been theorized as "the standpoint of the proletariat," in Lukacs' well-known phrase, which in turn has always meant that the revolution was to be made by workers who had wrest agency for their narratives from capital. Thus Mike Gold, editor of the *New Masses*, encouraged all workers to submit their personal writing for publication: "Everyone has a great tragic-comic story to tell. Almost everyone in America feels oppressed and wants to speak out somewhere. Tell us your story. It is sure to be significant."[12] Autobiographical writing, the sharing of the experience of exploitation, was a key for the popularization of a revolutionary political stand among workers. Indeed, as with African-American narratives in the testimonial tradition, exposing working conditions and exploring worker culture was to be one of the major forces for creating an autonomous worker identity on the basis of self-consciousness about the generality of worker experience.

Those who, for whatever reason, are able to make their lives as professional writers have very different interests in left-wing political organizations from those who write for consciousness raising, and thus their accounts of the relative utility or disutility of party membership have to be read in rather different terms; if few of them much liked Gold, who was widely perceived as the most orthodox of CP editors, one might begin by asking whether this is because their projects are so broadly different from his. Barbara Foley documents, among other things, that many writers turned, at least for a time, to Party critics for serious commentary and evaluation concerning how to make their writing more useful to the movement;[13] on the other hand, especially during the Popular Front period (1935–9), the Party turned to nonmember writers who were broadly supportive of socialism for political actions, high profile signatures on petitions, appearance at Party forums, and other specific tasks. Daniel Aaron, not a leftist himself, makes the point not only that the writers who were involved in more or less direct ways with the party were perfectly aware of who and what they were involving themselves with – there were no underhanded attempts to "use" writers – but that the writers in many cases may have gotten a great deal more out of their association with the Party than the Party got out of its association with the writers.[14] In the end, there is nothing complicated about the point: writers and intellectuals work in, with, or alongside a variety of movements at different moments of our lives for reasons that are compelling at the moment of association; our interests intersect with, but are not necessarily identical to, those of the political leaders of those movements, and this itself explains their suspicions of us, which we need neither sneer at, nor accept. In this context, the act of reading work by blacks associated with the CP, in particular, is first the act of looking carefully at what attracted them to the Party at a given point in time, and what they got from their participation in the Party, regardless of whether they stayed for life or left after a few years. It will be useful to chart the history of the development of US Communism in its relationship to African-American politics, such that one has a feel for the milieu; the outline that follows is, of course, much too broad for genuine historical narrative, but will help establish some basic context.

The people who formed the US affiliate of the Bolshevik Third Communist International ("Comintern") in the early twenties did so out of two basic contexts – the "old left" formations[15] of the pre-Great War period, including in their diversity the Industrial Workers of the World (whose founder, Bill Haywood, left the US, working as a mining engineer in the Soviet Union until he died in the 1920s) and the Bohemian intellectuals around the *Masses*, a Greenwich Village journal of art and politics in the 1910s; and a cross-section of newly demobilized young soldiers, from both working and professional class backgrounds. For African Americans attracted, whether for reasons of background or conviction, to socialist politics, the CPUSA emerged in the 1920s as the grouping with the greatest commitment to organizing black industrial workers, having a presence in black neighborhoods, and doing anti-racist work. Thus the African Blood Brotherhood, a group of several hundred militant socialists, predominantly Caribbean immigrants, with branches in New York and Chicago in the 1920s, negotiated a merger with the CPUSA, becoming the supporters of a nationalist tendency within the latter organization. Against the presumption that black politics took a back seat to pro-Soviet politics, as well as the presumption that US, and not European, marxists were uniquely able to comprehend the centrality of race to marxist politics, it was in fact the highest levels of the Comintern – specifically Lenin, Trotsky, and Stalin, all of whom *personally* studied and took positions on race in the US – that insisted on this central line for CPUSA organizing, and did so in the 1920s against notable opposition within the US Party.[16] This certainly should not be surprising to anyone with a passing acquaintance to Lenin's theory of imperialism, which, not incidentally, provided an explanation of why relatively peripheral Russia was more able to bring about a socialist revolution than relatively more developed England, France, or Germany. While Trotskyists and Stalinists would eventually split on the precise meaning of support for the national self-determination of black Americans, no one in this period who claimed to follow Leninist theory could ignore the centrality of black and anti-imperialist struggle to socialist struggle.

As is well known, the depression is the period when the CPUSA was largest, and when it could claim large numbers of intellectuals as members or fellow travelers. The first and most important reason for this is economics: the Russian economy, in contrast to the economy in which these intellectuals were living and working, was expanding at an unprecedented rate during the thirties, something which Trotsky himself took seriously even after being purged.[17] Continued CP support of autonomous black nationhood (the "Black Belt" thesis) justified the massive organizational resources put into work in both Harlem and the sharecropper movements of the south, as well as the organization of southern black industrial workers in cities like Atlanta which forms the immediate backdrop of Angelo Herndon's autobiography. Finally, it is the *early* depression period in which the

John Reed Clubs for proletarian writers, out of which Richard Wright emerged, were strongly pursued. On the other hand, in 1935 the inauguration of the "Popular Front Against Fascism," which *expanded* the appeal of the CP to white writers (and loosened the bounds of what would be considered pro-Communist writing), led to both the pulling back from anti-racist and black nationalist commitment (making it possible for Dos Passos, as one example of a racist left-wing writer, to be in the Communist sphere), and to the disbanding of the John Reed clubs – for the party no longer needed "proletarian literature" if it was aligned with a wide variety of professional writers. My point is not that the Popular Front line was right or wrong, but that its promulgation may have led, over the next ten years, to the *decrease* in alignment between African-American intellectuals and the Party. With the decreasing commitment to the politics of anti-racism and black self-determination came a corollary increase in the direct experience of racism within the Party. While previously some blacks were attracted to the party because it was the one place where they experienced genuinely respectful interaction with whites, this became a less compelling reason to remain a member after 1935.[18] It is in this context that it becomes possible to read Wright's account, in *American Hunger*, of leaving the Party not because of a break from its political agenda at all (and when that came, later, it was still not a break from marxism), but from a disinterest in having his writing career subject to the exigencies of a political organization's changing needs. It is the promulgation of the Cold War, and the adjustment to it by Wright and others, that makes this look different and more dramatic than the usual choice of artists who believe they have a social role to align with, and separate from, political movements in general.

The Popular Front period eventually replaced a revolutionary strategy with a gradualist strategy within the CPUSA, leading to its temporary disbanding during the period of alliance between the US and USSR in World War II. Thus it makes sense that post-World War II the reason why new black members and fellow travelers, such as W. E. B. Du Bois in his seventies and Paul Robeson in his thirties, were attracted to the Party was alignment in opposition to the Cold War military build-up in the US and outrage at the attempts to retain and reinforce British and French imperialism in the agreements which concluded the war. For these intellectuals and many others, only the Soviet Union provided a challenge to western imperialism that seemed powerful enough to matter. It is during this period that it becomes obvious to both leftist blacks, and white party members, that the Du Boisian and Leninist analyses of imperialism had begun to converge in previous decades and were now entirely merged. In this context, Robeson's newspaper *Freedom* became a new attempt to bring together black intellectuals who resisted the Cold War into a pro-Comintern, but not CPUSA controlled, intellectual formation.

In reading the above paragraphs, the most important point to retain is that there is no necessary consistency over four decades between the politics that would attract one to a black/marxist hybrid, and either pro-CP or anti-CP politics. Circumstances in the Party changed for African Americans, and not necessarily for the same reasons they changed for Anglo Americans or Eastern European immigrants. As a result there is also no consistency between the white Bolsheviks who broke from the CP as a result of the anti-Trotskyist purges, or the revelations of internal repression in the Soviet Union, and their support for or understanding of black politics in the US. Thus the fact that the influential American literary Trotskyists of the 1930s ultimately generated a pro-American cultural politics that became simple collusion with the Cold War[19] may, upon further research, have pushed certain African-American intellectuals toward the Comintern rather than alternative non-Comintern marxisms during the Cold War, regardless of their understanding of Stalin's terror – especially in light of the fact that Du Bois and Trotsky agreed that the Soviet *economy*, anyway, was socialist and beneficial to substantial numbers of Russian workers.

African-American subjectivity and Bolshevik theories

In the 1920s there were two, related, sources within orthodox marxist theory for analyzing the role of racial subjectivity in the construction of a proletariat: First, there is the theory of the unequal development of subjectivity that is implicit in all discussions of the relationship between the two major classes of "pure" capitalism, the bourgeois and the proletariat, and the breakdown of actual classes and class fragments in the real world; Marx's most famous account of this relationship is in *The Eighteenth Brumaire of Louis Napoleon*. Second, there is the theory of nationalism as a major, and perhaps necessary, stage of human development on the way to internationalism. Like the sociological theory of the process of racialized minoritization presented in *Dusk of Dawn*, and in a different form in chapter one of this book, both of these theories are spatially embedded in the theory of the globalist critique of political economy. The difference is that while racialization theorists like Du Bois and those who follow him presume that racialization cannot be fully explained by the logic of capitalism, deriving from social needs that become intertwined and inseparable from the growth of the capitalist economy but are logically accidental (or even antecedent) to it, more orthodox marxist positions, including the ones implicit in Herndon's and Robeson's narratives, presume that the logic of capital itself is enough to create not only proletarianization but also minoritization. The Du Boisian narrative was consistently outside the set of positions articulated by CP members during the period under discussion;[20] this leaves, broadly speaking, three possible positions that a black member or supporter of the Party could take concerning racial subjectivity:

(1) they could, like James Ford, Otto Hall, or William Patterson deny the significance of racial subjectivity to the politics of anti-capitalism altogether; this is, of course, the line the CPUSA is widely assumed to have insisted upon, quite without any knowledge or research on the part of those who make the assumption;

(2) they could, like the early African Blood Brotherhood and Harry Haywood, take a "national socialist" position, in which autonomous black nationalist organizing by the Negro proletariat – *not* the middle class – is a *necessary* moment of cultural and economic development (as nationhood is natural for all "peoples"), thus making the correct organizing strategy for (interracially organized) Communists the practical speeding up of this process of nationalist collectivization;

(3) or they could, as Paul Robeson ultimately did, take a more strictly *nationalist* line, whereby being Negro was already identical to being "proletarian" – Robeson would state that he was from a "working class people."[21] This line would be a key entry point to marxism for many who would start as black nationalists in the 1960s.

A short analysis of the writings of Leon Trotsky on literary subjectivity and racial subjectivity will help us understand the logic of these positions. Trotsky's *Literature and Revolution*, published in the Soviet Union in 1924 when the author could still reasonably hope that he was helping to set Comintern policy on art, is a reading of the relationship of a series of Russian authors and movements to the establishment of Soviet socialism. The book is dedicated most of all to the argument that writers, while not all equally friendly to the Revolution, cannot be judged according to the immediate political needs of the Revolution. Thus, while it's just as well that certain reactionary *émigrés* have left the country, the art of all writers, living in Russia or not, who do not specifically undermine the Revolution, should be tolerated by the state and appreciated for what it can contribute to an understanding of the emotional present and future. Because of the time and training it takes to produce, art will always be at a distance from the immediate organization of the new economy; only inasmuch as the Party demonstrates, through practical and long-term change in people's lives, that its work is deserving of support, will artists in general support the Revolution. Thus, if (as my epigraph to this chapter claims) nonmarxist but fellow traveling writers make the mistake of putting insufficient "idealogic distance" between themselves and the revolution – that is, if the subjectivity of their work is ultimately grounded in the material ways the revolution has affected them, rather than the ways it has affected the nation as a whole – this is a "social and not an individual trait." It is the fate of artists as a class fraction in a revolutionary situation. And, inasmuch as the experience of this class fraction is consonant with the experience of a cross-section of others affected by the Revolution, party intellectuals should read this work as a gauge of what the Revolution feels like for many on the ground.[22]

What makes Trotsky's analysis here pivotal for locating the tools that Bolshevik marxism brought to the analysis of race and nation is that the continuation of his chapter on fellow travelers links them to a "peasant nationalism" which is itself a romantic and subjectivist, but materially grounded, deviation. In this context, when one turns to Trotsky's later exploration of US racial conditions, as collected in the volume *Leon Trotsky on Black Nationalism and Self-Determination*, one is not surprised to find the analysis of racial subjectivity thought in the same terms as that of Russian peasant nationalism.[23] As with artists in *Literature and Revolution*, Trotsky expresses interest and sympathy toward the project of black subjectivist thinkers, and indicates that US Trotskyists should not set themselves up against black nationalists. Negroes are described as primarily a backward, peasant people with a sometimes progressive bourgeoisie which may contribute to certain positive changes on behalf of all black people before full integration of black and white working class movements is possible; in the meantime, the separate development of the races means that such integration might be considered undesirable by the mass of blacks. On the one hand, integration is not something that party organizers can expect from black people, but, on the other, black nationalism is not based on a sufficiently distanced reading of the social situation. Thus Trotsky insists that the "right" of self-determination for black Americans cannot be interfered with; however, he distinguishes carefully between this "right" to national autonomy, and the promulgation of the "slogan" of black self-determination, which he believes revolutionary socialists should not raise themselves.[24] For their own part, Trotskyist parties should organize and theorize interracially – C. L. R. James is one of Trotsky's collaborators in the text I'm referring to – in the hope that should white US workers begin to see their class interests accurately, the *right* of black self-determination will not turn into a self-generated *demand*.

In the period before 1935 the Comintern disagreed. According to "Black Belt" thesis supporter Harry Haywood, the "slogan of Right of Self-Determination here in the Deep South . . . destroys forever the white racist theory traditional among class conscious white workers which had relegated the struggle of black to a subsidiary position in the revolutionary movement.[25] Haywood attributes the success of this "correct" line to Stalin personally; according to CPUSA pamphleteer James Allen, Stalin demonstrates that a historically developed community which retains solidity over a long period of time, and lives together in a common territory with a common language and common economy inevitably becomes conscious of itself as a nation.[26] Since this is a *necessary*, and not a *possible*, stage in the process of socialist development, the only genuinely revolutionary line for the CPUSA is to promote this nationalist consciousness among the Negro proletariat.[27] There is no question that the membership of the CPUSA honored this thesis in practice less often than in theory, and further, that among Party members, the question of whether someone was white or black had no necessary connection to the carrying out of this thesis – which would appear to call the thesis into question to begin with. And of course, after 1935 the Black Belt thesis was shunted aside. Still, without any suggestion on my part that this idealist theory of nationalism was correct, I must report that Haywood, in his retrospective autobiography *Black Bolshevik*, claims convincingly not only that the days of the Black Belt thesis were the heyday of serious marxist structural analysis of the conditions of black agricultural and industrial workers, but that this analysis was the forerunner of many developments in black theory on the left-wing of the Black Power movement.

Ultimately, none of this should surprise us. It has been noted several times that Du Bois' 1915 *Atlantic Monthly* article "The African

Roots of the War" and Lenin's 1917 pamphlet *Imperialism: The Highest Stage of Capitalism* make exactly the same structural argument about the place of the "labor aristocracy" in the global economy, though Du Bois perceives this group in racial terms, and Lenin in national terms.[28] This is why when Du Bois finally breaks with black middle class politics, which doesn't happen until the Cold War, he finds his best allies in the CPUSA.

Two ways of representing the Negro male-as-proletarian: Angelo Herndon and Paul Robeson

Angelo Herndon's autobiography, *Let Me Live*, written, as the title implies, to raise funds and support for the Communist-led social movement backing Herndon's court defense on charges of "insurrection," provides a space for defining the intersection of race, class, and gender ideology in the southern US with the CP's commitment to organizing workers without regard to race.[29] Two important discussions of the situation of 1930s Communist organizing help to explain why. Robin D. G. Kelley argues that from the start the Communist plan to organize in the south, especially the industrial city of Birmingham, Alabama, was difficult because of the association of communism in the dominant imagination with free choice of acquaintance, which in the south was necessarily understood as free sexual choice among the races. The CPUSA's strategy of gathering an international movement in response to the frame-up of the Scottsboro nine for rape in 1932 reinforced this set of associations among racists and anti-Communists. In the southern imagination – and arguably the national imagination generally – communism meant interracialism and interracialism meant unacceptable sexual liaisons.[30] The Communist response to this social configuration required an alternative race-gender narrative. The alternative provided was deeply problematic, however, and Paula Rabinowitz's work, though it does not address race, helps to explain why:

> During the 1930s, class struggle in the United States was meta-phorically engendered through a discourse that re-presented class conflict through the language of sexual difference. The prevailing verbal and visual imagery reveled in an excessively masculine and virile proletariat posed to struggle against the effeminate and decadent bourgeoisie. Thus the potentially revolutionary struggles of the working class were recontained

within the framework of the eternal battle of the sexes within
domestic fiction.[31]

We have already seen, in the ex-colored man, someone who abandons blackness because the fact of lynching has made it inconsistent
with manhood; the example of Malcolm X in the next chapter will
fully elaborate this pattern within black male intellectual work in
which the process of bringing about community freedom is consistently equated with allowing the black male individual to "become a
man." As I have argued consistently, the identification with the
lynching victim *really does* effect psychological castration within a
patriarchal context; the problem is that such narratives attempt to
bring an end to castration anxiety, which makes sense only within
patriarchy, rather than an end to patriarchy. Angelo Herndon's narrative takes as its project the representation of a *racialized, yet uncas-
trated man*; in doing so, it not only exemplifies the masculinist engen-
dering of Communist narrative Rabinowitz describes, but opens the
possibility that black men are the privileged representatives of such a
process of remasculinization.

If black nationality is at the center of at least some Communist
organizing strategy in the 1930s, Herndon, *because* he is black, comes
to symbolize the *proletarian* outcome of a revolutionary domestic
romance in which the forces of opposition to the romance – southern
and northern anti-Communists, who are agents in the production of
feminized black male selves – are so particularly repressive that they
imprison black males merely *for being men*. In turn, prison becomes a
privileged space where a man proves his masculinity. *Let Me Live*, for
all its many flaws, inaugurates this particular pattern; after the slave
narrative but prior to *The Autobiography of Malcolm X* it is the central
prison text in black literature. No black feminist politics can permit
the heroic black male prisoner to represent freedom in this sense; and
yet no black feminist politics can ignore the grammar of black male
imprisonment, which remains *the* central element in the white supremacist gendering of black masculinity today.[32]

That Herndon's political predicament is a family romance is clear
from the start. On page one the six-year-old Herndon first "become[s]
conscious" by virtue of "tragedy"; the light-skinned mother who the
narrator "always thought beautiful" sings her sick child, Gelo, to
sleep and tells him that Jesus will make him well if he prays, even
while the family has no money to buy the medicine which is necessary to save his life.[33] The Oedipal problem is formed when Mother's
warmth and religiosity is not complimented by a strong male figure;

rather, Gelo's father is immediately contrasted with the successful domesticity of the pious mother (who presumably is not adversely affected by poverty) in this way:

> During the time of my illness I began to see my father in a new light. While my mother was demonstrative in her affection for us, he acted in a constrained and absent manner. Worry had made his face prematurely lined. It was only when he smiled that the essential kindness in the man was revealed. But he rarely smiled. Then I did not know why, but now I do know that it was overwork, under-nourishment and the burdens of daily living which had made a broken man out of him, although still young in years.[34]

This plausible depiction of black male social death forms the basis of the argument to follow: that the Communist Party can restore this poor family to its properly gendered structure. The adult Herndon, as retrospective narrator, is already present to give this fundamental interpretation of the family, not by placing it in a world historical setting, as in *Dusk of Dawn*, but through the representation of a perfectly idealized poverty. Christianity, which is feminine, has been introduced as the potential location of false consciousness for the young child. The structure of narrative substitution in the book, the reader already sees, will replace religion with Communism, which is masculine. A neighbor, in an example of class solidarity, contributes the necessary money to buy medicine, and Gelo survives.

Race is not mentioned at all amid the first chapter's class analysis, but rather than leave you wondering, in the second chapter Herndon moves immediately from the domesticity of his illness to a racist incident, which happens, of course, outside the home. Inasmuch as Herndon is in a family, it does not differ internally from any other proletarian family; inasmuch as he is in a neighborhood, a bunch of boys call him a "nigger." The racialized male internalizes his self-hatred, aided once again by his mother: asked what "nigger" means by her son, "a look of pain and indignation" comes onto her face, and she immediately quotes the Song of Songs on how God has asked the sun to burn black people, because they were vain sinners at some point in the past.[35] In addition to the text's rejection of prayer as a solution to poverty, then, black female reliance on feminine Christianity is portrayed as the direct cause of the internalization of biblically commanded racial self-hatred.

Yet little else in the later narrative suggests that racial self-hatred, or any alternative form of black identification, ever takes hold in the heroic Angelo Herndon. On the contrary, Herndon reports other events from early in his life which suggest the possibility of unity among the oppressed, both as mutually aiding each other (as with the money for the medicine already reported), or with the potential for solidarity through life experience. The language with which the plausibility of solidarity between blacks and Italian immigrants is represented is significant: "Mike was a solitary soul. A luxuriant Mediterranean plant from Sicily, he could not take root in the cold, impersonal soil of his new environment. Perhaps it was the warmth of my own Negro soul which struck a sympathetic accord in his expansive nature." Mike, it turns out, was a socialist in Italy, which the young Angelo associates, for reasons he can't quite explain, with having been a burglar.[36] Yet the plausibility of the cross-identification between Mike and Gelo depends not on Mike's identity as a socialist but on the identity of workers and poor people engaging in mutual aid, on the one hand, and through the common warmth of dark souls, on the other. The typical racialist shorthand which describes the unity of dark-skinned people as emotional is then used by analogy to describe the difference between the present cold, bourgeois world and the potentiality of a socialist world: "it was then that I fully became conscious of the inequalities in being a worker. It rankled in my young soul but it did not embitter me, for I was by nature full of gaiety and good spirits."[37]

Most strikingly, in terms of the text's large-scale repressive mechanisms, this encounter with Mike makes him *fully* conscious. Herndon's consciousness is persistently becoming "full" through the several similar experiences of identification narrated, making his decision to join the CP automatic, easy, and indeed unmediated as soon as he discovers the existence of the organization. In this way the book is hardly a *bildungsroman* at all, since it allows for no development, only the fullness of explained and assimilated consciousness in event after event, never allowing the possibility that Herndon has the slightest doubt about his own needs and desires. Thus the following:

> On a sultry evening in June, 1930, I was coming home from work when some soiled handbills, upon which people had trampled, caught my eye. I was startled by its headline, which read: "Would you rather fight or starve?" My friend and I ... read it over and over again, not believing our own eyes, as if we had been living in an evil dream all the time and suddenly awoke to reality with a bang.[38]

126

The unemployment council pamphlet is immediately represented as providing *revealed* truth. The material basis for the acceptance of its political position has been established, of course, but the apprehension of this truth arrives fully sprouted by the mere act of its enunciation. The religious replacement, Party for church, is entirely explicit, for he compares his position as listener to his first Communist speech to his experience at a younger age when he entered the church:

> Strange, only once before had ... a speaker ... moved me so deeply ... when my Uncle Jeremiah preached his first sermon and I ... piped in my nine-year-old voice: "I know religion is in me, Uncle Jeremiah." The emotional motivation in both cases was identical, but what a difference in their nature and in their aim! The change of my viewpoint was almost fabulous, emerging from the urge to escape the cruelties of life in religious abstractions into a healthy, vigorous, and realistic recognition that life on earth, which was so full of struggle and tears for the poor, could be changed by the intelligent and organized will of workers.[39]

The worker-speaker that moves him so much is white, but this does not provide any obstacle to belief or feeling of alienation he must get over, as Herndon shouts from the crowd "He's right! He does nothing but tell the truth. He's the first honest white man I've seen."[40] If, unlike in Trotsky, there is no messy subjectivity to be accounted for in the process of historical objectivity, this is because Communism has been structured entirely as a religion, however "realistic," not a critical politics. A bit later, in prison trying to forget his troubles, "suddenly flashed across my mind ... the faces of Karl Marx and Frederick Engels."[41] The possibility that marxist explanation might actually fit worker reality better than Christianity does under certain historical conditions is actually undermined by a text that can perceive the black worker's Communism as nothing other than a replacement Christianity.

The purpose of my critique of Herndon, here, is not to suggest that nothing is useful in this carefully wrought, in fact highly theorized replacement – after all, much of Kelley's discussion in *Hammer and Hoe* is devoted to demonstrating that Communist organizing in the south was effective in part because of the adaptation of already existing models of politico-religious thinking to the practicalities of labor organizing. What I wish to carry through is the further analysis of what this particular, constructed, autobiographical identity, in the context of a popular, and not primarily black, social movement, suggests about the ideal subject who is black, male, and Communist.

Herndon's self-portrayal after this point is nothing if not hypersubjective, lacking any position for self-critical reflection. This is because Herndon's subjectivity has, as Trotsky puts it, merged with the Revolution. For from the moment Herndon officially joins the party, at seventeen, he becomes *the* representative narrator, telling his own story and referring to it as everyone's story. During his first stay in prison he writes:

> I said to myself:
> "When they strike the helpless and the weak they strike me."
> Helpless myself, I began to brood on this insane business of living. For the first time I clearly saw that the white man's boastful civilization was a fraud. The few battened on the many and when the underdog dared question his evil lot he was beaten down without mercy.[42]

After a different arrest, Herndon remarks that he "fully understood the nature of the terrors that lay ahead of the working class in Birmingham."[43] The real pains and terrors he faced as an oft jailed fighter for justice never reflect *his* pains and terrors at all – they are always nothing but the pains and terrors of the class. They are always understood "fully." To the extent that this is one version of how a proletarian narrative should be written – and I can't overemphasize that this narrative is *atypical* in its orthodoxy – it is no wonder that Richard Wright sees Communist politics as the impossibility of individual subjectivity.

Herndon spends much of the period 1930–7 in and out of various Alabama and Georgia prisons. His position as prison narrator is always as meta-commentator, never as experiential narrator; incidents in prison are given as examples of the depravities of guards, the depravities of Negro prisoners (the prisons are segregated, so these are the only ones he knows), and most significantly, of the immediate response he gets from other prisoners when he makes speeches – always in the perfect, formal English of a pamphlet. No doubt it is true that "unless one has had the doubtful benefit of a stay in prison, it is hardly possible to grasp fully the viciousness of the place," but his own self-conscious singularity in prison, based on "the moral duty of acting in the light of my communist convictions," in fact makes his descriptions of the people he is supposedly changing the world on behalf of unreliable at best. In this context, the predictably homophobic descriptions of the depravity of prisoners on these same two pages take the place of any concern for the victims of rape that the heroic male proletarian might otherwise have.[44]

It is, however, not only in the lengthy prison sections that Herndon positions himself as a singular moral hero. He holds forth making all-too-clever speeches to judges and in front of juries; in spite of his own "repugnance" toward having to act this way, he constantly acts "shrewdly"; in one encounter after another he is brilliant while his white tormentors are merely violent, providing repeated opportunities "not to give my tormentors the satisfaction of betraying any sign of pain under their brutality"; he makes eloquent, impromptu speeches in front of the widest diversity of friends and foes.[45] In the long introductory section of this chapter, I resisted the underlying Cold War logic that presumes that books by Communist Party members or associates are uncomplicated, knee-jerk propaganda; such arguments are wrong, and particularly dangerous to the contemporary writing of left history and practice. Yet in this context it is important to see that the ways in which *Let Me Live* is a canned book may help us to identify a particular kind of left-wing sentimentality about race. The ongoing difficulty of thinking through the prison narrative as a generic form of African-American literature – something that becomes ever more urgent as the imprisonment of black men becomes an ever more central element in white supremacy – emerges from this sentimental masculinism. Women, of course, can be neither black nor socialist in this text, since they are either incidents to or active opponents of the heroic character himself. By posing the imprisoned black male as model proletarian, *Let Me Live* simultaneously retains the possibility of civil rights and black community organizing while justifying the most assimilationist narrative within US politics, not so much because "black subjectivity" disappears, but because blackness is idealized as the model for the general disappearance of subjectivity.

This text represents the possibility of certain constructions that retain their importance for me: black worker activism and self-education, starting locally in the struggle against white supremacist imprisonment but ultimately situating this struggle within a global politics. As such, its representation of racialized class position matters because it is a near precursor to the massively successful, and usefully complicated, presentation of black manhood in *The Autobiography of Malcolm X*, discussed in chapter six – and also the next important CP prison text, *Angela Davis: An Autobiography, With My Mind on Freedom*, discussed in chapter seven. The differences between the texts are also huge, and will be addressed at length.

By contrast, Robeson's *Here I Stand* begins with global politics – Robeson was a world-traveling musician and actor before he established any political identity at all – on the way to justifying an entirely different narrative of black civil rights politics. About the only thing Robeson and Herndon have in common is their "manhood." A little less than one-third the length of Herndon's book, about a life three times longer at the time of composition, its structure is both meticulously compressed and self-consciously unrevealing, with an opening essay of twenty-five pages which is about Robeson's childhood and moral development, and a 100-page personal account of his participation in international political and artistic currents in the 1950s. Further, in *Here I Stand* Robeson is not simply a "man" but a man's body. His huge, football-playing frame was central to the representation of all US blackness, if not all Africanness, in the period of his greatest fame, since his depictions of blackness and Africanness on stage and film were more widely known and respected than any other in the 1940s; and his refusal to break with the Communist Party was among the most visible public scandals of the Cold War.[46] In this context, the title of the book itself describes the way that the integrity of Robeson as *the* representative black man is the basis on which the argument of the book should be adopted. This integrity is always identified with blackness, rather than Communism – indeed, that Robeson's work with and on behalf of the Communist Party should be respected *because* of his blackness is what makes this black Communist subjectivity different from Herndon's.

The first words of the text are "I am a Negro," an assertion the apparent obviousness of which should give us pause: for a well-known actor, musician, and "notorious" Cold War communist to assert such a thing is to intend a specific challenge to those who would deny that "Negro" can be a proudly claimed identity. That the assertion contains masculine gender is demonstrated just as quickly in the text, since the first chapter (after the "prologue"), the one about his childhood, locates this acquired racial identity with his father, the patriarch, in its opening lines: "The glory of my boyhood years was my father. I loved him like no one in all the world. His people, among whom he moved as a patriarch for many years before I was born, loved him too. And the white folks – even the most lordly of aristocratic Princeton – had to respect him too."[47] The black father as figure of respect is one we have not seen in our previous autobiographies. Even where in autobiographical accounts there are respectable fathers, as with Ida B. Wells Barnett or Walter White, they are not mythologized or portrayed as *conservative* in the sense they appear here:[48] "I readily yielded to his quiet discipline. Only once did I disobey him." Father was a minister, well-known locally among white and black, with a "deep, sonorous basso, richly melodic and refined"; furthermore, "he was very broad of shoulder and his physical bearing reflected the rock-like strength and dignity of his character."[49] Robeson's description of his home life is built around the figure of the rock, central to conservative nationalism: the chapter title is "A Home in That Rock," from the name of a spiritual. At the same time he presents himself as the son who achieves for the sake of this rock of a father, Robeson moves at school among the white liberal elite of Princeton, New Jersey, where he is encouraged to "climb up if you can – but don't act 'uppity'. Always show that you are *grateful . . . Above all, do nothing to give them cause to fear you*."[50] Radical politics is, then, that social space in which the contradiction implicit in being caught between manhood and servility, being a humble rock, can work itself out. Thus the last sentence of this opening chapter, key to so many claims for identity politics, becomes clearly understandable: "All which came later, after Rutgers and Columbia law school – my career as an artist in America and abroad, my participation in public life, the views which I hold today – all have their roots in the early years recalled in this prologue."[51] The practice of black manhood identity, rather than party membership, is radical politics for Robeson, and the International Communist movement is merely the group of *his* admirers who support this practice.

Robeson's identification with Communism started as a result of his appreciation of the Soviet Union's support for African decolonization and depended ultimately on his notion of integrity, of not rejecting one's allies when under fire: one does not betray one's friends. According to his son, Paul Robeson, Jr.:

> The fact that Robeson viewed the Soviet Union and the world communist movement as reliable allies of colonial liberation movements led him to form a close alliance with Communists despite his private misgivings about the Stalinist purges of 1936–38 and his disagreement with the Communist Left's exaggerated emphasis on class priorities over "nationalist" priorities in the third world.[52]

However, what we must see in the identity-narrative of *Here I Stand* is not a refusal of class identity in favor of national identity, but, precisely, a redefinition of class identity ultimately made possible by the black nationalist interpretation of Stalin's definition of the emergent nation. In *Here I Stand* Robeson speaks freely of his ability to interpret folk songs from a variety of places in the world because of the "fact

that I came from a working-class people."[53] The very establishment of
the category "folk song" positions "class identity" onto *groups*, rather
than individuals, via the mediation of the category of "a people," of
whom he is a representative, or as Duberman describes him, an
"ambassador."[54] And it is in his role as ambassador that his refusal to
testify that he is not a member of the Communist Party (which in fact
he was not) is comprehensible. It is a matter of the personal integrity
of the "folk," rather than political identity with a worker's movement: "I have made it a matter of principle, as many others have
done, to refuse to comply with any demand of legislative committees
or departmental officials that infringes upon the constitutional rights
of all Americans." Herndon would have stated that the working class
does not cooperate with the forces of legal repression. Thus while
Robeson has "publicly expressed my belief in the principles of scientific socialism, my deep conviction that for all mankind a socialist
society represents an advance to a higher stage of life," he does not
"intend to argue for my political viewpoint, and, indeed, the large
question as to which society is better for humanity is never settled by
argument."[55]

Sterling Stuckey says that for Robeson, "nationalist self-exertion"
is the means for achievement of "humanist" goals.[56] Thus when
Robeson suggests that "the time is now" (title to chapter four) for
"the power of Negro action" (title of chapter five), the goal is to bring
about the end of US segregation at home and colonialism abroad,
since "America cannot survive if she insists upon bearing the burden
of the crumbling system of Imperialism." And this system will continue "as long as we permit it," with "we," again, referring specifically and exclusively to "Negroes": "I say that Negro action can be
decisive" is the next sentence.[57] The principles of scientific socialism
to which Robeson claims allegiance, are thus re-formed in this statement, as the decisive class actors are now a grouping built not around
the relationship to the mode of production but are rather a second
order representative of this relationship, defined in the social, not the
economic, field. There are no Communists in this narrative of agency,
except inasmuch as Robeson's social identity already makes him a
"Communist." In Robeson's articulations, that which Trotsky
thought would be permissible, but which he would not specifically
promote, in fact occurs: socialist agency requires the slogan, not the
right, of black identity; and in a twist of the formula, Robeson will
accept the *right* of white people to engage in pro-third-worldist action
with him, but he will not, in 1958, *advance it as a slogan*. Robeson's

chapter on the power of Negro action presents no special role for the Comintern in the bringing about of world revolution.

Prior to the 1960s the CPUSA was perceived by a cross-section of black intellectuals as the most practical space in which to work for black autonomist socialism. This was not, certainly, a large space, but it was a real one nonetheless. The form of the space that was carved out by Robeson is the direct precursor to Malcolm X in my narrative because it exhibits the identity politics of a popular figure of bourgeois demeanor which, when rearticulated by X, an imprisoned working class man with family ties to the Garveyists of the 1930s and membership in the Black Muslims in the 1960s, becomes the most widely disseminated public figuration of black revolutionary identity in the US in the twentieth century.

Part three

The dialectics of home: gender, nation, and blackness since the 1960s

6

Malcolm X and the grammar of redemption

> Every Negro boy – in my situation during those years, at least
> – who reaches this point realizes at once, profoundly, because
> he wants to live, that he stands in great peril and must find,
> with speed, a "thing," a gimmick, to lift him out, to start him
> on his way. *And it does not matter what the gimmick is* ... It was
> my career in the church that turned out, precisely, to be my
> gimmick. James Baldwin[1]

> Probably about 90 percent of young people get their first
> introduction to black history through the *Autobiography [of
> Malcolm X]*. Deidre Bailey[2]

> That feels like truth to me. Patricia Williams[3]

Introduction

This chapter hypothesizes two things that cannot be *proven*. Yet
much of the narrative presented in the three previous chapters has
been constructed to make them plausible, and the two concluding
chapters, which concern the potentiality for the emergence of a large-
scale feminist resignification of the present grammar of racialization,
are written in the wake of these hypotheses. Put briefly, they are
follows:

(1) It makes sense to view *The Autobiography of Malcolm X* as
simultaneously reflective and productive of the mass cultural structure of feeling which emerged as "blackness" in the mid-1960s.[4]
Inasmuch as the period 1956–74 can be said to be the moment of the
greatest alteration – which in no way should be read as "diminution"
– in racial consciousness in the twentieth century, it follows that an
understanding of the precise contours of this autobiography as educational narrative, as narrative of gendering, and as narrative of the

137

conditions of possibility of freedom, is a necessary element in the analysis of the moment of racialization we now inhabit.

(2) The power of Malcolm X's experience to achieve this centrality in black popular culture depends on the practice of redemption, as a stage in the narration of "freedom," it affords. In this I follow Hortense Spillers on Malcolm X closely:

> Through the loss of the mother ... to the institution of "insanity" and the state ... Malcolm and his siblings, robbed of their activist father in a kkk-like ambush, are not only widely dispersed across a makeshift social terrain, but also show symptoms of estrangement and "disremembering" that require many years to heal, and even then, only by way of Malcolm's prison ordeal turned, eventually, into a redemptive occurrence ...
>
> The project of liberation for African Americans has found urgency in two passionate motivations that are twinned – (1) to break apart, to rupture violently the laws of American behavior that make such syntax possible; (2) to introduce a new *semantic field/fold* more appropriate to his/her own historic movement ... The narrative of Malcolm El-hajj Malik El-Shabazz ... represent[s] both narrative ambitions.[5]

The possibility of an African-American cultural politics in opposition to not only white supremacy, but also mass imprisonment (increasingly for women as well as men), underemployment, and subproletarianization, requires these terms. To avoid them is to cede the field to a certain misogynist right-wing to which Malcolm X belonged for ten years, which may already have successfully organized the field of "redemption" as large apolitical "marches" in Washington, DC. Such events are not useless; nor are they, of themselves, politics; nor, of course, are they feminist. This chapter proposes that to the extent that we are political and feminist, we must read *The Autobiography of Malcolm X* to trace the paths to, and from, such events.

Narrative form and racial consciousness

The Autobiography of Malcolm X concludes with a short essay by Ossie Davis called "On Malcolm X," written in answer to a white interlocutor who wanted to know why a popular entertainer and nationally known supporter of Martin Luther King, Jr., chose to speak at X's funeral. First, he states, while many white people have asked him that question, no black person, regardless of her or his political disagreements with Malcolm, has. Davis goes on:

> Every one of the many letters I got from my own people lauded
> Malcolm as a man, and commended me for having spoken at his
> funeral. At the same time – and this is important – most of them
> took special pains to disagree with much or all of what Malcolm
> said and what he stood for. That is … they all … know that
> Malcolm – whatever else he was or was not – *Malcolm was a man!*
>   White folks do not need anybody to remind them that they are
> men. We do! This was his one incontrovertible benefit to his
> people.[6]

For Davis this manhood consists in particular of two further features:
the willingness to speak frankly to whites about racism, and its
corollary, the sense of complete freedom from racialized restraint he
demonstrated and, indeed, provided the space for others to achieve.
Davis is specific in claiming that Malcolm, if only in death – if only for
the moment of identification made possible by the act of speaking
about him – has liberated him:

> And if, to protect my relations with the many good white folks
> who make it possible for me to earn a fairly good living in the
> entertainment industry, I was too chicken, too cautious, to admit
> [my admiration for him] when he was alive, I thought at least
> that now, when all the white folks are safe from him at last, I
> could be honest with myself enough to lift my hat for one final
> salute to that brave, black, ironic gallantry, which was his style
> and hallmark … so absolutely absent in every other Negro man
> I know, which brought him, too soon, to his death.[7]

Davis' identification, as the last word within the book itself, should be
considered at the outset the ground of this narrative's claim to black
hegemony; the figure of Malcolm X in the media accomplished, for
Ossie Davis at least, what Herndon and Robeson specifically imagined the narrative of their bodies should do – exhibit the manhood of
the race. Since Michele Wallace's *Black Macho and the Myth of the
Superwoman*, it has therefore been typical for feminists to reevaluate
Davis' laudatory comments about Malcolm's X's manhood: ''Malcolm was the supreme black patriarch … and with him died the
chance for a black patriarchy.''[8]

If Malcolm X defines black masculinity and the phantasmatic potential for patriarchy in a way that has had ongoing appeal – and not
only for men – we will do well to determine why he is able to inhabit
this position so well. I will claim that he can do so only because his
narrative is much more open and flexible than the rules of patriarchal
manhood, his own and those attributed to him, might propose. Paul
John Eakin has argued that *The Autobiography of Malcolm X* exposes

the "limits of autobiography," understood as the single-voiced narrative of individual development, because it contains a narrative voice which, explicitly, changes as the text unfolds. The reasons for writing the book shift between the time when it was dedicated to Elijah Muhammad, which "motivates more than half of the *Autobiography* in its final version," and the exploration of a Pan-Africanist political identity apart from the NOI – and this shift is not covered over, but is presented for all to see.[9] Not only is this book, like all autobiographies, constructed to fit a notion of identity consistent with a particular narrative moment; it is constructed over a period in which two conflicting narrative agendas are at work, and the text, written by a *third* party, is *not* rewritten to contain the contradictions. When X tries to rewrite certain passages about his NOI days to reflect his later politics, Haley is instrumental in convincing him that to do so would take away from the power and significance of the book.[10] This has enormous consequences. If, as John Edgar Wideman argues, Haley-as-writer's "disappearance into Malcolm's voice permits readers to accomplish an analogous disappearing act ... open[ing] the boundaries of our identities ... to the higher ground of Malcolm's voice,"[11] and we know that there are at least two distinct "voices" into which we can enter – in a moment I will suggest that number is actually four – then we might posit that the power of this text to represent black masculinity is itself contingent on the multiple narratives of such masculinity it contains, narratives which are not unlimited but are open to particular and determinate forms of contention. Where such contention exists, feminist pedagogy will find openings.

The text contains four racial consciousnesses, each of which establishes a particular logic of identification for the reader. The first two, that of the seventh child in an impoverished but striving, Garveyist family, and that of the hustler, are both clearly retrospective – and yet the effectiveness of the narration depends on the reader's being invited to enter into the assumptions of the child and of the hustler during the parts of the text where they are narrated. For example, in the well-known "Mascot" chapter, where X describes one major mode of acceptance of black children in school as that of pet or mascot, the narrative is largely related not from the judgmental voice of the retrospective narrator but rather from the point of view of the happy child who really does take pleasure in being a mascot for a year. The particular sets of privileges he is introduced to from the position of mascot – his own room in the home of a white family, the attention of lots of children – are novel, and comfortable, in ways that shape Malcolm's experience: we hear the identity-formation that comes from "Malcolm we're just so *proud* of you!" as his patron says it.[12] Certainly the title of the chapter and the periodic intervention of a retrospective narrator – "it never dawned on them that I could understand, that I wasn't a pet, but a human being ... but I was no more than vaguely aware of anything like that [then]" – makes it clear to the reader the sharp limits implied by the position of mascot.[13] Yet even this position is not presented as devoid of pleasure.

Each subsequent narrative voice of the text gets its due, for better and worse. Malcolm the hustler, though denounced, is also narrated with relish; the rejection of hustling is only partially the rejection of the narrative voice of the hustler. During the entire period in Boston and New York prior to his stay in prison, X remains an entirely *likable* narrator: fun, combative, strong, sophisticated in his analysis of the hustling world. If this is true of the hustler section, which is narrated entirely retrospectively, all the more is it true of the NOI section, most of which was narrated by X to Haley while he was a minister of that religion. At the outset, we hear of the importance of the conversion to Islam in no uncertain terms:

> Today, when everything that I do has an urgency, I would not spend one hour in the preparation of a book which had the ambition to titillate some readers. But I am spending many hours because the full story is the best way that I know to have it seen, and understood, that I had sunk to the very bottom of the American white man's society when ... I found Allah and the religion of Islam and it completely transformed my life.[14]

This passage, especially in coming as the final words of the chapter preceding the conversion, creates the presumption within the narrative that the identity inhabited as a result of NOI membership and ministry is the single subject-position of the remainder of the book. Then, as the next eleven years are narrated, the stories are primarily about speeches he gives, orthodox theology, and the kind of absolute commitment that does not permit questioning. Information about the world also begins "the Honorable Elijah Muhammad teaches" – even as this information becomes more directly political and less theological after 1959, he continues to attribute his own political thinking to the voice of Muhammad. As in the previous sections, there are a certain number of insertions of clauses that call this narrative into question: within the account of the orthodox history of the NOI, the narrator mentions that he "would sit, galvanized, hearing *what I then accepted* ... as being the true history of our religion.''[15] But the power of the orthodox narrative does not disappear with these comments. Malcolm is, after all, in the middle of revealing to us his sins and his salvation, and the fact that he is only saved through Elijah Muhammad's intervention. These early interpolations can do little to interrupt the story of the passing of truth from prophet to prophet when the same page he writes ''Mr. Elijah Muhammad says that he sat listening with an open heart and an open mind – the way I was sitting listening to Mr. Muhammad. And Mr. Muhammad said he never doubted any word that the 'Savior' taught him.''[16] It is possible, in pages like these, to see lines that are clearly in the narrative voice as it was given to Haley initially, and others added later as commentary which call the authority of the earlier voice into question. There is no way of deciding from textual evidence which voice is to be believed.

Finally, we do get to the politics of 1964, including X's rejection of the subject-positions which precede it, but from the point of view of narrative identification it may provide less a supercession than a supplement to what comes before, depending perhaps on the social location of the reader. Indeed, the post-NOI voice still argues that mistaken as the reliance on Elijah Muhammad was, it was *necessary*; it is, according to this narrative, psychoanalytically impossible to become Malcolm El Hajj Malik El-Shabazz the internationalist revolutionary, without first becoming X – the specifically *blank* identity formed in the rejection of whiteness. If so, then even after the final transformation the text can be reappropriated into an NOI narrative, and for the same reasons it can be turned into an internationalist politics – because while the social conditions of black subproletarian men look a good deal like they did sixty years ago, different readers may themselves inhabit different social locations in the narrative. Thus, even at its conclusion the narrative of universalist Islam co-exists with, rather than replaces, the NOI narrative, with neither providing a single, clearly dominant subject-position for the book.

I see no reason to celebrate this as ''dialogism,'' nor to denounce it as incoherence. I think there is a certain amount of internal evidence, based on Haley's epilogue, where, as I've already mentioned, Haley takes it upon himself to scold X for changing parts of the original narrative, that X, had he lived, would have changed his life story at least as many times as Du Bois, in ways that would require a similar sort of analysis, focused on the theoretical implications of the changes. I do want to claim that the ability of so many to identify with the narrative is not so much opportunism on the part of African

Americans of several class positions, as it is a consequence of the multiple Malcolms that are narrated, and the multiple thematics (the political and identitarian content) that can be generated from them. *The Autobiography of Malcolm X* occupies a large cross-section of the field of black male working class experience.

Four narratives of the content of racial consciousness

What follows are four ways of reading the *Autobiography* as a *bildungsroman*, focusing broadly on themes that may have specific valences in regard to the black politics of the 1960s, and/or to now: the presentation of "truth," sexuality, race, and education. The logic, and illogic, of the paths from beginning to end of these narratives ground the politics of "black" "masculinity" today.

Narrative 1: The hustle and the truth

Ossie Davis claims to *trust* Malcolm X, because he tells the *truth*. Indeed, the white journalist M. S. Handler's introduction to the book is built around the trust/truth nexus:

> During [our] first encounter Malcolm sought to enlighten me about the Negro mentality . . . [T]he Negro had been trained to dissemble and conceal his real thoughts, as a matter of survival. He argued that the Negro only tells the white man what he believes the white man wishes to hear, and that the art of dissembling reached a point where even Negroes cannot truthfully say they understand what their fellow Negroes believe . . .
>
> Many of the Negro writers and artists who are national figures today revered Malcolm for what they considered his ruthless honesty in stating the Negro case, his refusal to compromise . . . One said, "Malcolm will never betray us. We have suffered too much from betrayals in the past."[17]

Our first agenda is to describe the content of this truth, or what must stand as truth for trust to occur. Doing so should not call into question whether X's text is, in fact, true – the opening paragraphs of this chapter reveal the precise sense in which I would claim that it is, and I wish to make no further claims in this regard. But not all things that are true necessarily become *trustworthy*, and so our goal must be to determine what it is about stating *this* truth that makes one a valued public figure.[18]

Malcolm asserts, amid a long analysis of the relationship between white liberals, the civil rights movement, and the oppression of black people,

> I'm telling it like it *is*! You *never* have to worry about me biting my tongue if something I know as truth is on my mind. Raw, naked truth exchanged between the black man and the white man is what a whole lot more of is needed in this country – to clear the air of the racial mirages, clichés, and lies this country's very atmosphere has been filled with for four hundred years.[19]

Clearly, telling it like it is, central to the book's rhetoric, is understood to be focused around "clearing the racial air." That is, the importance of the truth of Malcolm X's voice depends on the system of racial histories and events about which people do not talk. (*The Souls of Black Folk* opens: "Between me and the other world there is an ever unasked question... I seldom answer a word."[20]) X himself only asserts this truthfulness in contexts where he is making racial claims in particular: *truth is a matter of speaking frankly about race.* Thus, in his narrative voice, the truth comes up as follows: "The Honorable Elijah Muhammad is the first black leader among us with the *courage* to tell us – out here in public – something which when you begin to think of it back in your homes, you will realize we black people have been *living* with... Our *enemy* is the white man."[21] In prison, X emphasizes, he could not wait to spread *this* truth widely, and – importantly, for the meaning of trust – to tell it directly to white men.[22] Nor is it only himself, or even only black men, who can be credited with racial honesty in X's narrative: "Goldwater as a man, I respected for speaking out his true convictions – something rarely done in politics today. He wasn't whispering to racists and smiling at integrationists. I felt Goldwater wouldn't have risked his unpopular stand without conviction. He flatly told black men he wasn't for them."[23] Truth is not content, but form: the willingness to say directly to the other "I do not like you," whenever it is the case.

Where truth is the articulation of psychological positions, rather than the representation of an external world, it also is liberated from the category of the ethical: the first assertion that Malcolm is a truth teller in the text is "old Mrs. Adcock... was the one who... would tell me something I remembered a long time: 'Malcolm, there's one thing I like about you. You're no good, but you don't try to hide it. You are not a hypocrite.'"[24] Malcolm requires this fact, that he is no good and he will tell you about it, to center further claims at the opening and closing of the hustling sections that the reader should believe everything he has to say: at the moment of his first conk, by his own account his "first really big step toward self-degradation," he states that "when I say all of this I'm talking first of all about myself"; at the moment he describes the crime that put him in jail, he states, "I want to say before I go on that I have never previously told anyone my sordid past in detail . . . But people are always speculating – why am I as I am? To understand that of any person, his whole life, from birth must be reviewed."[25] The way you know he is telling the truth about race, X suggests, rests on the revelation of himself, in the past, as the most unreliable of people: a hustler, a liar, a gambler, and a violent criminal. And this, in turn, relies on the paradox of the "hustling society's first rule": "you never trusted anyone outside of your own close-mouthed circle, and you selected with time and care before you made any intimates even among these."[26] The identitarian rhetoric of the book, inasmuch as it is addressed to an audience of potential political allies, comes to this: trust me because I represent your (actual or potential) untrustworthiness. I have known it and lived it.

The content of this hustling society is not irrelevant for reasons that relate to X's analysis of America as the world's hustler. First, hustling is something that one must *learn*, explicitly: even in its earliest and perhaps most legitimate form, shining shoes, there's a specific set of ways that one must degrade oneself to make money, as X learns working his first ballroom in Boston:

> While you shined shoes, I learned, you also kept watch on customers inside, leaving the urinals. You darted over and offered a small white hand towel. "A lot of cats who ain't planning to wash their hands, sometimes you can run up with a towel and shame them" [, Freddie said.] Your towels are really your best hustle in here. Cost you a penny apiece to launder – you always get at least a nickel tip.[27]

This is a tiny example, but the narrative includes pages upon pages of detailed descriptions about how different hustles – pimping, numbers running, drug dealing – work, and how Malcolm learned how they work. These examples are brought together around a very specific sort of regret:

> Many times since, I have thought about it, and what it meant. In one sense, we were huddled in there, bonded together in seeking security and warmth and comfort from each other and we didn't know it. All of us – who might have probed space, or cured cancer, or built industries – were, instead, black victims of the white man's social system.[28]

This regret can be expressed at a great level of specificity: if only the numbers runners "had lived in another kind of society, their exceptional mathematical talents might have been better used."[29] Finally, the hustlers become the key to social movements for non-bourgeois black people because they are the only truly dangerous people in the black community, according to Malcolm, the only people who really disrespect the white power structure and thus the ones just ambitious enough to make anything happen.[30]

For all that, when X describes himself as a member of the hustling society he stresses two major characteristics: his beastliness and his servility to white people, the people with the real money. The beast metaphor should remind us that when X equates Islam, telling the truth, and "becoming a man" he is at least initially opposing these things to hustling, lying, and being an animal – none of which are yet gender specific. X states:

> I was a true hustler – uneducated, unskilled at anything honorable, and I considered myself nervy and cunning enough to live by my wits, exploiting any prey that presented itself. I would risk just about anything.
> ... As is the case in any jungle, the hustler's every waking hour is lived with both the practical and the subconscious knowledge that if he ever relaxes, if he ever slows down, the other hungry, restless foxes, ferrets, wolves, and vultures out there with him won't hesitate to make him their prey.[31]

The problem here is that the form of the rebellion that was, in his mind, to set him free psychically from the patronage of the white society instead led him to forms of behavior that are in fact demanded by that society – he is a mascot, an animal, at a new level. Shoeshining is still treating white people as your master, and the real profits in the numbers industry go to the white hustlers in "legitimate" banks who put up the money.

Malcolm's class identity, out of which the trustworthy ex-hustler develops, emerges out of an orthodox Americanist contradiction, the internal tension of the poor boy striving amid an attraction to the excitement of the life of "the people." The push for uplift is created not only by X's relative success in school from an early age, and the fact that his mother was college educated, but also as a result of moving to Boston to live with his sister Ella, in order to get away from the scenes of his earliest crimes. In this sense, we must remember that the class expectations of X's family are not unambiguous in the least – though poor, they attempt to achieve middle class status. The growth of X's commitment to the hustle, narrated in six short pages, is far more a choice among entrepreneurial options than it might have been for someone whose family history was more unambiguously proletarian. He depicts himself, a sixteen-year old midwestern transplant, wandering the streets of Boston, as follows:

> I went gawking around the neighborhood [where Ella lived] . . . I saw those Roxbury Negroes acting and living differently from any black people I'd ever dreamed of in my life. This was the snooty black neighborhood; they called themselves the "Four Hundred" and looked down their noses at the Negroes of the ghetto, of so-called "town" section where Mary, my other sister, lived.
>
> I'd guess that eight out of ten of the Hill Negroes of Roxbury, despite the impressive-sounding job titles they affected, actually worked as menials and servants. "He's in banking," or "He's in securities." It sounded as though they were discussing a Rockefeller or a Mellon – and not some gray-headed, dignity-posturing bank janitor, or bond-house messenger.
>
> I didn't want to disappoint or upset Ella, but despite her advice, I began going down into the town ghetto section. That world of grocery stores, walk-up flats, cheap restaurants, pool-rooms, bars, storefront churches, and pawnshops seemed to hold a natural lure for me.
>
> Not only was this part of Roxbury much more exciting, but I felt more relaxed among Negroes who were being their natural selves and not putting on airs.[32]

The key point to be made about this depiction is that, in practical terms, the distinction between the "bourgeois" and "working class" societies, both of which X will ultimately find objectionable, is not objective economic class (in the sense of relationship to the means of production), but relationship to the means of reproduction of the cultural and caste systems – that is, those whose daily lives and aspirations are (at whatever level) integrated, and those whose daily lives are not. For the younger Malcolm Little, and no doubt many poor blacks with some choices, this is rearticulated as the meaning of class: wage laborers (the marxist working class) are the "bourgeois," while hustlers (a subgroup of the marxist petty bourgeois) are "the people." For readings of the *Autobiography* that stop there, like Robin Kelley's, rather than following the political logic of the rest of X's life, X as hustler comes to stand in for "the black working class," and the "essentialist" NOI becomes other to "the working class." Such readings are no more desirable than those which defend the NOI on theological grounds.[33]

The NOI, and not Ella, is able to save X from the hustling life (and more specifically, prison, as I will discuss below) precisely because it offers reasons for adopting a nonhustling perspective that do not imply a change in Malcolm Little's phantasmatic class identification, and that, unlike either the mascot narrative or the hustling narrative, permit him to "be a man" by becoming *black*. The NOI, in this account, is made up of people with whom hustlers are able, in specific, to identify (whether or not they adopt the entire narrative of the religion). And by his own account, X's subsequent emergence as a "leader" is based on the fact that he could speak to the largest cross-section of black working class people, regardless of their position as employees or servants of white people or as independent and addicted hustlers who know his relationship to the game and respect him for it.

Finally, the hustling world's greatest psychological characteristic, and the one which, perhaps surprisingly, links class identification to humanism in the text, is violence. Frantz Fanon is well-known for the argument that the overcoming of the psychological debility of blackness in a racially split society requires the infliction of violence upon the oppressor, symbolically if possible, bodily if not. Malcolm's text sets up this argument in practical terms: the hustler "is internally restrained by nothing. He has no religion, no concept of morality . . . To survive, he is out there constantly praying on others"; he is therefore "actually the most dangerous black man in America."[34] As in Fanon's text, although through a slightly different argument, violence itself becomes an expression of *being human*: "if white people were attacked by Negroes – if the forces of law prove unable, or inadequate, or reluctant to protect those white from those Negroes – then those white people should protect and defend themselves from those Negroes, using arms if necessary. And I feel that when the law fails to protect Negroes from whites' attack, then those Negroes should use arms, if necessary, to defend themselves."[35] That they do this, is, in this argument, the *prerequisite* for obtaining respect as human beings: perhaps, X claims, if Negroes start defending themselves, white people will then start listening to Martin Luther King, and hasten the process of integration for those who want it.[36] The threat of violence is, then, the ultimate test of "truth" in the meaning it is given here.

Narrative 2: Sexuality and purity

That black humanism is defined by the institutionalization of violence is, then, the first stage of the argument leading back to gender
and patriarchy in X's text. This is not because women cannot engage
in violence – women do engage in a minority of the violence in the
text, and at the end of his life (specifically in his speeches) Malcolm X
publicly lauds specific women revolutionaries, in Cuba, Algeria, and
Mississippi. It is, however, because large portions of the text – those
where the narrative was constructed prior to 1964 – are explicitly
patriarchal, and because those moments of the text which permit the
questioning of patriarchy still do not repudiate it, that the black
working class male is the symbol and agent of a (psychical or bodily)
violence which remains patriarchal.[37]

Eugene Wolfenstein, Hilton Als, and Jan Carew have all theorized,
from radically different points of view, the centrality of X's mother,
Louise Little, an educated, near white West Indian woman, to the
construction of gender, family, and psychic community in the *Autobiography*.[38] Wolfenstein and Carew, in different ways, use Mrs. Little as
a figure of psychic and family connection and ongoing love: for
Wolfenstein this love is manifest, paradoxically, by Louise's abuse of
Malcolm as a child, ostensibly because his relatively light skin too
much resembled her own, while for Carew her figure is especially
useful for stressing the Pan-African origins of Malcolm's experience.
Als, by contrast, relates Louise Little as the text's Bertha Mason figure –
she is a West Indian mulatto who goes mad and is abandoned by her
family – suggesting the usefulness of the madwoman in the attic to
black nationalist patriarchy. Louise Little is, in fact, all of these things:
there is no contradiction between these positions when the narrative is
read from the point of view that it juxtaposes an NOI subjectivity and a
post-NOI subjectivity, one vicious, the other clearly sympathetic and
outraged at the abuse done to the mother. Even if Louise is not given
her due in the *Autobiography* – it is, for example, known that she was
every bit as much a Garveyist as her husband, yet X portrays his own
Garveyist legacy as of his father's line – her presence cannot be
summed up as the reflection of Malcolm's misogyny, if we read the
book as a whole. At very least, X is unambiguous that the combination
of grinding poverty and the racist white state destroyed Louise Little –
that is, while the narrative does not construct her as agent, it also, in the
end, constructs her as a specifically sympathetic victim, which is not
fundamentally different from the way it constructs most black men.

More significantly, reconsideration of his mother is in every way central to the process of writing of the book to begin with: Haley's afterword is clear that reflection on his mother's experience is the circumstance that permits him to tell his autobiography. After months of trying to get him to start talking, and two hours into a frustrating interview, Haley asked X, "I wonder if you'd tell me something about your mother?"

> Slowly, Malcolm X began to talk, now walking in a tight circle. "She was always standing over the stove, trying to stretch whatever we had to eat. We stayed so hungry that we were dizzy..." And he kept on talking until dawn, so tired that the big feet would often almost stumble in their pacing. From this stream of consciousness reminiscing I finally got out of him the foundation for this book's beginning chapters... After that night, he never again hesitated to tell me even the most intimate details of his personal life, over the next two years. His talking about his mother triggered something.[39]

At the time Haley is interviewing him, X has rarely seen his mother since she was institutionalized by the state, after the forcible break-up of her family, twenty-six years earlier. His last visit to her, the main narrative states, was in 1952, after his release from prison, and he won't go back because doing so "could make me a very vicious and dangerous person."[40] Yet, Haley reports in the epilogue, after Malcolm began to talk about his mother, he became intensely guilty about the fact that she was institutionalized, and, with the help of several siblings, he gets her out. He states: "Ever since we discussed my mother, I've been thinking about her. I realized that I had blocked her out of my mind – it was just unpleasant to think about her having been ... in that mental hospital."[41] It is also, of course, during this period of narrating the book to Haley that X breaks with Elijah Muhammad and the NOI. Thus, taking into account the afterword, the narrative connects the patriarchal family, with the father as the strong, dark black man who dies violently with the allegiance to Elijah Muhammad as father figure in the family which makes up the NOI. Releasing the mother – confronting guilt over her, and re-evaluating her importance in his life, is a direct precursor to his reconsideration of Elijah as patriarch. In turn, this produces the *plausibility* that X's narration could be rewritten with respect to gender. For all that, since *this* text never fully supersedes the NOI narrative with the internationalist narrative, merely leaving them to collide as competing versions, likewise both the misogynist and the emerging nonpatriarchal narratives appear together, with the misogynist one getting the bulk of the space in the *book*. Plausible or not, Malcolm X – less Alex Haley – did not produce this alternative narrative in the time he had left alive.

In chapter four I discussed some of the origins of the theory of cross-racial sexual desire as it appears in the texts of Ida B. Wells Barnett, James Weldon Johnson, and Walter White. The *Autobiography* confirms that interracial sex was a topic of conversation and analysis among hustlers in the 1940s, and the sense of transgression it brought was combined with, on the one hand, its use in the maintenance of white supremacy, and on the other, the misogyny with which he practiced it. First of all, working close to prostitutes, X claims, taught him who was "responsible" for male immorality: "domineering, complaining, demanding wives who had just about psychologically castrated their husbands," in this case both black and white. "More wives," he argues, "could keep their husbands if they realized their greatest urge is *to be men*."[42] In absolute contradiction to this, X continues that "most men, the prostitutes felt, were too easy to push around . . . The prostitutes said that most men needed to know what the pimps knew. A woman should occasionally be babied enough to show that the man had affection, but beyond that she should be treated firmly. These tough women said that it worked with *them*."[43] It seems that women don't want to let their men be men, which should be fine, since the men don't know how to be men anyway, but instead the men have to go to "tough" (in some way that is not explained) women, whose service, for which they are paid, is that they make men believe they are "letting men be men."

The instability in gendering produced by a society in which only prostitutes know how to perform this complicated dance also leads to interracial sex – the instability of race. On the one hand, Negro prostitutes "catered to monied white people's weird sexual tastes,"[44] while on the other, white women, in search of real men, and black men, in search of real women, seek out each other, without financial exchange, since this form of desire serves mutual needs for the formation of properly gendered couples.[45] X's own sexual desire for a white woman, Sophia, he can control, is thus simultaneously the desire for his light-skinned mother, and also the desire to do to that white mother figure what the (white) state has done to his actual mother. The state sends his mother to an institution for the insane; X leads Sophia to prison. The NOI theology, demanding love for dark skin, especially on the part of light-skinned blacks, provides X with a space for breaking this pattern. In such a sexual economy, the need to avoid "perversion" (the economy of which is based in Harlem, we must remember, because of the conjunction of white supremacy and sexual hypocrisy) and to promote love of blackness (which doesn't exist among *anyone* – white women want men, not blackness) can be comprehended. Breaking away from the hustling life must, therefore, not only mean breaking away from white women, but learning, as X insists, to "respect" black women. Likewise, it means demanding white respect of black women, which is not integration: "the white man's 'integrating' with black women has already changed the complexion and characteristics of the black race in America."[46] On the one hand, black men need to desire black women; on the other, such unilateral "respect" means respect for her *in her proper place*, where she can be "protected" – in the family.[47] If the hustler disrespects women as such, the patriarch respects "true love," which only Islam understands: "The Western 'love' concept, you take it apart, it really is lust." The "core" of true love, by contrast, is that "the true nature of man is to be strong, and a woman's true nature is to be weak, and while a man must at all times respect his women, at the same time he needs to understand that he must control her if he expects to get her respect."[48] Finally, if the hustling code is to trust no one and respect no life, the NOI code is to respect properly constituted authority, and to trust the word of Elijah Muhammad (and all who uphold his word) absolutely. X, who does not possess a name, is always wife to Muhammad's husband.

X did not, before he was shot, become broadly critical of this patriarchal structure, or its application to authoritarian political structure more widely, a fact with implications for his nationalism even at its very best. Even in the last year of his life Malcolm admires the well-orderedness of the right-wing Saudi monarchy and admires Ghanaian president Kwame Nkrumah not only for his social politics but for his security guards, which are a symbol of "respect for independent black men."[49] I want to mention two particular significances to this attachment to authority in terms of the social meaning of the text. First, the maintenance of this authoritarian stance creates a mystified version of what a family is. In saying this I am interested in being neither "anti-family" or "pro-family" as these positions are presently understood in the US. By his own account, Malcolm goes through an excruciatingly painful "divorce" from Elijah Muhammad, and of course it is probable that the Nation of Islam was directly responsible for his murder, a fact, if there ever was one, consistent with the way patriarchal families operate when the second in command leaves.[50] Since Muhammad had provided Malcolm with an idealized family structure which could replace the collapsed family structure of Malcolm's own upbringing, the psychic collapse and reconfiguration that resulted from the loss of this ideal community was once again total. The problem, which nothing in the narrative ever addresses, is not that families are not productive of "identity" or that community identifications do not share certain structures with family identifications – any psychoanalysis requires both these assumptions – but that for this very reason families and communities contain sharp internal tensions that often lead to destructive violence. That is to say, X's vision of blackness/family/community as locations of identity was not so much wrong with regard to the determinations of race, as it was naive in presuming that such socially determined identity leads to a peaceful community, rather than a divided one.

The second problem is that authority, even though it can be occupied by specific women at the end of the narrative, is always symbolized or corporatized by men. Dyson argues, reasonably, that the most unfortunate aspect of black nationalism's adoption of X in recent times has been the way that his image leads to an emphasis on men;[51] I would suggest that this is hardly because black women are invisible in the *Autobiography* – indeed, they are all over, and there are several examples of respect for them as political and religious individuals. If you are teaching the book, there is no difficulty at all reading Ella as a powerful "masculine" woman, given a surprisingly respectful presence even against the grain of the whole narrative. However, for women to occupy the space of authority as women would require an entirely new narrative, not local adjustments. It would start with the mother as a fully realized human being, and it would finally reject monarchism its Islamic guise, including in its manifestations in post-colonial Africa.

Narrative 3: From color to nation

That the Little family is deeply involved in the Garvey movement is a centrally important feature of the opening of the *Autobiography*.[52] The opening paragraphs describe the Little family being run out of their home in Omaha by Ku Klux Klan riders as a result of the Reverend Earl Little's Garveyist preaching; X states that the local white supremacists were threatened by Garvey's teaching that Negroes must "become independent of the white man."[53] Additionally,

X claims Garvey's legacy explicitly by referring to UNIA meetings he attended and by speaking of the pride he took in seeing Garvey's photograph, "a big black man dressed in a dazzling uniform with gold braid on it," and in hearing that he "had black followers not only in the United States but all around the world."[54] The specific rhetoric of black aristocracy present in the political structure of Garveyism is reproduced in specific in the NOI and holds great attraction for X, certainly forming part of his lasting desire for uniformed black men. Yet even after Earl Little dies, according to X as a result of his political activities,[55] Garveyists continued to visit the house (now in Lansing, Michigan) to talk to his mother, which – though this is not in the autobiography – reverberates with Jan Carew's suggestion that Louise Little, a light-skinned West Indian woman who explicitly chose black identification, was a political activist in her own right.[56] The location of these references to Garvey amid a narrative of a family experiencing political repression at the start of the *Autobiography* creates the context in which the later conversion of nearly all of the Little family to one or another nationalist framework is shown as an example of family continuity. Only the specific journey X takes – via prison – is exceptional within his family.

Elijah Muhammad's mythological history of race follows from the same psychological necessity as Garvey's version of black pride, going it one better by defining whiteness as the poor reflection of blackness, thus positioning whites at the center of the "problem" of race.[57] For X, pondering it in his prison cell, "the white man is the devil" just makes sense: upon hearing this phrase, "my mind was involuntarily flashing across the entire spectrum of white people I had ever known," trying out all the hardest test cases – the hardest of which is actually that of a Jewish hustler who had let him in on a substantial hustle, for no obviously selfish reason. Reginald, his brother convinces Malcolm that Hymie is no exception by explaining capitalist logic as white logic: "What is it if I let you make five hundred dollars to let me make ten thousand dollars."[58] Through the entire narrative X defends the value of the provocation in this exact phrase:

> When [a fellow inmate] was ripe – and I could tell – then away from the rest, I'd drop it on him, what Mr. Muhammad taught: "the white man is the devil."
>
> That would shock many of them – until they started thinking about it.
>
> I think that an objective reader may see how when I heard "the

white man is the devil," when I played back what had been my own experiences, it was inevitable that I would respond positively.[59]

What is taking hold, at this historical moment, and via a phrase more shocking than substantial, is the thinking through of the concept "white" by a class of people who have previously felt constrained from such thinking through. The mere process of thinking whiteness as negative to blackness is central to the ability to conceive critically of white supremacy as such. It is simultaneously important, then, that the notion be thought systematically – "unless we call one white man, by name, a 'devil' ... we are speaking of the *collective* white man's *historical* record" – but simultaneously that no individual be allowed to not think the proposition through, since each black individual is damaged, and each white individual is a beneficiary of this process.[60]

As soon as X adopts this position on whiteness, in prison, he recognizes the necessity of being able to justify it in sophisticated ways, and spends long hours in the library making himself into an organic intellectual. He learns, in a letter, the NOI story of the historical creation of the white man: the evil scientist, Mr. Yacub, creates chaos within the earthly paradise that is Mecca by learning how to create a white race of people from black stock. The brilliance of the story lies in its elaboration of what Harryette Mullen refers to as the necessity of blackness in the production of whiteness.[61] While the theology is Elijah Muhammad's, it is X who read Gregor Mendel while in prison in order to achieve a scientific understanding of how this could have happened, and thus elaborated the story greatly:

> From his studies, the big head scientist knew that black men contained two germs, black and brown. He knew that the brown germ stayed dormant as, being the lighter of the two germs, it was the weaker. Mr. Yacub, to upset the law of nature, conceived the idea of employing what we today know as the recessive genes structure, to separate from each other the two germs, black and brown, and then grafting the brown germ to progressively lighter, weaker stages. The humans resulting, he knew, would be, as they became lighter, and weaker, progressively also more susceptible to wickedness and evil. And in this way finally he would achieve the intended bleached-out white race of devils.[62]

X's pre-NOI experiences with whites were not, as far as one can tell from the text, unusually bad or debilitating; they mostly amounted to his being patronized at school and as a servant at various odd jobs – in other words, being treated typically within a white supremacist situation.[63] It is not until the moment of the conversion that Malcolm fully realizes that his escape to the hustling life, identified as black and anti-bourgeois, only got him further in. After he gets himself out of direct service work, the relatively few white people he interacts with are hustlers like himself; they are, however, the bigger and more powerful hustlers, the ones with capital to invest and really make a lot of money on the scene; they are the ones who call the shots. For all this, the final reason that positing the white man as devil works psychologically is because Malcolm is able to use the notion to displace his own set of choices, his own responsibility for hustling, onto the larger structure of the society, which, he discovers, is itself a *hustling society:* the set of relationships which have allowed him to use others to his own benefit have, in a far more dramatic sense, been using him. Only by doing this is X able to think of his previous activity not as rebellious toward whiteness, but as a black reflection of it; and he attempts to articulate what he takes to be a purer, blacker form of existence. All forms of relationship to white people are then corrupt, and the way to remake himself is to extricate himself from contact with white people to the greatest extent possible. His ability to change requires externalizing the source of evil, calling it white; coming to grips with the part of the evil that is internal to black cultures is simply not thinkable at this stage of X's narrative.[64]

If the narrative of black originality and authenticity then becomes a political strategy which permits the reinvention of self for a large number of black people at a determinate historical moment, it is important to remember that it is X who not only makes Muhammad's narration "scientific," but also he who – against its creator's intentions – politicizes it, turning it from a myth to an understanding of history with political consequences. What kind of mass political appeal is available, for the first time, through this particular rethinking of race? First, this political appeal is always framed as a class appeal: "You have tilled his fields! Cooked his food! Washed his clothes! You have cared for his wife and children when he was away. In many cases, you have even suckled him at your *breast*! You have been far and away better Christians than this slavemaster who *taught* you Christianity." This identity politics is quite specific, that is, addressed to a collective you who actually are *presently* serving white employers, most likely in the personal service roles most often reserved for African Americans, though possibly in industrial or even agricultural roles. He then states, "you have sweated blood to help

156

him build a country so rich that he can today afford to give away millions." And what is the specific offense that accrues from this argument, according to X? It is not that black workers don't get their share of the profits, but that "this white man has not got it in him to find the human *decency* ... to recognize us ... the black people who have done so much for him, as fellow human beings."[65] What is specific to black people, that makes their problems distinct from those of other *labor*, is precisely the dynamics of recognition. It is in this context that X can claim that white people have no right to ask integration of *us*, and it is merely a responsibility of whiteness – the premise, in the end, on which he will ask for white solidarity – that white men "subsidize a separate state," where the problem of recognition will not be an issue.[66] This will not happen, however, because the white man cannot face his crime: "every time he sees your face, he sees a mirror of his crime – and his guilty conscience can't bear to face it!"[67]

Finally, the most significant aspect of the turn toward politics and away from theology is that "white society" is no longer understood only as racial, but as national: white society becomes "America." This, in turn, contributes to the systemic critique rather than the critique of individual whites, since regardless of the individual agent, the workings of this materially constituted nation, "America," will produce white supremacist results; opposition to America is then opposition to white supremacy – and this opposition, X comes to see in 1964, is not necessarily "racial." Still, he does not revise his usage of the terms "white" and "black" as racial markers, precisely because what is at stake after 400 years of misrecognition in America, the hustling society, is not merely new recognitions, but a politics constructed outside the ideologm "America." Black politics must literally be un-American.

One peculiarity of the Nation of Islam is that, from the point of view of inventing and articulating international identitarian connections, it ties its followers to two related, but different, bodies: Africa, as the home of blackness, and the Middle East, as the home of Islam. Such "ties" are, for most members of the NOI, phantasmatic (as are the ties of most white Americans to Europe), but as with numerous black intellectuals before him, they become concretized through travel and study, until his final political organization, the Organization of African-American Unity (OAAU), was an attempt to model a US-based organization after the Organization of African Unity (OAU).[68] Meanwhile, he leaves the United States to go on the hadj to

Mecca and attempts to affiliate with orthodox Islam, and he finds himself not in black Africa but in a space that he perceives as containing multiracial harmony under the sign of truly universalist religion. In this context, within the autobiography he assigns to Islam, as such, the role of humanist philosophy:

> America needs to understand Islam, because this is the one religion that erases from its society the race problem. Throughout my travels in the Muslim world, I have met, talked to, and even eaten with people who in America would have been considered "white" – but the "white" attitude was removed from their minds by the religion of Islam. I have never before seen *sincere* and *true* brotherhood practiced by all colors together, irrespective of their color.[69]

Color-blindness as such is available through Islam, and, he suspects, through no other institutional mechanism. The family of religion, and the possibility of religious identification, has remained the only solution to political problems.

The large structure of the argument, at this point, is that African Americans can change themselves only through identification with blackness, and can change America only through solidarity and economic relations with Africa and the Middle East. Meanwhile, all people might look to Islam for the plausibility of an interracial solidarity which does not, as yet, exist, in the US. For African Americans, a commitment to internationalism rather than commitment to America is therefore a prerequisite of political leadership: "It was there in the Holy Land, and later in Africa, that I formed a conviction which I have had ever since – that a topmost prerequisite for any Negro leader in America ought to be extensive traveling in the nonwhite lands on this earth, and the travel should include many conferences with the ranking men of those lands."[70] For white Americans, a commitment to anti-racism means a commitment to Islam and/or Africa and/or the third world as such: if black people have spent too much energy identifying with America, *so have white people*. White Muslims have never had this problem. The consequence is that this version of anti-racist narrative *never becomes an integrationist narrative under the sign of "America."* In Africa X is able to agree with an "American white ambassador" that "American society makes it next to impossible for humans to meet in America and not be conscious of their color differences."[71] In this context X can continue to advocate separate black and white organizing in the US, and to strictly reserve interracial interaction for conditions that have been established autonomously of the determinations of "American society." At this point X has found the difficult path back to the politics of anti-colonial third worldism advocated by the late Du Bois and Robeson, which, as we have seen, was organic to the black movements of the 1930s and which was suppressed by the Cold War.[72]

Narrative 4: Of the training of black men

For all these arguments, finally, X matters – or is it merely the narrative form of this autobiography that matters? – because of his ability to *change*, and to do so in ways that illustrate the simultaneity of personal redemption and social change. One of the *Autobiography's* most cited passages, coming at the moment of the final conversion, to internationalism from the NOI, is "there was precedent in my life for this... My life had been a chronology of – *changes*."[73] Thus in this fourth, and last narrative of the themes in the *Autobiography*, I return to the problematic of personal transformation as it speaks to the contemporary formation of black male gender in the US educational apparatus, which is by no means the same as "in school." Prison is the key social institution through which black American men have been articulated for at least the last two decades.[74] If *The Autobiography of Malcolm X* did not quite invent the prison narrative as we know it, it nevertheless centered the prison experience, for the first time, as educational experience. George Jackson, John Edgar Wideman, Nathan McCall, Sonyika Shakur: the list of more recent black male autobiographers for whom prison is an educational institution is terrifyingly large, much larger than the names I've listed here. This is not even to mention rappers.

"School" has several referents within *The Autobiography of Malcolm X*, only the first of which is that state institution in which the ostensible purpose is to impart knowledge, and the unstated purpose is to reproduce the specific forms of social stratification. Indeed, X points to the integrated school as an early location where he was racialized – that is, the place where a color difference implicit in the single race home becomes explicit in the mixed race school. The state institution is thus directly implicated in the production of race. Being one of the few African Americans in a majority white school meant being called "'nigger' and 'darkie' and 'Rastus' so much that we thought those were our natural names. But [the white kids] didn't think of it as an insult; it was just the way they thought about us."[75] In this context, young Malcolm's 'adoption' by a white family in an all-white rural area following his mother's institutionalization, and his acceptance as the school 'mascot', are the educational process itself. Unfortunately, Malcolm Little, as an unusually smart kid, was sufficiently interested in learning that he didn't fully internalize this for an extended period of time. Because of this, more explicit mechanisms are necessary: a middle school English teacher, Mr. Ostrowski, tells him that being a lawyer is "no realistic goal for a nigger... Why don't you plan on carpentry?"[76] What matters in X's presentation of this tale, which is no doubt a distillation of multiple autobiographical events for dramatic purposes rather than a relay of literal truth, is that while Malcolm Little stops looking to school as a place for learning, he continues to seek the locations of learning – indeed, *schools* – which, unlike the public school, are there to train him. Thus within ten pages – a matter of months in the text – when Malcolm has moved to Boston and begun to shine shoes for money, the verb "to school" appears where the noun has disappeared:

> "Man you sure schooled me!" I said, and he laughed and knew what I meant. It hadn't taken me long on the job to find out that Freddie had done less shoeshining and towel-hustling than selling liquor and reefers, and putting white "johns" in touch with Negro whores. I also learned that white girls always flocked to the Negro dances.[77]

Everything about the content of the *Autobiography* I have discussed until now depends on precisely this language of education for its glue and continuity; every significant move in his life – not only the large-scale conversions, but also changing jobs or moving to New York, is redescribed the way Small's Paradise Bar is – as an "educational situation."[78] Thus the techniques of education in this narrative demand a materialist reading in which the organic intellectual transfers his scholarly pursuits between multiple institutions, seeking the cultural capital necessary to graduate and move on to a teaching position: black man as professor and pedagogue.[79]

It would be precisely wrong to assume that the state provides no educational institutions free of charge to young black men, because to do so would be to ignore the most significant educational institution in the text: prison. The specific meaning of prison in this text is *not* that it is the place of his oppression – in that sense, all America is a prison already – but rather that it is that place where a large number of black men are permitted to get together and exchange information and ideas. Upon entering, X quickly takes an interest in Bimbi, an intellectual who expounds on Thoreau and tells Malcolm that he "has

some brains" and "should take advantage of the prison correspondence courses."[80] When several members of his family convert to the
Nation of Islam after Malcolm is imprisoned, the foundations which
have already been laid through these conversations with Bimbi, his
enrollment in correspondence classes, and the excellent prison library
permit not only the conversion, but the passion in which Malcolm
begins religious study.

Precisely because prison affords both the time, and the level of
concrete day to day oppression, to make him come to grips with his
lack of a developed self, small acts of will are magnified many times.
For example, when first told not to eat pork by a brother on the
outside who has recently joined the Nation of Islam, Malcolm tries to
imagine the kind of scam this represents, and how it would perhaps
get him out of prison sooner. But, however insignificant it seems, the
practical experience of not eating pork "made me proud, in some odd
way [since] one of the universal images of the Negro ... was that he
couldn't do without pork."[81] In other words, the adoption of simple
rules of behavior which would create a sense of mental agility was
intrinsic to the sort of psychic change he needed to go through, and
was a necessary part of the larger transformation from animal to man,
criminal to religious activist. When the rest of the NOI theology was
introduced to him in a subsequent letter, given the sense of personal
strength he had developed and the time to think, the adoption of the
entire religion becomes possible.

Once having chosen to become a Muslim, Malcolm becomes active
and hardworking: "I have never been more busy in my entire life."[82]
X gets a job in the library, and sets out to become what is, by this
point, a stock figure in African-American narrations about prison –
the prison intellectual, who fills his time writing, studying law, and
honing his argumentative and rhetorical skills with other prison
intellectuals. In the sort of passage that mainstream educators dream
of, X waxes about his enlightenment:

> I have often reflected about the new vistas that reading opened
> to me. I knew right there in prison that reading had changed
> forever the course of my life. As I see it today, the ability to read
> awoke inside me some long dormant craving to be mentally
> alive. I certainly wasn't seeking any degree. My homemade
> education gave me, with every additional book that I read, a
> little more sensitivity to the deafness, dumbness, and blindness
> that was afflicting the black race in America.[83]

While prison is the state apparatus which provides the site of X's education, it is important that, since the state doesn't make any pretense that it is a "reformatory" (as it does with inmates under eighteen), X's religious institution (the NOI), provides the ideological narrative into which X is interpolated. With the state making no attempt to provide its own framework, the religion structures his learning unchallenged. What occurs is a transfer of authority: as with the move from mascot to hustler, where a self-denying recognition of racist white authority is replaced by the peer authority of a more senior hustler, here the authority of hustlers is replaced with that of Elijah Muhammad, a father figure who seems to offer both ego-fulfillment and the possibility of longer-term intellectual development. Prison has afforded the institutional conditions for this transfer of authority; it has not yet offered the material conditions necessary to the critique of all metaphysical authority, the moment toward the end of the book when X "realize[s] how very dangerous it is for people to hold any human being in such esteem." It takes twelve more years for this last transfer of authority, to "truth, no matter who tells it," because there is *no already existing institution through which it can take place*.[84] Thus Malcolm's final conversion is to the *potential* for a revolutionary social movement in the US, a potential which exists because of events external to X's narrative – the civil rights movement and third world decolonization in specific. Engagement with social and political movements, something not available to all people at all times, is the materially necessary condition for Malcolm X to surface as neither criminal nor fundamentalist.

I have remarked several times that X is not merely a student in the institutions described in the *Autobiography*, but always insists on his role as a pedagogue; this provides the other great theme that helps to explain why he is now so easily identified as an authority figure. Upon his conversion, in prison, X "had to start telling the white man about himself to his face"; upon his release from jail and membership in the Detroit Mosque, he immediately becomes concerned that there is insufficient recruitment and proselytization going on;

> It had become clear to me that Mr. Muhammad needed ministers to spread his teachings, to establish more temples . . .
> My decision came relatively quickly. I have always been an activist, and my personal chemistry perhaps made me reach more quickly than most ministers in the Nation of Islam.[85]

One of X's chief traits throughout is that of the man who aspires to achieve pedagogical authority regardless of his specific social situation. Clearly, a full reading to the end of the text, where X denounces all authority figures and asserts the importance of making one's own way to truth, brings about the oldest of pedagogical paradoxes, well-known to the Nietzschean text: if you follow my precepts, you will not follow me. Political leadership – the desire to make it possible for more people to attain anti-racist and anti-imperialist stances, requires Malcolm X to assert certain difficult to arrive at truths, in the knowledge that his is becoming, in the mid-1960s, a commonly held structure of feeling; but reliance on Malcolm X's assertions for one's understanding of truth means giving away the authority of one's own blackness. X has truly become an intellectual; you can tell by the fact that he discovers himself within this particular paradox, which he cannot go beyond.

The Autobiography of Malcolm X is a radical book about psychological process, though for all the effort is expends it still never gets quite where many of us wish it would. If academic intellectuals reject it because it doesn't, we refuse to learn the conditions of possibility for such a process to begin with. On the other hand, because the book is so convinced it can teach change through authoritative example, it leaves open the possibility that one of its clearly authoritarian voices will remain authoritative. Deirdre Bailey states that while practically all young poor African Americans claim X as an authority figure, this claim justifies any action: "They say, 'Hey, Malcolm sold drugs, I sold drugs. He pimped for a living, I had to pimp for a living. He was in jail. I was in jail.'"[86]

If I state that these four narratives are the structure of contemporary black masculinity for those who are its victims, I am not stating that they must, inevitably – or should, as a matter of ethics – settle comfortably within the metaphor of Malcolm X for all time. I merely claim that one necessary condition in the formation of a viable black politics is that something like Malcolm's personal process become available in the institutional spaces where proletarian and sub-proletarian black men live.

7

The political identity "woman" as emergent from the space of Black Power

Malcolm was the supreme black patriarch... The great black father was finally in our midst. But in 1965 black men murdered Malcolm, and with him died the chance for a black patriarchy.
Michele Wallace[1]

Meridian had walked until she wore herself out, and one thought had preoccupied her mind: "The only new thing now," she had said to herself, mumbling it aloud, so that people turned to stare at her, "would be the refusal of Christ to accept crucifixion. King," she had said, turning down a muddy lane, "should have refused. Malcolm, too, should have refused... All saints should walk away. Do their bit, then – just walk away. See Europe, visit Hawaii, become agronomists or raise Dalmatians."
Alice Walker[2]

I want to hold the notion... that movements provoke theoretical moments.
Stuart Hall[3]

Principally, this chapter weaves three specific women's constructions of blackness from the 1970s, in the wake of Malcolm X's manhood. Its central focus is the autobiographical work of Nikki Giovanni and Angela Davis from 1971 and 1974, work that does not name itself "feminist," but suggests the possibilities and limitations for a radical analysis of gender that would be consistent with Black Power's structure of racialization.[4] The form of autonomist feminism that emerges in the late 1970s with the Combahee River Collective, June Jordan (as analyzed in chapter one) and numerous others, I will suggest, emerges in the wake of particular limitations in these two texts. Something like this was suggested initially by Michele Wallace in her *Black Macho and the Myth of the Superwoman*, the third narrative that structures this chapter.[5] Wallace's problematic book, the first book of what

164

might now be called black feminist cultural studies, along with the anthology edited by Barbara Smith, *Home Girls*, which first appeared as an issue of *Conditions* in 1979, will in chapter eight come to represent two often polarized tendencies in the depiction of the intersection of blackness and feminism in the contemporary academy. I will suggest that while the tensions between Smith and Wallace are real, their differences can easily be caricatured by a lack of seriousness in those who fail to read Smith's black feminism as theorized, or Wallace's cultural studies as identitarian.

Up until this point I have placed a tremendous amount of stress on the intellectual history of black men. My reasons for doing so have not been the lack of autobiographies by black women from earlier periods – there are a number I could have written about – nor any sense that black men's autobiographies adequately represent black female subjectivity prior to the 1970s – clearly they do not. Rather, I have claimed that black men's texts have represented "blackness" as an oppositional politics in a deeply hegemonic sense, consistent with the patriarchal relations which have structured the US generally, and its processes of racialization in particular. In this context, what needs to be described is the position of women who attempt, in spite of the hegemonic space of masculine blackness so produced, to write themselves racially.[6] Precisely because media-savvy, urban Black Power in the later 1960s – built on a sense of manhood that emerges from an inadequate assessment of Malcolm X in writers like Baraka and Cleaver – is successful in galvanizing a mass identity movement, it provokes the need in thinking women, and eventually men, to address the interrelation of race and gender in a new way. Certainly it is possible, and for some purposes desirable, to locate the consistencies in the work of black women from Maria Stewart and Anna Julia Cooper to the present; however, for the purposes of my project I am interested in locating the specificity of the emergent women's identity provoked by the Black Power Movement.

Numerous historians of the "second wave" feminist movement have indicated that it was a relative latecomer to the mass movements of the 1960s. I have already recounted how the Cold War political climate destroyed pre-World War II civil rights and left-wing coalitions, making necessary the building of all new post-War groupings and alliances; likewise, the Cold War made for substantive historical discontinuity in struggles for the reconceptualization of gender, with its white suburban nationalism used to enforce a supposedly traditional gendering of the family, pushing women out of the positions in the work force they held both before and during the war.[7] It is important to recognize, as I discussed in chapter five, that the pre-War left was not simply corrupt, but far more complicated and mixed with regard to race than is generally acknowledged; likewise, the history of gender on the left would require a similarly differentiated narrative.[8] What does appear clear is that whereas the impetus for the formation of the New Left was in the overtly racialized Civil Rights movement, its formation included no similar critical understanding of the existence of a corrupt gender system. The ideologies of masculinity that emerged during this time, while not alien to prior movements or narratives, emerged with a virulence that had not previously been seen. Of course, it is necessary to demonstrate that Du Bois was patronizing to black women, that White pretended Wells Barnett didn't exist, and that Robeson's "manhood" is not distant from Malcolm X's; but it is also necessary to remember that Du Bois, White, and Robeson took as a matter of progressive doxa that the fight for women's rights, adequately understood or not, was also their fight as civil rights workers and/or Negro nationalists; and that this assumption disappeared from "black" struggle at the moment that "black manhood" emerged, in some ways usefully, as an issue of gendering in Malcolm X and others. Without this historical narrative as it emerges from the Cold War, one cannot explain why contemporary feminism, unlike earlier feminisms, is so often a response to the left in particular (rather than patriarchy in general) – and why the important contemporary narratives of black women are so often direct responses to previous narratives by black men.

Black Macho and the Myth of the Superwoman makes every mistake a black feminism emerging in such a context might make – it is no surprise that June Jordan, older than Wallace and a veteran of the movements Wallace criticizes, found it "unsubstantiated, self-demeaning [and] ahistorical."[9] Jordan was of course correct that Wallace failed, in 1978, to account for the black women's substantial and death-defying political participation from beginning to end of the 1960s movements. Wallace has, in her recent introduction, stated that her critique of "Black Macho," and the reception afforded her book, should always have been presented in terms of the "problem of representation,"[10] which my discussion interprets as the relationship between social movements, structures of feeling, and identity-producing media, one of which is popular autobiography. If our problem at present is to understand why Malcolm X has remained, in spite of feminist responses, central to the figure of "blackness," we can do worse than follow up on Wallace's identification of Giovanni and Davis as examples of "those few [women] who did manage to exercise some kind of influence" in the Black Power period but "did not concern themselves with the predicament of black women."[11]

I am concerned to demonstrate that Giovanni and Davis each have specific, and certainly too narrow, suggestions about how to assert the location of women in the context of Black Power, and that their suggestions read nicely in contrast to one another. Giovanni's woman is pure subject, proud single welfare mother, interested in the reactions of the individual to and in power; Davis' is pure object produced by the media gaze of global capital, a marxist intellectual who works hard to refuse specificity. Thus, these two women sit at an intersection that this book sets up for minority discourse theory in chapter one: I will demonstrate that Giovanni agrees with Bhabha that in cultural politics we are not "confronted with an ontological problem of being but with the discursive strategy of the moment of interrogation, a moment in which the demand for identification becomes, primarily, a response to other questions of signification and desire, culture and politics ... In place of the symbolic consciousness that gives the sign of identity its integrity and unity, its *depth*, we are faced with a dimension of doubling,"[12] while Davis, student of Adorno in Germany and Marcuse in San Diego, endlessly repeats that "The power of the status quo puts up facades into which our consciousness crashes. It must seek to crash through them. This alone would free the postulate of depth from ideology. Surviving in such resistance is the speculative moment."[13] It is through this contrast that the following analysis most doubles – even while deepening – the contrast between Zora Neale Hurston and Ida Wells Barnett in chapter four.

Black woman poet: subject

Nikki Giovanni is the only writer discussed in this entire book who really appears to believe that the personal is *the* political, and not merely that the personal is, among other things, political. *Gemini*, both an autobiography and a book of essays, is internally, and quite explicitly, inconsistent – the last words of the book are "I really do, I think" – and claims to defy a systematic politics – "the moment you institutionalize a problem you don't intend to solve it."[14] As a result, Giovanni most certainly cannot be said to speak for any particular politics; rather her autobiographical practice itself performs a black and female subjectivity the newness of which, entering the world, "invests the utterance of the 'present' ... with cultural and political value."[15] Giovanni's text therefore reproduces the performativity frequently claimed for *Dust Tracks on the Road*; it does so in a way that demonstrates the inadequacy of a performative politics that proclaims the impossibility of a determinate object.

Giovanni speaks racialization, the entry to "blackness," at a moment when this process is newly unproblematic – a sign that the Black Arts Movement has been successful in producing young artists for whom race is merely inhabited, rather than struggled for or resisted. Thus the essay "On Being Asked What It's Like To Be Black" opens with "I've always known I was colored. When I was a Negro I knew I was colored; now that I'm Black I know which color it is. Any identity crisis I may have has never centered on race."[16] The essay proceeds anecdotally with the life story of Giovanni's grandmother, Louvenia, whom Giovanni places at the identitarian center of her narrative as representative of the history of women's strong-willed, brave, and self-endangering resistance to racism.[17] Giovanni's portrayal of her young self as a tireless and slightly insane fist-fighter, taking on children bigger than herself and wrestling them to the ground is represented as a direct legacy of Louvenia's strength: "most of us [blacks] have a history of fighting," and "Folks in my home town still have a lot of respect for me dating back to those days."[18] It matters that Giovanni represents this as an aspect of blackness, neither feminine nor unfeminine, but something women, like men, have inasmuch as they are black.

The basic form of this chapter, like most of the chapters in *Gemini*, is to present a series of such character portraits – a grandmother, a self – which can then be established as "black" in the context of a movement of "anarchic" black youth; the anecdotes themselves then emerge as examples of how the truly free live, as it were, after politics. Thus the personal and family narratives give way, in this essay, to the following quotations:

> Through a series of discussions I was having with a social worker, I discovered I am not objective. Any feeling I may have for someone or something is based on how he or it relates to me ... There are no objective standards when it comes to your life; this is crucial. Objective standards and objective feelings always lead to objectionable situations. I'm a revolutionary poet in a prerevolutionary world.

And dealing with blackness as a cultural entity can only lead
to revolution... That's not a subjective thought, it's a fact. Facts
are only tools to gain control over yourself and other people. So
white folks develop facts about us; we are developing facts
about them. In the end it's always a power struggle...

I believe in logic. Logic is not an exercise to prove *"A* implies
B" but a spiritual understanding of the subjective situation and
the physical movement necessary to place life in its natural
order. Black people are the natural, hence logical, rulers of the
world. This is a fact. And it's illogical for me to assume any
other stance or to allow any other possibility. It's self-
negating...

I was trained intellectually and spiritually to respect myself
and the people who respected me. I was emotionally trained to
love those who love me. If such a thing can be, I was trained to
be in power – that is, to learn and act upon necessary emotions
which will grant me more control over my life... There is a real
possibility that I can be the first person in my family to be free.
That would make me happy. I'm twenty-five years old. A revolutionary poet. I love.[19]

"Blackness as a cultural entity" is the reactive, unmediated personal
opposition to contact with the nonblack;[20] inasmuch as it is the result
of shared family histories, such personal opposition is always already
collective. At the same time, the themes developed in the passages
quoted should appear consistent to anyone who has been concerned
with neo-Nietzschean social theory in recent years. The redescription
of logic as systemic deployment of power from within a subject-
position determined by no greater object than itself is used to generate an ethics of intersubjective mutuality constructed within the
framework of "blackness," but not ultimately tied to it, since the last
paragraph is about "respect" for individuals, not races. Race is thus
an arbitrary location of hegemony, in the sense Laclau and Mouffe
understand both "arbitrary" and "hegemony."[21] Likewise, the term
"respect," with its always implicit reference to Aretha Franklin, is in
fact conspicuous throughout black women's writing in the period.[22]
Yet no one – *no one* – reads *Gemini* as an example of contemporary
cultural theory. Perhaps this is because the theorist Giovanni mentions as an influence is Ayn Rand, or that this particular hegemonic
blackness also turns out, as one reads on, to be deeply homophobic,
anti-Semitic, and parochial. "The weak have made weakness a religion," claims Giovanni, and weakness, finally, is what her struggle is
against; whiteness, as she knows from Elijah Muhammad, is merely
its reflection.[23]

And *Gemini* is a genuine success in humorously and stylishly portraying strength. I did not understand how hilarious it is until I started reading passages out loud in a classroom among students who were completely antagonistic to the book; we giggled through an entire seventy-five minute class. The humor itself cannot be divorced either from its roots in the bohemian struggle to move outside middle class professionalism (while holding onto the image of a family that gives strength, as with Louvenia) or the power of a black female heterosexual talking publicly about her hard-won sexuality, her body, her pregnancy. In 1971 Giovanni was a successful performance poet whose well-watched TV and personal appearances were nearly unique among people called "poets" in the US; *Gemini* is the performance of someone who wants to be a *star*. In the essay "A Spiritual View of Lena Horne," "spiritual" is given direct resonance to a series of images around stars/constellations/astrological signs, like "Gemini" itself, and "star" has a very specific meaning:

> Innovators are the combined energies of the people. They frequently feel guilty about taking more than they give, which should not be. The innovator who isn't taking more from the people than she is giving has nothing to give... Many people feed into the one person who is/becomes the personification of the people. That's what stars are all about – a collection of mass gravitation.[24]

Another way of saying this appears early on in the book: "I had enough style not to be considered disgraceful."[25] If *Gemini*'s post-politics are about real or imagined fist-fights, its artistry is all style and innovation, persistent and willful misdirection, refusal to say what it means or mean what it says, deadly serious arguments made circular and confusing and noxious arguments made in the driest of tones. This is very hard to describe, but I will try to present the fabulous first chapter, "400 Mulvaney Street," in an attempt to bring these pieces together coherently.

The chapter opens with a return to Knoxville, where Giovanni was born, on a speaking engagement at the University of Tennessee, whose theater Giovanni claims to have personally integrated less than ten years earlier. Giovanni is happy to be coming home, suggesting that the relationship that artists have with their homes is generally fraught by suspicion and discomfort, and that she is hoping to avoid the "negative equation between the artist and home."[26] The narrative meanders to allow Giovanni the space to reflect on the building of the local airport, and the widening of the highway between the airport and the city (the governor, in from Nashville to see a UT football game, gets caught in traffic and misses the kick-off; the road widening starts the next day), which in turn leads to a larger consideration of the way the city has changed in her absence. Detailed descriptions of the old black downtown area give way to the description of 400 Mulvaney Street, the address of her grandparents' house. It is at this moment, without warning or narrative consistency, that Giovanni places what turns out to be the pivotal statement of the chapter: "something called progress killed my grandmother." Urban renewal – the building of a convention center, a new highway and its access roads – has destroyed Giovanni's landmarks, made impossible, and also doubly necessary, her nostalgia.[27]

Nostalgia in this context is a form of sublimated rage. Giovanni moves quickly into the story of how she was expelled from Fisk University – from which her father had graduated – for leaving the dorms to see her dying grandfather without waiting for the permission of the Dean of Students. That she could have gotten permission, but couldn't be bothered with the "bitchy" Dean, is acknowledged; principally she states: "I said I didn't need her permission to go home."[28] Grandfather died that spring and as a result of her expulsion Giovanni was there with her grandmother, who had never before lived alone. Giovanni nursed her grandmother, enrolled at a local black college, and watched as Mulvaney Street was slated for redevelopment and her grandmother was forced to move east to another house, one with "no familiar smell... No coal ashes from the fireplaces. Nowhere you could touch and say 'Yolande threw her doll against this wall'... Linden Avenue was pretty but it had no life."[29] Her grandmother lived in the new house just long enough to watch Nikki graduate from college, and Giovanni suggests that she would have lived much longer had she not been moved from her house.

The narrator returns to the speech at the University of Tennessee, reflecting on the house as a means to suggest that "there may be a reason why [Blacks] lack a collective historical memory." Unlike many of her contemporaries, however, she does not promote the restoration of such memory as a goal of black activism; rather she uses the reflection to shout: "This is the urgency – Live."[30] In being denied this memory by a redevelopment process over which the family has no control, the process of public nostalgia enacts the form of black living in the present as the process of claiming space as one's own in the *now*. And it is the storytelling itself, called by the name "black style," which provides continuity, which remains to occupy the space that the white American middle class gets from possession of property, *homes*. With 400 Mulvaney knocked down, the (black) style of Giovanni's storytelling is where she (and blacks generally) may find "home."

Later in the book Giovanni writes of this set of aesthetic and metaphorical relations in the following terms:

> Black is a sacrament. It's an outward and visible sign of an inward and spiritual grace. A poetry reading is a service. A play is a ritual. And these are the socially manifested ways we do things... When Black people have been recorders we have sought truth; when white people used these tools they sought dreams.
>
> We hear a lot about the Black aesthetic. The aesthetic is a dream a culture wishes to obtain.[31]

An insistent practitioner who refuses to systematize anything like *the* black aesthetic if doing so will ignore Smokey Robinson's falsetto (gender marker clearly intended),[32] Giovanni is able to provide a more widely convincing portrayal of the aesthetic meaning of blackness at a given moment than any of the more well-read men around her. It is in this context that we must understand three complicated truths about Giovanni's career after *Gemini*: (1) in her essay "Black Poems, *Poseurs*, and Power," originally published in *Negro Digest*, Giovanni published one of the most significant early criticisms of the masculinism of Black Power from within the movement. In this essay she takes on the militarism of the Newark movement, whose most well-known figure is Amiri Baraka, not for militancy itself but for the fact that "the people of Newark became more afraid of the Black candidates and their organization than they were of the present scandal-ridden Black hating organization."[33] (2) This fact, framed explicitly as the critique of Black Power masculinity in the essay, is for her in no way inconsistent with a reading of white supremacy which claims that "the weight of Blackness ultimately falls on Black men."[34] (3) Well-known movement men had decided, by 1972, that she was out of their control and started denouncing her work. Margaret McDowell and Virginia Fowler have already amply documented the fact that criticism of her work in the 1970s paid little attention to the poetry itself, relying instead on *ad hominem* attack.[35]

Thus while *Gemini* is, explicitly, not a feminist text, and intends to be aggressively offensive to both white women and all homosexuals (white feminists, it turns out, are only white women sexually attracted to black women anyway), it ends up generating a striking analysis of black women's political specificity in 1971. The following set of quotes are positioned as the book's major conclusion, prior to a short denouement:

> And I believe the white man is a natural man, that his anxieties and fears are the anxieties and fears of natural men, because I watch us going into the same syndromes. I'm forced now to admit the white woman is obviously a natural and perhaps superior piece cause I have watched and am watching our men go ape shit to get it... And we watch white women really get into what they're all about with their liberation movement. The white woman's actions have been for an equality movement first of all and secondly have been patterned after Black men's... But white women and Black men are both niggers and both respond as such. He runs to the white man to explain his "rights" and she runs to us. And I think that's where they are both coming from. Probably anyone of you knows a mixed couple – check it out. And the young white man doesn't know who he wants to be. He grows his hair long like his woman's; he dresses like our men and tries to run his home as Black women have.
>
> We Black women are the single group in the West intact. And anybody can see we're pretty shaky. We are, however (all praises), the only group that derives its identity from itself. I think its been rather unconscious but we measure ourselves by ourselves, and I think that's a practice we can ill afford to lose.[36]

As a declaration of psychological independence this passage is both clear about the extremely limited and fragile nature of that independence, and also entirely consistent with a series of similar declarations I will be exploring in the rest of this book: *we have no choice, as black women, since we have no one else with whom to identify.* This might be understood as the aestheticist, rather than left-wing, version of June Jordan's "Declarations of an Independence I Would Just as Soon Not Have," which I discussed in chapter one.

Finally, Giovanni depends on Angela Davis as the primary, actually named black female political figure in her whole book – "I fell completely and absolutely in love with the image and idea of an Angela Yvonne, though I have never met her and probably never shall."[37] In light of the fact that Giovanni provides an anti-Communist, anti-internationalist, anti-Semitic chapter in the guise of analyzing "Angela's case," articulating a politics directly offensive to everything that would appear in Davis' autobiography three years later, the words "image and idea" cannot be ignored. It would be impossible to imagine a quote less in keeping with Davis' self-portrayal than "People keep expecting Angela to be logical. But that's a twenty-six year old woman who probably had every reason to feel she could flow through life, find something/someone and be brainy and cute who suddenly found herself the most wanted woman in the world."[38] Davis will tell us, with a logic brainy, uncute, and utterly self-effacing, how she got to be that woman, as a means of justifying Communism as an internationalist narrative. Most centrally, she will speak of the despair of being known as an "image and idea" rather than as a person.

Black woman philosopher: object

Giovanni was a public figure when *Gemini* appeared, but the term "public figure" is entirely inadequate to describe the space from which *Angela Davis: An Autobiography* is written. In the Cold War, Communism provided the basic framework of media-constructed fear, and fellow traveling individuals like Paul Robeson were labeled Communist and stripped of their ability to perform and travel. For at least a short time, blackness was not the foregrounded narrative of white fear in the mass media. During the 1960s blackness is clearly the foregrounded narrative, though the suspicion that Communists orchestrate everything from behind never entirely disappears. In this context, Angela Davis, whose visual image on the famous FBI wanted posters is that of the perfect Black Power monster (not least because she is a woman who acts like a man), may also be the only media figure singled out as a Communist in the era. Fired from her teaching job as a professor of philosophy at UCLA by Reagan-appointed regents but reinstated by a court that defends the rights of university professors to be Communists, Davis' blackness represents key fears of right-thinking Americans even before she allegedly conspires in the August 7, 1970 shoot-out at the Marin County Courthouse. When, in particular, one reads in the original preface of *this* autobiography that "I was not anxious to write this book. Writing an autobiography at my age seemed presumptuous,"[39] it does not seem responsible to treat this statement from only a rhetorical point of view. There had already been several books about this twenty-eight year old woman published prior to the autobiography, including Regina Nadelson's *Who is Angela Davis?*, a truly silly and exploitative pop biography by a white ex-acquaintance, J. A. Parker's *Angela Davis: The Making of a Revolutionary*, an anti-Communist screed by someone not identified by profession or affiliation in the text, but who appears to be black from the occasional pronoun, and *If They Come in the Morning*, a collection Davis co-edited with Bettina Aptheker and several others as part of the political movement to get her out of jail, but published with the high-profile Davis listed as the author.[40]

Angela Davis: An Autobiography thus enters a discourse of blackness and communism already set by years of post-Cold War and post-Malcolm X imagery, and also one in which the visual and textual image of Davis herself has come to stand in for the intersection of these discourses. The visual meaning of Davis' image must be further emphasized. Davis has recently written about this phenomenon that "it is both humiliating and humbling to discover that a single gener-ation after the events that constructed me as a public personality, I am remembered as a hairdo."[41] This form of memory, as Davis goes on to discuss, is itself in many ways implicit in the public forms by which people like Giovanni attained awareness of her even during the movement, notably photographs of her first as a lecturer and speaker at rallies, and then on the famous posters. At the same time, there is an element to this history that is both gendered and microhistorical which cannot be ignored: Malcolm X's analysis of the conk is one of the most discussed sections of *The Autobiography of Malcolm X* to this day, yet one can hardly suggest that X is remembered for his hair in the same way that Davis is. Rather, he is well known for his manhood, a concept that, while it includes certain aspects of appearance, cannot be limited to them. Davis was hardly the first woman to wear a "natural" – at the time she first wore her big Afro she "was emulating a whole host of women – both public figures and women I encoun-tered in my daily life."[42] Yet she is remembered only through the photographs of her, a woman who is *down*, but not one with the complex attributes of "manhood," and therefore as what Giovanni wanted her to be, and she tried to reject: a style.

It is beyond the scope of my project to write the media history by which Davis becomes this figure, but it is surely noteworthy that autobiography is the means by which she attempts to counter, with extreme *reasonableness* and a sweater rather than a leather jacket on the cover, her media portrayal. Davis wrote an autobiography because she was a marxist intellectual, student of Marcuse and Adorno, concerned at the theoretical level about the ways in which popular imagery intercedes where analysis is necessary. She writes an "auto-biography" whose central concern is how she is gazed at, rarely acknowledging a self other than the effect of this gaze in its objectivity.

Prison as structuring black experience – again

Davis' narrative is a more self-conscious prison narrative than any other I have considered. No other text I describe takes prisons, trials, and the legal process itself as its focus, nor prisoners and their friends as its central protagonists, in the same way – surely not Herndon, for whom writing of the imminent world revolution seemed far more possible and thus writing of the local issue of prisoners' rights far less important, nor Malcolm X, for whom prison was the place of learning, and the telos of the narrative is what comes later. Yet by 1974, with the legacy of Herndon and X in the context of movements in which solidarity campaigns for George Jackson, Huey Newton, and a variety of other prisoners became major political struggles, the description and analysis of prison has become a starting point for the depiction of racialization. Thus when Angela Davis is on trial and held incognito in prison, and she wants to describe her bond with her codefendant Ruchell McGee with whom she could not have a more different class background, she writes: "when the superfices of our two lives were set aside, what they had in common could easily be seen. It all boiled down to the fact that we were Black and in our own ways had tried to fight the forces that were strangling our people."[43] We are the same because we are Black and on trial; being Black and being on trial are, fundamentally, the same thing. Being in jail is "being haunted by the spectres of all those sisters and brothers whose lives were eroding in other jails."[44] Blackness is metaphorized as being imprisoned to begin with; being in jail is ground zero of the experience of blackness.[45]

Angela Davis: An Autobiography does not start at birth, but underground, on the run, in a way that directly recalls Richard Wright's fiction, complete with the identification of all-pervasive fear as the central fact of existential being, a "fear so overwhelming ... the only thing I could compare it to was that sense of engulfment I used to feel as a child when I was left alone in the dark." Taking roads in a neighborhood she has been doing political organizing in, "tonight the way seemed strange, full of the unknown perils of being a fugitive." As she travels from city to city, looking up friends and safe houses, her "fears seemed to be confirmed in every straight-looking white man standing around."[46] Amid the dramatic, visually descriptive passages, in which Davis' wandering eyes take in airport security setups and highways, hotel lobbies, and car interiors, the book begins as the account of a media event, where cameras and newspaper headlines are the determinative texts constructing the actions of the paranoid subject. Soon she has been caught in the lobby of a New York hotel, the press notified in advance by the police: "As far as I could see, reporters and photographers were crowded into the lobby." Davis "tried hard not to look surprised."[47]

Following Davis' capture, but before she turns to the narrative of childhood and family, the bulk of the lengthy first section narrates her experiences in the New York City Women's House of Detention in Greenwich Village, where Davis was detained prior to the extradition hearings that would return her to California to stand trial. When Davis enters the jail, she tells us, "all the women were either Black or Puerto Rican."[48] This statement introduces not only a model for how women become jailed (including the information that white women who are arrested are generally released on their own recognizance), but also continues the narrative of Davis looking around, constantly describing anything and everything that will divert attention from her own situation. It's not that she neglects to inform us when she is illegally denied contact with her lawyer, but that this information is interspliced with information about a prisoner about to give birth but denied medical attention. When Davis is not able to refer to specific examples of the oppression of women around her, she reminds us that George Jackson has described worse conditions than her own. "I fought the tendency to individualize my predicament,"[49] she tells us, and this certainly represents her strategy of writing. Her most dramatic moment of the kind of identification I am describing occurs during a rally in the streets of Greenwich Village, outside the House of Detention, on her behalf. Davis, on the seventh floor, can hear the people below her yell "Free Angela," to which she responds by yelling "Free Vernell! Free Helen! Free Amy!"[50]

Davis continually assures her readers that "there were no degrees of better or worse" in jail, since "jail was jail." She speaks of the impossibility of getting used to prison – "familiarity with the routine in 4b did not diminish the horror of living behind bars" – and of the ways in which arbitrary force, rather than a rule-governed process, is necessary to the functioning of prisons: for example, "The centrality of commissary emerges from the deprivation which is such an important element of official control and authority. In jail you learn that nothing can be taken for granted; the normal need-fulfillment process is shattered."[51] For all this, running through the section is the idea that prison can be more rather than less human if the social interaction of the prisoners within, and the solidarity of a movement outside, can be felt by the imprisoned subject. Not surprisingly, Davis was initially placed in solitary and told that it was being done for her own safety, since the women on the floor hated her communism and would hurt her given the opportunity; also not surprisingly, Davis informs us that the opposite was the case, and that when by court order she was placed in a regular unit the women treated her as a celebrity and wanted to know what a communist was anyway. When she does get to the general population, Davis tells us about the many rituals of the women's house – themselves often different from those one generally sees in male-narrated accounts of prison – like the lights-off ritual whereby each woman shouts "goodnight" to the woman in the cell next to her, continuing down the line until all have expressed their solidarity. There is, in this portrayal, a real shift in the prison narrative from that of macho (i.e. Herndon) or self-improvement (Malcolm X) to the narrative where the conditions of prison are described as psychologically debilitating, but also creating the conditions of solidarity.

What this narrative most justifies is Davis' version of movement politics as described later in the book. Davis wants to argue that movements for bail, parole, and any other form of release of prisoners are in principle good Black and Communist politics, which is why she has been particularly involved in organizing around Rap Brown, the Soledad Brothers Defense Committee, and others for years before her own case becomes so important. Her presentation of this is very important in terms of the large structure of the book:

> I had profound reservations about devoting so much of the energy of the campaign to the single question of [my] bail. In the first place, I had been certain that there would not be the flimsiest chance of victory. In the second place, I thought the political content of the bail issue too weak. It did not permit people to express their resistances to the *system* of repression, which was not only behind my own imprisonment but was why so many others were languishing in prison.
>
> The participation of so many people had been in itself phenomenal, but what impressed me most and what convinced me of the correctness of the bail fight was the way in which the people who waged the fight began to evolve politically. Many of them began to involve themselves in other areas of the campaign. Once they had been exposed to the realities of the prison and judicial systems, they were forced to give serious consideration to the political repression we spoke about.[52]

Prisoner issues are identificatory issues: Davis, as prisoner and as the image of a prisoner, wants participants in a movement to first identify

178

her with all other prisoners and second, identify as prisoners themselves such that they work to free all prisoners. The best political
strategy, as it develops in this text, is the one that identifies blacks,
and specifically black women, as real and metaphorical prisoners, as
a way into the objective analysis of societal oppression which places
poor black women at the bottom of an oppressive totality, still to be
theorized.

The "I" as a series of events

I have already stated that *Angela Davis: An Autobiography* exhibits
none of the desire for self-revelation of other autobiographies, and
does not begin from the point of view that personal experience *should*
be an element in the justification of a politics. In her 1988 introduction
to the book, Davis states this ever more clearly: "I did not really write
about myself ... I attempted to utilize the autobiographical genre to
evaluate my life in accordance with what I considered to be the
political significance of my experiences."[53] While politics often motivates African-American autobiography at the outset, no other autobiography discussed in this book – not even *Dusk of Dawn* – follows this
procedure with the rigor and formal commitment of Davis'. We have
seen that the narrative opens not with when "I was born" but with
when "I became a widely known public figure"; I have not mentioned that the date, August 9, 1970, appears at the left margin prior to
this narration. This would be unremarkable if the date turned out to
correspond to a diary entry or was a strategy built on the fictionalization of the diary form, as occurs in a variety of autobiographies. But
as we follow the dates that open sections throughout the book, we
realize that their referents are not Davis' diaries, if such exist, nor
even events we might consider "personal" in her life. They are,
consistently, dates that you can cross-reference with the newspaper:
the dates of public events. August 9, 1970 is the day after the Marin
County Courthouse shooting, the day Davis went underground. The
next date is the date of her arrest, and then the date of her extradition
to California. Time passes, daily experience is recounted between the
appearance of these dates but in a synchronic form; diachrony is
figured as news, and personal narrative, where present, is therefore
figured as the interstices of time itself. In the sections of the book
where these dates do not appear (significantly less than a quarter of
the 400 pages), Davis narrates her childhood and educational history;
in all the sections narrated about Davis older than sixteen, whether

she is describing her high school or a friendship, the events of her life are dated by the news of King's death, the Birmingham church bombing, the Watts riot, George Jackson's death. "Angela Davis" is developed as a character only inasmuch as she responds to historical crisis.

What complicates this picture and may help to explain it, is that the short second section of the book (thirty-five pages) which concerns Davis' childhood potentially tells a story quite distinct from that of the prisoner-identification that constructs the book's opening. In this section, we learn that Davis grows up as the child of politically active people, associating with red diaper babies, bohemians, and internationalist leftists from an early age. Constructing her book around this narrative would, of course, direct attention to the ground of her specificity within the black movement, and threaten to distinguish her, to make her not like other prisoners. That is, there appears to be a constitutive relationship between the fear of being not quite an authentic black woman prisoner and the desire to narrate "black woman prisoner" as a category of political identification.

Thus if Davis has been at pains to describe herself as like other black women, as nonindividuated among them, it is in this section where we discover a series of remarkable things that place her, literally, on the border between racial formations. Daughter of a small-business owner and a teacher, Davis' middle class home in Birmingham sits at the *exact* location where the border between white and black neighborhoods is defined – indeed, it was her family, in moving into that house in what had been a white neighborhood, that caused the line to be drawn where it was.[54] Not surprisingly, Davis experienced nothing but hostility from local whites growing up; yet her parents were committed to teaching her that white people and black people had a history of working together, even, sometimes, in the south:

> Every time I said "white lady" or "white man" anger clung to my words. My mother tried to erase the anger with reasonableness. Her experiences had included contacts with white people seriously committed to improving race relations... She had worked to free the Scottsboro Boys and there had been whites – some of them Communists – in that struggle. Through her own political work, she had learned that it was possible for white people to walk out of their skin and respond with the integrity of human beings... I did not know what she was talking about.[55]

But Davis does know what her mother is talking about; within pages we learn more of these political contacts, who include friends in New

York who are involved in various left movements and who afford Davis as a child not only the exposure to certain political ideas, but also simply the imagination that she can leave Birmingham. New York becomes an object of her desire from a very young age, and in addition to spending a fair amount of time there as a child, she attends an alternative high school there for two years.[56] In turn, the experience of white contacts outside Alabama combined with her excellent book-learned French – which itself demonstrates something about her class aspirations in the US context – allows her as an adolescent to engage in such practice political revolts as posing as a Martiniquean to get waited on in a downtown Birmingham shoe store.[57]

The self of international Communism

Marxist theory, and traveling in a specific, already existing network of international Communist activism, provides the narrative glue that will hold together the specificity of Davis with the generality of prison blackness. The communist self is presented as one in which difference and identity are narrated such that neither term is permitted to absolutely replace the other, and where identity appears not as pre-given, but rather through a politically explicit process of stabilization. We must therefore be careful in reading the opening paragraph, where Davis argues that autobiography "would require a posture of difference," and therefore her book needs to develop how the "most essential fact" is that "the forces that have made my life what it is are the very same forces that have shaped and misshaped the lives of millions of my people."[58] Note that this has *not* made her life identical to the lives of others; rather the same forces have formed her that have formed others. The purpose of writing about oneself in terms of identity, then, is that one has already been differentiated – by the bourgeois media, for example – and the writing will show that this particular, historical form of differentiation can only be explained with reference to the real, outside forces that shape all selves.[59] This will explain the text's regular emphasis not only on the social forces that place Davis in jail, but also on those social forces that create black women whose social positions look very different from Davis', but who now identify strongly with her – the respectable grandmother who provides a safe house when she's underground, the prison guard who apologizes that it's the best job she can get.

This explains how black women come to share an identification; it does not explain how a specific black woman, Angela Davis, comes to a specific analysis of the politics of this identification. The autobiography suggests that this latter accomplishment is first of all made possible by *travel*: the Communist is an internationalist inasmuch as she knows north and south, Europe as well as the US, elite education as well as racist oppression, Herbert Marcuse as well as her cellmates. Indeed, traveling contributes to her intellectual analysis of the world system even as it keeps her from particular moments of political action. Davis leaves Birmingham for New York during the Montgomery Bus Boycott, the US for Germany during the Watts Riots, won't work with the patronizing white pseudo-marxists at Brandeis because she identifies herself with international marxist youth who attend conferences in Europe. She is never in the one place that would cause her to act politically in a given location until she has experienced years of the totalization made possible by movement. Everywhere she finds herself she has a reference point somewhere else; in London she is commenting about the relationship of African-American to Black-British oppression; among and to African Americans she speaks of the brave struggles of the Cuban people as a way of preventing what she takes to be narrow nationalism. In part five she would not have joined the Communist Party except for the all-black organizing cell she works with, but among Black activists she is always openly Communist and considers working in an anti-Communist environment a grave political error.[60]

Davis recounts the history of her direct political engagement against her awareness that until 1967 she has not been present at the events that have directly affected her comrades. She explains her return to the United States to study with Herbert Marcuse at University of California, San Diego in terms of the isolation this has brought: "The more the struggles at home accelerated, the more frustrated I felt at being forced to experience it all vicariously. I was advancing my studies, deepening my understanding of philosophy, but I felt more and more isolated."[61] The years of traveling and scholarship, preparing for politics, are over; upon arrival in California, the narration ceases to say anything about whether she did any intellectual work, what she read, what she hoped to write about in her dissertation. Practical politics becomes the focus, the text negotiating the different Black and/or Communist organizations in southern California as she searches for the one with the most coherent political strategy or accountable leadership structure. In an analysis that links

Davis to the African Blood Brotherhood, Davis knows that for day to day work she will have to be a Black nationalist, and she joins the Black Panthers and SNCC. Simultaneously, she demonstrates that international solidarity is not other than nationalism, but a component part of what it means to do nationalist work: the major on-campus work she does at UCSD is to help found Lumumba-Zapata College, a pan-third worldist unit of the university organized across Black/Chicano racial lines and including white leftist groups as well.[62] What party membership seems to mean, then, in this text, is not the acceptance of specific instructions from a movement vanguard, but rather a network in which to discuss global political questions while working in movement organizations, questions that lead one to advocate certain strategic choices rather than others. Blackness becomes the name of a politics, while marxism is maintained as a theoretical framework, and the CP is a support network that will be there long after the current struggles have faded.

This would end my account of the communist self in this autobiography were it not necessary to return to the fact that Davis became a notorious figure as a communist. As she states, "the psychological impact of anti-communism on ordinary people in this country runs very deep. There is something about the word 'communism' ... that evokes not only the enemy, but also something immoral, something dirty."[63] A fully adequate account of this would require an account of American anti-communism. In this location all I can do is recount the relationship between Davis' notoriety and her membership in the Communist Party, something which matters because while her image as black woman with Afro and gun provides the all-important visual phantasm around which the right could construct an enemy, the immediate excuse for her notoriety was never her relationship to the Black Panthers or to SNCC, but rather her being hired to teach philosophy in the California system while being a member of the Communist Party.

According to a prospective juror at Davis' trial, being interviewed under oath, it is well-known that Communists are "sneaky."[64] That this juror is lying about herself, claiming to have many black friends when she is a notorious racist in her home town helps us inflect the meaning of this sneakiness. J. A. Parker, the author of *Angela Davis: The Making of A Revolutionary*, stresses exactly this Communist sneakiness in his defense of the Reagan regents' policy that communists should not, in fact, be allowed to teach in the University of California system, referring to Professor Marcuse as "a master of the polemics of obscurity" and Davis' use of language as "different from that which is generally accepted in rational discourse."[65] The actual firing of Davis followed the planting of an FBI agent to follow her actions with the LA Black Panthers. After being spied on, Davis received a formal letter from the Regents asking if she was a member of the CP. Sneakily, she stated publicly and without hesitation that she was. While the autobiography thus makes it a point to contrast Davis' presumed sneakiness with the complete transparency of the anti-Communists around her, she also informs us of the more serious effects of the discourse of anti-communism on her life – like death threats. Indeed, Davis loses her apartment when her landlord accuses her of hypnotizing him on behalf of the Communists, who are "able to brainwash people." Thus, if being constructed as a violent black radical makes Davis paranoid, being constructed as a Communist contributes a great deal to the kinds of paranoid fantasies others have of Davis. The landlord becomes so paranoid that he actually does make an attempt on her life. The psychic links between such fantasies and repressed sexuality are then drawn out through the discovery of love poems written by the landlord to Davis during a weekend she was supposedly holding him captive and brainwashing him.[66]

Yet Davis' Communist self finds it just as difficult to theorize sexuality as her landlord finds it impossible to talk about his titillation over Communism. In striking contrast to Giovanni, X, and most of her contemporaries, Davis' public narrative has persistently resisted sexuality as an aspect of black politics. After all this then, we return to the question which structures this chapter: where is the challenge of gender in this self? The answer, to the extent that any is available from Davis, appears in personal letters to George Jackson.

Gender, emotion, and the narrative of George Jackson

When, in 1974, Angela Davis wrote that she was not a "'real' person separate and apart from the political person,"[67] this statement is in part a reaction to what she considered to be the mistakes of the feminist movement and the slogan "the personal is the political." She says as much in the 1988 introduction in her comments about some of the ways in which she has changed in the ensuing years, about her increasing understanding of why this slogan was powerful, even while she continues to oppose it.[68] In this context it makes sense to see the centrality of the categories of race and class in Davis' autobiography (even as she exemplifies repeatedly the "universality" of women's situation) as resulting from her sense that these are the identifications that have broad, explanatory power, while gender is personal, emotional and sexual, and explains little or nothing about the world *as a whole*. The book's remarkable and inconsistent critique of women in homosexual relationships in the Women's House of Detention in Greenwich Village is the clearest sign of this under-standing of gender/sexuality together: the prevalence of homosex-uality in jail, Davis assures us, comes not from the prevalence of women who are "actual" homosexuals in jail, but as a way of coping and creating family networks within jail, networks which are unre-lated to the heterosexual matrices these women will rejoin when back on the streets. The apparently neutral narrator of an understandable but regrettable situation, Davis tell us,

> Certainly [homosexuality] was a way to counteract some of the pain of jail life; but objectively, it served to perpetuate all the bad things about the House of Detention. "The Gay Life" was all-consuming; it prevented many of the women from developing their personal dissatisfaction with the conditions around them into a political dissatisfaction, because the homosexual fantasy life provided an easy and attractive channel for escape.[69]

That Davis exhibits the traditional distinction between political and private concerns, with its concomitant assumption that those who attend to private pleasure at all must be doing so as a way of avoiding politics, is not surprising. Why other forms of community building, like saying goodnight to each other, are praised, while homosexual kinship networks are disparaged, is of course unexplained. The *Auto-biography* is, however, fairly consistent in its treatment of all gender-ing this way: for example, her marxist version of women's equality appears clearly in the critique of "an unfortunate syndrome among some Black male activists – namely to confuse their political activity with an assertion of their maleness."[70] If gender *politics* is entirely absent from *Angela Davis: An Autobiography*, however, gender *analysis* does, eventually, appear. What is striking in the context of this cri-tique, is the particular form that an analysis of the objective position of black women appears in the text: as the lengthily quoted text of a letter from Davis to George Jackson, read aloud by the prosecuting attorney at her trial. The attorney is trying to prove that Angela Davis participated in the Marin shoot-out because she and George Jackson were in love; the narrator will acknowledge only that her interest in Jackson is political. The DA is wrong that Davis planned the shoot-out; but from the book's own evidence, he's right about the romance.

In *Black Macho* Michelle Wallace suggested that the reason why Davis provided an acceptable female symbol of the Black Power movement is that "when she finally plunged herself into Movement activity, she reached right over all the possible issues that might have been considered relevant to her own experience to the issue of the plight of the black male 'political prisoner'. She even fell in love with a man who had made it eminently clear that he considered black women enslaving."[71] One must be careful quoting Wallace here: there is no need to sneer at black male political prisoners, nor to disparage Davis' real political commitments, to nevertheless see that what Wallace hoped to do in 1978 was make clear the psychological issues, the desires and paranoias, that formed some part of women's political action during Black Power. After all, Davis does not discuss this.

Four-fifths into the longest section of the book, where Davis talks about her life as a political organizer, she narrates the formation of the Soledad Brothers Defense Committee and informs us that "I knew that I had too many responsibilities to assume a major role in the defense committee."[72] Thus we are bound to note the particular language with which she recounts the fact that she became the main organizer of that Defense Committee in spite of her already over-whelming commitments: "I was paralyzed by the thought of the absolute irreversibility of [Jackson's decade in prison] ... A determination began to swell in me to do everything within the limits of the possible to save George from the gas chamber"; "Though I knew that I would have to push myself to the very limits of my capabilities, it did not even enter my mind to step down. The exhilaration I felt in experiencing all this energy and enthusiasm could have persuaded me to drop everything else"; upon seeing Jackson, through the glass barrier at the prison, for the first time: "George looked even more vibrant than I had imagined ... His shoulders were broad and mus-cular, his tremendous arms sculptures of an ancient strength, and his face revealed the depth of his understanding of our collective condi-tion ... I could hardly believe the refreshing beauty of his smile"; "My communications with George become more regular ... a per-sonal intimacy also began to develop between us."[73] George Jackson is portrayed as the sexual unconscious of certain political decisions by Angela Davis – and this statement is true even if (as I certainly do) we find Davis' political choices defensible on other grounds. Davis doesn't exactly deny that this time, keen political commitment does in fact take the form of a love affair, but she cannot acknowledge that there is any significance to this. My point, in resurrecting this analysis, which I presume it is obvious is not a reflection on Angela Davis, the present individual, now, is to demonstrate exactly what black feminism, including Davis' own subsequent version, was, and is, up against. The most intellectually engaged black female political figure of the period was engaged in a politics structured at the outset by the desire for gendered black manhood. That Davis herself, and any number of others, have, so far as one can tell from their writings, gotten over this, does not mean that the US has as a whole.

So what of "the black woman" in *Angela Davis: An Autobiography*? In the passages quoted from the correspondence of Jackson and Davis we may piece together the following analysis: first, Jackson had changed his understanding of women's capacities and roles in the revolution (as he had presented it in *Soledad Brother*) and was particularly concerned that Davis publicize this fact among black women, to whom he apologizes for his earlier sexism. Davis is sufficiently concerned to publicize this that she mentions it twice in the *Autobiography*.[74] Second, the passages reprinted from her letters to Jackson are the only examples of passionate personal writing in what is otherwise dispassionate anti-autobiographical prose: "I am standing in the little glass cubicle downstairs, standing, waiting, loving, desiring and then hot cold rage when the chains begin to rattle as you slowly descend the stairs... I'm supposed to rip off the chains. I'm supposed to fight your enemies with my body, but I am helpless, powerless."[75] Third, it is within the texts of these letters – generally within the prosecuting attorney's speech, quoting from them – that the only analysis of the intersection of race and gender in this otherwise race/class autobiography appears. Davis' analysis, which starts from Jackson's premise that under present conditions Black men do feel castrated by Black women, but that this is not the responsibility of individual Black women, concludes:

> For the Black female, the solution is not to become less aggressive, not to lay down the gun, but to learn how to set the sights correctly, aim accurately, squeeze rather than jerk and not be overcome by the damage. We have to learn how to rejoice when pigs' blood is spilled.
>
> Women's liberation in the revolution is inseparable from the liberation of the male.[76]

In the end third-worldist marxism was to assume that gender equality was just that, a simple process of men and women engaged in the same action in the context of the revolution: shooting. (Nor am I claiming that there is something in every case unethical about women, or men, shooting.) What had yet to be theorized as black *feminism* was the notion of a gendered psychology productive of difference within race/class identity.[77]

8

Home and profession in black feminism

I think that a whole lot of what's going on in my work is a kind
of *theorizing through autobiography* or through storytelling.
bell hooks[1]

Only the [black] female stands *in the flesh*, both mother and
mother-dispossessed. This problematizing of gender places
her, in my view, *out* of the traditional symbolics of female
gender, and it is our task to make a place for this different
social subject. In doing so, we are less interested in joining the
ranks of gendered femaleness than gaining the *insurgent*
ground as female social subject. Actually *claiming* the
monstrosity (of a female with the potential to "name") ...
might rewrite after all a radically different text for female
empowerment.
Hortense Spillers[2]

In fact, not play, the absence of black women from any kind of
romantic or professional archetype is a complicated
phenomenon.
Patricia Williams[3]

Gemini opens by challenging "the negative relationship between the
artist and home," a relationship which the last pages indicate could
be rethought with a healthy dose of black women's self-identity;
Angela Davis provides the image of a black woman as political
worker who articulates the whole world as her home in a way that is
historically improbable – though Hurston's anthropology indicates
that a rather different version of it was not impossible – prior to Black
Power. Neither phrases the problematic of home as specific to black
women: Giovanni's category is the artist, while Davis makes clear
that political participation is in the very act of travel. Largely because
of the current prominence of postcolonial theory, we have become
used to the notion that contentions over identity, both as a concept

and as a project, are contentions over notions of home and migration, the subject's relationship to family and nation, the "community" against projects demonstrating that community, like Freud's family, is internally contradictory. At the moment of the major articulation of a specifically "black" *feminism*, around the turn of the 1980s, the metaphor of home, as that which must be found, or escaped, by black women, becomes a central frame for contention. Claims about home are, consistently, constructed autobiographically.

My first goal in this concluding chapter will be to describe the tension between the way that Barbara Smith forms the particular objectification "black feminist" out of home in two pieces of writing from the volume *Home Girls*, its general introduction and the short piece – it is hard to tell whether it is supposed to be fiction or autobiography – called "Home," and the way that Michelle Wallace opposes this version of home by providing a rather different narrative of origins. However, Wallace does not break from Smith's notion of home entirely. To suggest something about why this is, I will read *Talking Back* by Wallace's contemporary bell hooks, whose work, like Wallace's, is sharply criticized in *Home Girls*, and in which the notion of home is equally ambivalent, for its psychological theory of the writing of autobiography. Read together, Wallace and hooks suggest that the possibility of transforming home – of making it consistent with travel – itself relies on a reformulation and working through of, rather than a utopian break from the concept.[4] What, however, requires the contemporary academic to leave home, I will suggest, is precisely *professionalization*, the class term which, to the extent the academy can be metaphorized as a "dwelling," implies something rather distinct from the narrative of home. I will not argue that no one "lives" (or writes) at home, but rather that "we" – academics, who are likely most of my readers – don't. Thus the problems of hooks' work emerge less in the theory and practice of autobiography she first promulgated, than in her persistent refusal to address the implications of her own professional emergence via the academic star system.

Autobiography, home, and the critique of home

Barbara Smith introduces *Home Girls* with the comment that it was "undoubtedly at home that I learned the rudiments of Black feminism, although no such term even existed then."[5] Home, in the autobiographical opening to the volume's introduction, is a two-family working class house in Cleveland full of women, six in all, plus one uncle who moved out because his wife, Smith's Aunt LaRue, was "too wrapped up in her family." Smith states:

> The women in my family, and their friends, worked harder than any people I have ever known before or since, and despite their objective circumstances, they believed. My grandmother believed in Jesus and in sin, not necessarily in that order; my mother believed in education and in books; my Aunt LaRue believed in beauty and in books as well; their arguments aside, they believed in each other...
> Needless to say, they believed in home.[6]

Black feminist thought, in this narrative, emerges from the success and love of a family as women's community, rather than from the break with a patriarchal family. It emerges from a community that has "never been fools [because] we couldn't afford to be."[7] It requires an autobiographical voice in which the autonomy of black women at home makes for easy compatibility between the politicized promotion of black women's continued independence and already given family structures within the black community. This is emphatically not, Smith soon tells us, the claim that the black community is a matriarchy with black women having some kind of control over social or economic resources; rather it is the claim that because black women have always had to take far more control of their lives than the dominant culture supposes women should, the roots of their political strength will come from a space already materially available to them as *black* women.

Smith is sufficiently certain of this model in black communities that she states "I suspect most of the contributors to *Home Girls* learned their varied politics and their shared commitment to Black women from the same source I did."[8] Inasmuch as Audre Lorde, on the first page of *Zami: A New Spelling of My Name*, which is excerpted in *Home Girls*, answers the question "to whom do I owe the power of my voice?" with "it is the images of women ... that lead me home,"[9] Smith's comment is surely not idiosyncratic.[10] On the other hand, Michelle Cliff's "If I Could Write This In Fire I Would Write This In Fire," also in *Home Girls*, would appear to challenge Smith, since the struggle for autonomy in that autobiographical essay is developed after migration in the fight against male relations. Smith has been widely accused of a too easy nostalgia by more recent feminists, and the real political problems with the creation of such a mythology of the strength of home for black women – the ways in which it can be made consistent with a "family values" politics – are at the center of the debate. Unfortunately, responses to narratives like Smith's are generally caricatures, in no way thinking through the carefully coded rearticulations of race and gender that Smith attempts to effect within the notion of home.[11] After all, the words that my ellipses leave out in the above quotation from the opening of *Zami* were "kind *and cruel.*"[12] When we move away from the introduction and to Smith's story "Home," her construction of home becomes quite complex and far more ambivalent than we might expect.

This six-page story starts with a dream in which Smith, living in Boston, recalls the house in Cleveland she still thinks of as her home and which has no equivalent in her current, mobile life. Already the lack of the reproduction of this version of home in her generation, then, is a conspicuous premise of the story called "Home." She dreams, in particular, of Aunt LaRue, the woman who taught her what she now considers her black feminism, but also of all the other women in that house who raised her. All these women are now dead, and the actual house in Cleveland is occupied by others, so this is definitely very much a dream of a place slipping away, even a dream Smith considers *childish*:

> [It is] my childish desire to see a face that I'm not going to see ... To know that home existed. Of course I know they're gone, that I won't see them again, but there are times when my family is so real to me, at least my missing them is so real and thorough, I feel like I have to do something, I don't know what. Usually I dream.[13]

In the wake of this opening reverie, Smith narrates a conversation about their present home with her partner, Leila, regarding this nostalgia, and Leila takes on the voice of cynical reason – "You're so crazy. You can bet that whoever lived here in 1945 wasn't colored or two women either."[14] But Leila's anti-nostalgia, including a mild complaint about her own mother, falls on deaf ears, and Smith continues to daydream, this time about phoning La Rue for the purpose of asking her questions about the family's history:

> Every week or so Leila talks to her mother. It's hard to overhear them. I try not to think about it, try to feel neutral and act like it's just a normal occurrence, calling home. After battling for years, Leila and her mother are very close ... My family, like most, was great at keeping secrets. But I'd always planned when I got older and they couldn't treat me like a kid to ask questions and find out. Aunt LaRue died suddenly, a year after I'd been out of college and then it was too late to ask a thing.
> For lack of information I imagine things about them.[15]

Home, here, is a place that one makes peace with as a way of proceeding; home is a place of secrets; home is a place where certain people, but not others, are useful informants – this last point is of particular importance when we discover that Aunt LaRue died before Barbara Smith came out as a lesbian, so Smith is actually fantasizing the image of a relative who would have been supportive of her sexuality, unlike her living relations. That her own mother is not supportive of her is itself a constituent part of Smith's imagination of LaRue as the locus of home: "Most of my friends have such passionate, complicated relationships with their mothers... I'd like to have a woman on my side who brought me here. Yes, I know it's not that simple, that I tend to romanticize, that it can be hell especially about coming out... I always imagine that with my aunt, it would have been all right."[16]

In the last two pages the story moves away from the imagined home in Cleveland to the "sometimes" where the building of a home with Leila feels the same as the imagination of a past home:

> Until I knew her, I though it wasn't possible to have [the feeling of home] with another woman, at least not for me. But I think we were raised the same way. To be decent, respectful girls. They taught us to work. And to rebel...
> When we first started living together I would get déja vu, waves of feelings that I hadn't had since I'd lived in that other place, home.[17]

At its end, the story "Home," as well as the existence of the book *Home Girls*, is the nonnostalgic, performative accomplishment of a new version of home that differs, historically, from the older version of home. It is woman-centered, like the previous one, but not in denial of the possible sexual implications of such homosociality. It is rebellious in ways that are necessarily discontinuous with the earlier home because that earlier home was both where the rebellion was seeded, and one of the places rebelled against. It is, finally, conscious of its own articulation as a useful fantasy. Fear of its failure makes it hard, consistently, to accomplish in the world. For all that, the persistent creation of home is a project worth doing.

And yet, the obvious response is that not every black feminist's autobiographical statements support Smith's vision of their own homes. Indeed, it is interesting to note that even as Michele Wallace republishes several older essays about the work of her mother, the artist Faith Ringgold, in her essay collection *Invisibility Blues*, the autobiographical statements which lace both her critical essays in that book and her recent introduction to the new edition of *Black Macho and the Myth of the Superwoman* demonstrate that learning black feminist politics from or alongside one's mother in no way implies a nostalgic relationship to home. And while I have suggested in several ways throughout this book that the present tendency to ignore Smith and the *Home Girls* group in the present academy is often misrecognized by recent writers as the replacement of an older, essentialist black feminist politics with a more properly theoretical account of race and gender, I do want to suggest here that a different and more subtle change occurred between the subgeneration of the so-called essentialists like Smith, June Jordan, and Barbara Christian, and that of Michelle Wallace and bell hooks.[18] That shift is the introduction of the complicated rereading of the mother-figure (and thus of home) as sometimes inspirational and independent, and simultaneously as implicated in the reproduction of the patriarchy.[19] The possibility of this move, as we have just seen, is already available, though refused, in Smith's "Home."

For Wallace and hooks, at the intersection where the experience of movement building has not yet given way to a fully professionalized approach to writing, autobiographical reference continues to be a mode of theory. Wallace and hooks begin to articulate the partiality of the tool of autobiography, in a period where personal history is a means toward self-questioning as well as self-justification, standpoint rather than objectivity is assumed as a framework for judgment, and the conscientiousness of persona – the taking on of roles – is central to autobiographical writing. All of these things have been present in earlier black autobiography but only in their contemporary feminist guise are they, themselves, central to understanding the category of race.

In the introduction to *Invisibility Blues* Michele Wallace states her project in the 1980s to have been "to comprehend [black women's] high visibility together with their almost total lack of voice"[20] – that is, to square the publicity received by Alice Walker when *The Color Purple* won the Pulitzer Prize or the success Oprah Winfrey has attained, while continuing to stress the almost total absence of black women from control of capital and from positions of real management of cultural institutions. Race/gender are seen, in these essays, as the reifications of a visual field that hides the depth of social practice in specific ways which continue to produce the black female subject as other, even while masking this fact amid the photography of diversity. Wallace makes the further claim that because race/gender systems do this in conjunction, black women's simultaneous coding as subordinate within different dominative axes means that the attempt to form a depth analysis can easily be miscalculated through the overemphasis on a particular problem of personal history. That is, as a young black woman experiencing this form of subordination, her solution was to take on "Black Macho" outside of a nuanced picture of the history of the racialized social movements that preceded her own book. And while *Invisibility Blues* will continue the pattern of self-reference by referring to Wallace's own image and fame in illustrating this point, this time she knows that her experience, however important in constructing her theory, is an example, not the truth:

> A black woman writer who wants to write seriously about contemporary cultural issues and how they are socially constructed ... is faced with an almost insurmountable problem: if she takes a scholarly or academic approach, she will find herself virtually outside of language and without authority ... On the other hand, if she takes a colloquial "entertainment" approach – as I did in *Black Macho* – then she will be read widely, but only to be attacked and ostracized. Either way cuts the possibility of constructive commentary – in the work itself, or in the criticism of that work – down to zero.[21]

At the moment that Wallace makes this argument, in the context of the backlash to *Black Macho* and *The Color Purple*, it should be possible to see two adjustments as having been made in the history of race-experience: first, it is no longer obvious to Wallace that the divergence between forms of authority based on academic work and forms of authority based on autobiographical description, which has been the subject of this entire book, is still a characteristic of all black racial experience; instead, it has become primarily the characteristic of black feminist experience. Second, that as a direct result of this fact, the autobiographical claims of women will be attacked first of all *within* the "family," by men who metaphorize the race as a family.[22]

Though Wallace does not make note of this, *Black Macho* achieved much of its power from being laced with its rhetoric of autobiography – and this autobiography is highly unflattering to both of her parents as individuals. In particular, and in a way that contradicts the form of the black feminist analysis that *Home Girls* made possible, this twenty-eight-year old author opens the second half of her book with "By the time I was fifteen there was nothing I dreaded more than being like the women in my family."[23] The analysis she pursues in this section of the book, generationally specific to those who went through adolescence and college in the late 1960s and early 1970s, concerns the contradiction between being raised in struggling but relatively middle class homes by hardworking and autonomous black women who want her to be the same kinds of proto-feminists that Smith claims the women in her family raised her to be, and living the kinds of racial narratives being pursued in the aftermath of Malcolm X in which a new subject of desire – the patriarchal black man modeled on Malcolm's image – has come into being for hetero-sexual black women. In other words, the self-contained model of black womanhood that Nikki Giovanni half-seriously proposes at the end of *Gemini* – we are the only group that measures ourselves by ourselves – ceases, for Wallace as a teenager, to be desirable pretty much as soon as it is articulated. For Barbara Smith, Malcolm X never becomes a *sexual* icon – as he does (via George Jackson) for Angela Davis, and for Michele Wallace. Giovanni's concluding pages nar-rated Black Power as that which produced black women as the only potentially autonomous identity-position in the US; Wallace's psychoanalytical model produces the opposite conclusion: the black woman "has yet to become what she is."[24]

I am suggesting that in the seven years between the experiences recounted in *Gemini* and in *Black Macho*, the condition of blackness itself has changed, such that these two women (both twenty-eight when their books are published) read identical phenomena through different lenses. Obviously, this is not the claim that subgenerational differences are anything like a complete explanation for differences between individuals – obviously Giovanni, Davis, and Smith are all arguing from points of divergence that can be explained in other terms – but I want to suggest that it is plausible that the emergence of the critique of family as such is articulated by women who, in the wake of a movement, experience the work ethic of Smith's family of proto-black feminists not as righteously autonomous but as lonely and bitter Superwomen. Wallace will then be accused by Linda Powell in *Home Girls* of knowing nothing about how hard black women work, and while Powell's criticisms of *Black Macho* are often simply correct, she also has missed the point: Wallace the teenager and adult wants a fantasized love and respect, not the dubious privilege of overwork in the guise of super-autonomy.

Thus Wallace's more recent persona, explored autobiographically in the introduction to the new edition of *Black Macho* as well as through the rethinking of her own media image in *Invisibility Blues*, argues that black feminism cannot be a family-based politics. Black women are not those that supported her own form of revolt, and cannot be counted on for sisterly solidarity. This does not mean that "black women" are not an oppressed social group or that politics does not require a fight that does, in fact, address the specific ways that black womanhood is a subordinated subject-position. Inhabiting the social space of black women, however, is a distinct fact from solidarity with those whose space one shares; rather it may provide the framework for, precisely, articulating the tensions which appear within the space itself. A rough chart of the seventies using Giovanni, Davis, Smith, and Wallace might then be built as follows:

Giovanni: Black Power activist;
Subject

Smith: Wallace:
civil rights activist;   adolescent during Black
dialectician of home   Power period;
                                dialectician of the critique of
                                home

Davis: Black Power activist;
Object

Autobiographical practice in the work of bell hooks

In the above chart, bell hooks would occupy the identical position to Michele Wallace. The remainder of my analysis will use hooks' elaborately theorized autobiographical writing – which, I suspect it will surprise no one, forms the genetic origin of this book – on the way to exploring the limitations of autobiography as a professional strategy. This analysis, however, is quite distinct from one that would imagine that the autobiography of racialization can be gone beyond in all social locations. Rather, it suggests that certain formulas for the production of such autobiography, in becoming professionalized, are necessarily removed from the field of the production of new non-professional social identities. To use Gramscian terminology, professional intellectuals, who in late capitalism are the "traditional intellectuals" of the bourgeoisie, cannot re-embed that which has been removed from organic spaces simply by stating our good faith.

Bell hooks' essay, "Writing Autobiography" is a narrative of what she calls, throughout *Talking Back*, "self-recovery," a term she uses intentionally to reverberate with self-help and recovery discourses, while trying to give it a firmer theoretical basis.[25] For hooks, self-recovery is a necessary part, though by no means the whole, of politicization; it is the part of the narrative of the formation of community that happens when the individual is alone. Hooks starts with the wish to kill history, specifically the history of the self which causes anguish:

> To me, telling the story of my growing up years was intimately connected with the longing to kill the self I was without really having to die. I wanted to kill that self in writing . . . It was clearly the Gloria Jean of my anguished childhood I wanted to be rid of, the girl who was always wrong, always punished . . . by writing the autobiography, it was not just this Gloria I would be rid of, but the past that had a hold on me, that kept me from the present. I wanted not to forget the past but to break its hold. This death in writing was to be liberatory.[26]

This passage does and does not reverberate with others discussed to this point in the book; certainly Malcolm X uses his autobiography as a way of transcending the past and loosening its hold on him, yet the specific forms of ambivalence expressed by hooks require the acknowledgment that this project, the project of remembering, is a painful one, and thus not one to relish. And if for Smith the project may avoid strict autobiography in favor of a fantasy of the supportive home as grounding for a present politics, for hooks the process of writing autobiography itself *is* the pain: "until I began to try and write an autobiography, I thought that it would be a simple task this telling of one's story. And yet I tried year after year, never writing more than a few pages."[27]

This short essay has three distinct parts: four introductory paragraphs in which hooks lays out the specific psychological obstacles to writing an accurate autobiography, three paragraphs in which she relates apparently random vignettes, which, in recurring within memory, are specifically evocative for her; and then a six-paragraph reconsideration of what the *practice* of recalling these vignettes has meant. In the first part, pain and writing conspire to make accuracy problematic: she must write, soon, because "each year, a moment seemed less and less clear . . . yet I could not begin though I had begun to confront some of the reasons I was blocked." In contrast to writing, "talk[ing] about one's life," considerably less rigorous a project, was easy, not "frightening." Even at the point of writing this piece, hooks is "afraid to express in writing the experience that served as a catalyst for [her] block to move."[28] This experience is a love affair, about which hooks tells us nothing but that her lover "was in some mysterious way a link to [her] past," perhaps he smelled like her Uncle Pete, though this does not explain why walking with him and hearing a train causes her to imagine being stopped at a railroad crossing. Reflecting on this, hooks remarks:

> Each day I sat at the typewriter and different memories were written in short vignettes. They came in a rush, as though they were a sudden thunderstorm. They came in a surreal, dreamlike style which made me cease to think of them as strictly autobio-graphical because it seemed that myth, dream and reality had merged. There were many incidents that I would talk about with my siblings to see if they recalled them. Often we remembered together a general outline of an incident but the details were different for us. This fact was a constant reminder of the limita-tions of autobiography, of the extent to which autobiography is a very personal story telling – a unique recounting of events not so much as they have happened but as we remember and invent them.[29]

It matters that, precisely, what this understanding does not lead to, in the conclusion of the essay, is the repudiation of autobiography or self as an explanation for the generation of political practice; on the contrary, it turns out that it is precisely this project of fictionalization – but rigorous fictionalization, which includes comparing her recol-lection of events among others who recall them differently, and a commitment to honesty about how the phantasms with which one lives affect one's current perceptions – performs the necessary task of enabling future speech. Thus, in the end, hooks says "I felt as though I had an overview not so much of my childhood but of those experien-ces that were deeply imprinted in my consciousness. Significantly, that which was absent, left out, not included was important." Most importantly concerning the effect of writing autobiography is that "in the end I did not feel as though I had killed the Gloria of my childhood. Instead I had rescued her. She was no longer the enemy within, the little girl who had to be annihilated for the woman to come into being." In such an argument the "joining of fragments" makes the "narrative whole again," and is therefore "liberating."[30]

The implications of such a description of autobiographical practice are as follows: first, the basic format of a psychoanalytical model, in which the personal history is recounted for the purpose of liberating the self from what constrains its practice, is affirmed; second, the lack of ability to confirm the truth of events in no way calls into question the need to rigorously express the truth as one remembers it; and third, in the end the purpose of such a model is to re-center the self in a way that helps to explain and promote certain practical and/or political choices. The roots of this re-centered self are retained in the history of the self; its traces are not eliminated, but rather are altered in small ways that permit the recovery of that which is most useful. Thus it is a psychoanalytic narrative that in no way denies the fact of split subjectivity as a phenomenon, but can see no reason to privilege or celebrate splitness as such. Indeed, the invention of a new, unsplit self is a prerequisite of writing for at least this narrator.

If black feminist writing before bell hooks' *Talking Back* had often been personalist, in the sense that experience in the black and women's movements was the basis for the retheorization of politics, *Talking Back* nevertheless is the book that gives this pattern its fullest and most complex presentation. This is possible at least in part because hooks, unlike Giovanni, Davis, or Smith wrote two books that were entirely nonautobiographical and nonpersonalist prior to this one; *Talking Back*, in contrast to her first two, was to be the one in which "I was doing things differently – and what was slowing me down had to do with disclosure, with what it means to reveal personal stuff."[31] Although, she says, she had always been able to talk about herself, the idea that personal writing was not *racially* acceptable had long been ingrained in her consciousness: "One of the jokes we used to tell about the 'got everything' white people is how they just tell all their business, just put their stuff right out there. One point of blackness then became – like how you keep your stuff to yourself, how private you could be about your business."[32] In this narrative, this notion of privacy is consistently articulated to feminist theory about the private as the location of the specific oppression of women within the race: as a child she internalized that, "madness, not just physical abuse, was the punishment for too much talk if you were female," leading to the claim that "unlike other forms of domination, sexism directly shapes and determines relations of power in our private lives ... in that most intimate sphere of relations – family."[33] It matters a great deal that her mother is the one portrayed as most interested in silencing hooks' autobiographical narrative, telling her, "'You talk too much about the past. You don't just listen.' And I do talk. Worse, I write about it."[34] Thus, hooks argues, the politics of writing personal accounts as theory moves to a location rarely explored in previous black feminist autobiographical works – the gendering of the family, including the mother's role in patriarchal gendering, and the psychological turmoil of individual relationships.

Hooks consistently articulates her personal history as a history of blackness, and femaleness, in specific; and as such sees her recovery as a necessarily black and feminist one. But asserting one's race/ gender as *necessary* does not mean asserting the ethically positive qualities of blackness itself; that is, rootedness is not a politics which implies that one's roots are all *good*, merely that they are the material that one works from. Thus it is very important, in assessing hooks' model of an identitarian politics (which, she claims, is *not* "identity politics"), that her assertion of blackness as fundamental in our period is not ideal; rather, it asserts that blackness is the social location in which patriarchally constructed families develop affective ties which, in addition to opposing white supremacy, may reinforce patriarchy. Indeed, women, in this model, become not only the victims of patriarchy – though they may be that – but also its agents:

> This speculation does not place women outside the practice of domination, in the exclusive role of victim. It centrally names women as agents of domination, as potential theoreticians, and creators of a paradigm for social relationships wherein those groups of individuals designated as "strong" exercise power both benevolently and coercively over those designated as "weak."[35]

The response, in this context, to both the right-wing idea that properly constructed families are the location of the transmission of positive values, and to the anti-authoritarian idea that families are necessarily oppressive, is to see families as simultaneously both: "family relations may be, and most often are, informed by acceptance of a politic of domination, [and] they are simultaneously relations of care and connection."[36] In this context, the specific meaning of feminist emphasis on personal history is that it addresses us at a level of attention to our socially and psychically constructed selves more fundamentally than other mass-based movements; while the emphasis within black feminism on naming the socially constructed self (as, for example, "black woman") is not simply a matter of self-assertion or promotion but rather the necessary grounds for a self criticism, for elaborating the limits our raced-gendered histories place on us.

In this context we might try to make sense of hooks' account of the writing of her first book, *Ain't I a Woman*, a book in which hooks specifically and intentionally objectifies the issues under discussion through a third person historical account of black women's history; it is, as well, Gloria Watkins' first published work using the pseudonym bell hooks.[37] The genesis of the book begins with the experience common to students of college age of trying to find accounts of oneself in books, which, hooks makes clear, is not specific to black women in any way – though the particular problems of racial and gender subordination are experienced in specific ways by black women. In this context, hooks' inability to gain support to write *Ain't I a Woman*, even within Women's Studies, led her to identify with the black women who worked on campus in nonprofessional positions, and with her colleagues who were telephone operators, a job she held to help pay for school. Political action, in this environment, is more than a matter of merely finding a place to write, a location of support; it is in the ability to imagine oneself as representative of a subordinate group because, on the one hand, only the members of that group have provided any support for one's work, and, on the other, because you are the only member of that group in your graduate program. Two important, and contradictory, things result from the point of view of the writing subject of the book: "I was speaking most directly to black women ... [and] placing myself and other black women at the speaking center"; but, alternatively

> I was certainly adamant in *Ain't I a Woman* that black women had much to gain through participation in a feminist movement, even though I was equally adamant in my criticism of dominant tendencies in the movement that I felt undermined its importance. I did not see my book as representing "the" feminist work or "the" black female statement on feminism. It was and remains a polemical piece.[38]

What seems of the greatest practical importance is that the phantasmatic production of "black woman" as a category of political readers or supporters, unavailable in graduate school, was itself necessary for the possibility of any writing to take place – only after writing two books in the guise of this objectification, this category, was hooks able to discover how much these books concerned her personal needs, her autobiography.

A similar process is at work in the construction of the persona of bell hooks, the pseudonymous alternative to her birth name, Gloria Watkins. Gloria is a name she "associate[s] with frivolity and dizziness," and "though I am sometimes dizzy and quite frivolous, I was afraid then that this name would take me over, become my identity before I could make it what I wanted it to be."[39] Gloria, the young girl, long before she began writing *Ain't I a Woman?* used the pseudonym because "it had a strong sound" and because it was a family name, of a great grandmother who had the reputation of "a strong woman, a woman who spoke her mind." As the book developed, the psychic splitting took a different form; Gloria was a person "not particularly concerned with politics," and bell hooks provided the possibility of writing that was politically oriented.[40] Thus in the case of the pseudonym, like the voice in the text, it is precisely the act of objectification, of a consciously formed personal identity paralleling the group identity formation "black women," that provides the space to engage in an explicitly political and polemical project, and to overcome her "fear of expression."[41] Thus if the polemic in "On Self-Recovery" is about the need for black women to "move from seeing ourselves as objects to acting as subjects,"[42] this is undercut by the later analysis that such "action" was always already dependent on a prior objectification of the self. Bell hooks does not eliminate Gloria Watkins any more than the category black women eliminates the differences among "black women"; rather, it is itself the name of a productive public identity without which intellectual work, for at least this particular black female subject, is not possible.

Taken as autobiography this is a fascinating and politically useful account. Yet *Talking Back*, published in 1989, sits at a watershed moment not only of academic black feminism, but of the institutionalization of the name "bell hooks." For once Gloria Watkins went about revealing personal information under that sign, the entire elaborate distinction between Gloria and bell began to break down, as bell, in her books – which as of this writing include two full autobiographies – began to speak for Gloria, and her existence as an institutionalized public identity lost its meaning. The painful psychoanalysis which produced bell hooks from Gloria Watkins has not been followed up by an engagement with the question of the professionalization of bell hooks. That is, if "bell hooks," in Talking Back, is a concept, not a person, by 1989 this concept has become an explicitly professionalized one. Yet by its failure to acknowledge the class aspect of its development in subsequent work, hooks' writing has become decreasingly politically engaged.

Hooks' work on the surface places class, capitalism, and academic institutions firmly in the middle of contemporary considerations of racial identity; it is necessary for me to describe how it does so, especially in the context of what I take to be her specifically anti-marxist account in the recent *Outlaw Culture*. "Through much of my graduate school career," hooks says, "I was told that 'I did not have the proper demeanor of a graduate student.'"[43] In a different essay, she reports:

> Like many working-class folks [my parents] feared what college
> education might do to their children's minds even as they unen-
> thusiastically acknowledged its importance. They did not un-
> derstand why I could not attend a college nearby, an all-black
> college... And even though they reluctantly and skeptically
> supported my educational endeavors, they also subjected them
> to constant harsh and bitter critique.[44]

Hooks uses this not to defend an anti-intellectual position with regard to doing social critique, but rather as a position from which to
question how such a critique gets made and whether there are critical
languages used by non-intellectuals which might in turn help to
articulate the ambivalence of class and academic mobility in her
intellectual work. Searching for a language which will not be immediately dismissed either by her working class family, on the one hand,
or her colleagues, on the other, she views the use of critical theory as a
class issue,[45] and one directly related to the question of pedagogy at
multiple levels: the question of how to introduce social theories that
could help students to change their lives to those who are scared of it,
the question of how to read everyday language as itself theoretical,
and, most importantly, the question of making the academy responsible, in class terms, to its own staff, and to those workers who need
its research or legitimation outside it. It is in this context that hooks
consistently stresses the difficulty of "struggling to educate for liberation in the corporate university."[46]

I share not only this broad political framework, but also a considerable amount of hooks' experience with regard to class in the
university – with differences that are not solely a matter of race and
gender, of course. Yet it is frustrating that hooks never develops the
meaning of "corporate" in the phrase I just quoted, or her understanding of the critique of "capitalism" as it appears in, for
example, the phrase "white supremacist capitalist patriarchy," her
persistent description of the mode of cultural production that we
want to bring an end to. While hooks is often convincing in her
analysis of subjectification within patriarchy and white supremacy
as systems of domination, it is entirely unclear in her work precisely what the critique of capitalism means, or who, it is imagined, will
oppose it. Unlike Du Bois or Robeson, the patriarchal men who
nevertheless worked hardest to comprehend why capitalism was
necessarily colonial, but like Malcolm X in his final year, when he
persistently oscillated between the question of whether socialism in
the decolonizing nations was necessary, or merely one of several

alternatives, hooks provides no generalized analysis of the meaning of capitalism.

This matters in two different ways in her work. On the one hand, in the context of a recent interview with Ice Cube, she is unwilling to be even mildly critical of something she refers to as "black capitalism"; while she states that "black capitalism is not black self-determination," she also states that "that doesn't mean we don't need black capitalism."[47] In the context of her persistent disavowal of capitalism through her work, it would be helpful to see an argument for why such a thing might be necessary, or what, in particular, is meant by it. Likewise, in her critique of the movie *Paris is Burning*,[48] it is clear that she dislikes the film in two ways that intersect the critique of capitalism: that the black drag queens represented in it are, in reproducing ruling class elegance, in love with a specific representation of class power; and in her concern that the profits made by the filmmakers and distributors of the film will not go to benefit these drag queens, who are themselves actually quite poor, but rather will end up largely in white hands, with the black men exploited as usual. Both of these concerns are useful and important. And yet they leave open the question of whether capitalism is problematic largely by virtue of its representations, and whether equitably distributed profits from the film would be an adequate to challenge to capitalism. Minimally, the question that must be confronted is the one Du Bois was unable to answer in *Dusk of Dawn*: how is it plausible to set up a separate black economic structure in the US; and regardless of its plausibility, aren't the consequences of advocating black capitalism merely the perpetuation of exploitation?

The second matter, however, is the crux: her most recent essay on class, which appears in the recent *Outlaw Culture*, published five years after *Talking Back*'s class analysis, is rather different in tone and content. In this essay the problem of class adjustment is no longer a matter of making the corporate university accountable to currently working class people, as it was in *Talking Back*; rather it is solely the problem of "class elitism" on the part of African-American intellectuals. That is, in contrast to the earlier book, in which hooks suggests that her work is motivated by identification with the black female staff members at various universities and the phone company, here she identifies herself with black professionals, whose attitudes toward the "poor" (*not* the "workers" – they are no longer agents at all in this essay) she hopes to reform. In this text hooks' criticism does not address capitalism at all, but merely "class power and class divisions among black folks," as though professionals merely losing their "bourgeois mind-set" is what is at issue.[49] In such a framework, "class" is produced in an anti-systemic manner as simply a subject-position removed from any relationship to the means of production. This is why the movement from a working class rural Kentucky household to a professional job in New York City has no bearing, apparently, on hooks' self-perception of her class position: she *still* claims to be "working class." I am not, as will be clear below, suggesting that differences in "class origin" might not, under some circumstances, generate different identifications, but "class origin" is not hooks' category; "class" is.

Leaving home for the academy

The difficult tension in the conclusion to my book is between the success of black feminism in producing a professional discourse necessary to the political and personal aspirations of a cross-section of racialized individuals, not all of whom are black women, and the lack of appearance of a large-scale social movement which would change the apparatus of racialization beyond the reproduction of Malcolm's image, in forms that were once tragic, and now would be farce were it not for the melancholy they produce. A scholarly book can point to such a tension; it cannot resolve it. It is in this context that the recent backlash against autobiographical writing among radical intellectuals has developed and should be made sense of. And while I continue to be interested in the complicated and dialectical analysis of the autobiographies of prisoners, niggas, welfare queens, bitches and hoes, and sometimes even students and professionals – none of which are being produced in large numbers, least of all when their subjects are women – I am equally sympathetic to the argument, made variously by Ann DuCille, Gina Dent, and many others, that to the extent that autobiography may have been a useful strategy in the past, within the academy this moment has come resolutely to an end. Whatever else our professional work may or may not be, it is not home, and we must not act like it is.

This book opened with the statement that identity politics – and therefore the pervasive demand to speak autobiographically – is always already identified with black women, and its conclusion no doubt demonstrates that one cannot write a book describing the determinants of this claim without also reproducing the identification. Ann DuCille's essay "The Occult of True Black Womanhood:

Critical Demeanor and Black Feminist Studies" is no doubt the best-known essay to theorize this at the moment of my writing, and its form, too, illustrates the problem. Stringing together a long series of frustrating examples of the means by which black women are now being marginalized even within "black feminist studies," DuCille is particularly concerned to criticize a number of writers who are not black women for the demeaning nature of their autobiographical explanations of how they became qualified and good-hearted enough to write books about black women. Her argument, with which I have no interest in disagreeing, is that professional competence in black feminist studies be the measure of books written in this field. Conspicuously, however, the explanation for why such professional competence should replace the prevalence of the confessional is couched not only in an autobiographical account of DuCille's own emergence as a black feminist – that is, the history of black feminist studies recounted is narrated simultaneously with the narrative of when DuCille first encountered particular ideas and concerns – but also via the categories of emotional stress and exasperation: "I have a burning need to work through on paper my own ambivalence"; "I am troubled, even galled, by what at times feels like the appropriation and co-optation of black women"; "I know I am misbehaving."[50] Somewhat optimistically, DuCille's essay attempts to go beyond herself and her contemporaries, who are "too set in our ways, too alternatively defensive and offensive," to announce the dawning of a new generation of scholars professionally competent enough to "grapple less with each other and more with issues, to disagree without being disagreeable"[51] because we will understand that "the most important questions [are] about professionalism and disciplinarity; about cultural literacy and intellectual competence."[52] (And suddenly there will be high paying jobs for every one of us, producing no jealousy, competition, nor hunger for power.) I don't think I *want* DuCille's essay to be correct any less then she does, but I hope I will be understood as friendly if I ask whether she has demeaned herself as much as those she criticizes have demeaned her by presenting herself as so emotionally unstable while her intellectual "daughters," and their friends, are such superior human beings? DuCille apologizes over and over for talking about how raced-gendered autobiography constitutes the very reason for her desire that we escape autobiography. Who is demanding this apology from this black woman? Black feminist theory must continue to take on that question.

DuCille is not the only person who has recently published an essay against confessional discourse that is itself couched in autobiography. "Missionary Position," by a scholar of the generation DuCille hopes so much from, Gina Dent, appears in the anthology collected by Rebecca Walker, *To Be Real*, an anthology that presents itself as bringing this new generation to voice.[53] Her argument, which in some ways is a counter-allegory of my book, is that feminism, the space in which the theorization of the autobiographical in our present period has been most centrally located, has found itself caught in a confessional mode in which the staged narration of self has become more significant than engagement with those outside of the confessing congregation. Stressing the large number of women whose daily lives exhibit the acceptance of feminist tenets, but who would not consider calling themselves feminists because of a perception that the ritual of feminist confession is irrelevant to their daily practice (the religious metaphor is precisely the grounds of her claim here), Dent recounts her experience at a feminist conference in which she asked a question about the relevance of consciousness raising to women whose daily lives, for material and personal reasons, continue to be lived in the sex work professions. Who believes that the consciousnesses of these women must be "raised," and to what end? The violence with which her serious, and not antagonistic, question was met by the ex-prostitute telling the story of her conversion to feminism leads Dent to want to rethink the politics of storytelling in terms of the consideration of local circumstance and meaning. Dent does not oppose the telling of stories of oppression, but rather wonders what theoretical problems might be hidden by a too broad political attachment to particular forms of storytelling.

The sense in which this is a counter-allegory for my project is as follows: I have argued for the practical ability of the interaction of self-representation within political moments and movements to reconstitute the meaning of blackness in a variety of important ways, some of which are predictable within the grounds of the autobiography itself, others of which are in excess to it. I have also suggested that in the aftermath of Black Power, women's autobiographies have opened up multiple readings of gendered blackness without succeeding in dislodging Malcolm X from the psychological center of racialization. Dent's argument would suggest that for a new generation of feminist practice, the stage at which listening to any given autobiographical account is transformative is now deeply mediated by the overabundance of the form – some of us have heard certain stories often enough to want to ask different questions about them, including

why they have stopped increasing the numbers who identify with a
radical political community. The moment of the act of theorizing
autobiography within the academy may also be the moment at which
the act of autobiography becomes problematic to teach; this fact may,
by virtue of historical association, be of particular consequence for
those inhabiting the category of black women in the present generation. In other words, the professionalism of black women as critics
creates a reaction against the history of autobiographically constructed race/gender at precisely the moment that it becomes possible for
white men of Dent's generation to perceive ourselves as just another
local category, to be academically trained in African-American and
feminist studies, and indeed to spend our research lives theorizing
the subjective marginality of our socially empowered position.

I take this argument with the greatest seriousness, though even
now I must emphasize it is countered by other possibilities. It may
alternatively be that we are just now beginning to get the kinds of
narrations of black women as professionals that Barbara Omolade
considers central for the release of black women from positions of
obligation and service.[54] That Omolade cites Patricia Williams' *The
Alchemy of Race and Rights* as an example of such professional narrative – and that Williams, as quoted in the epigraph to this chapter,
speaks of the need for such professional (and romantic) archetypes –
may provide an additional gloss of the *specific* kinds of non-mission-
ary, but still "autobiographical," narrations that might co-exist with
Dent's comments.

Throughout this book my problem has been how to incorporate the
problematic of DuCille's essay, which I clearly do not see as in the
process of fading away, into a professional narrative that is not a
confessional. Let me tell you a story. I have made use of Robyn
Wiegman's *American Anatomies* regularly throughout this book, especially in chapters one and four, where specific arguments of hers
and specific arguments of mine overlap, but also elsewhere. Though
Wiegman's assumptions are Foucaultian, and mine marxist, our positions within the field of race theory seem to me very close. The first
time I read her book – and in the first completed draft of this book – I
decided Wiegman was black, I wanted, needed her to be black.[55]
There are two moments in her book where, in a coded manner,
Wiegman indicates that she is white; I ignored both. In spite of real
differences between Wiegman and myself, *American Anatomies* is the
immediately prior book that is closest to the theory of racialization
presented in this book. I do not know whether this means that

collectively she and I represent an emerging "white" tendency in the field, but it seems to me that a race theory unwilling to ask that question is no better than one that presumes that autobiographies of racialization represent the transparent truth.

Coda: notes toward the objectification of myself

> I try to put together the two parts of my life, as many first-generation intellectuals do. Some use different means – for instance, they find a solution in political action, in some kind of social rationalization. My main problem is to try and understand what happened to me. My trajectory may be described as miraculous, I suppose – an ascension to a place where I don't belong. And so to be able to live in a world that is not mine I must try to understand both things: what it means to have an academic mind – how such is created – and at the same time, what was lost in acquiring it. (Pierre Bourdieu)[56]

> To confront them is not to represent (*vertreten*) them but to learn to represent (*darstellen*) ourselves. (Gayatri Spivak)[57]

> Afro-American culture has long been the starting point for white self-criticism in the US. (Michele Wallace)[58]

There is much I could say about the particular history of my coming to write this book, some of which has been said in the acknowledgments, and much more of which has been said in the statement that became the afterword of the version of this book filed as my dissertation. But over the last two years of rewriting it became clear to me that the inclusion of such a statement is precisely not what is needed to conclude this book.

Two things are at stake in the determinate construction of my own subjectivity here, now:[59] first, the question of its *objectification*, that is, the description of the conditions of its production; and second, the specification that such an objectification for a white, Jewish American, male radical of working class origins is produced not merely out of self-reflection but out of a particular and historically common representation of the African-American female intellectual as other. I am not the first person socially positioned to learn in a particular way to objectify myself through the process of reading African Americans, as several African Americans have let me know. The "high" theorists who have explained this to me most persistently since I began graduate school are Pierre Bourdieu and Gayatri Spivak. It should be clear that in citing them here I am not claiming identity with either one.

With regard to my Bourdieu quotation, the "ascension" to my present position, which has certainly been a royal pain, has nevertheless in no way been "miraculous"; and to the extent my multiple consciousness has been produced through a process not entirely unlike the one he describes, it comes from the collision not only of my class marginality at birth with the "academic" mind, but also my race/gender central-ity at birth with a different type of marginality, the always already having-been-read by black women. With regard to my quotation from Gayatri Spivak, it will be clear that although I consider this argument, the pivotal one in "Can the Subaltern Speak?," fundamentally correct, I simultaneously disagree strongly with her suggestion, in the section that immediately follows in that essay, that Jacques Derrida is a model white male (Jewish!) example of the representation of the (economic/aesthetic) self as the outcome of the (political) representation of the subaltern. Indeed, I have found a neo-marxist dialectical humanism much more convincing than deconstruction as an approach to such self-representation through other-representation.

One of the strands of narrative in this book has been the emergence of the representation of whiteness in black discourse. On this, Du Bois' mock dialogues with white friends, Elijah Mohammed's folk tale about the invention of the white race, bell hooks' depiction of the black gaze at whiteness, are pivotal. I turn in conclusion to Paule Marshall's 1969 novel *The Chosen Place, The Timeless People*, in which certain of the details of my subject-position are objectified via the character of Saul Amron.[60]

Amron is a character created by an African-American woman writer of Caribbean descent, who is both narrated from the third person and also viewed through the eyes of two black Caribbean women characters, Leesy Walkes and Merle Kinbona. The narrator presents him as an anthropologist of the best imaginable short: rad-ical in his knowledge of the economics, history, ecology, and psychol-ogy of colonial oppression, broad in his identification with the need for revolution, narrow and focused in his awareness of the extreme limits of what he can actually do, limits which do not force him to conclude that he can do nothing. As a young man in the 1930s he was a revolutionary and spoke of total transformation; in his early years as a professional anthropologist he created programs for the recon-struction of the economy of the places he studied that were altogether too big to receive funding and which, because of their scope, would have been bureaucratic in implementation had they been funded. In the 1960s he is project coordinator for a small development corporation funded by "progressive" American industry, figuring out what small-scale work can be done in collaboration with the sugar workers of the Bournehills district of Bourne Island for their own benefit. His most notable success comes when the sugar refinery that has processed the canes of these smallholders is closed by Kingsley and Co., the holding company that (we discover over the course of the novel) essentially controls the entire lives of the people of Bournehills. He and his partner, Allen Fuso, use the funds at their disposal and the analytical tools of their training to see that the farmers are able to transport their crop to the refinery on the other end of the island. This is little, but it is unambiguously good, an example of what a committed outsider with attentiveness to local circumstances can do for a specific group of people. (I will return to the fact that he fails to follow up this small-scale success.)

Leesy Walkes is the subaltern, to the extent that such a noun can be represented via characterization in a novel. She meets Spivak's criteria in the following ways: she is produced by the author as the one least represented in the social hierarchy even of her local community, Bournehills, being elderly, female, widowed in an accident at the refinery a generation earlier, and not presently able to work in the fields. She is unsympathetic to the claims and desires of even the other women laborers in her district, and so suspicious of all machines and all outsiders that she will not have her few canes (which were harvested by her nephew) transported in Saul's convoy but rather insists on using a goat cart. Pure *différance*, not only with regard to Saul, but with regard to her nephew Vere (who fixes cars) and Gwen (able-bodied, many-offspringed leader among the women sugar workers), Leesy is one of the few characters in the book whom Marshall does not *know* from the inside, other than to represent her as having no consciousness beyond the rejection of everything that marginalizes her. She does not speak, because of internal constraints literally *cannot*, in the presence of anyone higher in the social hierarchy than herself.[61] Even toward the women she does speak to she is nasty and cynical, yelling "you think you's the only body can read a newspaper, Mary Griggs?" at the woman who asks whether she's heard of Saul's plans for Bournehills.[62] This is what happens when Saul approaches the group in which she is standing:

> Offering his hand, saying simply that he was glad to meet them, he sought, in the brief moments he spent with each, to penetrate the tunnel of their eyes, to get at what lay there. And

under cover of the darkness he felt them assessing him: his outer self first – his large, somewhat soft white body that had never known real physical labor, the eyes that had gone numb after his first wife's death, the coarse hair that had begun to recede at the temples. They saw even farther, he sensed; their gaze discovering the badly flawed man within and all the things about him which he would gladly have kept hidden: his deep and abiding dissatisfaction with himself, for one, his large capacity for failing those closest to him, his arrogance, born of that defensive superiority which had been his heritage as a Jew, his selfishness – for in everything he did, no matter how selfless it might appear, he was always after raising his own stock...

All during the rest of the evening, part of his mind, his thoughts, dwelt on them. He found himself wanting to return to the beach and speak further with them. If he could have done it without appearing impolite, he would have liked to probe deeper into those eyes, to understand the meaning of the expression there.[63]

If Leesy or any of her companions says anything to Saul, Marshall does not tell us what it is, perhaps because Saul really can't hear it. We do, however, get this from Leesy's voice, talking to herself, several pages later, when no one is present:

> "But I wonder why these people from Away can't learn, yes," Leesy said... "Every time you look here comes another set of them with a big plan... And they always got to come during crop when people are busy trying to get their few canes out the ground and over to Cane Vale, always walking about and looking, the lot of them, like they never seen poor people before. I tell you they're some confused and troubled souls you see them there."

> "And it's not that the gentleman tonight doesn't look like he means well ... He talked direct. He's a man, you can see, don't put on no lot of airs like some of them who come here calling themselves trying to help. And he's the first one ever said he wanted to go out in a cane field and see for himself how we have to work. You can tell he's a decent somebody. But what's the use? He'll never get to know this place. He'll never understand it. Bournehills! Change Bournehills! Improve conditions! Ha!" Her laugh was full of a secret knowing. "The only way you could change things around here would be to take one of Bryce-Parker's bulldozers from the conservation scheme and lay the whole place flat flat flat and then start fresh."

> After a long silence, broken only by the sound of her tangled breathing (it seemed about to fail at any moment), she said, "Multimillions!" and sucking her teeth, slept.[64]

Saul Amron had just explicitly denied that his project was funded with any "multimillions."

Merle Kinbona is the intellectually brilliant black island native with the elite British education, fired from her teaching position on the island for her radical politics, rather incompetent operator of an out of the way inn in an old plantation house in Bournehills, constantly struggling for basic sanity, with whom Saul falls deeply in love, the person oppressed but not subaltern who is Saul's equal or better. The woman who really *represents* (*vertreten* and *darstellen*, for better or worse) Bournehills for him. You can tell that this dyad is the center of the novel because the concluding chapter of each of its four sections presents a dialogue between the two. Merle comes to love Saul too, but not half as much as he loves her, which means she sees him as alternatively a beautiful friend and a pathetic failure. She represents him in the following ways before they sleep together:

> "This was your first encounter with the gentleman," she said, "but how do you think someone like myself feels who's seen him come and put on his little show every year now for the past eight years?"
>
> "I know," he said, "I know how difficult it is for you living here."
>
> "No, you don't," she said. "You don't have a clue." She spoke flatly, simply stating a fact there was no disputing."
>
> ... "I'm not nearly as hopeless as you believe."
>
> She turned away, refusing for the moment to argue the point... Then, her profile to him, Merle said – and she spoke in the same flat, emotionless tone – "'No, you have no idea what it's like living here, in a place where you sometimes feel everything came to a dead stop donkeys' years ago and won't ever move again ... and where some little shriveled up man in a safari suit still drops in once a year to remind you who's boss. You feel so helpless at times you want to scream like a mad woman or rush out and murder somebody."[65]

But then:

> "Sometimes you come close to being what we call in Bournehills real people. Yes," she said quickly, as though afraid he would deny it. "You almost come like one of us at times. Maybe it's the techniques you have to learn in your business on how to get in with people. But I don't think so. Or perhaps it's because you're a Jew and that's given you a deeper understanding. After all, your people have caught hell far longer than mine. But I doubt it. Because I got to meet quite a few Jews in London: the East End was overrun with them in my time; people were saying

they were taking over England" – he found himself laughing despite his sudden discomfort at that familiar old saw – "and although one or two of them became my very close friends, most of them were as bad as the English and had no use for black people. Some of them, in fact, behaved worse toward us than the English. You would have thought they would have been more sympathetic, having gone through so much themselves. But it seems suffering doesn't make people any better or wiser or more understanding."[66]

They sleep together only after, at a bar the night of the island's carnival, Merle "interviews" the anthropologist, mercilessly, in a way that makes him profoundly uncomfortable, that undoes him psychologically for at least a short time: "'I don't know if I like being interviewed by you,' he said. 'I didn't think you would,' she said. 'Go on.'"[67]

In the period after they start having their affair, Merle represents him as follows:

> ... "I like you a lot, you know. Even though I'm using you."
> "Really?" he said, and dropped her arm. "How?"
> She bent on him a fond, sad smile. "Why, you're my new Juju man from Harley street [i.e., psychologist], don't you know that, love?"[68]

But when Cane Vale is closed down, and Merle has her most dramatic breakdown of the entire book, she still lights into the most convenient white man available:

> "Do something, but oh, Christ, don't just stand there with your head hanging down doing nothing. Oh, blast you. Blast all of you. You and Sir John and Hinds and the Queen and that smooth high-toned bitch of a wife you've got and that other bitch who tried to turn me into a monkey for her amusement. Look, don't come near me, you hear. I don't want to see not a white face today. Not one! *Fix it!*"[69]

Ah, which reminds me that I haven't mentioned that Saul is married ... and that yes, in the long run the affair with Merle ends that relationship. And without recounting that part of the plot in detail here, this too becomes the issue about smart, sincere white men who want to help, because while Saul does in fact "fix it," accomplishing what little he can for the people of Bournehills, he also is forced to leave the island permanently when his wife offers Merle money to get out of her life – Merle refuses not because she loves Saul, but because she won't take bribes from white people – and ends up bringing the entire development project down with her, writing letters to the US to get the project's funding lifted. Harriet Amron imagines that going home will save her marriage. My apologies for this representation of a white woman as the end of the project, but I promise all the white men other than Saul are far worse than Harriet. Indeed, Merle even identifies explicitly with Harriet's pain when she sees her losing her husband.

If, in the end, Saul says "I'm more convinced than ever now that that's the best way: to have people from the country itself carry out their own development programs whenever possible. Outsiders just complicate the picture,"[70] he is talking about a situation of pure power. What it means to say that multinational capital controls a significant portion of the lives of the people of Bournehills is to say that the carrying out, or not, of specific, useful, small-scale projects for a few thousand people depends on the stability of the personal life of a single anthropologist from "away."

No one book objectifies any situation adequately for a huge number of people, let alone thirty years after it is published. The relationship between black and white in African-American Studies at present is hardly identical to the relationship of a US-based anthropologist to the Caribbean district he works in. And I am, obviously, not saying that white people have no business in African-American Studies. But a race theory that turns the matter into one of pure professionalism is not, finally, a race theory. Until African Americans are as well-represented in the teaching of Shakespeare and literary theory, and in Chinese Studies, and in physics, and as students in well-funded elementary schools as white Americans are, us white folk have nothing special to be proud of by our presence in African-American Studies. We are neither "good" nor "bad," but we are "a problem" – and how *does* it feel to be a problem? We continue to need the honesty to objectify ourselves in the mirror of our particular others, and to choose our ethical battles in the context of the reality of those objectifications.

Notes

1 What is identity politics? Race and the autobiographical

1 Lorraine Hansberry, *To Be Young, Gifted, and Black* (New York, Signet, 1969), 256.

2 Frantz Fanon, *Black Skin, White Masks* (New York, Grove, 1967), 232, emphasis mine.

3 Gayatri Spivak, "Can the Subaltern Speak?," in L. Grossberg and C. Nelson, eds., *Marxism and the Interpretation of Culture* (Urbana, University of Illinois Press, 1988), 308.

4 Micaela di Leonardo, "White Ethnicities, Identity Politics, and Baby Bear's Chair," *Social Text* 41 (winter 1994), 165.

5 Reference to "distribution" of "power" is always fraught since the term power has been conceptualized as flow of energy, rather than distributed quantity, by strains of poststructuralist theory which follow Foucault. As my use of this term may strike some as anachronistic, I want to say that the term seems to me appropriately used in both senses. See Michel Foucault, *The History of Sexuality: An Introduction* (New York, Vintage, 1978), 93ff. and Gayatri Spivak's reinsertion of Foucault into the marxian theory of value: *Outside in the Teaching Machine* (New York, Routledge, 1993), 76.

6 See, for example, Lawrence Grossberg, *We Gotta Get Out of This Place* (New York, Routledge, 1992); Peter Erickson, "State of the Union," *Transition* 59, 104–9. This is a corollary to Ann DuCille's important account of the production of black women as the privileged site of difference within contemporary white feminist and black male discourses. Ann DuCille, "The Occult of True Black Womanhood: Critical Demeanor and Black Feminist Studies," in E. Abel, B. Christian, and H. Moglen, eds., *Female Subjects in Black and White* (Berkeley, University of California Press, 1997). It is possible that my argument will have something of the same effect within marxism, even as it attempts to ask in a rigorous way "what does black feminism have to teach marxism?" and "what does an analysis that is marxist and black feminist look like?"

7 Angela Davis reminds us that a typical activity of many "nationalist" organizations in California during the late 1960s was to form "internationalist" coalitions with Chicano, Native American, and other nationalist or internationalist groups. "Black Nationalism: The Sixties and the Nineties," in G. Dent, ed., *Black Popular Culture* (Seattle, Bay Press, 1992). Likewise, Michael Eric Dyson's distinction between racially conscious politics and racially exclusive politics is useful here. Malcolm X, in Dyson's terms, moved from the latter to the former while remaining a "nationalist." *Making Malcolm: The Myth and Meaning of Malcolm X* (New York, Oxford University Press, 1995). Today, as in the 1960s, black nationalism is frequently enunciated as a variety of pragmatic politics: "'Are all white people terrorizing Black people?' It doesn't matter [in my context]." Haki R. Madhubuti, *Black Men: Obsolete, Single, Dangerous?* (Chicago, Third World, 1990), vi. Finally, it must be remembered that even the least sophisticated of those who advocate that a given identity group "should" unite politically have perfectly good psychosocial and economic arguments, in their own terms, for why various members of the group do not do so (e.g., "selling out"). They too have thought through the question of the sociological process of political group formation in a way that goes beyond that which is attributed to them by straw arguments.

8 June Jordan, *Technical Difficulties* (New York, Vintage, 1994), 139–46.

9 Toril Moi, "Feminism, Postmodernism, and Style: Recent Feminist Criticism in the United States," *Cultural Critique* 9 (spring 1988), 15, emphasis in original.

10 This phenomenon is called "the rules of racial standing" in Derrick Bell, *Faces at the Bottom of the Well* (New York, Basic, 1992), chapter 6; the form, though certainly not the content, of this argument is elaborated in the sociologicization of speech act theory in Pierre Bourdieu, *Language and Symbolic Action* (Cambridge, Mass., Harvard University Press, 1991), chapter 1.

11 Di Leonardo, "White Ethnicities," 166.

12 *Ibid.*, 186.

13 Patricia Williams, *The Alchemy of Race and Rights* (Cambridge, Mass., Harvard University Press, 1991), 256–7.

14 Judith Roof and Robyn Wiegman, eds., *Who Can Speak? Authority and Cultural Identity* (Bloomington, Indiana University Press, 1995), 152–3.

15 Ernesto Laclau and Chantal Mouffe, *Hegemony and Socialist Strategy* (New York, Verso, 1985).

16 Though, as Colin Sparks points out, Hall's earliest work, in the late 1950s and through most of the 1960s, was in no way marxist, and his most practical work (unlike his theory) during his marxist decades never confronted issues differently from his earlier and later nonmarxist work. Colin Sparks, "Stuart Hall, Cultural Studies, and Marxism," in D. Morley and K. H. Chen, eds. *Stuart Hall: Critical Dialogues in Cultural Studies* (New York, Routledge, 1996). At present, Hall clearly imagines himself to have broken sharply from marxism; see, e.g., "Cultural Studies and Its Theoretical Legacies," in Morley and Chen, *Stuart Hall*, 262–75, where, without any exploration, he accuses

marxism of never having had a nonreductive theory of ideology while ignoring his own previous work which claimed the opposite, and "The Afterlife of Frantz Fanon: Why Fanon? Why Now? Why *Black Skin, White Masks?*," in A. Read, ed., *The Fact of Blackness* (Seattle, Bay Press, 1996) where it is simply presumed that the current productivity of *Black Skin, White Masks* rather than *Wretched of the Earth* in Fanon studies can be explained by the former's incipient poststructuralism. That *Black Skin, White Masks* factually was incipiently marxist (since that's where Fanon's thinking took him) seems not to have occurred to Hall in this formulation. Also ignored is that there are plenty of alternative positions in Fanon studies which claim *Black Skin, White Masks* for Sartrean existentialism – one might as well claim that Sartre was incipiently poststructuralist.

17 Lawrence Grossberg, "On Postmodernism and Articulation: An Interview with Stuart Hall," in Morley and Chen, eds., *Stuart Hall*, 141.

18 Stuart Hall, "Cultural Identity and Diaspora," in P. Williams and L. Chrisman, eds., *Colonial Discourse and Postcolonial Theory* (New York, Columbia University Press, 1994), 392.

19 *Ibid.*, 394.

20 Eric Olin Wright, *Classes* (New York, Verso, 1985); Pierre Bourdieu, *Distinction: A Social Critique of the Judgment of Taste* (Cambridge, Mass., Harvard University Press, 1984).

21 See Wright, *Classes*, 201ff. This book does not propose a fully adequate theory of class subjectivity for African-American Studies. At this point, however, I would suggest that such a theory would necessarily have to accommodate the following elements: (1) objective class position as understood in the terms of historical marxism – by which there has never yet been a "black bourgeoisie," or class of large black capital holders; (2) a reconsideration of the proper unit of class analysis, in Wallersteinian terms, as the household (where economic decisions are made); this account also sees "ethnicity" as, among other things, a joint economic strategy; (3) the question of class trajectory, as Bourdieu among others understands it, in which upward or downward mobility (individual, household, or ethnic) is accounted for; and (4) the related question of class origin, as discussed by bell hooks, for example.

22 Raymond Williams, *Marxism and Literature* (New York, Oxford University Press, 1981), 83–9.

23 See, for example, Linda Alcoff, "Philosophy and Racial Identity," in *Radical Philosophy* 75 (1996), 5–14; Patricia Hill Collins, *Black Feminist Thought: Knowledge, Consciousness and the Politics of Empowerment* (London, Harper Collins, 1990); Sandra Harding, "Rethinking Standpoint Epistemology: What is 'Strong Objectivity'?," in L. Alcoff and S. Potter, eds., *Feminist Epistemologies* (New York, Routledge, 1993). Embedded here is the problem of the status of the object in contemporary philosophy, a discussion which cannot be taken up here. I will merely say that the currently standard line about Adorno, that he was a proto-Derrida, and what a shame he didn't finish the argument, seems to me exactly wrong. In fact, as Peter Dews has shown, taken

seriously, the Adornian dialectic provides a still necessary resistance to the operations of deconstruction, by providing language for the critique of identity without forgetting that difference, taken to its extreme point, becomes conceptually self-identical. Theodor Adorno, *Negative Dialectics* (New York, Continuum, 1994), 146–51; Peter Dews, *The Limits of Disenchantment* (New York, Verso, 1995), chapter 1; Peter Dews, *Logics of Disintegration* (New York, Verso, 1987), chapter 1. Still, if even Adorno's discussion is more suspicious of identity than mine appears to be in this chapter, it is in part because he is, specifically, constructing the negative in European philosophy, a project which has its counterpart in constructing (and I do mean to emphasize that word) the positive in *minority* discourse as defined by Abdul Jan-Mohamed, "Negating the Negation as a Form of Affirmation in Minority Discourse: The Construction of Richard Wright as Subject," *Cultural Critique* 7 (fall 1987), 245–66. No one has yet developed the applicability of Adorno's position to minority discourse or post-colonialism with the grace, articulateness, and brilliance that Spivak has developed Derrida's position. A first, very important attempt at challenging Spivak via Adorno has been made in Asha Varadharajan, *Exotic Parodies: Subjectivity in Adorno, Said, Spivak* (Minneapolis, University of Minnesota Press, 1995), but on its own terms her book is clearly less accomplished than Spivak's work, and is therefore unlikely to convert those who do not already hold our position.

24 One of the primary mystifications of our present moment is, of course, the idea that the contemporary discourses of Foucault and Derrida are non-Eurocentric while the work of Marx and historical marxism is Eurocentric. If Foucault and Derrida, tied to explicitly European genealogies, can be made useful for third worldist feminism, then why exactly shouldn't Marx be made useful for third worldist feminism as well, at the historical moment when third world women are emerging as the largest section of the industrial proletariat? Tim Brennan comments similarly in "A Symposium on Whiteness," *Minnesota Review* 47 (1996), 119.

25 The traditional marxist contrast between a "class for itself" and a "class in itself" is laid out clearly by Marx in this work, in which the politically acting social classes in 1848 in France are shown to be many and varied while it is claimed that only specific ones, the bourgeois and the proletariat, are "world historical," able to bridge the gap between class-in-itself and class-for-itself. Karl Marx, *The Eighteenth Brumaire of Louis Bonaparte* (New York, International Publishers, 1963). Gayatri Spivak has provided a productive way into that text in "Can the Subaltern Speak?," demonstrating that for Marx the relationship between membership in a class and political participation are linguistically distinguished in German by different terms for "representation" as portrait or equivalent (as money stands for a commodity) and "representation" as proxy (as a politician or party represents a constituent). In relating this analysis immediately to autobiography I will be accused of ignoring Spivak's "Marxist skepticism of concrete experience as the final arbiter" of truth or politics, "Can the Subaltern

Speak?," 281. In my account "autobiography" is not "concrete experience," but its determinate recall. What I hope the dialectical approach
to identity politics explored in this chapter will make possible is an
equally marxist skepticism about the refusal to acknowledge class
experience as an empirical moment within a dialectic. I believe it is
this refusal that underwrites all manner of challenge to "experience"
in contemporary criticism. As marxists at least since Lukacs have
known, experience need not be the *final* arbiter of anything to be
recognized as a *moment* in the arbitration of representations.

26 Thus early socialist feminism's insistence on a "sex/gender system"
mappable through the terminology of psychoanalysis. See Juliet
Mitchell, *Women's Estate* (New York, Vintage, 1971); Gayle Rubin,
"The Traffic in Women: Notes on the Political Economy of Sex," in K.
V. Hansen and I. J. Philipson, eds., *Women, Class and the Feminist
Imagination* (Philadelphia, Temple University Press, 1990).

27 Cedric Robinson, *Black Marxism: The Making of the Black Radical Tradition* (London, Zed Press, 1983).

28 This term is that of Immanual Wallerstein, who also conceives of the
expansion of capitalism in basically geographical terms.

29 Paul Gilroy, *The Black Atlantic: Modernity and Double Consciousness*
(Cambridge, Mass., Harvard University Press, 1994), chapter 6; Bruce
Simon develops this point in "Traumatic Diaspora: Paule Marshall's
The Chosen Place, The Timeless People," unpublished paper.

30 In Jameson's reading of Althusser, ideology is a psychic structure,
determined within the context of social identity, more or less adequate for the translation of the "real" into the knowledge of the
subject. Because it has no outside within discourse, ideology is always
itself also a part of the real. Frederic Jameson, *The Political Unconscious*
(Ithaca, New York, Cornell University Press, 1981). Jameson is equally
useful in his consideration of Lukacs' dialectical account of realism,
strikingly different from the common caricature of realism as "the
real" itself. *"History and Class Consciousness* as an 'Unfinished Project,'" in *Rethinking Marxism* 1:1 (1988) 49–70. My most adequate
attempt to conceptualize ideology will come in chapter three, where I
discuss Du Bois' 1940 theory of race as it intersects with the theory of
ideology.

31 Becky Thompson and Sangeeta Tyagi, eds., *Names We Call Home:
Autobiography on Racial Identity* (New York, Routledge, 1996), xii.

32 bell hooks, *Talking Back: Thinking Feminist, Thinking Black* (Boston,
South End, 1989), 159. Autobiography as process has, with African-
Americanist scholarship, also been articulated in Valerie Smith, *Self-
Discovery and Authority in Afro-American Narrative* (Cambridge, Mass.,
Harvard University Press, 1987).

33 Gilroy, *The Black Atlantic*, 69.

34 William Andrews, *To Tell a Free Story: The First Century of Afro-
American Autobiography, 1760–1865* (Urbana, University of Illinois
Press, 1986); JoAnn Braxton, *Black Women Writing Autobiography* (Phil-
adelphia, Temple University Press, 1989); Stephen Butterfield, *Black
Autobiography in America* (Amherst, University of Massachusetts

Press, 1974); David Dudley, *My Father's Shadow: Intergenerational Conflict in African American Men's Autobiography* (Philadelphia, University of Pennsylvania Press, 1991); V. P. Franklin, *Living Our Stories, Telling Our Truths: Autobiography and the Making of the African American Intellectual Tradition* (New York, Oxford University Press, 1996); Sidonie Smith, *Where I'm Bound* (Westport, Conn., Greenwood, 1974); Valerie Smith, *Self-Discovery and Authority*.

35 James Olney, "Introduction" to *Autobiography: Essays Theoretical and Critical* (Princeton, New Jersey, Princeton University Press, 1980).

36 Gilroy, *The Black Atlantic*, 69.

37 Dudley, *My Father's House*, notes this phenomenon as well, but appears to attribute the writing of autobiography among black male political leaders to a strictly psychological – Oedipal, via Harold Bloom's category the "anxiety of influence" – jockeying for "leadership." I am far from unwilling to engage in Oedipal speculation, but the narrowness of the point of view from which Dudley does so prevents any elaborated social analysis of (for example) the relationship between Booker T. Washington and W. E. B. Du Bois.

38 Henry Louis Gates, Jr., "Writing 'Race,' and the Difference It Makes," in H. L. Gates, ed., *"Race," Writing and Difference* (Chicago, University of Chicago Press, 1985), 11.

39 Hortense Spillers, "Mama's Baby, Papa's Maybe: An American Grammar Book," in *Diacritics* 17: 2 (1987), 65–81; Robyn Wiegman, *American Anatomies: Theorizing Race and Gender* (Durham, N.C., Duke University Press, 1995).

40 Arguments regarding the pursuit of "autonomy," like the argument of Barbara Smith in *Home Girls*, are often accused of essentialism on the grounds that they suppose the construction of a particular group that stands in well-defined opposition to other groups. In fact, arguments constructed in terms of autonomy nearly always suppose the opposite – because there are no sharp lines of distinction between us and them, and yet certain patterns of power dispersal that are not to our advantage happen when we talk to them, we must consciously move toward an autonomous strategy. A recent philosophical argument for this position can be found in Patricia Huntington, "Toward a Dialectical Concept of Autonomy," in *Philosophy and Social Criticism* 21: 1 (1995), 37–55.

41 Phillip Bryan Harper, *Are We Not Men? Masculine Anxiety and the Problem of African-American Identity* (New York, Oxford University Press, 1996); bell hooks, *Black Looks: Race and Representation* (Boston, South End, 1992), chapter 6; Kobena Mercer, *Welcome to the Jungle* (New York, Routledge, 1993); Marcellus Blount and George Cunningham, eds., *Representing Black Men* (New York, Routledge, 1996).

42 Barbara Smith, "Toward a Black Feminist Criticism," in *Conditions* 2 (1977), 27.

43 June Jordan, *Civil Wars* (Boston, Beacon, 1981), 115–21.

44 *Ibid.*, 115.

45 *Ibid.*, 115–16.

46 *Ibid.*, 115.

47 *Ibid.*, 116.
48 *Ibid.*, 117–18.
49 *Ibid.*, 120.
50 *Ibid.*, 121.
51 *Ibid.*, 115, emphasis mine.
52 *Black Skin, White Masks*, 115.
53 "A Cultural Legacy Denied and Discovered: Black Lesbians in Fiction by Women," in B. Smith, ed., *Home Girls* (New York, Kitchen Table, 1983), 114–15.
54 In Bourdieu, the habitus is defined as follows:

> As an acquired system of generative schemes objectively adjusted to the particular conditions in which it is constituted, the habitus engenders all the thoughts, all the perceptions, and all the actions consistent with those conditions, and not others. The paradoxical product is difficult to conceive, even inconceivable, only so long as one remains locked in the dilemma of determinism and freedom, conditioning and creativity ... Because the habitus has an endless capacity to engender products – thought, perceptions, expressions, actions – whose limits are set by the historically and socially situated conditions of its production, the conditioned and conditional freedom it secures is as remote from a creation of unpredictable novelty as it is from a simple mechanical reproduction of initial conditionings.

Pierre Bourdieu, *Outline of a Theory of Practice*, trans. R. Nice (New York, Cambridge University Press, 1977), 95. I will have cause to return to this quotation in particular in the context of W. E. B. Du Bois' attempt to find a proper metaphor for describing the workings of race in chapter three.
55 Houston Baker, "Caliban's Triple Play," in H. L. Gates, ed., *"Race," Writing, and Difference*, 384ff. I am, for example, always amazed by the lack of consideration given the continuance of residential segregation in the US by those most committed to the idea of cultural hybridity. See Douglas Massey and Nancy Denton, *American Apartheid: Segregation and the Making of the Underclass* (Cambridge, Mass., Harvard University Press, 1993); and Robert Bullard, J. Eugene Grigsby, and Charles Lee, eds. *Residential Apartheid: The American Legacy* (Los Angeles, CAAS Publications, 1994).
56 Michael Hanchard emphasizes the "nonaffordance of public dignity" as key to the understanding of race. "Black Cinderella? Race and the Public Sphere in Brazil," in Black Public Sphere Collective, eds., *The Black Public Sphere* (Chicago, University of Chicago Press, 1995), 178–9.
57 Wiegman, *American Anatomies*, 23.
58 Judith Butler, *Gender Trouble* (New York, Routledge, 1990), 22.
59 Jean-Paul Sartre, *Critique of Dialectical Reason*, vol. I, trans. A. Sheridan-Smith (London, NLB, 1976), 231. Sartre's elaborates as follows:

> One worker reads, another agitates, another finds time to do both, another has just bought a scooter, another plays

the violin, and another does gardening. All these activities are constituted on the basis of particular circumstances, and they constitute the objective individuality of each person. But still, in so far as they are located, in spite of themselves, inside a framework of exigencies that cannot be transcended, they simply realize everyone's class-being. Everyone makes himself signify by interiorizing, by a free choice, the signification with which material exigencies have produced him as a *signified being*. Class-being, as practico-inert being mediated by the passive synthesis of worked matter, comes to men through men; for each of us it is our being-outside-ourselves in matter, in so far as this produces us and awaits us from birth, and insofar as it constitutes itself through us as a future-fatality, that is to say as a future which will necessarily realize itself through us, through the otherwise arbitrary actions which we choose. It is obvious that class-being does not prevent us from realizing an individual destiny (each life is individual), but this realization of our experiences until death is only one of several possible ways (determined by the structured field of possibilities) of producing our class being. (*Ibid.*, 238–9)

For the following section I am addressing Sartre's position in *Critique of Dialectical Reason* and Bourdieu's in *Outline of a Theory of Practice* as in all practical terms compatible. Bourdieu's critique of Sartre in the latter text refers exclusively to *Being and Nothingness*, a text which is quite distinct in its conception of the social. Additionally, since I also employ the terminology of Adorno on and off, I should note that his "constellation," *Negative Dialectics* 162ff., applies to the relation between social categories I am taking from Sartre and Bourdieu in the manner that Hall might otherwise use "articulation." Yet it is preferable to articulation precisely for being structural rather than performative.

60 Brackette Williams, "The Impact of the Precepts of Nationalism on the Concept of Culture: Making Grasshoppers of Naked Apes," in *Cultural Critique* 24 (Spring 1993), 189, 191. Michael Berube accuses the rightists who argue for the need for a "common culture" of consistently conflating "culture" with "society," and thus failing to see that we may share a common society while being culturally multiple, even fragmented. *Public Access: Literary Theory and Cultural Politics* (New York, Verso, 1994), 230. I would add to this an additional claim that Berube would probably disagree with: that the nation-state and economy are active in the systemization of the relations among this cultural multiplicity, in turn structuring (without fully determining) which individuals will attain which acculturations.

61 James Baldwin, *The Fire Next Time* (New York, Dell, 1961), 11.

62 Sigmund Freud, *Group Psychology and the Analysis of the Ego* (New York, Norton, 1959), 61.

63 *Ibid.*, 50.

64 All immigrants (white, black, and other), and people who are neither black nor white, enter this system at a variety of predetermined points, mostly in the mid-section between black and white but sometimes, as with dark-skinned Chicanos in California and the Southwest, or Hmong and certain other southeast Asians, competing with blacks for the very bottom of the structure. Immigrant placement in the system of US racialization needs an account of its own, outside the scope of this book. I am aware that, from the point of view of immigrant subjectivity my book, no doubt like Spillers' "American grammar" and Wiegman's "American anatomies," will look quite inadequate. For all that, just as my book is consistently suspicious of all attempts to discover in hybridity and middle-ness the loci of transcendence, it is suspicious of those positions that find immigrant positions "outside" the logic of white and black. Precisely because the American grammar is, like all psychoanalytic grammars, much more rigid than is often acknowledged, East Asians in the second generation, as one example, generally get forced into certain already existing racial roles (which look a great deal like the ones Jews, Slavs, and other southern and eastern Europeans occupied at the turn of the twentieth century), rather than forming new ones.

65 Joel Kovel, *White Racism: A Psychohistory* (London, Free Association, 1988); Bell, *Faces at the Bottom*.

66 The texts that invented whiteness studies, such as Ruth Frankenberg, *White Women, Race Matters: The Social Construction of Whiteness* (Minneapolis, University of Minnesota Press, 1994) and David Roediger, *The Wages of Whiteness: Race and the Making of the American Working Class* (New York, Verso, 1991), do not make the mistake of imagining whiteness apart from the black gaze; but as whiteness studies has developed autonomy as a field it has become possible to do so.

67 V. N. Volosinov, *Marxism and the Philosophy of Language* (Cambridge, Mass., Harvard University Press, 1973).

68 *Ibid.*, 69.

69 *Ibid.*, 88.

70 *Ibid.*, 89.

71 Joe Wood, "Malcolm X and the New Blackness," in J. Wood, ed., *Malcolm X: in Our Own Image* (New York, St. Martin's, 1992), 14, emphasis in original.

72 The choice to go with a lower case 'b' for black relies entirely on the style of dominant intellectual publications. If the capitalized 'B' appeared more consistently in the work of African Americans I respect, I would certainly have gone with it, but given that almost none of the work I cite in this book, autobiographical, critical or theoretical, uses it, I decided against it.

73 Hortense Spillers, "Moving on Down the Line: Variations on the African-American Sermon," in D. La Capra, ed., *The Bounds of Race* (Ithaca, NY, Cornell University Press, 1991), 57. I apologize for the audacity implied in the relationship I perhaps set up between myself and "the black community." Given that my professional life depends on this community (and to some extent its continued subordination, a

situation about which I am not proud), I hope it will be read as an attempt to be of service.

74 Wahneema Lubiano and Gerald Horne have discussed the ways that African-American Studies can be – and has been – an autonomous intellectual field related to a larger, international project of cultural politics. Lubiano, "Mapping the Interstices Between Afro-American Cultural Discourse and Cultural Studies: A Prolegomenon," in *Callaloo* 19:1 (1996), 68–77; Horne, "Who Lost the Cold War? Africans and African Americans," in *Diplomatic History* 20:4 (fall 1996), 613–26.

75 Jameson, *The Political Unconscious*, 13. A more recent example of the procedure to which I aspire is Ato Sekyi-Otu's brilliant *Fanon's Dialectic of Experience* (Cambridge, Mass., Harvard University Press, 1996), in which the author correctly asserts the primacy of narrative practice to Fanon's theorization of politics and psychology.

76 *The Black Atlantic*, 127.

77 Grace Lee Boggs, "The Black Revolution In America," in T. Cade, ed., *The Black Woman* (New York, New American Library, 1970), 212. The risk of such a position is that, because I claim marxism, I will be misunderstood as claiming that narratives of African-American subjectivity refer to the local in contradistinction to narratives of "the working class," which are global. Wahneema Lubiano, in "Shuckin' Off the African American Native Other: What's Po-Mo Got To Do With It," in *Cultural Critique* 18 (spring 1991), 149–86, has elaborated the critique of this construction of local/global. In fact, my position is that there is no general working class subject as yet, though one hopes one might emerge; and that any other instance of contemporary subject-formation – i.e. union organizing of US-based white male workers – is as "local" as the formation of African-American identity narratives.

78 *Fanon's Dialectic of Experience*; similar arguments were made earlier in Patrick Taylor, *The Narrative of Liberation: Perspectives on Afro-Caribbean Literature, Popular Culture, and Politics* (Ithaca, N.Y.: Cornell University Press, 1989) and my own "Decolonization as Learning: Practice and Pedagogy in Frantz Fanon's Revolutionary Narrative," in H. Giroux and P. McLaren, eds., *Between Borders: Pedagogy and the Politics of Cultural Studies* (New York, Routledge, 1994).

79 Ellen Meiksins Wood, "Back To Marx," in *Monthly Review* 49:2 (June 1997), 1–2.

80 *That* is the meaning of Fanon's statement, "national consciousness, which is not nationalism, is the only thing that will give us an international dimension." *Wretched of the Earth* (New York, Grove, 1963), 247. People familiar with Homi Bhabha's work will certainly note that all through this chapter I have been reading Fanon quite differently than he does; compare my analysis of this quote, for example, to Bhabha, "Introduction," *Nation and Narration* (New York, Routledge, 1990), 4.

81 My understanding of Nietzsche's work and its relationship to contemporary academic politics is exactly that of Terry Eagleton: see *Ideology: An Introduction* (New York, Verso, 1991), chapter 6 and *The Ideology of the Aesthetic* (London, Blackwell, 1990), chapter 9.

82 *The Black Atlantic*, 85.

2 African-American autobiography and the field of autobiography studies

1 Pierre Bourdieu, *Homo Academicus* (Stanford, Calif., Stanford University Press, 1988), 193.
2 Philippe Lejeune, *On Autobiography* (Minneapolis, University of Minnesota Press, 1989), 131–2.
3 In dialectical terms, "referentiality" is of course aligned with the object. The adjective "distributive" refers to position within a "field" of knowledge, and is meant to imply that positions on these axes possess, at any historical moment, certain amounts of cultural capital, Bourdieu, *Language and Symbolic Action*, 14–17, 57–61. The principle argument of this chapter does not concern the Bourdieuian economy of the field, but an argument that did would not be distant from mine here.
4 Several prior accounts have surveyed this field; indeed it may be that autobiography, having been a relatively recent and relatively marginal addition to the catalogue of literary genres to survey, demands in particular that all those who attend to any one example of it take the time to consider it generically. (It would, for example, be unusual for a new paper on *The Bluest Eye* to cite work in the history and theory of the novel, while a new paper on *I Know Why the Caged Bird Sings* would be quite likely to cite work in the history and theory of autobiography.) By far the best survey of the criticism of autobiography is Laura Marcus' *Auto/biographical Discourses: Theory, Criticism, Practice* (New York, Manchester University Press, 1994). Her organizational schema for understanding contemporary theories of autobiography overlaps with, while differing significantly from, mine: Marcus devotes an entire chapter to what I call "the axis of subjectivity," though she frames this discussion in psychoanalytical rather than sociological terms; I, meanwhile, organize psychoanalytic issues as questions of reference and truth, a topic which is for her a derivative of the consideration of autobiographical form.
5 Nancy Miller, *Getting Personal: Feminist Occasions and Other Autobiographical Acts* (New York, Routledge, 1991).
6 Marjanne Goozé, "The Definitions of Self and Form in Feminist Autobiography Theory," in *Women's Studies* 21 (1992), 411–29.
7 H. David Brumble, *American Indian Autobiography* (Berkeley, University of California Press, 1988); Hertha Wong, *Sending My Heart Back Across the Years: Tradition and Innovation in Native American Autobiography* (New York, Oxford University Press, 1992).
8 Wong, *Sending My Heart*, 7.
9 Paul DeMan, "Autobiography as De-Facement," in *Modern Language Notes* 94: 5 (1979), 919–30.
10 Quoted in Doris Sommer, "'Not Just a Personal Story': Women's *Testimonios* and the Plural Self," in B. Brodzki and C. Schenk, eds., *Life/Lines: Theorizing Women's Autobiography* (Ithaca, N.Y., Cornell University Press, 1988), 107.
11 Lejeune, *On Autobiography*, 4.

12 *Ibid.*, 13–14.
13 *Ibid.*
14 James Olney states with surprise that no one has ever actually provided a definition around the presence or absence of the word "autobiography," either in the title, the text, or the criticism of the text. "Introduction," to *Autobiography: Essays Theoretical and Critical* (Princeton, N.J.: Princeton University, 1980), 6.
15 DeMan, "Autobiography as De-Facement," 922.
16 *Ibid.*, 922–3.
17 *Ibid.*, 921–2.
18 My reading of DeMan's overstatement of the difference between his claims and those of Lejeune is consistent with John Guillory's more programmatic rejection of DeMan: See *Cultural Capital* (Chicago, University of Chicago Press, 1993), 227–9 on the detachment of DeMan's terminology from a genuine materialism, and 242–4 on the notion of "institution" in DeMan and others associated with him.
19 See, for example, Caren Kaplan's use of autobiography as an "outlaw genre," which permits essays in development economics to stand in for autobiographies of subaltern subjects, "Resisting Autobiography: Out-Law Genres and Transnational Feminist Subjects," in S. Smith and J. Watson, eds., *De/Colonizing the Subject: The Politics of Gender in Women's Autobiography* (Minneapolis: University of Minnesota Press, 1992); and Houston Baker's claim to "stylized scholarly recollection," which I discuss in the next section.
20 Robert Folkenflik, ed., *The Culture of Autobiography: Constructions of Self-Representation* (Stanford, Calif., Stanford University, 1993); Smith and Watson, *De/Colonizing the Subject*; Olney, *Autobiography*.
21 Claudia Tate, *Black Women Writers at Work* (New York, Continuum, 1983), 23.
22 Houston Baker, *Workings of the Spirit: The Poetics of Afro-American Women's Writing* (Chicago, University of Chicago Press, 1991), 49–50.
23 DeMan, "Autobiography as De-Facement," 920.
24 Wahneema Lubiano, "But Compared To What? Reading Realism, Representation and Essentialism in *School Daze, Do the Right Thing* and the Spike Lee Discourse," in Blount and Cunningham, *Representing Black Men*, 183. There is a big difference between suggesting that "realism" is but one strategy, and by no means always the most effective one, of representing a life, and the claim that reference may simply drop from discussions of life-writing: "In contrast to the Nietzschean reference of poststructuralism ... Lacan insists on psychoanalysis as a truth-experience: his thesis that truth is structured like a fiction has nothing at all to do with a poststructuralist reduction of the truth-dimension to a textual 'truth-effect,'" Slavoj Zizek, *The Sublime Object of Ideology* (New York, Verso, 1989), 154.
25 Janet Varner Gunn, *Autobiography: Toward a Poetics of Experience* (Philadelphia, University of Pennsylvania Press, 1982); Paul John Eakin, *Touching the World* (Princeton, New Jersey, Princeton University Press, 1992).
26 Eakin, *Touching the World*, 30, 50.

27 *Ibid.*, 5.
28 Gunn, *Autobiography*, 119.
29 Gunn, "A Politics of Experience: Leila Khaled's *My People Shall Live: The Autobiography of A Revolutionary,*" in Smith and Watson, eds., *De/Colonizing the Mind.* Gunn's analysis of narrative construction remains far from the poststructuralism that pervades Smith and Watson's volume otherwise.
30 Eakin, *Touching the World*, 36.
31 This is a problem shared by Michael M. J. Fischer's well-known "Ethnicity and the Postmodern Art of Memory," in J. Clifford and G. E. Marcus, eds., *Writing Culture: The Poetics and Politics of Ethnography* (Berkeley, University of California Press, 1986), where as "post-modern ethnographer" Fischer chooses "memory arts" that appeal to his sense of the diversity of cultural contexts, while explicitly denying that he has any grounds to pick among them or to analyze how the ethnographer chooses such "arts" beyond the power of "juxtaposition." In doing so Fischer forgets that he is the ethnographer-agent who decides what gets to count as "ethnic"; Betty Bergland reminds him that the chooser of "ethnic" texts which are representative of "their" "cultures" should not ignore questions of which ethnic texts get to serve the function of representativeness: "Postmodernism and the Autobiographical Subject: Reconstructing the 'Other,'" in K. Ashley, L. Gilmore, and G. Peters, eds., *Autobiography and Postmodernism* (Amherst, Mass., University of Massachusetts Press, 1994).
32 Lejeune, *On Autobiography*, 131.
33 Georges Gusdorf, "Conditions and Limits of Autobiography," in Olney, ed., *Autobiography*, 29.
34 *Ibid.*, emphasis mine.
35 Kaplan, "Resisting Autobiography," 117–18.
36 Gusdorf, "Conditions and Limits," 39, 45, 46.
37 *Ibid.*, 42.
38 Carolyn Heilbrun, *Writing a Woman's Life* (New York, Ballantine, 1988); Arnold Rampersad, "Biography, Autobiography, and Afro-American Culture," in *Yale Review* 73:1 (1983), 1–16; Albert Stone, *Autobiographical Occasions and Original Acts* (Philadelphia, University of Pennsylvania Press, 1980). For Heilbrun biography and autobiography can be analyzed together for the study of narrative subjectivity.
39 Stone, *Autobiographical Occasions*, 10.
40 It is also significant that the term "America" plays a special role in this process for Stone, and there is nothing accidental historically about the relationship of "autobiography" to "America," as much work on Benjamin Franklin's autobiography attests. I have written about autobiography and "America" in the entirely different context of Carlos Bulosan's *America is in the Heart*: "Why is America in the Heart?," in *Critical Mass: A Journal of Asian-American Cultural Criticism* 2:2 (summer 1995).
41 Sommer, "Not Just a Personal Story," 110.
42 Both quoted in *ibid.*, 107.
43 *Ibid.*, 109.

44 Leigh Gilmore, "The Mark of Autobiography: Postmodernism, Autobiography, and Genre," in Ashley, Gilmore, and Peters, eds., *Autobiography and Postmodernism*, 6.

45 Francoise Lionnet, *Autobiographical Voices: Race, Gender, Self-Portraiture* (Ithaca, N.Y., Cornell University Press, 1989), 3.

46 *Ibid.*, 9.

47 My brief account of Lionnet here ignores the obvious facts that Augustine was black (but what could that mean in this context?) and that Nietzsche's work is directly related to the development of poststructuralist theory. Since Lionnet's argument about the relationship between race, gender, and metissage is largely presented in principle rather than through a reading of people who agree or disagree with her, it is hard to know what exactly to say about the actual content of her readings.

48 Sidonie Smith, *Subjectivity, Identity, and the Body: Women's Autobiographical Practices in the Twentieth Century* (Bloomington, University of Indiana Press, 1991). Smith's long and interesting career includes one of the early works on black autobiography, *Where I'm Bound*, a thematic account of black subjectivity that precedes the move to theory, and an earlier work of feminist theory, *A Poetics of Women's Subjectivity* (Bloomington, University of Indiana Press, 1987). This analysis addresses only her most recent work.

49 Smith, *Subjectivity*, 4.

50 *Ibid.*, 20, 21, 22.

51 In fact, issues of intersubjectivity come up in a number of specific textual analyses, especially the one of Virginia Woolf's work. My point is that, in the introductory chapter, the promise of such intersubjectivity is not referred to; only the fact of split subjectivity is seen as a significant feature of women's autobiography. The assumption that we must always refuse to chart collective formations of subjectivity, on principle as necessarily essentialist, prevents making any sort of case for the value of specific forms of women's (or a subgroup of women's) intersubjectivity where it occurs or where there is an attempt to forge it.

52 Quoted in Smith, *Subjectivity*, 108.

53 *Ibid.*, 112.

54 *Ibid.*, 109.

55 *Ibid.*, 124–5.

56 *Ibid.*, 139.

57 *Ibid.*, 141.

58 *Ibid.*, 142.

59 If there was any doubt about this before, Moraga's *The Last Generation* (Boston, South End, 1993) makes the centrality of Chicana identity and community absolutely clear.

60 Stephen Butterfield, *Black Autobiography in America* (Amherst, Mass., University of Massachusetts Press, 1974), 3.

61 *Ibid.*, 7.

62 See Paul Gilroy, *There Ain't No Black in the Union Jack* (Chicago, University of Chicago Press, 1987), chapter 5, on the continuous use of

blackness and diasporic consciousness in African-British social movements even as the specific meanings of this consciousness change.

63 Michael Eric Dyson, *Reflecting Black* (Minneapolis, University of Minnesota Press, 1993), 141.

64 William Andrews, "African-American Autobiography Criticism: Retrospect and Prospect," in P. J. Eakin, ed., *American Autobiography:
Retrospect and Prospect* (Madison, University of Wisconsin Press, 1991),
196.

65 *Ibid.*, 208.

3 Three theories of the race of W. E. B. Du Bois

1 W. E. B. Du Bois, *Black Folk Then and Now* (New York, Henry Holt,
1939), 1.

2 V. N. Volosinov, *Marxism and the Philosophy of Language*, 13.

3 W. E. B. Du Bois, *The Autobiography of W. E. B. Du Bois* (New York,
International Publishers, 1968), 12.

4 W. E. B. Du Bois, *Dusk of Dawn: An Essay Toward an Autobiography of a
Race Concept* (New Brunswick, New Jersey, Transaction, 1984), xxix.

5 The original speech appears as "A Pageant in Seven Decades," in P.
Foner, ed., *W. E. B. Du Bois Speaks: Speeches and Addresses 1890–1919*
(New York: Pathfinder, 1970), 21–72.

6 Du Bois, *Dusk of Dawn*, xxix–xxx.

7 Du Bois, *The Souls of Black Folk* (New York, Signet Classics, 1969), xi,
43. These two statements may be said to inaugurate the discourse of
"postcolonialism" as it is now practiced in the US academy – especially when one recognizes that "the color line" as Du Bois conceived it
through most of his life is not within the US, but is international. It is
in many ways instructive to compare the question "How does it feel to
be a Problem?" with its Fanonian corollary, the statement "Look, a
Negro," the childhood basis of the psychological understanding of
race in *Black Skin, White Masks*, 109. Du Bois' question addresses not
the general problematic of the Negro child, but rather a very specific
social location, that of the adult black intellectual who inhabits the
social position of being a "problem." This formulation, and the theory
of double consciousness that follows from it, conform to the idea of
postcolonialism as a discourse of intellectual position, looking, for
example, like a precise and direct precursor of Gayatri Spivak's definition of postcolonialism as an "impossible 'no' to a structure, which
one critiques, yet inhabits intimately," *Outside in the Teaching Machine*,
60. I have developed this, with particular care given to the relationship between *Souls* and Homi Bhabha's *The Location of Culture*, in the
forthcoming "Postcolonialism After W. E. B. Du Bois."
Once one starts by viewing Du Bois as the first theorist of what is
now called postcoloniality, it is a small jump to seeing that he is
among the twentieth century's most innovative theorists, not "just" a
significant African-American theorist. His work is directly engaged
with Hegelian thought from his time as a student in Berlin in 1892–4.
As more serious philosophical work is done on Du Bois, it becomes

less and less reasonable to refer to him as a "pragmatist"; Shamoon Zamir, *Dark Voices: W. E. B. Du Bois and American Thought, 1888–1903* (Chicago, University of Chicago Press, 1995), has done the most careful reconstruction of his early intellectual influences, showing that the choice of Hegel over James was decisive and early; and Sandra Adell, *Double-Consciousness/Double Bind: Theoretical Issues in Twentieth Century Black Literature* (Urbana, University of Illinois Press, 1994) has provided a detailed philosophical account of the relationship of Du Boisian double consciousness to the forms of consciousness described in the *Phenomenology of Spirit*.

In the 1930s Du Bois began a direct and fruitful engagement with marxism (a discourse we know he was aware of in a limited way from 1892 and which appears in his work from at least 1909), adding to his theoretical concerns the relation of individual and group subject-position to the structure of the international economy. Cedric Robinson suggests that Du Bois was uniquely well-positioned to chart a marxist course of some originality in the 1930s:

> Undaunted by the political concerns of blacks in the American Communist Party which frequently manifested themselves as a search for ideological orthodoxy in their work and writings, Du Bois had little reason or awareness for cautiously threading an ideological position... In so doing, he was articulating in theoretical terms the intersections between the black radical tradition and historical materialism only vaguely hinted at in the formal organizations of his time. (*Black Marxism*, 289–90)

Robinson addresses only the 1935 study *Black Reconstruction*. Those who have worked on *Dusk of Dawn* have in general shown no interest in its status as a work of marxist theory. The closest thing to an exception to this characterization is Bernard Magubane's *The Ties That Bind: African American Consciousness of Africa* (Trenton, N.J., Africa World, 1987).

8 Du Bois, *Dusk of Dawn*, 3.

9 See also Barbara Foley, *Radical Representations: Politics and Form in US Proletariat Fiction, 1929–1941* (Durham, N.C., Duke University Press), for an evaluation of autobiographical writing that uses similar structures, and Frederic Jameson, *Marxism and Form* (Princeton, New Jersey, Princeton University Press, 1973), for the general discussion of the attempt to write narrative which shares the form of its theoretical claims.

10 Du Bois, *Dusk of Dawn*, 3.

11 *Ibid.*, 4. Double consciousness is thus a *fact* of black intellectual life, before it is a *value:* thus it would be inappropriate to read doubleness as some sort of privileged "third space" of mediation or brokerage between otherwise undoubled spaces. Gilroy articulates the continuing significance of Du Bois' concept of double consciousness in *The Black Atlantic*, 127ff.

12 Though it seems that he does not understand Freud in depth, Du Bois makes several suggestions of the usefulness of psychoanalytic theory

to his conception of a racial unconscious. I suspect that, had he theorized it explicitly, he would have moved in the direction of marxists like Althusser, Jameson, and Eagleton, all of whom in different ways see the description of the unconscious as being appropriate first of all to a theory of ideology. Volosinov, as my epigraph to this chapter suggests, is the sociolinguist who grounds the connections between social class, ideology, language and the unconscious as depicted in this chapter.

13 Du Bois, *Dusk of Dawn*, 7.

14 Du Bois, *Autobiography*, 12.

15 My term "marginality" here follows from Phillip Bryan Harper, *Framing the Margins: On the Social Logic of Postmodernism* (New York, Oxford University Press, 1994); "formation" follows from Michael Omi and Howard Winant, *Racial Formations in the United States from the 1960s to the 1990s*, 2nd edn. (New York, Routledge, 1994).

16 For a historical account of the success of middle class identification with *The Souls of Black Folk* and the theory of double consciousness in particular, see Kevin Gaines, *Uplifting the Race: Black Leadership, Politics, and Culture in the Twentieth Century* (Chapel Hill, University of North Carolina Press, 1996), 9ff. Indeed, Gaines goes on to argue that for Du Bois and other members of the Negro middle class during this period, increasing class stratification among Negroes was itself a sign of Negro progress, since this meant greater resemblance between Negroes and whites, *ibid.*, chapter 6.

17 W. E. B. Du Bois, *Darkwater: Voices From Within the Veil* (New York, Shocken, 1969), 5.

18 *Ibid.*, 11.

19 *Ibid.*, 5, 6, 7, 7.

20 *Ibid.*, 6.

21 It wasn't, particularly. Du Bois' mother had had an affair with her cousin, resulting in an illegitimate half-brother that Du Bois never met; his father left when he was an infant because the "great clan" didn't like him. Lewis suggests that long after Du Bois' stated political positions became pro-erotic in the 1920s and pro-working class in the 1930s he continued to be personally embarrassed by these facts. David Levering Lewis, *W. E. B. Du Bois: Biography of A Race, vol. I* (New York, Henry Holt, 1993), 21–2.

22 Du Bois, *Darkwater*, 11–12.

23 Du Bois, *Dusk of Dawn*, 15.

24 *Ibid.*, 14.

25 *Ibid.*, emphasis in original.

26 *Ibid.*, 14, 16.

27 *Ibid.*, 19. Mrs. Du Bois seems to be the obvious reference in this passage from *Dusk*, already cited above: "autobiography ... assumes ... too little in the reticences, repressions, and distortions which come because men do not dare to be absolutely frank."

28 Sacvan Bercovitch, *The Puritan Origins of the American Self* (New Haven, Conn., Yale University Press, 1974).

29 Arnold Rampersad, *The Art and Imagination of W. E. B. Du Bois* (New

York, Schocken, 1976).

30 Anthony Appiah, "The Uncompleted Argument: Du Bois and the Illusion of Race," in Gates, ed., *"Race," Writing, and Difference*, 21–37.

31 Du Bois, *Dusk of Dawn*, 221.

32 Willie L. Baber, "Capitalism and Racism," in *Critique of Anthropology*, 12:3 (1992). Like commodities in marxist analysis, race appears here as a fetish, and Eagleton's analysis of commodity fetishism applies: human subjects' socially constructed conditions of existence are "now inherent in social reality itself. It is not simply a question of the distorted perception of human beings, who invent the real world in their consciousness and thus *imagine* that commodities control their lives. Marx is not claiming that under capitalism commodities *appear* to exercise a tyrannical sway over social relations; he is arguing that they actually do," Terry Eagleton, *Ideology*, 85.

33 Omi and Winant, *Racial Formations*, 55–6; Du Bois, *Dusk of Dawn*, 127, 136. It should be clear from this that I, like Omi and Winant and numerous others, consider Anthony Appiah's argument in "The Uncompleted Argument" to be quite wrong both with regard to his reading of *Dusk of Dawn* and with regard to contemporary meanings of race. Indeed, as Holt and Outlaw have demonstrated, even the 1897 essay "The Conservation of Races" doesn't conform to Appiah's rather simplistic reading, Thomas C. Holt, "The Political Uses of Alienation: W. E. B. Du Bois on Politics, Race, and Culture, 1903–40," in *American Quarterly* 42:2 (June 1990), 301–23; Lucien Outlaw, "'Conserve' Races? In Defense of W. E. B. Du Bois," in B. Bell, E. Grosholz, and J. Stewart, eds., *W. E. B. Du Bois: On Race and Culture* (New York, Routledge, 1997), 15–37. Houston Baker, "Caliban's Triple Play"; Anita Haya Goldman, "Negotiating Claims of Race and Rights: Du Bois, Emerson, and the Critique of Liberal Nationalism," in *Massachusetts Review* 35:2 (summer 1994), 169–201; Robert Gooding-Williams, "Outlaw, Appiah and Du Bois's 'The Conservation of Races,'" in Bell, Grosholz and Stewart, *W. E. B. Du Bois*, 39–56; and Lott, Tommy L., "Du Bois on the Invention of Race," in *Philosophical Forum*, XXIV:1–3 (fall-spring 1992–3), 166–87, have all, like me, joined the growth industry of opposition to Appiah's position, which nonetheless continues to get cited as the truth about Du Bois by scholars not especially interested in either Du Bois or race theory. For reasons I can't imagine, I am the only of all these writers to provide an alternative reading *Dusk of Dawn*.

Finally, I would like to frame what's wrong with Appiah's essay in terms that should be – but I'm afraid will not be – clear to theorists of race in general. Appiah's argument assumes a basic premise, from Russelian (analytic) logic, which he uses to test Du Bois and all other race theorists. That premise is "either there is race, or there is not race, but not both." Only if this statement is considered true are we required to agree with Appiah's argument that there is nothing useful we can do with the concept of race. Dialectics, phenomenology, critical theory, and deconstruction are several among many philosophical logics which challenge the necessity of this premise. Individuals who feel comfortable operating in these logics will know how to respond to Appiah's essay.

34 Du Bois, *Dusk of Dawn*, 25–6.

35 *Ibid.*, 22.

36 *Ibid.*, 10, 14.

37 *Ibid.*, 14.

38 *Ibid.*, 23, emphasis mine.

39 Race as a fetish, then, in the sense I noted in footnote 32, can be given a history by articulating Du Bois' explanations of the genesis of racial feeling and self-identity to the category of "habitus," as described by Pierre Bourdieu in *Outline of a Theory of Practice*. I have replaced "the habitus" with "race" in this quote to elaborate Du Bois' position:

> As an acquired system of generative schemes objectively adjusted to the particular conditions in which it is constituted, [race] engenders all the thoughts, all the perceptions, and all the actions consistent with those conditions, and not others. The paradoxical product is difficult to conceive, even inconceivable, only so long as one remains locked in the dilemma of determinism and freedom, conditioning and creativity ... Because [race] has an endless capacity to engender products – thought, perceptions, expressions, actions – whose limits are set by the historically and socially situated conditions of its production, the conditioned and conditional freedom it secures is as remote from a creation of unpredictable novelty as it is from a simple mechanical reproduction of initial conditionings. (Pierre Bourdieu, *Outline of a Theory of Practice*, 95)

Omi and Winant's theory of "racial formation" intersects well with this Marxian-Bourdieuian epistemology.

40 There are, of course, also cultural inheritances that many black and nonblack Americans take from Africa. The point of emphasizing this particular genesis of twentieth century black identity is to indicate that, however much of an African cultural legacy is maintained, its particular coding as "black" and "racial" is the legacy of the veil.

41 See, for example, Penny Von Eschen, *Race Against Empire: Black Americans and Anticolonialism, 1937–1957* (Ithaca, N.Y., Cornell University Press, 1997).

42 Lewis notes that the economic argument of Lenin's *Imperialism* pamphlet was anticipated in articles Du Bois wrote for the *Crisis* in 1914–15, and in his book *The Negro*. W. E. B. Du Bois, 503–4.

43 Du Bois, *Dusk of Dawn*, 51.

44 *Ibid.*, 67.

45 Anthony Appiah's argument against the argument of *Dusk* is based largely on this passage, so what follows is the argument that supplements my statement about Appiah in note 33.

46 Of course, simultaneously he rejects the idea of the primitive as a temporal designation: "primitive men are not following us afar, frantically waving and seeking our goals; primitive men are not behind us

in some swift footrace. Primitive men have already arrived.", *Dusk of Dawn*, 127.

47 *Ibid.*, 117–30.
48 *Ibid.*, 117.
49 The problem of memory in Toni Morrison's novels is a much noted place to begin thinking about this issue. For example, both Satya Mohanty, "The Epistemic Status of Cultural Identity: On *Beloved* and the Postcolonial Condition," *Cultural Critique* 24 (1993), and Barbara Christian, "Fixing Methodologies: *Beloved*", in *Cultural Critique* 24 (1993) address the memory of Africa in their accounts of *Beloved*; see also Gilroy, *The Black Atlantic*, chapter 6, whose extended treatment of the memory of slavery takes Morrison's "not a story to pass on" as his chapter title.
50 Du Bois, *Dusk of Dawn*, 13.
51 *Ibid.*, 130–2.
52 *Ibid.*, 133.
53 hooks, *Black Looks*, 167.
54 Du Bois, *Dusk of Dawn*, 152–3.
55 Available in *Ibid.*, 319–22.
56 Many of his proposals are ones which are later articulated as "nationalist," but Du Bois himself rejects the term as senseless (possibly in reaction against the CPUSA description of the Black Belt as a "nation"). Further, since he never recommends that black people already intertwined with white economics or politics disentwine (any more than he argues that he is not implicated in the work of white intellectuals), his plan can't really be called "segregation" either – making coherent use of already existing segregation is the most accurate description of his recommendations.
57 Du Bois, *Dusk of Dawn*, 179.
58 *Ibid.*, 186–7.
59 *Ibid.*, 199–200.
60 *Ibid.*, 219.
61 Rampersad, *Art and Imagination*, 241–4, reads *Dusk* as more or less a repetitious plea for an ethical community, and not as adding anything in particular to Du Bois' corpus of ideas. While I obviously disagree with this general assessment, it is at this moment – the pleas for certain humanist ethical ideals as seen through the metaphor of African tribal community – that Rampersad's reading is most to the point.
62 Du Bois, *Dusk of Dawn*, 322.
63 Du Bois, *Autobiography*, 11.
64 Space prevents me from discussing the long section on the Soviet Union in *Dusk of Dawn*; in short, in 1940 he considered the Soviet Union such an inspiring example that it was possible to organize a society with the express intent of eliminating poverty, and says that his trip there in 1926 convinced him that the revolution was first of all a good thing; he also criticizes Stalin's purges; and most importantly, he indicates that so-called international communism doesn't adequately understand conditions in the United States and provides no program relevant to black Americans.

65 Gerald Horne, *Black and Red: W. E. B. Du Bois and the Afro-American Response to the Cold War* (Albany, New York, SUNY, 1986).
66 Du Bois, *Autobiography*, 21.
67 *Ibid.*, 36.
68 *Ibid.*, 57–8, entire passage italicized in original.
69 It is because I take seriously the notion of marxist social science, to which Du Bois contributes during the 1930s and 1940s, that I note this: the socialist political argument in *Dusk of Dawn* is sociological; the Communist political argument in the *Autobiography* is theological.
70 W. E. B. Du Bois, *Autobiography*, 58
71 In this sense, *contra* Appiah, Du Bois did, in fact "complete" the "scientific" argument about race, through the frame of Marxist-Leninist science. Appiah's essay strategically ignores Du Bois' writing after *Dusk of Dawn*, perhaps because to include it would necessitate Appiah admitting that his position, and that of the Communist Du Bois are the same.
72 Du Bois, *Autobiography*, 277.
73 *Ibid.*
74 *Ibid.*, 279.
75 *Ibid.*, 279–81.
76 Wells-Barnett's explicit discussions of sexuality, and her marginalization by black male leaders, is discussed in the next chapter. For further analysis of Du Bois' conflicted sexuality and the relationship between his increasing comfort, late in life, in discussing sexuality (including homosexuality) with his relationship to women, see V. P. Franklin, *Living Our Stories*, 260ff.
77 Even among the most important black feminists of the first half of the twentieth century only Pauline Hopkins and Ida B. Wells Barnett had much to say about the *sexualized* (as opposed to *gendered*) construction of race. Du Bois' position on women is best seen as rather similar to that of Anna Julia Cooper, in *A Voice from the South*; meanwhile, for Zora Neale Hurston racial meaning is entirely abandoned (in the sense Appiah currently endorses) for the description of southern black culture, through a lens that I continue, unpopularly, to see as conditioned as much by Boasian anthropology as her own "roots." For a fair, and not very sympathetic view of Du Bois' intellectual work on women, see Patricia Morton, *Disfigured Images: The Historical Assault on Afro-American Women* (New York, Praeger, 1991), chapter 4.
78 Bell hooks' *Talking Back*, which I address at length in chapter 8, is particularly helpful in elaborating the significance of the public/private distinction in this analysis; she appears to take her position from that of 1970s socialist feminism rather than feminist deconstruction.
79 Certainly during the 1920s he is now known to have had affairs with women with whom he worked professionally, like Jessie Fauset. I await the next volume of Lewis' biography for the details.
80 Massey and Denton, *American Apartheid*.
81 See Bernice Johnson Reagon, "Coalition Politics: Turning the Century," in Barbara Smith, *Home Girls*, 356–68; and also Smith's introduction to that volume.

82 The absence of a concept of historicization or dialectics in a given autobiography is actually of no consequence here. One learns the ideological backdrop of the narrative as much by the absence or implicitness of the parallel narratives of history as by their explicit presentation – as we have seen by addressing gender in the Du Boisian analysis.

4 The gender, race, and culture of anti-lynching politics in the Jim Crow era

1 James Weldon Johnson, *Along This Way* (New York, Penguin, 1990), 78.
2 Zora Neale Hurston, *Dust Tracks on the Road* (New York, Harper Perennial, 1991), 151.
3 Walter White, *A Man Called White* (New York, Viking, 1948) 1.
4 Ida B. Wells Barnett, *Selected Works of Ida B. Wells Barnett*, T. Harris, ed. (New York, Oxford University Press, 1991), 246.
5 This claim is very close to Farah Griffin's argument in *Who Set You Flowin'? The African-American Migration Narrative* (New York, Oxford University Press, 1995) that lynching is the central trope in black fiction explaining why a character leaves the south for the north. Though I do not focus on this fact, it matters that all the narratives discussed in this chapter are south to north migration narratives.
6 Wiegman, *American Anatomies*, chapter 3; Sandra Gunning, *Race, Rape, and Lynching: The Red Record of American Literature 1890–1912* (New York, Oxford University Press, 1996).
7 The word "ritual" here is taken from Trudier Harris' *Exorcising Blackness: Historical and Literary Lynching and Burning Rituals*, (Bloomington, Indiana University Press, 1984), and may be used in the production of a structural anthropology of US white supremacy deeply consistent with Wiegman's "anatomy."
8 Wiegman, *American Anatomies*, 82.
9 *Ibid.*, 86, emphasis mine.
10 Gunning, *Race, Rape, and Lynching*, 104.
11 This should in no way imply that privatizing the depiction of race provides an adequate account. Indeed, I would suggest that this is what happens in Hurston's "How it Feels to be Colored Me"; I will discuss Hurston below.
12 Abdul JanMohamed suggested this phrase to me.
13 James Weldon Johnson, *The Autobiography of an Ex-Colored Man*, in *Three Negro Classics*, ed. John Hope Franklin (New York, Avon, 1965). In fact, a considerable amount of evidence for Johnson's authorship began to emerge prior to the 1927 edition. The most noteworthy example of this evidence is that the opening of the 1922 introduction to Johnson's quite well-known *The Book of American Negro Poetry* reproduces the analysis of the American Negro's four major contributions to US culture almost word for word from the 1912 *Autobiography*. While noticing the continuity between *Autobiography* and other writings by Johnson makes it slightly more difficult to consider the 1912

text as autobiography, it also makes it considerably more difficult to consider the text as *ironic* as a whole.

14 Joseph T. Skerrett, "Irony and Symbolic Action in James Weldon Johnson's *The Autobiography of an Ex-Colored Man*," in *American Quarterly* 32: 5 (winter 1980), 540–58; Roxanna Pisiak, "Irony and Subversion in James Weldon Johnson's *The Autobiography of an Ex-Colored Man*," in *Studies in American Fiction* 21: 1 (1993), 83–96.

15 Benjamin Lawson, "Odysseus's Revenge: The Names on the Title Page of *The Autobiography of an Ex-Colored Man*," in *Southern Literary Journal* 21: 2 (spring 1989), 97.

16 Johnson, *Along This Way*, 238.

17 Berube suggests that it is only because the identity of the author is, initially, unknown that the book might be an effective political intervention: its status as autobiography is necessary to its production of fear in a white public, *Public Access*, 257. The real irony of Johnson's fiction, which can be lost on literary critics whose profession fundamentally privileges the study of irony, is that reading the text "ironically" requires knowing the truth that it is nonrepresentational to Johnson's life. Skerrett knows this, and thus reads the text's ironies in a way that depends on a side reading of *Along This Way*.

18 Johnson, *Ex-Colored Man*, 436–8.

19 I agree with Amy Robinson that "passing is not ... a strategy that evades the dominant terms of representation and the necessities of referential claims of identity"; it is, like drag, its twin in her account, "a strategy of the social field rather than a utopian theoretical space of ... subversion." "It Takes One to Know One: Passing and Communities of Common Interest," in *Critical Inquiry* 20 (summer 1994), 730. My account here assumes and I hope extends this argument, by pointing out the obviously determinative role of skin color, as against the common contemporary tendency to read all forms of changeable identity performance as equally available to all. For further commentary on passing as an activity that reproduces race, see Harryette Mullen, "Optic White: Blackness and the Production of Whiteness," in *Diacritics* 24: 2–3 (summer-fall 1994), 71–89; and on the ambivalent, not inherently progressive (or reactionary) politics of drag, see Carole-Anne Tyler "Boys Will Be Girls: The Politics of Gay Drag," in D. Fuss, ed., *Inside/Out: Lesbian Theories, Gay Theories* (New York, Routledge, 1991), 32–70.

20 Johnson, *Ex-Colored Man*, 393.

21 *Ibid.*, 511.

22 This distinction would be further aligned to the axes white-rational-heterosexual and black-creative-queer. I note this in response to Phillip Bryan Harper, *Are We Not Men?*, 111–13, who suggests, correctly, that the Ex-Colored Man's life as a [black] musical performer is embedded in an apparently homosexual relationship to a white patron, a relationship that ends when he leaves to seek his "manhood." I am, however, in sharp disagreement with Harper's conclusion that after the lynching this search for manhood is abruptly ended. As I will argue below, only by passing for white, marrying, and becoming a

banker, can the narrator end up a "man."

23 Plausible theoretical grounds for a definition of race built around affective intensity appear in Brian Massumi's essay "The Autonomy of Affect," in *Cultural Critique* 31, 83–109, in which immediate response to a visual cue (as with skin-color) is said to bring about a certain psychic intensity regardless of the vector of the intensity, its emotive or ethical content.

24 Johnson, *Ex-Colored Man*, 395.

25 *Ibid.*, 404.

26 *Ibid.*, 396.

27 *Ibid.*, 441, 440.

28 David Levering Lewis argues that the Harlem Renaissance idea that the development of black art will be the means of access to social justice was brought to Harlem by Charles Johnson, founder of the journal *Opportunity*, and pursued through the various literary awards given by *Opportunity*, *Crisis*, and others during the 1920s. *When Harlem was in Vogue* (New York, Vintage, 1979), 45–9, 89–98. It seems clear that this idea of art for uplift was generated widely and simultaneously by a variety of liberal thinkers.

29 Johnson, *Ex-Colored Man*, 403, 433.

30 *Ibid.*, 476–7.

31 *Ibid.*, 500.

32 *Ibid.*, 499.

33 Gunning, *Race, Rape, and Lynching*, 25.

34 Ida B. Wells Barnett, *Crusade for Justice: The Autobiography of Ida B. Wells*, ed. A. M. Duster, (Chicago, University of Chicago Press, 1973); White, *A Man Called White*.

35 All five narrators in this chapter come from family backgrounds which in marxist terminology are petit bourgeois; I do not consider this irrelevant to the argument here.

36 Wells Barnett, *Crusade for Justice*, 64–5.

37 *Ibid.*, 66.

38 The book Wells Barnett was writing in 1930 was never completed, and the version we have now as *Crusade for Justice* was edited and published by her daughter, Alfreada Duster, in 1973. The title is Duster's. My own further discussion of the shape of this autobiography is necessarily limited by the fact that it cuts off in mid-sentence several years before Wells Barnett reached her own present. What I am describing is a rough draft of an unfinished book.

39 Cleanliness – not as a metaphor but as an educational process of bourgeoisification – is a significant value to several Negro autobiographers in this period, with Booker T. Washington being its most notable advocate. See *Up From Slavery*, in J. H. Franklin, *Three Negro Classics*, 122–3.

40 White, *A Man Called White*, 5.

41 Charles Martin, *The Angelo Herndon Case and Southern Justice* (Baton Rouge, Louisiana State University Press, 1976), 17.

42 White, *A Man Called White*, 11.

43 White's agenda as a novelist is also constructed by lynching. His first

novel, *The Fire in the Flint*, which had a following in the Renaissance period, is a piece which informs white northern readers that even light-skinned, professional black men are subject to lynch law.

44 Edward Waldron, *Walter White and the Harlem Renaissance* (Port Washington, N.Y.; National University Publications/Kennikat, 1978), 168 n.40.

45 See *Selected Writings of Ida B. Wells Barnett*, 20–8. Gunning suggests that Wells Barnett's transgressions of feminine decorum opened the door for a variety of white and also black writers to publicly question her femininity, *Race, Rape, and Lynching*, 82–5. It is noteworthy, in fact, that Wells Barnett was not a stranger to accusations of sexual impropriety long before she became an anti-lynching campaigner; her 1892 Memphis Diary indicates that as a single, thirty-year-old professional woman she was regularly responding to insinuations of immorality. It seems plausible both that her well-known defensiveness, and her pathbreaking willingness to go on the offensive against the sexual mores of white men, are connected to her own ambivalence about the stern sexual orthodoxies she upheld as a bourgeois Christian: "I am an anomaly to myself as well as to others: I do not wish to be married, but I do wish for the society of gentlemen." Miriam Decosta-Williams, ed., *The Memphis Diary of Ida B. Wells* (Boston, Beacon, 1995), 80.

46 Johnson, *Ex-Colored Man*, 460–1.

47 Johnson, *Along This Way*, 170; Johnson repeats and elaborates this same point, 309–13.

48 White, *A Man Called White*, 94, 98, describing his own *Rope and Faggot: A Biography of Judge Lynch* (New York, Arno Press and the New York Times, 1969).

49 White, *Rope and Faggot*, x.

50 *Ibid.*, 40, 55, 82, emphasis in original.

51 *Selected Writings of Ida B. Wells Barnett*, 161, 145–50 and *passim.*, 34–7. Wells Barnett would eventually agree with White that the true "foundation" of lynching was economic, but not until *Crusade for Justice*, 64, which of course White could not have read. It seems likely that Wells Barnett would have read *Rope and Faggot*.

52 *Selected Writings of Ida B. Wells Barnett*, 223.

53 Decosta-Williams, *Memphis Diary*, 12.

54 Barbara Christian, "The Race for Theory," in *Cultural Critique* 6 (1987), 51–64.

55 Gloria Hull, *Color, Sex and Poetry: Three Women Writers of the Harlem Renaissance* (Bloomington, Indiana University Press, 1987), chapter 1.

56 Wells Barnett, *Crusade for Justice*, 220.

57 Without doing documentary research, this narrative can be reconstructed from Mildred Thompson, *Ida B. Wells Barnett: An Exploratory Study of an American Black Woman, 1893–1930*, Black Women in United States History series, D. C. Hine, ed. (Brooklyn, Carlson Publishing, 1990), who writes both about the fact of her exclusion from standard black political histories and also of some of the people she could not get along with; Robert Zagrando, *The NAACP Crusade Against Lynching, 1909–50* (Philadelphia, Temple University Press, 1980) and Char-

les Kellogg, *NAACP, a History of the National Association for the Advancement of Colored People* (Baltimore, Johns Hopkins University Press, 1967), who mention her in passing in their histories of the early NAACP, and Lewis, *W. E. B. Du Bois* who reconstructs Du Bois' 1910 shutting Wells Barnett out of the group of forty race leaders, 396–7.

58 Thompson, *Ida B. Wells Barnett*, 1. Thompson's biography is, as its title states, "exploratory." Wells Barnett is probably the most significant African-American figure yet to be the subject of a full-length biography.

59 Johnson, *Along This Way*, 413.

60 *Ibid.*, 136.

61 *Ibid.*, 68.

62 *Ibid.*, 120–1.

63 *Ibid.*, 151.

64 *Ibid.*, 21, 31, 45.

65 *Ibid.*, 412.

66 *Ibid.*, 165–70.

67 *Ibid.*, 390.

68 Vron Ware, *Beyond the Pale: White Women, Racism and History* (New York, Verso, 1992), 190–7.

69 Zora Neale Hurston, *Their Eyes Were Watching God* (New York, Harper Perennial, 1990).

70 Deborah Plant, *Every Tub Must Sit on its Own Bottom: The Philosophy and Politics of Zora Neale Hurston* (Urbana, University of Illinois Press, 1995); Lionnet, *Autobiographical Voices*.

71 Priscilla Wald, "Becoming 'Colored': The Self-Authorizing Language of Difference in Zora Neale Hurston," in *American Literary History* 2:1 (spring 1990), 79–100; Samira Kawash, *Dislocating the Color Line: Identity, Hybridity, and Singularity in African American Literature* (Stanford, Calif., Stanford University Press, 1997).

72 Wald, "Becoming 'Colored,'" 81; similarly 96–7.

73 Kawash, *Dislocating the Color Line*, 208.

74 Plant, *Every Tub Must Sit on its Own Bottom*, 4.

75 *Ibid.*, 10.

76 Hurston, *Their Eyes*, 1.

77 Zora Neale Hurston, *Dust Tracks on the Road*, 5–6.

78 *Ibid.*, 158.

79 *Ibid.*, 165–9.

80 *Ibid.*, 207.

81 William Maxwell, "'Is it True What They Say About Dixie?' Richard Wright, Zora Neale Hurston, and Rural/Urban Exchange in Modern African-American Literature," in B. Ching and G. Creed, eds., *Knowing Your Place: Rural Identity and Cultural Hierarchy* (New York, Routledge, 1997), 71–104.

82 Hazel Carby, "The Politics of Fiction, Anthropology, and the Folk: Zora Neale Hurston," in M. Awkward, ed., *New Essays On Their Eyes Were Watching God* (Cambridge, Cambridge University Press, 1990).

83 Hurston, *Dust Tracks*, 127.

8. *Ibid.*, 130.

85 *Ibid.*, 144.
86 Doing so helps Hurston to maintain an idealized account of the south. And while my reading of *Dust Tracks* does not fully account for its southernism, in light of how delighted people are to have discovered an anti-imperialist narrative that was cut from *Dust Tracks* because of World War II, it should be mentioned that, in a manner quite typical of much southern ideology, this romanticization of "folk" culture replaces abstract "travel" for any sense of place or the issues intrinsic to places traveled. Such a politics, while it appropriately argues for the cultural continuity between the US south and the Caribbean, is perfectly capable of any kind of military opportunism and interventionism – Hurston supported the US invasion of Haiti in 1938. Her argument about Japan is, of course, that they are simply doing in their "sphere of influence" what the United States has been doing all along in its own. This is certainly an accurate enough argument, but it is unattached to anything except a sort of "boys will be boys" disdain, and hardly provides the grounds for a sustained critique of imperialism.
87 This disdain for working women who are not versions of herself is not general to her earlier short stories. "Sweat" is particularly valuable for its portrayal of a black woman as worker. Even by *Their Eyes*, however, Hurston's portrayals of black women as, principally, competition for her heroines starts to become the predominant mode – the dialogue with Pheoby, whose "bosom friendship" with Janie is stated but never illustrated in the entire narration of Janie's years in Eatonville notwithstanding.
88 Hurston, *Dust Tracks*, 87.
89 *Ibid.*, 30.
90 *Ibid.*, 4, 117, 128–9, 161–3.
91 *Ibid.*, 141, 152.
92 *Ibid.*, 151.
93 And even Barbara Johnson admits that *Their Eyes Were Watching God* ends with a "search for wholeness, oneness, universality and totalization" which "can never be put to rest." *A World of Difference* (Baltimore, Johns Hopkins University Press, 1987), 164. *Dust Tracks* ends exactly the same way.
94 Pierre Bourdieu, *The Rules of Art*, trans. S. Emanuel (Stanford, Calif., Stanford University Press, 1996); *Homo Academicus*.
95 Barbara Christian, "The Highs and Lows of Black Feminist Criticism," in H. L. Gates, ed., *Reading Black, Reading Feminist* (New York, Meridian, 1990), 44–51; "The Race for Theory."

5 Representing the Negro as proletarian

1 Richard B. Moore, *Richard B. Moore, Caribbean Militant in Harlem: Collected Writings 1920–72*, W. B. Turner and J. M. Turner, eds., (Bloomington, Indiana University Press, 1988), 155.
2 Leon Trotsky, *Literature and Revolution* (Ann Arbor, Mich., Ann Arbor Paperbacks, 1960), 91.

3 Richard Wright, *The Outsider* (New York, Harper and Row, 1991), 197.
4 Karl Marx, *The Economic and Philosophical Manuscript of 1844*, ed. D. J. Struik (New York, International Publishers, 1964), 180.
5 Mary Frances Berry and John Blassingame, *Long Memory: The Black Experience in America* (New York, Oxford University Press, 1982), 223.
6 Manning Marable, *Race, Reform and Rebellion: The Second Reconstruction in Black America, 1945–1982* (Jackson, University of Mississippi Press, 1984), 18.
7 Mark Naison, *Communists in Harlem During the Depression* (New York, Grove, 1983); Robin D. G. Kelley, *Hammer and Hoe: Alabama Communists During the Great Depression* (Chapel Hill, University of North Carolina Press, 1990); Horne, *Black and Red*.
8 Horne, "Who Lost the Cold War?"; Brenda Plummer, *Rising Wind: Black Americans and US Foreign Affairs, 1935–60* (Chapel Hill; University of North Carolina Press, 1996); Von Eschen, "Challenging Cold War Habits: African Americans, Race, and Foreign Policy," in *Diplomatic History* 20: 4 (fall 1996), 627–38; Von Eschen, *Race Against Empire*.
9 Foley, *Radical Representations*; Paula Rabinowitz, *Labor and Desire: Women's Revolutionary Fiction in Depression America* (Chapel Hill, University of North Carolina Press, 1991); Alan Wald, *The New York Intellectuals* (Chapel Hill, University of North Carolina Press, 1987).
10 Angelo Herndon, *Let Me Live* (New York, Random House, 1937); Paul Robeson, *Here I Stand* (Boston, Beacon, 1988).
11 The most sustained elaboration of the psychology of American anti-Communism to what I, following Spillers, call the "American Grammar Book" is Joel Kovel's *Red Hunting in the Promised Land: Anticommunism and the Making of America* (New York, Basic Books, 1994), which, like his more well-known *White Racism: A Psychohistory*, describes the specifically US contours of a particular logic of vilification. Barbara Foley develops the relationship between this logic and African-American Studies in "The Rhetoric of Anticommunism in *Invisible Man*," *College English* 59: 5 (1997), 530–49. Until it is understood that the current expectation within the academy that marxist critique immediately and ritually distance itself from the history of the Soviet Union is the legacy of Cold War social psychosis, having nothing to do with either the content of contemporary marxist thought or with any actual knowledge about the history of the Soviet bloc on the part of those holding the expectation, marxist politics is not possible. Within African-American Studies this should be easy to comprehend, since we know well that racist logic holds that black public figures are always responsible to distance themselves from other, "bad," blacks in order to be taken seriously.

It must become obvious to everyone that murderous governments have been the norm in the twentieth century. Leaving aside the global death toll caused strictly by "economic matters," like malnutrition, enclosure and misuse of land, etc., the US government has murdered or directly funded the murders of as many dissident professionals and activists on "our" side as the Soviets did on "theirs." "Our" success has been to make most of them Latin American or Asian; of the hundreds who have, in fact, been US "citizens," the success has been to limit the killing to black and Native American communities. Ward Churchill has pointed out that the percentage of Pine Ridge residents murdered in the 1970s is comparable to the percentage of Salvadorans murdered in the 1980s. Likewise, Brenda Plummer says: "The reality of 1947 was that parts of the United States could match Stalinist terror blow for blow. The South and North alike played host to forced labor, lack of due process, intolerance of dissent, atrocious prisons and mental hospitals, hunger and malnutrition. Vital statistics from the US Census Bureau indicate that Afro-American infant mortality and life expectancy rates continued to hover at Soviet levels. Crude death rates were higher," Plummer, *Rising Wind*, 183.

Dissident whites holding US passports have, in fact, been quite lucky in our anomalous positions as the tolerated – which perhaps means nothing more than unfeared – opposition.

12 Cited in Foley, *Radical Representations*, 87.

13 *Ibid.*, 46–54.

14 Daniel Aaron, *Writers on the Left: Episodes in American Literary Communism* (New York, Columbia University Press, 1992).

15 Today the 1930s are referred to as the "Old Left," another aspect of the nomenclature of anti-marxism. Every US "Old Left" already had an old left, despite the repetitious claims of American exceptionalism.

16 Richard B. Moore, *Selected Writings*, 47–58; Harry Haywood, *Black Bolshevik: Autobiography of an Afro-American Communist* (Chicago, Liberator Press, 1978), chapter 8–10.

17 Walter Rideout, *The Radical Novel in the United States, 1900–1954* (New York, Columbia University Press, 1992), 158. Alan Wald states that those Trotskyists who sought a position simultaneously anti-Stalin and pro-Communist during the 1930s and 1940s urged a limited defense of the Soviet Union as a deformed worker's state run by a corrupt and unnecessary governmental body, but with an economy making a successful transition to socialism.

18 Haywood, *Black Bolshevik*, 352–8, 586–98.

19 Wald notes this as a relatively minor feature of the move of Trotskyist theorists away from marxism after World War II, *The New York Intellectuals*, 217. However, from my point of view it is precisely the racist and imperialist logic of Americanism, linked as it is with the success stories of white immigrants (and nearly all Wald's "New York Intellectuals" are children of Jewish immigrants), which already appeared in their work in the 1930s, that *best* accounts for the turn of these intellectuals to Cold Warriorism. In fact, this Americanism is what is consistent between the specific 1930s Trotskyists who became Cold Warriors, and the specific 1930s CP members (like Earl Browder, who touted the line "Communism is twentieth century Americanism") who dissolved the party in 1944.

20 Du Bois' occasional writings about the CPUSA prior to World War II confirm that he thought this, in spite of his enthusiasm for Russian socialism; and the fact that the *Autobiography* abandons *Dusk*'s narra-

tive of the autonomy of racialization reconfirms that he, and not the set of possibilities within the CP, changed.

21 Robeson, *Here I Stand*, 54.

22 Trotsky, *Literature and Revolution*, chapter 2.

23 Leon Trotsky, *Leon Trotsky on Black Nationalism and Self-Determination* (New York, Pathfinder, 1978).

24 *Ibid.*, 30, 42.

25 Haywood, *Black Bolshevik*, 234, 238.

26 James Allen, *Negro Liberation* (New York, International Publishers, 1938), 5.

27 The CP's explanation, then, for why to oppose the Garveyists is in this clause: the Party would claim that Garvey is not developing nationalist consciousness among the proletariat, but among the petty bourgeois.

28 W. E. B. Du Bois, "The African Roots of the War," in *Atlantic Monthly* 115 (May 1915), 707–15, reprinted in H. Aptheker, ed., *Writings by W. E. B. Du Bois in Periodicals Edited by Others, vol. II, 1910–1934* (Millwood, New York, Kraus Thomson Organization Ltd., n.d.); V. I. Lenin, *Imperialism: The Highest Stage of Capitalism* (New York, International Publishers, 1939). It happens that Lenin knew Du Bois' work before Du Bois knew Lenin's work; in *Capitalism and Agriculture in the US* Lenin cites the Du Bois-penned US government reports from the 1890s on southern agriculture; Lenin notes their "remarkably detailed descriptions ... unavailable ... in any other country," quoted in Herbert Aptheker, *Annotated Bibliography of the Published Writings of W. E. B. Du Bois* (Millwood, New York, Kraus Thomson Organization Ltd., 1973), 501.

29 Information on the history of the Angelo Herndon case and its place in the history of southern repression of both black and communist movements is provided in Martin, *The Angelo Herndon Case*. Surprisingly, Martin barely mentions the existence of *Let Me Live* at all in his account. More generally, however, he describes the differing strategies for attaining justice in the south adopted by the NAACP, who would rely on the courts without success, and the CP, whose manypronged social movement approach, in which the court is presumed to be one, perhaps minor, sphere of action, is far more effective in obtaining justice. In this sense *Let Me Live*, unlike most autobiographies discussed in chapters three, four, and five, follows quite explicitly in the slave narrative tradition of texts written to produce specific social effects due to their production for an already constituted social movement.

30 Kelley, *Hammer and Hoe*, 78ff.

31 Rabinowitz, *Labor and Desire*, 8.

32 Thus – as I have stated repeatedly – while the issues I address here more closely overlap with Phillip Bryan Harper's *Are We Not Men?*, the politics I espouse more closely resembles that of Hortense Spillers' "Mama's Baby, Papa's Maybe."

33 Herndon, *Let Me Live*, 3, 5.

34 *Ibid.*, 7.

35 *Ibid.*, 10–11.
36 *Ibid.*, 19–20.
37 *Ibid.*, 20.
38 *Ibid.*, 73.
39 *Ibid.*, 78.
40 *Ibid.*, 77.
41 *Ibid.*, 153.
42 *Ibid.*, 99.
43 *Ibid.*, 147.
44 *Ibid.*, 209, 215.
45 *Ibid.*, 112–13, 131, 150, 213ff.
46 Kenneth M. Cameron, "Paul Robeson, Eddie Murphy, and the Film Text of 'Africa,'" in *Text and Performance Quarterly* 10 (1990), 282–93; Martin Duberman, *Paul Robeson* (New York, Alfred A. Knopf, 1989), chapters 14–18.
47 Robeson, *Here I Stand*, 6.
48 Sterling Stuckey, *Slave Culture: Nationalist Theory and the Foundations of Black America* (New York, Oxford University Press, 1987). I refer to Robeson's, and Stuckey's, cultural nationalism as conservative in the etymological sense, as defined by the conservation of a set of putatively proletarian or "folk" cultural values from the past.
49 Robeson, *Here I Stand*, 9.
50 *Ibid.*, 20.
51 *Ibid.*, 27.
52 Robeson, Paul, Jr., "Paul Robeson," in M. J. Buhle, P. Buhle, and D. Georgakis, eds., *The Encyclopedia of the American Left* (Chicago, St. James, 1990), 655.
53 Robeson, *Here I Stand*, 54.
54 Duberman, *Paul Robeson*, 422.
55 Robeson, *Here I Stand*, 39, 40.
56 Stuckey, *Slave Culture*, 326.
57 Robeson, *Here I Stand*, 65, 90.

6 Malcolm X and the grammar of redemption

1 James Baldwin, *The Fire Next Time*, 37–8, emphasis in original.
2 Deidre Bailey, "The Autobiography of Deidre Bailey: Thoughts on Malcolm X and Black Youth," in Wood, ed., *Malcolm X*, 233. Bailey is identified as a "student and activist," and her presence in this book, amid some of the most well-known African-American intellectuals in the US, is clearly intended to present an "authentic" view of contemporary black youth.
3 Williams, *The Alchemy of Race and Rights*, 97.
4 Malcolm X and Alex Haley, *The Autobiography of Malcolm X* (New York, Ballantine, 1992). "Structure of feeling" is, of course, Raymond Williams' term, and in his own view its use is always a "cultural hypothesis, actually derived from attempts to understand such [seeming individual] elements [as style] and their connections in a generation or period, and needing always to be returned ... to

evidence," *Marxism and Literature*, 132–3. For, "what we are defining is a particular quality of social experience and relationship … which gives the sense of a generation or a period," *Ibid.*, 131.

5 Spillers, "Mama's Baby, Papa's Maybe," 76, 79.
6 X and Haley, *Autobiography*, 457–8.
7 *Ibid.*, 459–60.
8 Michele Wallace, *Black Macho and the Myth of the Superwoman* (New York, Verso, 1990), 37.
9 Paul John Eakin, "Malcolm X and the Limits of Autobiography," in Olney, *Autobiography*, 183.
10 X and Haley, *Autobiography*, 476.
11 John Edgar Wideman, "Malcolm X: The Art of Autobiography," in Wood, ed., *Malcolm X*, 107.
12 X and Haley, *Autobiography*, 38.
13 *Ibid.*, 32–3.
14 *Ibid.*, 174.
15 *Ibid.*, 239 (my italics).
16 *Ibid.*
17 *Ibid.*, xi–xii, xiii–xiv.
18 I take bell hooks' emphasis on "truth" in *Sisters of the Yam* (Boston, South End, 1993) to be addressed to the conditions under which a black woman's experiential reality becomes comprehensible as truth – that is, regardless of epistemological or ontological considerations, that which is "known" by a given black woman is significantly less likely to become "knowledge," even to herself, than that which is "known" by a given white man (and notwithstanding his relationship to the means of production).
19 X and Haley, 314.
20 Du Bois, *The Souls of Black Folk*, 43–4.
21 X and Haley, 288–9.
22 *Ibid.*, 212.
23 *Ibid.*, 430.
24 *Ibid.*, 18.
25 *Ibid.*, 64, 65, 173.
26 *Ibid.*, 101.
27 *Ibid.*, 56.
28 *Ibid.*, 104.
29 *Ibid.*, 135.
30 *Ibid.*, 359.
31 *Ibid.*, 125–6.
32 *Ibid.*, 48, 49, 51.
33 Robin D. G. Kelley, "The Riddle of the Zoot: Malcolm Little and Black Cultural Politics During World War II," in Wood, ed., *Malcolm X*. Kelley's article, which is ostensibly about Malcolm X, primarily uses his text as a springboard for writing about black male popular culture in the 1930s and 1940s, in and of itself a worthy project. However, Kelley claims that the zoot suits, conks, and cultural elements that X refers to as self-hatred are actually precisely signs of black working class cultural creativity and identity. This argument simply does not

take X's position seriously: X does not deny that black working class (Kelley's category) hustlers like himself are trying to form rebellious identities; he suggests, however, that certain kinds of rebellion are not capable of bringing either happiness to the rebel or benefit to those who share the black working class identity; rather, the people who engage in them become bitter, addicted, and ultimately incapable of using their substantial intellects. (Indeed, it may be because they have substantial powers of intellect that they may have gotten to that position, rather than taking a less rebellious course to begin with.) Thus even if these forms of rebellion are *political*, they are by no means a replacement for a *politics*.

For Kelley's position, which is dominant in cultural studies at present, the defense of two further constructs is at stake: "the black working class" and "popular culture." Kelley is so committed to reminding us that zoot suits and conks are an example of working class resistance that he ignores that the Nation of Islam is also an example of working class resistance, and to exactly the same extent – which is why traditional marxists would likely label *both* "petty bourgeois." (Kelley corrects this mistake in "House Negroes on the Loose: Malcolm X and the Black Bourgeoisie," *Callaloo* 21:2 (1998), 419–35, which I read as this went to press.) As to the latter, I acknowledge no second place to Kelley in my admiration for, and defense of, black popular culture. I merely suggest we do hip hop – and the black working class – no favor if we act like there is no difference in political valence between Snoop Doggy Dogg and Pharcyde, let alone Aceyalone – to stick only to examples from LA in the mid-1990s. What Kelley provides is a demonstration that Malcolm X's subculture in the 1940s is in some sense resistant to the dominant society. What he does not provide is a reason for someone who admires Malcolm X's third worldism – or, for that matter, someone who loathes his misogyny – to admire that resistance more than Malcolm's later analysis of it.

The most precise account, neither celebratory nor denigrating, of hip hop's politics appears in an article devoted to arguing (usefully enough) that it's time to stop talking so much about hip hop's politics and start working more on its aesthetics. See Tim Brennan, "Off the Gangsta Tip: A Rap Appreciation, or Forgetting About Los Angeles," in *Critical Inquiry* 20 (summer 1994), 685–9.

34 X and Haley, *Autobiography*, 358–9.
35 *Ibid.*, 422.
36 *Ibid.*, 435.
37 The desire to re-read the end of X's life, despite limited evidence, as proto-feminist is explicit in Angela Davis, "Meditations on the Legacy of Malcolm X," in Wood, ed., *Malcolm X*; bell hooks, *Yearning: Race, Gender and Cultural Politics* (Boston, South End, 1990); hooks, *Outlaw Culture: Resisting Representations* (New York, Routledge, 1994); and in my own work; what limited evidence there is for the justifiability of this desire is provided in William Sales, *From Civil Rights to Black Liberation: Malcolm X and the Organization of Afro-American Unity* (Boston, South End, 1994), and Jan Carew, *Ghosts in Our Blood: With*

Malcolm X in Africa, England and the Caribbean (Chicago, Lawrence Hill, 1994). Patricia Hill Collins, like me, maintains that the narration of violence in this text is patriarchal without dismissing the possibility that feminism may support the violence of women and men in some instances, "Learning to Think for Ourselves: Malcolm X's Black Nationalism Reconsidered," in Wood, ed., *Malcolm X*.

38 Eugene Wolfenstein, *The Victims of Democracy: Malcolm X and the Black Revolution* (London, Free Association, 1989); Hilton Als, "Philosopher or Dog?" in Wood, ed., *Malcolm X*; Carew, *Ghosts in Our Blood*.

39 X and Haley, *Autobiography*, 449. Wolfenstein points out that this depiction of Haley's makes the sessions between X and Haley strongly resemble the psychoanalytic process, *The Victims of Democracy*, 285.

40 X and Haley, *Autobiography*, 26.

41 *Ibid.*, 452.

42 *Ibid.*, 107, emphasis in original. Note that grammatically, the second "their" could refer to the wives as well as the husbands, and this is no less ambiguous in the original context. Would we, as feminists, want this pronoun to refer to the women as well as, or instead of, the men?

43 *Ibid.*, 107–8.

44 *Ibid.*, 130. Perhaps the most serious difficulty in understanding this text as potentially oppositional at this moment comes from the fact that for Malcolm, sleeping with white women is not "subversive," but rather fits neatly in the reproduction of white supremacy. But "subversion of identity" theses can't address the fact that the sexual freedom of Harlem in this period was not an example of something unambiguously good for the people who lived in Harlem, but rather an example of the dominant society placing its sexually marginal and its racially marginal in the same location for its own convenience and to the benefit of neither. Potentially, we might hope, a common articulation between anti-racism and anti-heterosexism can be formed from the Harlem experience, especially when articulated by people both African-American and gay/lesbian. More traditionally, however, it has led to well-grounded suspicions on the part of black community members that they are being used for the sexual services white people can pay for but not openly acknowledge, and from there sometimes to participation in the most virulent strands of homophobia.

Russell Simmons is able to argue to Marlon Riggs that the image of the NOI Malcolm X as positive black manhood was a necessary part of his own development, which he cannot and does not want to abandon even in light of coming out: "Didn't you, when you were a child, feel proud when you saw the Muslim brothers on the corner? I know I did. Because you so rarely saw that image of a black man – well-dressed, confident, assured, articulate – doing something for the community and himself." Riggs does not argue that such an image was unimportant, but objects to the notion that such an image remains important: "the problem is that we haven't recognized that the particularities of that moment have ceased – have changed," and, of course, it is now necessary to construct an alternative, gay-positive black masculinity, Ron Simmons and Marlon Riggs, "Sexuality, Television and Death: A

Black Gay Dialogue on Malcolm X," in Wood., ed., *Malcolm X*, 138. And yet it's not obvious that key particularities of that moment have ceased. As long as the ghettoization and imprisonment of sub-proletarian black men continues, we can expect that neither blackness as such nor masculinity as such will disappear from their socialization process. The suppression of X in the name of sexuality movements, rather than a direct working through and rearticulation, will simply reinforce our existing colonial relationship to the ghetto.

Riggs' film *Black is ... Black Ain't* is, of course, a fabulous example of such a rearticulation, and a particularly good classroom companion to *The Autobiography of Malcolm X*.

45 X and Haley, *Autobiography*, 111.
46 *Ibid.*, 318.
47 On the importance of family, and the relationship of family to com-munalist rhetoric in the NOI of Malcolm X's period, see E. U. Essien-Udom, *Black Nationalism: A Search for an Identity in America* (Chicago, University of Chicago Press, 1962), chapters 4 and 6.
48 X and Haley, *Autobiography*, 267, 260.
49 *Ibid.*, 410.
50 *Ibid.*, 358. Though Elijah Muhammad certainly ordered X's death, it remains likely that agencies other than the NOI also wanted him dead, and either assisted in his murder or did not prevent it when they could have. X thought this would be the case in the last several weeks of his life, *ibid.*, 495.
51 Dyson, *Making Malcolm*, 96.
52 Numerous nationalist writers have noted the continuity between Garveyism and the NOI; for example, Theodore G. Vincent, *Black Power and the Garvey Movement* (San Francisco, Ramparts Press, 1972); Essien-Udom, *Black Nationalism*; Carew, *Ghosts in Our Blood*; and Harold Cruse, *The Crisis of the Negro Intellectual* (New York, Quill, 1984).
53 X and Haley, *Autobiography*, 5.
54 *Ibid.*, 9.
55 Bruce Perry, *Malcolm: The Life of a Man Who Changed Black America* (Barrytown, New York, Station Hill, 1991) denies that Earl Little really was pushed from the streetcar because of his political activities, suggesting instead that he was out committing adultery. It is, of course, important to X that he represent the story of his father's death in political terms even as he explicitly acknowledges that the story is hearsay: "Negroes in Lansing have always whispered..." X and Haley, *Autobiography*, 13. As far as I can tell, there is no more or less reason to take Perry's word than X's.
56 Carew provides the most extensive documentation of the extent of the family's Garveyist activities, culled from conversations with Malcolm X at the very end of his life, interviews with several brothers who were also involved in the NOI, and an investigation into Louise Little's early life.
57 Both Du Bois and James Baldwin had, in different ways, called into question the presentation of race issues as a "Negro problem" rather

than a "white problem" prior to Elijah Muhammad, but it seems accurate to me to say that only Malcolm X's popularization of Muhammad's "the white man is the devil" via the mass media, and the anger provoked by this phrase, had the effect of getting a large number of people (white or black) to think through such a claim.

58 X and Haley, *Autobiography*, 184.

59 *Ibid.*, 211, 436.

60 *Ibid.*, 369, emphasis in original.

61 Mullen, "Optic White."

62 X and Haley, *Autobiography*, 191.

63 My narrative in the next three paragraphs is in basic agreement with Eugene Wolfenstein's more exhaustive recreation of X's claim that America is the hustling society. *The Victims of Democracy*, chapter 5.

64 How this relates to the activity of black intellectuals who do not share the same set of psychic necessities is the difficult issue that James Baldwin, whose writing provides the shadow of this entire chapter, grappled with in regard to X. Baldwin treats X very much the way he treats his younger self in *The Fire Next Time* – as someone trying to escape a ghetto situation and needing a gimmick, and therefore using the religious materials available to him to chart a plausible path out. See *The Fire Next Time*, 80–111, and "Malcolm and Martin," in David Gallen, ed., *Malcolm X: As They Knew Him* (New York, Carroll and Graff, 1992), 257–79. Baldwin's strong personal identification with X is confirmed by Leeming, who says Baldwin saw X as a "soul mate," *James Baldwin: A Biography* (New York, Henry Holt, 1994), 295. In turn, it is useful to imagine a Malcolm X who survived saying of himself retrospectively, paraphrasing my epigraph to this chapter from Baldwin, "it was my career in the Nation of Islam that turned out, precisely, to be my gimmick."

65 X and Haley, *Autobiography*, 292–3, emphasis in original.

66 *Ibid.*, 293. Thus the demand for reparations is marxian in that it is a version of the restorative demand of all socialism, that surplus-value be returned to its producers; but it goes beyond such a demand in its insistence that such a restoration is meaningful only under certain social circumstances.

67 *Ibid.*, 234.

68 The meaning of this model to X is not clear, inasmuch as the actual OAAU was a Harlem-based membership organization, primarily made of ex-NOI members who remained loyal to him; his speeches on the subject of the organization are thus contradictory. On the one hand, he apparently wanted to build an organization of organizations – a black leadership coalition that would attempt to navigate their different politics; but X knew he could not do this, since few African Americans with institutional power of any sort in 1964 would risk it through participating in an initiative of his. On the other, his international celebrity (which was just that – it was not access to funds or the immediate ability to mobilize large numbers of people) demanded some affiliation, Malcolm X, *By Any Means Necessary* (New York, Pathfinder, 1970). This problem was by no means unique to Malcolm

X among leaders of radical movements in the age of media-based internationalism: see Frederic Jameson's analysis of the rise and fall of Detroit's League of Revolutionary Black Workers, *Postmodernism, or the Social Logic of Late Capitalism* (Durham, N.C., Duke University Press, 1990), 412–18.

69 X and Haley, *Autobiography*, 391.
70 *Ibid.*, 398.
71 *Ibid.*, 427.
72 The Vietnam War, on the verge of escalation as Malcolm X dies, is instrumental in the largest grassroots flourishing of pan-third-world-ist identification in African-American history, as a substantial number of black soldiers were unable to see any reason to prefer the US to the Vietnamese. The black literature of the Vietnam War, almost entirely absent from current African-American Studies, makes this clear. See Michael Bibby, *Hearts and Minds: Bodies, Poetry, and Resistance in the Vietnam Era* (New Brunswick, N.J., Rutgers University, 1996).
73 X and Haley, *Autobiography*, 390, emphasis in original. bell hooks is my immediate predecessor in stressing this: see *Yearning; Outlaw Culture*. In general, the narrative of the personal "quest" is the most commonly written about topic on the *Autobiography*; see John Groppe, "From Chaos To Cosmos: The Role of Trust in *The Autobiography of Malcolm X*," in *Soundings* 66:4 (1983), 437–49; Albert Stone, *Autobiographical Occasions*; Robert Penn Warren, "Malcolm X: Mission and Meaning," in Gallen, *Malcolm X: As They Knew Him*, 201–12; Wolfenstein, *The Victims of Democracy*.
74 This reading of black male imprisonment overlaps strongly with Clarence Lusane, *Race In the Global Era* (Boston, South End, 1997), chapter 6, which also includes relevant statistics. The runaway prison industrial complex is, of course, not exclusively an issue for black men; but the strongly disproportionate rates at which black men are imprisoned, the ways black men are interpolated socially as always already likely to be criminals, and the centrality of these to the American grammar of "security," join the issues of criminal justice, racial justice, and social justice in a particularly tight bind.
75 X and Haley, *Autobiography*, 12.
76 *Ibid.*, 43.
77 *Ibid.*, 58.
78 *Ibid.*, 100.
79 Listeners of hip hop will recognize this as a central thematic of the form.
80 *Ibid.*, 178. X writes that he was placed in a model liberal prison with particularly good facilities for his education. This is definitely not the experience of most contemporary prisoners.
81 *Ibid.*, 156.
82 *Ibid.*, 170.
83 *Ibid.*, 179.
84 *Ibid.*, 421.
85 *Ibid.*, 212, 225, 243.
86 Bailey, "The Autobiography of Deidre Bailey," 234.

7 The political identity "woman" as emergent from the space of Black Power

1 Wallace, *Black Macho*, 37.
2 Alice Walker, *Meridian* (New York, Pocket, 1976), 151.
3 Stuart Hall, "Cultural Studies and its Theoretical Legacies," 283.
4 Nikki Giovanni, *Gemini: An Extended Autobiographical Statement on My First Twenty-Five Years of Being a Black Poet* (New York, Penguin, 1971); Angela Davis, *Angela Davis, an Autobiography: With My Mind on Freedom* (New York: International Publishers, 1988).
5 I follow Robyn Wiegman in wanting to reassert, at this late date, the significance of the analysis in *Black Macho* not as a challenge to the negative reviews of black feminists like June Jordan (in *Civil Wars*, 163–8) or Linda Powell (in Smith, ed., *Home Girls*, 283–92), but to recapture what was new in Wallace's psychoanalytical framework in 1978: "In particular, Wallace is concerned with the ideological and political fracturing that arises when black disenfranchisement is cast in terms of a denied masculinity, as the capitulation of Black Power to patriarchal notions of masculinity consequently cast the black woman as matriarch, willing helpmate to the black man's cultural castration," *American Anatomies*, 109.
6 This approach differs a great deal from that of Madhu Dubey, *Black Women Novelists and the Nationalist Aesthetic* (Bloomington, Indiana University Press, 1994). Dubey, like myself in this last section, is interested in women's response to patriarchal nationalism in the 1970s, and reads novels by Gayle Jones, Toni Morrison, and Alice Walker as a response to the aesthetic theories of Stephen Henderson, Addison Gayle, and others. It is easy to agree that black women novelists rarely, if ever, followed the aesthetic principles of the nationalist critics in the 1970s. A more complicated problem is to account for the ways that black women did and did not challenge the *political* nationalism of the 1960s – for example, it seems to me that the best of 1960s political nationalism remains in the work of Toni Morrison, Toni Cade Bambara, and others, even as they use this analysis to feminist ends.
7 Sara Evans, *Personal Politics* (New York, Vintage, 1979); Alice Echols, *Daring to Be Bad: Radical Feminism in America, 1967–75* (Minneapolis, University of Minnesota Press, 1989); Elaine Tyler May, *Homeward Bound: American Families in the Cold War Era* (New York, Basic, 1988).
8 Angela Davis' *Women, Race and Class* (New York, Vintage, 1980), as a book engaged with the history of the US left, was written in clear awareness of this.
9 Jordan, *Civil Wars*, 167.
10 Wallace, *Black Macho*, xix.
11 *Ibid.*, 162.
12 Homi Bhabha, *The Location of Culture* (New York, Routledge, 1994), 49–50.
13 Adorno, *Negative Dialectics*, 17.
14 Giovanni, *Gemini*, 149, 148.

15 Homi Bhabha, *The Location of Culture*, 215.

16 Giovanni, *Gemini*, 24.

17 Mary Helen Washington, "Teaching *Black Eyed Susans:* An Approach to the Study of Black Women Writers," in G. Hull, P. B. Scott, and B. Smith, eds., *But Some of Us are Brave* (Old Westbury, New York, The Feminist Press, 1982), 208–220 noted the prevalence of such a grandmother figure in black women's writing of the 1970s, citing Alice Walker and Toni Morrison among others.

18 Giovanni, *Gemini*, 29.

19 *Ibid.*, 29–33.

20 In contrast to the attempt at the systematization of black poetry by Stephen Henderson, this could be taken as the model of aesthetic blackness proposed in the most well-known anthology of the Black Arts Movement, L. Jones and L. Neal, eds., *Black Fire* (New York, William Morrow, 1968). Compare the passages I have just quoted to the words of the poet then still known as Leroi Jones from the years immediately proceeding Giovanni's book: "The Black Artist's role in America is to aid in the destruction of America as he knows it. His role is to report and reflect so precisely the nature of the society, and of himself in that society, that other men will be moved by the exactness of his rendering and, if they are black men, grow strong," Jones, "state/ment," in *Home: Social Essays* (New York, William Morrow, 1966), 251. What is specifically remarkable about this passage from Jones, consistent with Giovanni's prose, is the way that the representation of blackness, this social experience that has been newly created out of a history of Negroness and a series of political movements, brings growth simply by its coming into existence, mediated by nothing. The poem "Black Art," *Black Fire*, 302–3, inflicts wounds to whites in the same manner.

21 Ernesto Laclau and Chantal Mouffe, *Hegemony and Socialist Strategy*.

22 June Jordan, *Civil Wars*, 144; Patricia Hill Collins, *Black Feminist Thought*, 107–8.

23 Giovanni, *Gemini*, 130–1.

24 *Ibid.*, 88

25 *Ibid.*, 7.

26 *Ibid.*, 4.

27 *Ibid.*, 5. Mulvaney Street is now one of these access roads. Giovanni says of "400 Mulvaney Street," the chapter's title, and her memories of it, "All gone, not even to a major highway but to a cutoff of a cutoff" *ibid.*, 10. Sitting in Oakland, California, when I read this book originally, this was an obscure line. Sitting in downtown Knoxville less than half a mile from the spot where the house would have been, I can attest to its literal truth: what would be the 400 block of Mulvaney Street is an access road to the James White Parkway, which itself is the connecting road between the airport highway and Interstate 40.

28 *Ibid.*, 7.

29 *Ibid.*, 10.

30 *Ibid.*, 12.

31 *Ibid.*, 98.

32 *Ibid.*, 106.

33 *Ibid.*, 108.

34 *Ibid.*, 104.

35 Margaret McDowell, "Groundwork for a More Comprehensive Criticism of Nikki Giovanni," in J. Weixlmann and C. J. Fontenot, eds., *Belief vs. Theory in Black American Literary Criticism* (Greenwood, Flo., Penkevill, 1986), 135–60; Virginia Fowler, *Nikki Giovanni* (New York, Twayne, 1992).

36 Giovanni, *Gemini*, 143–4.

37 *Ibid.*, 71.

38 *Ibid.*, 84.

39 Angela Davis, *Autobiography*, xv.

40 Regina Nadelson, *Who is Angela Davis?* (New York, Peter H. Wyden, 1972); J. A. Parker, *Angela Davis: The Making of a Revolutionary* (New Rochelle, N.Y., Arlington House, 1973); Angela Davis, *If They Come in the Morning* (New York, New American Library, 1971).

41 Angela Davis, "Afro Images: Politics, Fashion and Nostalgia," in *Critical Inquiry* 21 (autumn 1994), 37.

42 *Ibid.*, 38.

43 Angela Davis, *Autobiography*, 293.

44 *Ibid.*, 327

45 The image of being behind a barrier has been present in my narrative since my reading of *Dusk of Dawn*. Prison as an organizing theme of autobiographical blackness could itself provide the structure for a book-length project. All major treatments of slave narrative have made use of this theme; most important among writers who have linked slave narrative to twentieth-century prison writing is H. Bruce Franklin, *Prison Literature in America*, 2nd edn. (New York: Oxford University Press, 1989).

46 Angela Davis, *Autobiography*, 4–5, 13.

47 *Ibid.*, 17.

48 *Ibid.*, 19.

49 *Ibid.*, 28.

50 *Ibid.*, 65.

51 *Ibid.*, 20, 33–4, 50. This becomes the central argument about prison conditions in the most well-known recent prison narrative, John Edgar Wideman, *Brothers and Keepers* (New York, Penguin, 1984).

52 Angela Davis, *Autobiography*, 336.

53 *Ibid.*, viii.

54 *Ibid.*, 78.

55 *Ibid.*, 79–80.

56 *Ibid.*, 82–4.

57 *Ibid.*, 86–7.

58 *Ibid.*, xv.

59 Because Adorno is often positioned as an early version of the post-structuralist critique of identity, it is interesting in this context to look at Adorno's account of identity, *Negative Dialectics*, 146–51. In Adorno's argument for anti-identitarianism, difference is that which resists the force of the compulsion to identity inherent in sociality,

especially the sociality of the administrative state. Still, the "ideal of identity" is not escapable, nor can it be discarded. In this context, as Davis knows, minority discourse, that which has been forced by the administrative state into the position of nonidentity, already stands in a different relationship to identity than does philosophy. Davis has already been differentiated – the entire purpose of her figure in the media is to stand as the principle of differentiation. Her assertion of identity therefore occurs at a different location in the dialectic from Adorno's assertion of differentiation.

60 Angela Davis, *Autobiography*, 150, 187.

61 *Ibid.*, 144.

62 *Ibid.*, 197. Davis' recent formulation of this problematic, with which I am in substantial agreement, is that black nationalism is "a very complex and contradictory project that had emancipatory moments leading beyond itself," Angela Davis, "Black Nationalism: The Sixties and the Nineties," in G. Dent, ed., *Black Popular Culture*, 323. Davis writes the history of nationalism as neither adequate to its object nor reactionary and a thing that we should somehow be able to do without.

63 *Ibid.*, 222.

64 *Ibid.*, 354.

65 J. A. Parker, *Angela Davis*, 87, 89.

66 Angela Davis, *Autobiography*, 241–5.

67 *Ibid.*, xv.

68 *Ibid.*, viii.

69 *Ibid.*, 55.

70 *Ibid.*, 161.

71 Michele Wallace, *Black Macho*, 164.

72 Angela Davis, *Autobiography*, 255.

73 *Ibid.*, 254, 258, 263–4, 268.

74 *Ibid.*, 62, 317.

75 *Ibid.*, 311.

76 *Ibid.*, 373–4.

77 Though this is, properly speaking, a side issue to my narration of blackness, Juliet Mitchell's *Women's Estate* had by 1971 provided a useful articulation of socialist feminism, one that informs my analysis of Davis here. For Mitchell as for Davis, women's oppression occurs at the level of marxist analysis referred to as ideology; however, having a complex psychoanalytic account of ideology, including its perpetuation within revolutionary movements, she refuses the solution of a class politics that denies the constitutive role of gender differentiation in political action itself. Mitchell's early work, like Gayle Rubin several years later, continues to be worth consulting because it illustrates a particular road not taken in the theorization of marxism and feminism since the early 1970s – one especially neglected in the US. Needless to say, until extremely recently only black women (including Davis in subsequent work) had made any serious attempt to articulate marxian, psychoanalytic, *and* race/socioanalytic categories.

8 Home and profession in black feminism

1 bell hooks, *Outlaw Culture*, 209, emphasis in original.
2 Hortense Spillers, "Mama's Baby, Papa's Maybe," 80.
3 Patricia Williams, *The Rooster's Egg: On the Persistence of Prejudice*, (Cambridge, Mass., Harvard University, 1995), 185.
4 This conclusion is written in the wake of Michele Wallace's *ad hominem* attack on bell hooks, "For Whom the Bell Tolls," *Village Voice* (November 7, 1995), but I have no interest in adjudicating between the two. I am, on the contrary, interested in noting that Wallace and hooks are very close in both age and career path (having both become famous by writing books which were not traditionally "academic" but which became attractive to cultural studies and media studies, and only later becoming institutionalized as tenured academics), and actually appear at a theoretical level a great deal closer than almost any other pair of contemporary black feminist intellectuals. In this context – and in light of the ambivalences in their psychoanalytical treatments of home – Wallace's essay about hooks appears consistent with my (and her) analysis of the tensions one finds at "home."
5 Barbara Smith, "Introduction," to *Home Girls*, xx.
6 *Ibid.*, xx–xxi.
7 *Ibid.*, xxv.
8 *Ibid.*, xxii.
9 Audre Lorde, *Zami: A New Spelling of My Name* (Freedom, Calif., The Crossing Press, 1982), 3.
10 Another possible intertext is June Jordan's poem, "Moving Toward Home", which provided the title for her book *Living Room*.
11 Deborah Chay "Rereading Barbara Smith: Black Feminist Criticism and the Category of Experience," in *New Literary History* 24 (1993), 635–52, provides precisely the kind of reassessment of Barbara Smith's work ("Toward A Black Feminist Criticism," which I do not read here) to which I object strongly. Chay starts her essay by setting up a parallel between Steven Heath's well-known essay "Difference," and Smith's essay, both published within a year (1977–8). While both essays are purported to be important to "the setting of a new cultural agenda," the parallel quickly breaks down, as it becomes clear that Chay's agenda will be to criticize Smith's essay because "black feminist criticism['s] newly won ... status in academic and associated areas" makes it necessary for theory to redirect black feminist criticism, *ibid.*, 635–36. One might immediately wonder why the redirection of poststructuralism for identical reasons might not be in order. There is nothing in my agenda that prevents the material analysis of what has changed between 1977 and the present, as a means of contextualizing Barbara Smith's work; however, linking Heath to Smith in this case is a way of not engaging with Smith's project at all, but rather using it as a convenient whipping post with no audience other than that of the already converted. In this context Smith's reply to Chay – which can only be called nasty – is entirely in order. In response to specific points of Chay, not otherwise covered in this

chapter: (1) It is not true that Smith attempts "to establish a critique based on the explicit refusal of antecedent histories" (*ibid.*, 636), inasmuch as she goes out of her way to suggest that antecedence for the black feminist subject might yet come from the history of intellectual production by black women, if only someone would bother to read it; Smith also acknowledges that however she might attack the sexism of the black men or the racism of the white women, both the black and feminist struggles immediately preceding her own movement were necessary in creating the historical space for her own work. (2) While Chay is correct in noting that Smith's account of the concept of "identity" must be considered inadequate for a contemporary academic account (*ibid.*, 637–38), this in no way makes illegitimate the claim that the presence or absence of black women as critics of literature written by black women may constitutively change the content of that criticism; an account of social identity that would explore the reasons for this can be written. (3) The claim that "Smith cannot account for the ideological construction of experience," a category on which she relies, is also true. Nor does she attempt to make such an account. Chay, in turn, cannot account for the way that social experience itself, including the experience of race, gender, movement participation, and existence outside of a professional academic setting, are themselves constituent factors in the interpolation of ideology. (4) Finally, Chay's essay is built around a series of rhetorically nasty adjectives. When she wants to criticize experience as a category of evidence, she makes it "incontestable." When she needs Smith to be a realist she makes her position "uninflected." Can we be clear? Experience is, precisely, a category of evidence; it is not "incontestable." Realist representation is conceivable, and, I argue, often desirable; it is not "uninflected." *And nothing in Barbara Smith's writing states or implies otherwise.* Smith inflects, self-consciously, without dissimulation. Why, in order to inflect, we hope, "better," do we have to make a target of Smith?

The essay which directly precedes my analysis of how to read the history of recent black feminist intellectual production is Barbara Christian, "But What Do We Think We're Doing Anyway: The State of Black Feminist Criticism(s) or My Version of a Little Bit of History," in C. Wall, ed., *Changing Our Own Words* (New Brunswick, N.J., Rutgers University Press, 1989).

12 Lorde, *Zami*, 3, emphasis mine.
13 Smith, "Home," in *Home Girls*, 64–5.
14 *Ibid.*, 65.
15 *Ibid.*, 66.
16 *Ibid.*, 67.
17 *Ibid.*, 68.
18 Of course it matters a great deal that Wallace and hooks are criticized explicitly in the essays collected in *Home Girls* – Wallace for writing of the history of the civil rights movement in ways that are dismissive to the women who worked in it and for being historically inaccurate in general, and hooks for failing to consider lesbian movements in *Ain't I a Woman?*
19 Due to space considerations, I do not consider in this chapter Itabari

Njeri's *Every Good-Bye Ain't Gone* (New York, Vintage, 1990), the most dramatic recent example of a text in which the abandonment of the mother-figure is the ground for feminist politics.

20 Michele Wallace, *Invisibility Blues: From Pop to Theory* (New York, Verso, 1990), 5.
21 *Ibid.*, 223.
22 Paul Gilroy, "It's a Family Affair," in G. Dent, ed., *Black Popular Culture*, 303–16, has most recently and powerfully discussed the prevalence of the family trope within racial nationalism. It is not insignificant that, while critical of facile notions of mutually beneficial community that the use of kinship terms promotes (and the violent splits it may mask), Gilroy performs a limited defense of those terms. In this he appears consistent with the home-positive critics; meanwhile Wahneema Lubiano points out in a commentary that Gilroy's take differs from the long-standing feminist critique of the family, (in Dent, *Black Popular Culture*, 331).
23 Wallace, *Black Macho*, 89.
24 *Ibid.*, 176.
25 bell hooks, *Talking Back*, 155–9; "self-recovery" is elaborated on 28–34.
26 *Ibid.*, 155.
27 *Ibid.*
28 *Ibid.*, 156.
29 *Ibid.*, 157.
30 *Ibid.*, 159.
31 *Ibid.*, 1.
32 *Ibid.*, 2.
33 *Ibid.*, 7, 21.
34 *Ibid.*, 73.
35 *Ibid.*, 20
36 *Ibid.*, 21.
37 *Ibid.*, 150–4, 160–6.
38 *Ibid.*, 154.
39 *Ibid.*, 160.
40 *Ibid.*, 161.
41 *Ibid.*, 162.
42 *Ibid.*, 27.
43 *Ibid.*, 58.
44 *Ibid.*, 75.
45 *Ibid.*, 35–6.
46 *Ibid.*, 102.
47 bell hooks, *Outlaw Culture*, 126.
48 bell hooks, *Black Looks*, chapter 9.
49 bell hooks, *Outlaw Culture*, 152.
50 Ann DuCille, "The Occult of True Black Womanhood," 26, 30, 44.
51 *Ibid.*, 50.
52 *Ibid.*, 31.
53 Gina Dent, "Missionary Position," in R. Walker, ed., *To Be Real: Telling the Truth and Changing the Face of Feminism* (New York, Anchor, 1995), 61–75.

54 Barbara Omolade, *The Rising Song of African-American Women* (New York, Routledge, 1994), 58–9.
55 Wiegman has told me this was not idiosyncratic on my part.
56 Pierre Bourdieu and Terry Eagleton, "Doxa and Common Life: An Interview," in S. Zizek, ed., *Mapping Ideology* (New York, Verso, 1994), 272.
57 Gayatri Spivak, "Can the Subaltern Speak?," 288–9.
58 Michele Wallace, *Invisibility Blues*, 193.
59 Knoxville, Tennessee: December 6, 1996, 4:30 pm. Revised January 2, 1998, 10:00 am.
60 Paule Marshall, *The Chosen Place, The Timeless People* (New York, Vintage, 1992). I never teach a survey class in black literature without including either *Native Son*, in which Max provides an adequate objectification of myself, or *The Chosen Place, The Timeless People*. The point is precisely that white teachers who try to *explain* to skeptical students how we could possibly be qualified to teach African-American literature classes set ourselves up as fools; but that in no way means that there aren't relevant ways of representing one's social position.
61 After reading this, my friend Bruce Simon referred me to Hortense Spillers' second article on Marshall's novel, "Black, White, and in Color, or Learning How To Paint: Toward an Intramural Protocol of Reading," in J. Cox and L. Reynolds., eds., *New Historical Literary Study: Essays on Reproducing Texts, Representing History* (Princeton, N.J., Princeton University Press, 1993). In this article, Spillers discusses the character of "the Canterbury woman," who is *not* the "subaltern" – i.e., she who cannot speak – but, as Spillers refers to her, the "nameless," she who cannot be spoken. It will be necessary, as part of a longer project which attempts to articulate the determinate relationship between the marxist "proletariat" and the category "woman of color," to compare the (deconstructively derived) woman who cannot speak with the (psychoanalytically derived) woman who cannot be spoken. I cannot do that here.
62 Marshall, *The Chosen Place*, 136.
63 *Ibid.*, 137–8.
64 *Ibid.*, 142–3.
65 *Ibid.*, 228.
66 *Ibid.*, 262.
67 *Ibid.*, 324.
68 *Ibid.*, 360.
69 *Ibid.*, 390.
70 *Ibid.*, 467.

Works cited

Aaron, Daniel, *Writers on the Left: Episodes in American Literary Communism*, New York, Columbia University Press, 1992.

Abel, Elizabeth, Barbara Christian, and Helene Moglen, eds., *Female Subjects in Black and White*, Berkeley, University of California Press, 1997.

Adell, Sandra, *Double-Consciousness/Double Bind: Theoretical Issues in Twentieth-Century Black Literature*, Urbana, University of Illinois Press, 1994.

Adorno, Theodor, *Negative Dialectics*, New York, Continuum, 1994.

Alcoff, Linda, "Philosophy and Racial Identity," in *Radical Philosophy* 75 (1996), 5–14.

Allen, James, *Negro Liberation*, New York, International Publishers, 1938.

Andrews, William, "African-American Autobiography Criticism: Retrospect and Prospect," in P. J. Eakin, ed., *American Autobiography: Retrospect and Prospect*, Madison, University of Wisconsin Press, 1991, 195–215.

   To Tell A Free Story: The First Century of Afro-American Autobiography, 1760–1865, Urbana, University of Illinois Press, 1986.

Appiah, Anthony, "The Uncompleted Argument: Du Bois and the Illusion of Race," in H. L. Gates, ed., *"Race," Writing, and Difference*, Chicago, University of Chicago Press, 1986, 21–37.

Aptheker, Herbert, *Annotated Bibliography of the Published Writings of W. E. B. Du Bois*, Millwood, New York, Kraus Thomson Organization Ltd., 1973.

Baber, Willie L., "Capitalism and Racism," in *Critique of Anthropology*, 12: 3 (1992), 339–64.

Baker, Houston, *Workings of the Spirit: The Poetics of Afro-American Women's Writing*, Chicago, University of Chicago Press, 1991.

   "Caliban's Triple Play," in H. L. Gates, ed., *"Race," Writing, and Difference*, Chicago, University of Chicago Press, 1986, 381–95.

Baldwin, James, *The Fire Next Time*, New York, Dell, 1963.

Bell, Bernard, Emily Grosholz, and James Stewart, eds., *W. E. B. Du Bois: On Race and Culture*, New York, Routledge, 1997.

Bell, Derrick, *Faces at the Bottom of the Well: The Permanence of Racism*, New York, Basic, 1992.

Bercovitch, Sacvan, *The Puritan Origins of the American Self*, New Haven, Yale University Press, 1974.

Bergland, Betty, "Postmodernism and the Autobiographical Subject: Reconstructing the 'Other'," in K. Ashley, L. Gilmore and G. Peters, eds., *Autobiography and Postmodernism*, Amherst, University of Massachusetts Press, 1994, 130–66.

Berry, Mary Frances, and John Blassingham, *Long Memory: The Black Experience in America*, New York, Oxford University Press, 1982.

Berube, Michael, *Public Access: Literary Theory and Cultural Politics*, New York, Verso, 1994.

Bhabha, Homi, *The Location of Culture*, New York, Routledge, 1994.

"Introduction" to H. Bhabha, ed., *Nation and Narration*, New York, Routledge, 1990.

Bibby, Michael, *Hearts and Minds: Bodies, Poetry and Resistance in the Vietnam Era*, New Brunswick, N.J., Rutgers University Press, 1996.

Blount, Marcellus, and George Cunningham, eds., *Representing Black Men*, New York, Routledge, 1996.

Boggs, Grace Lee, "The Black Revolution in America," in T. Cade, ed., *The Black Woman*, New York, New American Library, 1970, 211–23.

Bourdieu, Pierre, *The Rules of Art*, trans. S. Emanuel, Stanford, Calif., Stanford University Press, 1996.

Language and Symbolic Power, John B. Thompson, ed., Cambridge, Mass., Harvard University Press, 1991.

Homo Academicus, Stanford, Calif., Stanford University Press, 1988.

Distinction: A Social Critique of the Judgment of Taste, Cambridge, Mass., Harvard University Press, 1984.

Outline of a Theory of Practice, trans. R. Nice, New York, Cambridge University Press, 1977.

and Terry Eagleton, "Doxa and Common Life: An Interview," in S. Zizek, ed., *Mapping Ideology*, New York, Verso, 1994, 265–77.

Braxton, JoAnn, *Black Women Writing Autobiography*, Philadelphia, Temple University Press, 1989.

Brennan, Tim, "Off the Gangsta Tip: A Rap Appreciation, or Forgetting About Los Angeles," in *Critical Inquiry* 20 (summer 1994), 663–93.

et al., "A Symposium on Whiteness," in *Minnesota Review* 47 (1996), 115–31.

Brumble, H. David, *American Indian Autobiography*, Berkeley, University of California Press, 1988.

Bullard, Robert, J. Eugene Grigsby, and Charles Lee, eds., *Residential Apartheid: The American Legacy*, Los Angeles, CAAS Publications, 1994.

Butler, Judith, *Gender Trouble: Feminism and the Subversion of Identity*, New York, Routledge, 1990.

Butterfield, Stephen, *Black Autobiography in America*, Amherst, University of Massachusetts Press, 1974.

Cameron, Kenneth M., "Paul Robeson, Eddie Murphy, and the Film Text of 'Africa,'" in *Text and Performance Quarterly* 10 (1990), 282–93.

Works cited

Carby, Hazel. "The Politics of Fiction, Anthropology, and the Folk: Zora Neale Hurston," in M. Awkward, ed., *New Essays on Their Eyes Were Watching God*, Cambridge, Cambridge University Press, 1990.

Carew, Jan, *Ghosts in Our Blood: With Malcolm X in Africa, England and the Caribbean*, Chicago, Lawrence Hill, 1994.

Chandler, Nahum, "The Figure of the X: An Elaboration of the Du Boisian Autobiographical Example," in S. Lavie and T. Swenebourg, eds., *Displacements, Diaspora, and Geographies of Identity* (Duke, 1996), 235–71.

Chay, Deborah, "Rereading Barbara Smith: Black Feminist Criticism and the Category of Experience," in *New Literary History* 24 (1993), 635–52.

Christian, Barbara, "Fixing Methodologies: *Beloved*," in *Cultural Critique* 24 (1993), 5–14.

"The Highs and Lows of Black Feminist Criticism," in H. L. Gates, ed., *Reading Black, Reading Feminist*, New York, Meridian, 1990, 44–51.

"But What Do We Think We're Doing Anyway: The State of Black Feminist Criticism(s) or My Version of a Little Bit of History," in C. Wall, ed., *Changing Our Own Words*, New Brunswick, N.J., Rutgers University Press, 1989.

"The Race for Theory," in *Cultural Critique* 6 (1987), 51–64.

Collins, Patricia Hill, *Black Feminist Thought: Knowledge, Consciousness and the Politics of Empowerment*, London, Harper Collins, 1990.

Cruse, Harold, *The Crisis of the Negro Intellectual*, New York, Quill, 1984.

Davis, Angela, "Afro Images: Politics, Fashion and Nostalgia," in *Critical Inquiry* 21 (autumn 1994), 37–45.

"Black Nationalism: The Sixties and the Nineties," in G. Dent, ed., *Black Popular Culture*, a project by M. Wallace, Seattle, Bay Press, 1992.

Women, Race, and Class, New York, Vintage, 1980.

Angela Davis: An Autobiography, New York, International Publishers, 1974.

If They Come in the Morning, New York, New American Library, 1971.

Decosta-Williams, Miriam, ed., *The Memphis Diary of Ida B. Wells*, Boston, Beacon Press, 1995.

DeMan, Paul, "Autobiography as De-Facement," in *Modern Language Notes* 94: 5 (1979), 919–30.

Dent, Gina, "Missionary Position," in R. Walker, ed., *To Be Real: Telling the Truth and Changing the Face of Feminism*, New York, Anchor Books, 1995, 61–75.

Dews, Peter, *The Limits of Disenchantment*, New York, Verso, 1995.

Logics of Disintegration, New York, Verso, 1987.

Di Leonardo, Micaela, "White Ethnicities, Identity Politics, and Baby Bear's Chair," in *Social Text* 41 (winter 1994), 165–91.

Duberman, Martin, *Paul Robeson*, New York, Alfred A. Knopf, 1989.

Dubey, Madhu, *Black Women Novelists and the Nationalist Aesthetic*, Bloomington, Indiana University Press, 1994.

Du Bois, W. E. B., *Dusk of Dawn: An Essay Toward an Autobiography of a Race Concept*, New Brunswick, N.J., Transaction Publishers, 1984.

W. E. B. Du Bois Speaks: Speeches and Addresses 1890–1919, ed. P. Foner, New York, Pathfinder, 1970.

The Souls of Black Folk, New York, Signet Classics, 1969.
Darkwater: Voices From Within the Veil, New York, Schocken, 1969.
The Autobiography of W. E. B. Du Bois, New York, International Publishers, 1968.
"The Negro Mind Reaches Out," in A. Locke, ed., *The New Negro*, New York, Athenum, 1968, 385–414.
Black Folk Then and Now, New York, Henry Holt, 1939.
"The African Roots of the War," in *Atlantic Monthly* 115 (May 1915), 7–15, reprinted in H. Aptheker, ed., *Writings by W. E. B. Du Bois in Periodicals Edited by Others, Volume II, 1910–1934*, Millwood, New York, Kraus Thomson Organization Ltd., n.d.
DuCille, Ann, "The Occult of True Black Womanhood: Critical Demeanor and Black Feminist Studies," in Abel, Christian, and Moglen, eds., *Female Subjects*.
Dudley, David, *My Father's Shadow: Intergenerational Conflict in African American Men's Autobiography*, Philadelphia, University of Pennsylvania Press, 1991.
Dyson, Michael Eric, *Making Malcolm: The Myth and Meaning of Malcolm X*, New York, Oxford University Press, 1995.
Reflecting Black, Minneapolis, University of Minnesota Press, 1993.
Eagleton, Terry, *Ideology: An Introduction*, New York, Verso, 1991.
The Ideology of the Aesthetic, London, Blackwell, 1990.
Eakin, Paul John, *Touching the World*, Princeton, N.J., Princeton University Press, 1992.
Echols, Alice, *Daring to Be Bad: Radical Feminism in America, 1967–75*, Minneapolis, University of Minnesota Press, 1989.
Erickson, Peter, "State of the Union," in *Transition* 59 (1993), 104–9.
Essien-Udom, E. U., *Black Nationalism: A Search for an Identity in America*, Chicago, University of Chicago Press, 1962.
Evans, Sara, *Personal Politics*, New York, Vintage, 1979.
Fanon, Frantz, *Black Skin, White Masks*, New York, Grove, 1967.
Wretched of the Earth, New York, Grove, 1963.
Fischer, Michael M. J., "Ethnicity and the Postmodern Art of Memory," in J. Clifford and G. E. Marcus, eds., *Writing Culture: The Poetics and Politics of Ethnography*, Berkeley, University of California Press, 1986.
Foley, Barbara, *Radical Representations: Politics and Form in U.S. Proletariat Fiction, 1929–1941*, Durham, N.C., Duke University Press, 1993.
"The Rhetoric of Anticommunism in *Invisible Man*," *College English* 59:5 (1997), 530–49.
Folkenflik, Robert, ed., *The Culture of Autobiography: Constructions of Self-Representation*, Stanford, Calif., Stanford University, 1993.
Foucault, Michel, *The History of Sexuality: An Introduction*, New York, Vintage, 1978.
Fowler, Virginia, *Nikki Giovanni*, New York, Twayne Publishers, 1992.
Frankenberg, Ruth, *White Women, Race Matters: The Social Construction of Whiteness*, Minneapolis, University of Minnesota Press, 1994.
Franklin, H. Bruce, *Prison Literature in America*, 2nd edn., New York, Oxford University Press, 1989.
Franklin, V.P., *Living Our Stories, Telling Our Truths: Autobiography and the*

Making of the African American Intellectual Tradition, New York, Oxford University Press, 1995.

Frazier, E. Franklin, *Black Bourgeoisie*, New York, Free Press, 1957.

Freud, Sigmund, *Group Psychology and the Analysis of the Ego*, New York, Norton, 1959.

Gaines, Kevin, *Uplifting the Race: Black Leadership, Politics, and Culture in the Twentieth Century*, Chapel Hill, University of North Carolina Press, 1996.

Gallen, David G., ed., *Malcolm X: As They Knew Him*, New York, Carroll and Graff, 1992.

Gates, Henry Louis, Jr., "Writing 'Race', and the Difference It Makes," in H. L. Gates, ed., *"Race," Writing and Difference*, Chicago, University of Chicago Press, 1985.

Gilmore, Leigh, "The Mark of Autobiography: Postmodernism, Autobiography, and Genre," in K. Ashley, L. Gilmore, and G. Peters, eds., *Autobiography and Postmodernism*, Amherst, University of Massachusetts Press, 130–66.

Gilroy, Paul, *The Black Atlantic: Modernity and Double Consciousness*, New York, Oxford University Press, 1994.

"It's a Family Affair," in G. Dent, ed., *Black Popular Culture*, pp. 303–16, Seattle, Bay Press, 1992.

There Ain't No Black in the Union Jack, Chicago, University of Chicago Press, 1987.

Giovanni, Nikki, *Gemini: An Extended Autobiographical Statement on My First Twenty-Five Years of Being a Black Poet*, New York, Penguin, 1971.

Goldman, Anita Haya, "Negotiating Claims of Race and Rights: Du Bois, Emerson, and the Critique of Liberal Nationalism," in *Massachusetts Review* 35: 2 (summer 1994), 169–201.

Goozé, Marjanne, "The Definitions of Self and Form in Feminist Autobiography Theory," in *Women's Studies* 21 (1992), 411–29.

Griffin, Farah, *Who Set You Flowin'? The African American Migration Narrative*, New York, Oxford University Press, 1995.

Groppe, John D., "From Chaos To Cosmos: The Role of Trust in *The Autobiography of Malcolm X*," in *Soundings* 66: 4 (1983), 437–49.

Grossberg, Lawrence, *We Gotta Get Out of This Place*, New York, Routledge, 1992.

Guillory, John, *Cultural Capital*, Chicago, University of Chicago Press, 1993.

Gunn, Janet Varner, "A Politics of Experience: Leila Khaled's *My People Shall Live: The Autobiography of a Revolutionary*," in S. Smith and J. Watson, eds., *Decolonizing the Subject*.

Autobiography: Toward a Poetics of Experience, Philadelphia, University of Pennsylvania Press, 1982.

Gunning, Sandra, *Race, Rape, and Lynching: The Red Record of American Literature 1890–1912*, New York, Oxford University Press, 1996.

Hall, Stuart, *Stuart Hall: Critical Dialogues in Cultural Studies*, D. Morley and K. H. Chen, eds., New York, Routledge, 1996.

"Cultural Identity and Diaspora," in P. Williams and L. Chrisman, eds., *Colonial Discourse and Postcolonial Theory*, New York, Columbia University Press, 1994, 392–403.

Hanchard, Michael, "Black Cinderella? Race and the Public Sphere in Brazil," in Black Public Sphere Collective, eds., *The Black Public Sphere*, Chicago, University of Chicago Press, 1995, 169–89.

Hansberry, Lorraine, *To Be Young, Gifted, and Black*, New York, Signet, 1969.

Harding, Sandra, "Rethinking Standpoint Epistemology: What is 'Strong Objectivity'?," in L. Alcoff and S. Potter, eds., *Feminist Epistemologies*, New York, Routledge, 1993.

Harper, Phillip Bryan, *Are We Not Men? Masculine Anxiety and the Problem of African American Identity*, New York, Oxford University Press, 1996.

  Framing the Margins: On the Social Logic of Postmodernism, New York, Oxford University Press, 1994.

Harris, Trudier, *Exorcising Blackness: Historical and Literary Lynching and Burning Rituals*, Bloomington, Indiana University Press, 1984.

Haywood, Harry, *Black Bolshevik: Autobiography of an Afro-American Communist*, Chicago, Liberator, 1978.

Heilbrun, Carolyn, *Writing a Woman's Life*, New York, Ballantine, 1988.

Herndon, Angelo, *Let Me Live*, New York, Random House, 1937.

Holt, Thomas, "The Political Uses of Alienation: W. E. B. Du Bois on Politics, Race, and Culture, 1903–40," in *American Quarterly* 42:2 (June 1990), 301–23.

hooks, bell, *Outlaw Culture: Resisting Representations*, New York, Routledge, 1994.

  Sisters of the Yam: Black Women and Self-Recovery, Boston, South End, 1993.

  Black Looks: Race and Representation, Boston, South End, 1992.

  Yearning: Race, Gender, and Cultural Politics, Boston, South End, 1990.

  Talking Back: Thinking Feminist, Thinking Black, Boston, South End, 1989.

Horne, Gerald, "Who Lost the Cold War? Africans and African Americans," in *Diplomatic History* 20:4 (fall 1996), 613–26.

  Black and Red: W. E. B. Du Bois and the Afro-American Response to the Cold War, Albany, New York, SUNY, 1986.

Hughes, Langston, *I Wonder as I Wander*, New York, Hill and Wang, 1993.

Hull, Gloria, *Color, Sex and Poetry: Three Women Writers of the Harlem Renaissance*, Bloomington, Indiana University Press, 1987.

Huntington, Patricia, "Toward a Dialectical Concept of Autonomy," in *Philosophy and Social Criticism* 21:1 (1995), 37–55.

Hurston, Zora Neale, *Dust Tracks on the Road*, New York, Harper Perennial, 1991.

  Their Eyes Were Watching God, New York, Harper Perennial, 1990.

Jackson, George, *Soledad Brother*, New York, Bantam, 1970.

Jameson, Frederic, *Postmodernism, or the Social Logic of Late Capitalism*, Durham, N.C., Duke University Press, 1990.

  "*History and Class Consciousness* as an 'Unfinished Project,'" in *Rethinking Marxism* 1:1 (1988), 49–70.

  The Political Unconscious, Ithaca, N.Y., Cornell University Press, 1981.

Works cited

Marxism and Form, Princeton, N.J., Princeton University Press, 1973.

JanMohamed, Abdul, "Negating the Negation as a Form of Affirmation in Minority Discourse: The Construction of Richard Wright as Subject," in *Cultural Critique* 7 (fall 1987), 245–66.

Johnson, Barbara, *A World of Difference*, Baltimore, Johns Hopkins University Press, 1987.

Johnson, James Weldon, *Along This Way*, New York, Penguin, 1990.

   The Autobiography of an Ex-Colored Man, in *Three Negro Classics*, ed. John Hope Franklin, New York, Avon, 1965.

   The Book of American Negro Poetry, 1st edn., New York, Harcourt, Brace & World, 1922.

Jones, Leroi, *Home: Social Essays*, New York, William Morrow, 1966.

   and Larry Neal, eds., *Black Fire*, New York, William Morrow, 1968.

Jordan, June, *Technical Difficulties*, New York, Vintage Books, 1994.

   Civil Wars, Boston, Beacon, 1981.

Kaplan, Caren, "Resisting Autobiography: Out-Law Genres and Transnational Feminist Subjects," in S. Smith and J. Watson, eds., 1992

Kawash, Samira, *Dislocating the Color Line: Identity, Hybridity, and Singularity in African American Literature*, Stanford, Calif., Stanford University, 1997.

Kelley, Robin D. G., *Hammer and Hoe: Alabama Communists During the Great Depression*, Chapel Hill, University of North Carolina Press, 1990.

   "House Negroes on the Loose: Malcolm X and the Black Bourgeoisie," in *Callaloo*, 21:2 (1998), 419–35.

Kellogg, Charles, *NAACP, a History of the National Association for the Advancement of Colored People*, Baltimore, Johns Hopkins University Press, 1967.

Kovel, Joel, *Red Hunting in the Promised Land: Anticommunism and the Making of America*, New York, Basic Books, 1994.

   White Racism: A Psychohistory, London, Free Association, 1988.

Laclau, Ernesto and Chantal Mouffe, *Hegemony and Socialist Strategy*, New York, Verso, 1985.

Lawson, Benjamin Sherwood, "Odysseus's Revenge: The Names on the Title Page of *The Autobiography of an Ex-Colored Man*," in *Southern Literary Journal* 21 : 2 (spring 1989), 92–9.

Leeming, David, *James Baldwin: A Biography*, New York, Henry Holt, 1994.

Lejeune, Philippe, *On Autobiography*, Minneapolis Press, University of Minnesota, 1989.

Lenin, V. I., *Imperialism: The Highest Stage of Capitalism*, New York, International Publishers, 1939.

Lewis, David Levering, *W. E. B. Du Bois: Biography of A Race*, vol. I, New York, Henry Holt, 1993.

   When Harlem Was in Vogue, New York, Vintage, 1979.

Lionnet, Francoise, *Autobiographical Voices: Race, Gender, Self-Portraiture*, Ithaca, N.Y., Cornell University Press, 1989.

Lorde, Audre, *Zami: A New Spelling of My Name*, Freedom, Calif., The

Crossing Press, 1982.

Lott, Tommy L., "Du Bois On the Invention of Race," in *Philosophical Forum*, XXIV: 1–3 (fall-spring 1992–3), 166–87.

Lubiano, Wahneema, "Mapping the Interstices Between Afro-American Cultural Discourse and Cultural Studies: A Prolegomenon," in *Callaloo* 19:1 (1996), 68–77.

"But Compared To What? Reading Realism, Representation and Essentialism in *School Daze, Do the Right Thing* and the Spike Lee Discourse," in M. Blount and G. Cunningham, eds., *Representing Black Men*, New York, Routledge, 1996, 173–204.

"Discussion [of Paul Gilroy]" in G. Dent, ed., *Black Popular Culture*, Seattle, Bay Press, 1992, 331.

"Shuckin' Off the African American Native Other: What's Po-Mo Got To Do With It," in *Cultural Critique* 18 (spring 1991), 149–86.

Lusane, Clarence, *Race in the Global Era: African Americans at the Millennium*, Boston, South End, 1997.

Madhubuti, Haki R., *Black Men: Obsolete, Single, Dangerous?* Chicago, Third World, 1990.

Magubane, Bernard, *The Ties That Bind: African-American Consciousness of Africa*. Trenton, N.J., Africa World, 1987.

Marable, Manning, *Race, Reform and Rebellion: The Second Reconstruction in Black America, 1945–1982*, Jackson, University of Mississippi Press, 1984.

Marcus, Laura, *Auto/biographical Discourses: Theory, Criticism, Practice*, New York, Manchester University Press, 1994.

Marshall, Paule, *The Chosen Place, The Timeless People*, New York, Vintage, 1992.

Martin, Charles H., *The Angelo Herndon Case and Southern Justice*, Baton Rouge, Louisiana State University Press, 1976.

Marx, Karl, *Capital*, vol. I, trans. S. Moore and E. Aveling, New York, International Publishers, 1967.

The Eighteenth Brumaire of Louis Bonaparte, New York, International Publishers, 1963.

Massey, Douglas and Nancy Denton, *American Apartheid: Segregation and the Making of the Underclass*, Cambridge, Mass., Harvard University Press, 1993.

Massumi, Brian, "The Autonomy of Affect," in *Cultural Critique* 31 (1995), 83–109.

Maxwell, William, "'Is it True What They Say about Dixie?' Richard Wright, Zora Neale Hurston, and Rural/Urban Exchange in Modern African American Literature," in B. Ching and G. Creed, eds., *Knowing Your Place: Rural Identity and Cultural Hierarchy*, New York, Routledge, 1997, 71–104.

May, Elaine Tyler, *Homeward Bound: American Families in the Cold War Era*, New York, Basic, 1988.

McDowell, Margaret, "Groundwork for a More Comprehensive Criticism of Nikki Giovanni," in J. Weixlmann and C. J. Fontenot, eds., *Belief vs. Theory in Black American Literary Criticism*, Greenwood, Flo., Penkevill, 1986, 135–60.

Works cited

Mercer, Kobena, *Welcome to the Jungle*, New York, Routledge, 1993.

Miller, Nancy, *Getting Personal: Feminist Occasions and Other Autobiographical Acts*, New York, Routledge, 1991.

Mitchell, Juliet, *Women's Estate*, New York, Vintage, 1971.

Mohanty, Satya, "The Epistemic Status of Cultural Identity: On *Beloved* and the Postcolonial Condition," *Cultural Critique* 24 (1993), 41–80.

Moi, Toril, "Feminism, Postmodernism, and Style: Recent Feminist Criticism in the United States," in *Cultural Critique* 9 (spring 1988), 3–24.

Moore, Richard, *Richard B. Moore, Caribbean Militant in Harlem: Collected Writings 1920–72*, W. B. Turner and J. M. Turner, eds., Bloomington, Indiana University Press, 1988.

Moraga, Cherrie, *The Last Generation*, Boston, South End, 1993.

Loving in the War Years, Boston, South End, 1983.

Morton, Patricia, *Disfigured Images: The Historical Assault on Afro-American Women*, New York, Praeger, 1991.

Moses, Wilson, *The Golden Age of Black Nationalism, 1850–1925*, New York, Oxford University Press, 1978.

Mostern, Kenneth, "Postcolonialism After W. E. B. Du Bois," forthcoming.

"Why is America in the Heart?," in *Critical Mass: A Journal of Asian-American Cultural Criticism* 2: 2 (summer 1995).

"Decolonization as Learning: Practice and Pedagogy in Frantz Fanon's Revolutionary Narrative," in H. Giroux and P. McLaren, eds., *Between Borders: Pedagogy and the Politics of Cultural Studies*, New York, Routledge, 1994.

Mullen, Harryette, "Optic White: Blackness and the Production of Whiteness," in *Diacritics* 24: 2–3 (summer-fall 1994), 71–89.

Nadelson, Regina, *Who is Angela Davis?* New York, Peter H. Wyden, 1972.

Naison, Mark, *Communists in Harlem During the Depression*, New York, Grove, 1983.

Njeri, Itabari, *Every Good-Bye Ain't Gone*, New York, Vintage, 1990.

Olney, James, ed., *Autobiography: Essays Theoretical and Critical*, Princeton, N.J., Princeton University Press, 1980.

Omi, Michael and Howard Winant, *Racial Formation in the United States from the 1960s to the 1990s*, 2nd edn., New York, Routledge, 1994.

Omolade, Barbara, *The Rising Song of African American Women*, New York, Routledge, 1994.

Parker, J. A., *Angela Davis: The Making of a Revolutionary*, New Rochelle, New York, Arlington House, 1973.

Patterson, William, *The Man Who Cried Genocide*, New York, International Publishers, 1971.

Perry, Bruce, *Malcolm: The Life of a Man Who Changed Black America*, Barrytown, New York, Station Hill, 1991.

Pisiak, Roxanna, "Irony and Subversion in James Weldon Johnson's *The Autobiography of An Ex-Colored Man*," in *Studies in American Fiction* 21: 1 (1993), 83–96.

Plant, Deborah, *Every Tub Must Sit on its Own Bottom: The Philosophy and Politics of Zora Neale Hurston*, Urbana, University of Illinois Press, 1995.

Plummer, Brenda, *Rising Wind: Black Americans and US Foreign Affairs, 1935–60*, Chapel Hill, University of North Carolina Press, 1996.

Rabinowitz, Paula, *Labor and Desire: Women's Revolutionary Fiction in Depression America*, Chapel Hill, University of North Carolina Press, 1991.

Ramparsad, Arnold, "Biography, Autobiography, and Afro-American Culture," in *Yale Review* 73 : 1 (1983), 1–16.

The Art and Imagination of W. E. B. Du Bois, New York, Schocken, 1976.

Read, Alan, ed., *The Fact of Blackness: Frantz Fanon and Visual Representation*, Seattle, Bay Press, 1996.

Rideout, Walter, *The Radical Novel in the United States, 1900–1954*, New York, Columbia University Press, 1992.

Robeson, Paul [Sr.], *Here I Stand*, Boston, Beacon, 1988.

Robeson, Paul, Jr., "Paul Robeson," in M. J. Buhle, P. Buhle, and D. Georgakis, eds., *The Encyclopedia of the American Left*, Chicago, St. James, 1990, 654–6.

Robinson, Amy, "It Takes One to Know One: Passing and Communities of Common Interest," in *Critical Inquiry* 20 (summer 1994), 715–36.

Robinson, Cedric, *Black Marxism: The Making of the Black Radical Tradition*, London, Zed, 1983.

Roediger, David, *The Wages of Whiteness: Race and the Making of the American Working Class*, New York, Verso, 1991.

Roof, Judith and Robyn Wiegman, eds., *Who Can Speak? Authority and Critical Identity*, Bloomington, University of Indiana Press, 1995.

Rubin, Gayle, "The Traffic in Women: Notes on the Political Economy of Sex," in K. V. Hansen and I. J. Philipson, eds., *Women, Class and the Feminist Imagination*, Philadelphia, Temple University Press, 1990.

Sales, William W., *From Civil Rights to Black Liberation: Malcolm X and the Organization of Afro-American Unity*, Boston, South End, 1994.

Sartre, Jean-Paul, *Critique of Dialectical Reason*, vol. I, trans. A. Sheridan-Smith, London, NLB, 1976.

Sekyi-Otu, Ato, *Fanon's Dialectic of Experience*, Cambridge, Mass., Harvard University, 1996.

Simon, Bruce, "Traumatic Diaspora: Paule Marshall's *The Chosen Place, The Timeless People*," unpublished paper.

Skerrett, Joseph T., "Irony and Symbolic Action in James Weldon Johnson's *The Autobiography of an Ex-Colored Man*," in *American Quarterly* 32 : 5 (winter 1980), 540–58.

Smith, Barbara, ed., *Home Girls: A Black Feminist Anthology*, New York, Kitchen Table / Women of Color Press, 1983.

"Toward A Black Feminist Criticism," in *Conditions* 2 (1979), 25–43.

Smith, Sidonie, *Subjectivity, Identity, and the Body: Women's Autobiographical Practices in the Twentieth Century*, Bloomington, University of Indiana Press, 1991.

Where I'm Bound, Westport, Conn., Greenwood, 1974.

and Julia Watson, eds., *De/Colonizing the Subject: The Politics of Gender in Women's Autobiography*, Minneapolis, University of Minnesota Press, 1992.

Smith, Valerie, *Self-Discovery and Authority in Afro-American Narrative*,

Works cited

Cambridge, Mass., Harvard University Press, 1987.

Sommer, Doris, "'Not Just A Personal Story': Women's *Testimonios* and the Plural Self," in B. Brodzki and C. Schenk, *Life/Lines: Theorizing Women's Autobiography*, Ithaca, New York, Cornell University Press, 1988.

Spillers, Hortense, "Black, White, and in Color, or Learning How To Paint: Toward an Intramural Protocol of Reading," in J. Cox and L. Reynolds, eds., *New Historical Literary Study: Essays on Reproducing Texts, Representing History*, Princeton, New Jersey, Princeton University Press, 1993.

"Moving on Down the Line: Variations on the African American Sermon," in D. La Capra, ed., *The Bounds of Race*, Ithaca, New York, Cornell University Press, 1991, 39–71.

"Mama's Baby, Papa's Maybe: An American Grammar Book," in *Diacritics* 17: 2 (1987), 65–81.

Spivak, Gayatri, *Outside in the Teaching Machine*, New York, Routledge, 1993.

"Can the Subaltern Speak?," in L. Grossberg and C. Nelson, eds., *Marxism and the Interpretation of Culture*, Urbana, University of Illinois Press, 1988.

Stone, Albert, *Autobiographical Occasions and Original Acts*, Philadelphia, University of Pennsylvania Press, 1980.

Stuckey, Sterling, *Slave Culture: Nationalist Theory and the Foundations of Black America*, New York, Oxford University Press, 1987.

Tate, Claudia, *Black Women Writers at Work*, New York, Continuum, 1983.

Taylor, Patrick, *The Narrative of Liberation: Perspectives on Afro-Caribbean Literature, Popular Culture, and Politics*, Ithaca, New York, Cornell University Press, 1989.

Thompson, Becky and Sangeeta Tyagi, eds., *Names We Call Home: Autobiography on Racial Identity*, New York, Routledge, 1996.

Thompson, Mildred I., *Ida B. Wells Barnett: An Exploratory Study of an American Black Woman, 1893–1930*, Black Women in United States History series, D. C. Hine, ed., Brooklyn, Carlson Publishing, 1990.

Trotsky, Leon, *Leon Trotsky on Black Nationalism and Self-Determination*, New York, Pathfinder, 1978.

Literature and Revolution, Ann Arbor, Mich., Ann Arbor Paperbacks, 1960.

Tyler, Carole-Anne, "Boys Will Be Girls: The Politics of Gay Drag," in D. Fuss, ed., *Inside/Out: Lesbian Theories, Gay Theories*, New York, Routledge, 1990, 32–70.

Varadharajan, Asha, *Exotic Parodies: Subjectivity in Adorno, Said, Spivak*, Minneapolis, University of Minnesota Press, 1995.

Vincent, Theodore G., *Black Power and the Garvey Movement*, San Francisco, Ramparts Press, 1972.

Volosinov, V. N., *Marxism and the Philosophy of Language*, Cambridge, Mass., Harvard University Press, 1973.

Von Eschen, Penny, *Race Against Empire: Black Americans and Anticolonialism, 1937–1957*, Ithaca, N.Y., Cornell University Press, 1997.

"Challenging Cold War Habits: African Americans, Race, and Foreign

Policy," in *Diplomatic History* 20:4 (fall 1996), 627–38.

Wald, Alan, *The New York Intellectuals*, Chapel Hill, University of North Carolina Press, 1987.

Wald, Priscilla, "Becoming 'Colored': The Self-Authorizing Language of Difference in Zora Neale Hurston," in *American Literary History* 2:1 (spring 1990), 79–100.

Waldron, Edward W., *Walter White and the Harlem Renaissance*, Port Washington, New York, National University Publications/Kennikat, 1978.

Walker, Alice, *Meridian*, New York, Pocket Books, 1976.

Wallace, Michele, "For Whom the Bell Tolls," in *Village Voice*, November 7, 1995.

Invisibility Blues: From Pop To Theory, New York, Verso, 1990.

Black Macho and the Myth of the Superwoman, New York, Verso, 1990.

Wallerstein, Immanuel, *Historical Capitalism with Capitalist Civilization*, New York, Verso, 1995.

Ware, Vron, *Beyond the Pale: White Women, Racism, and History*, New York, Verso, 1992.

Washington, Booker T., *Up From Slavery*, in J. H. Franklin, ed., *Three Negro Classics*, New York, Avon, 1965.

Washington, Mary Helen "Teaching *Black Eyed Susans:* An Approach to the Study of Black Women Writers," in G. Hull, P. B. Scott, and B. Smith, eds., *But Some of Us are Brave*, Old Westbury, New York, The Feminist Press, 1982, 208–20.

Wells Barnett, Ida B., *Selected Works of Ida B. Wells Barnett*, compiled by T. Harris, New York, Oxford University Press, 1991.

Crusade for Justice: The Autobiography of Ida B. Wells, ed. A. M. Duster, Chicago, University of Chicago Press, 1973.

White, Walter, *Rope and Faggot: A Biography of Judge Lynch*, New York, Arno Press and the New York Times, 1969.

A Man Called White, New York, Viking, 1948.

Wideman, John Edgar, *Brothers and Keepers*, New York, Penguin, 1984.

Wiegman, Robyn, *American Anatomies: Theorizing Race and Gender*, Durham, N.C., Duke University Press, 1995.

Williams, Brackette, "The Impact of the Precepts of Nationalism on the Concept of Culture: Making Grasshoppers of Naked Apes," in *Cultural Critique* 24 (spring 1993), 143–91.

Williams, Patricia, *The Rooster's Egg: On the Persistence of Prejudice*, Cambridge, Mass., Harvard University Press, 1995.

The Alchemy of Race and Rights, Cambridge, Mass., Harvard University Press, 1991.

Williams, Raymond, *Marxism and Literature*, New York, Oxford University Press, 1991.

Wolfenstein, Eugene Victor, *The Victims of Democracy: Malcolm X and the Black Revolution*, London, Free Association, 1989.

Wong, Hertha, *Sending My Heart Back Across the Years: Tradition and Innovation in Native American Autobiography*, New York, Oxford University Press, 1992.

Wood, Ellen Meiskins, "Back To Marx," in *Monthly Review* 49:2 (June

1997), 1–9.

Wood, Joe, ed., *Malcolm X: In Our Own Image*, New York, St. Martin's, 1992.

Wright, Eric Olin, *Classes*, New York, Verso, 1985.

Wright, Richard, *The Outsider*, New York, Harper and Row, 1991.

X, Malcolm, *By Any Means Necessary*, New York, 1970.

 and Alex Haley, *The Autobiography of Malcolm X*, New York, Ballantine, 1992.

Zagrando, Robert L., *The NAACP Crusade Against Lynching, 1909–50*, Philadelphia, Temple University Press, 1980.

Zamir, Shamoon, *Dark Voices: W. E. B. Du Bois and American Thought, 1888–1903*, Chicago, University of Chicago Press, 1995.

Zizek, Slavoj, *The Sublime Object of Ideology*, New York, Verso, 1989.

Index

Aaron, Daniel 116
Abel, Elizabeth 104
Adell, Sandra 232 n.7
Adorno, Theodor 167, 175, 220 n.23,
    224 n.59, 256–7 n.59
African American (term) 22–3
African-American studies 11–12,
    30–31, 45, 50–53, 112–15, 206–10
    periodization in 83–84
African Blood Brotherhood 117, 120,
    183
Allen, James 122
Als, Hilton 149
American (identity) 42, 61, 63–64,
    157–59
Anderson, Benedict 5
Andrews, Williams 11, 52–53
anthropology 107–08
anti-communism 76, 113–14, 123,
    244–45 n.11
anti-racism 14, 20–22
Appiah, Anthony 64, 234–35 n.33, 235
    n.45, 237 n.71
Aptheker, Bettina 175
articulation 7–8, 30
autobiography 10–13, 57–60, 82, 87–88,
    99–100, 106, 139–40, 191, 193–94
    and Communist practice 115
    African-American Autobiography
        Studies 30–31, 45, 50–53
    autobiography studies 28–53 *passim*
    bell hooks' theory of 197–203
    bildungsroman 28, 32, 99–100

collaborative 43–45
collective 32
Native American Autobiography
    Studies 29–30
of professional academics 206–11
Women's Autobiography Studies
    29–30, 45–50

Bailey, Deidre 137, 163
Baker, Houston 37
Baldwin, James 20, 23, 137, 251–52
    n.57, n.64
Bambara, Toni Cade 37, 87, 254 n.6
Baraka, Amiri 165, 172, 255 n.20
Barthes, Roland 39
Bell, Derrick 21
Bergland, Betty 229 n.31
Berube, Michael 224 n.60, 239 n.17
Bhabha, Homi 167, 226 n.80, 231 n.7
Bibby, Michael 253 n.72
Black (term) 22–23
blackness 10, 18–21, 38, 52, 89, 114–15,
    137–38, 152, 154–57, 167–72, 174,
    175–76, 183, 196–97, 201
    as style 172, 175
Black Arts movement 168, 172
Black Belt thesis 113, 117–18, 122
black feminism 12–13, 13–17, 26–27,
    30, 86–87, 97–98, 104, 106, 110–11,
    164–67, 186–88, 189–97, 200–01,
    203, 206–09
black masculinity 14, 84–85, 98, 124,
    137–38, 140, 163

Index

black men 13–14, 92, 142–43, 151–52, 173
  and educational institutions 159–63
  and imprisonment 124, 127–29, 159–63
black nationalism 9–10, 12, 21, 73, 113, 120, 121–22, 131–32, 152–53, 182–83, 218 n.7, 236 n.56
Black Panther Party 183
Black Power 52, 85, 122, 164–67, 172, 186, 196, 208
black professional class 61, 72–74, 110–11, 147
black women 4, 14–17, 52, 152–53, 164–67, 173, 178, 187–91, 195, 202–03
  and professions 207–09
black working class 10, 120, 123–39, 143, 145–48, 156–57, 203–04
Blount, Marcellus 14
Boaz, Franz 107
Boggs, Grace Lee 24
Bontemps, Arna 104
Bourdieu, Pierre 8–9, 17, 26, 28, 110–11, 210–11, 223 n.54, 224 n.59, 235, n.39
Braxton, Joanne 11, 52
Brown, H. Rap 178
Brown, Sterling 104
Brumble, H. David 30
Bruss, Elizabeth 36
Butterfield, Stephen 11, 51

capitalism 4, 9–10, 25–27, 96–97, 119–23, 205–06, 216
Carby, Hazel 107
Carew, Jan 149, 154
charisma 20
Chay, Deborah 258–59 n.11
Christian, Barbara 97, 104, 111, 194
Civil Rights Movement 113, 166
class (see also black professional class, black working class) 8–10, 25, 101–02, 108–09, 119–20, 131–32, 146–48, 184–85, 205–06, 219 n.21
Cleaver, Eldridge 165
Cliff, Michelle 191
coalition 15–16, 81–82

Cold War 76, 113–15, 118–19, 129–33, 174, 178, 181–84
Collins, Patricia Hill 249–50 n.37
colored (term) 22–23, 88–91
Combahee River Collective 164
communism 12, 75–78, 114–15, 123–33, 174, 178, 181–84
Communist International (Comintern) 76, 113, 116–17, 119, 120–21, 131
Communist Party, USA 76, 92, 113, 115–19, 122–23, 183
Cooper, Anna Julia 165, 237 n.77
Cullen, Countee 68
culture 7–8, 18–21, 84, 108–10
Cunningham, George 14

Davis, Angela 12, 110, 129, 164, 166–67, 173–74, 174–88, 189, 196, 197, 200, 218 n.7
Davis, Ossie 138–39
DeMan, Paul 31, 35–36, 37–38, 40
Dent, Gina 206, 208–09
Derrida, Jacques 211, 220 n.23, n.24
Determination 7–11, 30, 37–38, 65, 82
Dews, Peter 220 n.23
Dialectics 17, 21, 23–25, 31, 58, 81, 82, 197
Digable Planets 26
Di Leonardo, Micaela 3–5
Dos Passos, Jon 118
Douglass, Frederick 12, 61, 63
Duberman, Martin 132
Dubey, Madhu 254 n.6
Du Bois, W.E.B. 12, 22, 23, 24, 90, 94, 98–99, 107, 109–10, 111, 118, 119, 142, 159, 166, 204, 211, 251 n.57
  and gender 78–80
  "The African Roots of the War" 122–23
  Autobiography 75–80
  Crisis 24, 69, 99
  Darkwater 57, 61–64, 100
  Dusk of Dawn 18, 21, 34, 57–60, 64–75, 88, 100, 111, 119–20, 125, 179, 205
  The Souls of Black Folk 24, 57, 60, 88, 144
  "The Souls of White Folk" 6
DuCille, Anne 104, 206–07, 209
Dudley, David 11

Dyson, Michael Eric 218 n.7

Eagleton, Terry 226 n.81, 234 n.32
Eakin, Paul John 38–40, 44, 45, 139
Ellison, Ralph 114
essentialism 5, 21, 64, 81, 222 n.40
    anti-essentialism 7, 49, 109

Fanon, Frantz 3, 17, 25, 148, 219 n.16,
    226 n.80, 231 n.7
Farrakhan, Louis 20
Fauset, Jessie 82
Federal Bureau of Investigation 174
feminism (see also black feminism) 9,
    13, 25, 44, 46–50, 82, 84–85, 138,
    165–66, 172–73, 200, 201
Field (i.e. Bourdieuian theory) 110–11,
    227 n.3
Fischer, Michael M.J. 229 n.31
Foley, Barbara 114, 116
Folkenflik, Robert 36
Ford, James 113, 120
Foucault, Michel 18, 217 n.5, 220 n.24
Fowler, Virginia 172
Franklin, Aretha 169
Franklin, V.P. 11
Freedom 23, 138
Freud, Sigmund 20, 78, 190

Gaines, Kevin 233 n.16
Garveyism 140, 149, 153–54
Gates, Henry Louis, Jr. 12
Gilmore, Leigh 29, 45–46, 47
Gilroy, Paul 10, 11, 24, 27, 50, 51, 232
    n.11, 260 n.22
Giovanni, Nikki 12, 110, 164, 167–74,
    184, 189, 196, 197, 200
Global, The 23–27, 58, 74–75, 76–77,
    119–20, 129–30, 167, 182–83
Gold, Mike 115–16
Gomez, Jewelle 17
Gooze, Marjanne 29
Gramsci, Antonio 197
Griffin, Farah 238 n.5
Guillory, John 228 n.18
Gunn, Janet Varner 38–39, 40
Gunning, Sandra 84, 85, 92, 241 n.45
Gusdorf, Georges 40–42, 43, 44, 48, 49,
    51, 58

Haley, Alex 45, 140, 142, 150
Hall, Otto 120
Hall, Stuart 7–8, 164
Handler, M.S. 143
Hansberry, Lorainne 3
Harper, Phillip Bryan 14, 239 n.22, 246
    n.32
Harris, Trudier 238 n.7
Haywood, Bill 116
Haywood, Harry 113, 120, 122
Heilbrun, Carolyn 42, 48
Herndon, Angelo 114, 117, 120,
    123–29, 130, 132, 176, 178
home 170–71, 189–97
homosexuality 128, 172–73, 185, 192,
    250–51 n.44
hooks, bell 11, 13, 14, 22, 23, 27, 71, 99,
    189, 190, 194, 197–206, 211, 259
    n.18
Hopkins, Pauline 85, 237 n.77
Horne, Gerald 76, 114
Hughes, Langston 114
Hull, Gloria 97
Humanism 21, 134, 148, 158, 211
Hurston, Zora Neale 48–50, 84, 86–87,
    99, 103–11, 168, 189, 237 n.77
    Their Eyes Were Watching God 103,
    106
    Dust Tracks On A Road 104–05

Ice Cube 26, 205
Ice T. 26
identification 4, 16–17, 19, 20, 26,
    32–33, 34–35, 39–40, 45, 50, 51,
    59–60, 67, 73–74, 88–89, 126–28,
    130, 138–43, 148, 152–53, 163, 169,
    191–92, 210–16
    and lynching 84, 91–92, 94, 102
    and passing 87–92
    and prison 124, 128–29, 159, 163,
    176–79
    and pseudonyms 201–03
identity politics 3–7, 14–17, 51–52, 60,
    81–82, 88, 115, 127, 137–38, 156–57,
    167, 178–82, 201
ideology 82, 221 n.30
immigration 42, 225 n.64
imperialism 43–44, 76, 117, 118–19,
    122–23, 132, 243 n.86

Index

individuality 32, 41–43, 51–52, 99–100, 177
industrial workers of the world 116
institutionality 31, 36–37
irony 71, 87–88, 107

Jackson, George 159, 176, 177, 180, 184–88, 196
Jacobs, Harriet 42
James, C.L.R. 122
Jameson, Fredric 24, 221 n.30
JanMohamed, Abdul 220 n.23, 238 n.12
John Reed Clubs 118
Johnson, Barbara 243 n.93
Johnson, James Weldon 12, 22, 83, 84, 86, 87–88, 109–10, 111, 151
  Along This Way 87, 95, 99–103
  The Autobiography of An Ex-Colored Man 23, 35, 87–92, 95, 103
Jordan, June 4–5, 7, 15–17, 164, 166, 173, 194

Kaplan, Caren 36–37, 41
Kawash, Samira 105
Kelley, Robin D.G. 114, 123, 127, 147, 248–49 n.33
King, Martin Luther, Jr. 12, 138, 148, 180
Kovel, Joel 21, 244 n.11

Laclau, Ernesto 7, 169
Lawson, Benjamin 87
Lejeune, Philippe 28, 31, 33–36, 40
Lenin, V.I. 117, 123, 235 n.42
Leninism 119
Lewis, David Levering 233 n.21, 240 n.28
Lionnet, Françoise 45–47, 48, 104
Little, Earl 153–54
Little, Louise 149–50, 154
Lorde, Audre 191–92
Lubiano, Wahneema 38, 226 n.74, n.77, 260 n.22
Lukacs, Georg 115
Lusane, Clarence 253 n.74
lynching 12, 14, 84–87, 91–92, 94, 102
  anti-lynching politics 85–86, 92–95
  history of writing about 95–99

Magubane, Bernard 232 n.7
Marable, Manning 113–14
Marcus, Laura 227 n.4
Marcuse, Herbert 167, 175, 182, 183–84
Marshall, Paule 211–16
Marx, Karl 9, 10, 25, 26, 112, 220 n.24, n.25
marxism 8–10, 25–27, 74–75, 82, 112–23, 167, 181, 183, 187–88, 217 n.6, 220 n.24
masculinity (see also black masculinity) 13–14, 91–92, 123–24, 138–39, 151
Mason, Charlotte Osgood 109
Mason, Mary 36
Masses 116–17
Massumi, Brian 240 n.23
Maxwell, William 107
McCall, Nathan 159
McDowell, Margaret 172
McGee, Ruchell 176
Mercer, Kobena 14
Miller, Nancy 29
Mitchell, Juliet 257 n.77
modernity 18
Moglen, Helene 104
Moi, Toril 5
Moore, Richard 112
Moraga, Cherrie 40, 44, 48–50
Morrison, Toni 236 n.49
Moses, Wilson 113
Mouffe, Chantal 7, 169
Ms. 15
Muhammed, Elijah 140, 141–42, 144, 150, 152–56, 162, 169, 211
Mullen, Harryette 155
multiculturalism 20

NAACP 24, 63, 72, 73, 74, 76, 86, 92, 95, 98–99
Nadelson, Regina 174
Naison, Mark 114
narration 13, 23–27, 38–39, 41–43, 138–43, 159, 199–200, 208–10
Nation of Islam 140–41, 147–48, 149, 150, 151–52, 154, 157, 159, 161–62
nationalism (see also black nationalism) 5, 21, 119–22
native American studies 29–30

278

negritude 17
Negro (term) 22–23, 69–70, 130
Newton, Huey 176
New York 21 32
Nietzsche, Frederick 47
Nietzscheanism 26, 105, 108, 163, 169
Nkrumah, Kwame 152

objectification 201–03
Olney, James 11, 29, 36
Omi, Michael 65
Omolade, Barbara 209
organization of African unity 157

Pan-Africanism 67, 68–69, 157–58
Parker, J.A. 174–75, 183–84
passing 87–92, 94–95, 102
Patterson, William 120
Plant, Deborah 104–05, 106
Plessy v. Ferguson 83
Plummer, Brenda 114, 245 n.11
politics (see also identity politics) 3–4,
    6–7, 16–17, 20–21, 72–75, 83, 87,
    104–05, 138, 156, 208
  of autobiography 10–11, 43–45,
    105–06, 199
Popular Front 116, 118–19
poststructuralism 7, 29, 38, 46–47, 105
Powell, Linda 196
power 3, 31, 217 n.5
Presley, Elvis 19
prison 124, 127–29, 154–55, 157–63,
    176–79
professionalization 190, 197, 203–04,
    206–10, 216
property 173
psychoanalysis 20, 32, 104, 123–25, 142,
    153, 196, 198–200
  of anti-communism 183–84

Rabinowitz, Paula 114, 123–24
race (see also African American, black,
    blackness, colored, identification,
    Negro, whiteness) 5–6, 7–12,
    17–22, 24–25, 49, 80–82, 83, 100–03,
    137–38, 153, 169, 195
  and ambivalence 88–89
  and culture 19–20, 73, 85–87, 89–90,
    101–02, 109–10

and Du Boisian sociology 57–60,
    64–65
and recognition 66–67, 70–71, 157
and the public/private split 200
and the theory of ideology 10,
    232–33 n.12, 234 n.32
as habitus 17, 65–69, 235 n.39
as political identity 23, 52, 72–75
as skin color 5–6, 18–20, 49–50
psychology of 10–11, 69–72, 84, 86–87,
    88–89, 92, 125–26
race studies 29
narration of the 'real' 30–31, 144
Ramparsad, Arnold 42, 63
rape 85, 93, 95, 97, 98, 123
referentiality and the 'real' 28, 31–32,
    33–40, 106, 143–45, 199, 220–21
    n.25
religious identity 77, 124–27, 141–42,
    157–58, 162
revolution 25–26, 76, 112, 117, 121–22,
    162, 187–88
Riggs, Marlon 250–51 n.44
Robeson, Paul 12, 24, 114, 118, 119,
    120, 129–33, 139, 159, 166, 174, 204
Robinson, Amy 239 n.19
Robinson, Cedric 10, 232 n.7
Robinson, Smokey 172
Rodriguez, Richard 40, 44
Roof, Judith 6
Rosenblatt, Roger 36
Rubin, Gayle 251 n.77

Sartre, Jean-Paul 18, 223–24 n.59
school 65–66, 89, 131, 140–41, 159–61,
    203–04
Sekyi-Otu, Ato 25
sexuality 79–80, 96–97, 104, 123–24,
    151–52, 185, 186–87, 193, 237 n.77,
    250–51 n.44
Shakur, Sonyika 159
Simmons, Russell 250–51 n.44
Simon, Bruce 261 n.61
slave narrative 11, 41–42, 52, 124
Smith, Barbara 14, 165, 190–94, 196,
    197, 198, 200, 222 n.40
Smith, Sidonie 11, 36, 39–40, 42, 44, 45,
    47–50
Smith, Valerie 11

Index

SNCC 183

social movements 15–16, 21, 24–27, 81–82, 162, 164, 178, 182–83

Soledad Brothers Defense Committee 178, 186

Sommer, Doris 32–33, 43–45, 48, 51, 80

Sparks, Colin 218 n.16

Spillers, Hortense 13–14, 20, 23, 138, 189, 261 n.61

Spivak, Gayatri 3, 210–11, 220 n.23, 220–21 n.25, 231 n.7

Sprinker, Michael 36

Stalin, Joseph 117, 119, 122, 131

Steele, Shelby 105

Stewart, Maria 165

Stone, Albert 42–43, 44, 45

Stuckey, Sterling 132

subjectivity (see also we-subjects) 28–29, 32–33, 40–50, 121–22, 129, 168, 210

    black communist 119–23

    diasporic 11, 49

    split, mixed or hybrid 45–50, 200

Tate, Claudia 37

testimonio testimony, 32, 43–45

Third Worldism 26, 67, 132, 162, 183, 187

Thompson, Becky 10

totality 24–26, 59

trauma 10–11

Trotsky, Leon 112, 117, 119, 120–22, 128, 132

Tyagi, Sangeeta 10

Van Doren, Carl 100

Van Vechten, Carl 87

Varadharajan, Asha 220 n.23

Violence 148, 149, 152–53, 187–88

Visuality 18, 175, 194–95

Volosinov, V.N. 22, 57

Von Eschen, Penny 114

Wald, Alan 114, 245 n.17

Wald, Priscilla 105

Waldron, Edward 95

Walker, Alice 87, 164, 194

Walker, Rebecca 208

Wallace, Michele 104, 139, 164–65, 166–67, 186, 190, 193–97, 210

Washington, Booker T. 12, 68, 102, 109

Washington, Mary Helen 103

Watson, Julia 36, 42

we-subjects 22–23, 32–33, 44–45, 50–51

Wells Barnett, Ida B. 12, 14, 79–80, 83, 84, 86–87, 92–99, 100, 101, 103, 104, 110–11, 130, 151, 166, 167, 237 n.77

White, Walter 14, 83, 84, 86–87, 92–99, 100, 101, 130, 151, 166

white supremacy 17–18, 155–56

whiteness 6, 19–22, 70–71, 88–92, 142, 154–57, 167, 173, 209–10, 211

Wideman, John Edgar 140, 159

Wiegman, Robyn 6, 14, 18, 84–85, 209–10

Williams, Brackette 19

Williams, Patricia 5–6, 137, 189, 209

Williams, Raymond 9, 247–48 n.4

Winant, Howard 65

Winfrey, Oprah 194

Wolfenstein, Eugene 149

Wong, Hertha 30

Wood, Ellen Meiskens 25

Wood, Joe 23

Wright, Eric Olin 8–9

Wright, Richard 104, 107, 112, 114, 118, 128, 175

X, Malcolm 12, 14, 22, 23, 25, 43, 44, 45, 115, 124, 129, 133, 137–63, 164, 165, 175, 176, 178, 184, 196, 204, 208

Zamir, Shamoon 231–32 n.7

Zizek, Slavoj 228 n.24